AT ONE
WITH ALL
LIFE

*For Gaia, Mother of Earth, who has inspired, challenged,
taught and humbled me.*

AT ONE
WITH ALL
LIFE

A Personal Journey in
Gaian Communities

Judith L. Boice

Findhorn Press

© 1989 Judith Boice
First published 1990 by Findhorn Press, The Park, Findhorn, Forres IV36 0TZ,
Moray, Scotland

ISBN 0 905249 74 7

Set in Times on Mackintosh SE.
Design by Claudia Klingemann; layout by Claudia Klingemann and
Philip Mielewczyk, Bay Area Graphics.
Cover illustration by Claudia Klingemann; chapter illustrations by Harley Miller.
Printed and bound by Billings & Sons, Worcester, UK
Printed on recycled paper

Acknowledgements

Thanks to Sandra Kramer and Findhorn Press for their patient, dedicated work in manifesting this book. I acknowledge Lella Russell Smith, a sister-spirit to whom I am indebted for hours of creative, visionary conversation that led to many of the basic concepts underlying this book. Thanks to my sister Ruth and her husband Eric for providing a home when I needed one. My love to Phoebe Reeve for the Deva of EarthLove that has provided a language for sharing Earth wisdom. To Phyllis Rodin, my gratitude for reading the manuscript and believing in my writing, for encouraging me to birth this work into the world. Thanks to Alan for your continuing love and support. Thank you David for your unwavering love, encouragement, patience and support. Thanks, Mom and Dad, for the many years of love and encouragement, and for providing what every traveller longs for—a home address where the door is always open.

I would like to acknowledge with gratitude the sources of the quotes used in this book:
Page 256-7: *From the Beginning of Life to the Day of Purification: The Hopi Story*, by Don Katchongva. Hopi Land and Life, Rte 9, Box 78, Santa Fe, NM 87501, USA.
Page 257: *Voices of Our Ancestors*, by Dhyani Ywahoo © 1987. Reprinted by arrangement with Shambhala Publications, 300 Massachusetts Avenue, Boston, MA 02115, USA.
Page 260: 'Mester Stoorworm' in *Scottish Folk Tales*, by Ruth Manning-Sanders. London: Methuen's Children's Books, 1986, pp. 84-5.
Page 263: *Who Speaks for Wolf*, by Paula Underwood Spencer, A Tribe of Two Press, 1983, pp. 31-32.
Page 265-6: Gary Snyder: *The Real Work*. Copyright © 1980 by Gary Snyder. Reprinted by permission of New Directions Publishing Corporation.
Page 266: *If You Want to Write* © 1987 by the Estate of Brenda Ueland. Reprinted by permission of Graywolf Press.
Page 267: *Japanese Woodworking Tools: Their Tradition, Spirit and Use*, by Toshio Odate, Taunton Press, 1984.

To the Creator, I offer thanks for the Life that lives through me. Thanks for the wood that heats my home, the water that cleanses my body, the food that nourishes me, the air that sustains me, the animals and plants that teach me, the humans who love and challenge me. For the Seen and Unseen Beings who have taught me and guided my journey, I offer my gratitude: to the Spirit of Vision Mountain, the Angel of the Findhorn Foundation, the Mother in Auroville and the Dreamtime of Australia.

Note
A few of the names of people in this book have been changed.

Contents

JOURNEYING

I have walked far
I have walked long
Seeking the Self
That has always been
In the very Heart of me

I have walked far,
I have walked long
Searching for the Home
Whose door opens
In my very Centre

I have walked far
I have walked long
Searching for Wisdom
That has always been
The Reflection of Me
In Every Thing

INTRODUCTION
Provisions for the Journey

". . . That's what an Expedition means. A long line of everybody. You'd better tell the others to get ready, while I see if my gun's all right. And we must all bring Provisions."
"Bring What?"
"Things to eat."
"Oh!" said Pooh happily. "I thought you said Provisions. I'll go and tell them."

(A.A. Milne, *Winnie the Pooh.*)

Sitting in this one-room cabin in Western Massachusetts, listening to a thunderstorm booming among the summer-green trees, the cold of winter seems far away. Here, during the iciest months of the year, I sat in front of my computer wearing three sweaters, a hat and sometimes gloves, writing this book. The thermometer on the desk barely reached 50°F on the coldest days no matter how many logs I fed into the woodburning stove. In these conditions, I relived the journey of the last six years of my life—a journey that began with a single question.

As a student at Oberlin College, I constructed a lot of theories, partly out of inspiration and mostly out of desperation. The model of the world presented in text books and lectures stimulated me. Actually 'stimulated' is incorrect. The models infuriated me, and I was determined to use the tools of academia to reveal its inadequacies. I would moan to my advisor about the amount of theory in my courses. I wanted more experiential learning.

"But Judy," my advisor would say, "you've got to learn their language before you can argue with them." So I learned the language of economists and sociologists and psychologists and scientists in order to be 'effective' in their world.

Through my classes and papers I was searching for something I could believe in. For 'Woman, Man and Nature' class I researched women's leadership in the environmental movement. The project implied singling out a woman and researching her career. But as I studied the women's movement where it intersected with environmental activism, I discovered a type of leadership that defied the definition, and therefore the detection, of those recording history. Women tend to organise in groups that downplay the importance of a single leader. They tend to work more cooperatively and more inclusively than male-dominated groups. I wondered if the difference in the way the groups organised and exercised leadership had to do with their sex or their concern for the Earth or both. I decided to explore the issue from a new angle, collecting my own data instead of relying on writings from the past.

I sent a written questionnaire accompanied by a blank cassette tape to ten women involved in spiritual communities connected with the Earth. Their responses confirmed my hunch that a strong relationship with the Earth influences a group's structure; it tends to be less hierarchical and more cooperative. After the first flush of excitement, though, a thought niggled. I had the perspective of only one person in each community. How did the other members view the community? Even more insistent was the thought, 'How would I view the community?' As a student, I was weary of the world of conjecture and analysis, the art of dissecting inspiration into lifeless bits, and I longed for direct experience.

In the autumn of my senior year at Oberlin College, I received a grant from the Mellon Foundation to live in 'a spiritual community with Earth connections to evaluate whether the connection with the Earth manifests in different forms of group structuring and leadership'. The grant covered my airfare and expenses to live at the Bear Tribe, a Native American Medicine Society outside Spokane, Washington, during 'January Term', a month set aside for individual projects. I had a lot of theory to justify my journey, but what I really wanted was to live in a community, to experience it deeply and know its guts. I had to know first hand if these communities fulfilled my expectations or if I had romanticised them beyond recognition.

Living at the Bear Tribe both confirmed and contradicted my expectations of community. I wanted to experience other groups as well to know how they answered the challenge of living in a supportive way upon the Earth. This book addresses four communities that have emerged from the vision stage and are now functioning, autonomous beings, all at different levels of growth and maturity, and exploring their relationship with the world. When I began planning the book, I wanted to include all of the communities that I felt qualified, but I also wanted to give an *in-depth view* of what community living is really like. I had a lot of theories, but only a couple of years' experience in a student cooperative at Oberlin College. I wanted to look at this beast of a Gaian community from the inside out, instead of reporting as a critical observer.

When I made the commitment to living in these communities, I soon realised that I would need years in each one to fully understand its subtle workings. I would need time for the essence of the community's vision to become a part of me, so that the purpose could speak through me, instead of needing to quote it from a charter or trust deed.

This journeying story is also an account of the *inner transformations* that take place when someone says 'yes' to living in a community. I began to notice that everyone who lives in a community seems to go through a similar pattern of triumphs and challenges. None of the books about community I could find ever said very much about how the members actually lived from day to day, how they felt about living there, and what the challenges were.

Quickly I came to know that community living is some of the hardest work that anyone could ever undertake. Building Utopia takes a lot of effort. At times, yes, the work is joyous and rewarding; at other times the building requires slogging through swamps that humanity has chosen to ignore for thousands of years.

When first joining a community, people usually enter a blissful 'honeymoon' period—they have found their Place, their People, they are finally loved and understood and accepted. Here, at last, is a collection of dreamers as mad as they—what a relief! This honeymoon/homecoming may last a few months, a few weeks or a couple of days—it seems to shorten with each new community I enter. Perhaps I now know where to look for the cracks and imperfections.

After the blissful honeymoon people usually experience the first pangs of disillusionment. The diehards will ride the waves, but the curiosity seekers quickly bail out. The disillusionment lasts for varying lengths of time, too, depending on how stubborn and/or perceptive the person is.

Then comes the slough of despond. Whatever is going wrong in my life, I'm sure it's the community's fault. I seem to have lost my sense of individuality. My creativity, my inner schedule, my sweat and tears and heartbeat seem to be regulated by the pulse of the community. I struggle internally against what I see as a need to 'conform'. I get sick. I become depressed. I resist like hell. I wish now that I had bailed out earlier because the waves are getting *really* rough, and I'm extremely sea-sick.

Gradually the storm passes. I surrender to the rhythm of the community and find that my Self still survives intact. In fact, I now have a lot more energy, and the effort that I put into the collective overflows into my own personal efforts. I find a balance between my individual needs and the needs of the collective. After the earlier rough waves I learn, by necessity, that I need to take care of myself first or I will have nothing to give to the group.

Claiming power. I've survived the bliss of new beginnings, the disillusionment, the dark night of the soul, and the first glimmerings of the far end of the tunnel. Now I fully enter the community, re-formed by the journey through the Abyss. Although the daily roller coaster of emotional ups and downs continues, my basic ability to move and be effective within the collective remains stable.

That synopsis could be a brief telling of 'Everywoman's' journey in community. This story, though, is particularly about Gaian communities.

'Gaia', the name of the Greek Goddess of the Earth, has recently re-entered common usage as a result of James Lovelock's 'Gaia Hypothesis'. NASA commissioned Lovelock, a British scientist, to create a definition for 'life' that could be used as a yardstick for measuring the presence or absence of life on other planets with the aid of the newly created space probes. In the process of researching a definition for life, Lovelock used the planet Earth as a model for an 'alive' planet. In the end Lovelock came to the conclusion that the Earth is indeed alive and as a *planet* has a type of consciousness that allows it to operate as a self-regulating organism.

The Earth's oceans, for example, have remained at a remarkably stable level of salinity for millions of years. The planet's overall temperature has remained within a couple of degrees for many millions of years, contrary to the steadily increasing temperature curve that a scientist would predict for a world with such conditions. Lovelock showed that the planet Earth has the ability to regulate its own macro-systems. It has a unifying intelligence that allows it to function as an *organism*, a unified whole, with a complex set of interlocking systems, much like our own human bodies. NASA was not particularly impressed by Lovelock's findings, but other scientists and a remarkable number of theologians grasped the importance of the hypothesis.

If the Earth is recognised as having a unifying consciousness, we can no longer view it as inert matter expressly made for manipulation by human beings. The Earth moves from the status of a disjointed collection of unrelated environments or 'natural resources' to that of a self-regulating, conscious, integrated whole. Humans then begin to see themselves as part of a larger whole, not as elevated masters of an inert structure designed for them to dominate and then to escape from.

I have defined Gaian communities as those that support the life, health and diversity of the planet. Three criteria for identifying Gaian communities are:

1. Commitment to 'right relationship' with the Earth.

Right relationship begins by asking the question, 'Who is my next door neighbour? With whom am I relating most directly?' If we look more closely at the question, we find that our 'next door neighbour' has much broader meaning than the human in the closest habitable dwelling. With an expanded definition of 'neighbour', I find the pine trees outside my window, the daffodils just pushing their leaves through the soil, even the chair on which I sit and the clothes that warm and protect my body, much more immediate neighbours than the human dwellers separated from me by a network of walls and windows and shrubbery.

My relationship with that neighbouring human *is* of paramount importance, *and* I expand my sense of kinship to encompass all of the beings that surround me. Once I conceive of these other-than-human-beings as 'kin' or 'neighbours', I recognise our relatedness and need for mutual support. I respect you because you are worthwhile in and of yourself. I honour you as neighbour. I acknowledge you as kin on the same planet, fellow occupant of the same neighbourhood. When I relate to the beings around me with respect, I am open to a state of deep listening, which is another aspect of 'right relationship'. I value that you have a perspective on life different from my own and am willing to listen to your life experience.

2. Commitment to working on oneself and one's relationship with others.

The primary goal of working on oneself is to gain *self-awareness*, a knowledge of and responsibility for one's inner workings. My emphasis on groups incorporating self-work stems from a belief that any kind of meaningful change originates in self-change, an individual's shift in awareness. This holds true for any sort of transformation, on any scale, i.e. in one-to-one relationships, in family dynamics, or political, social, spiritual or planetary change—all begin with individuals who shift their conceptual framework of the world.

As an example in the political arena, the passage of the Civil Rights Act in the US did not fundamentally change the treatment of people of colour by the white majority. Only individual realisation of the worth of all races of humanity can bring about a true change. When enough individuals change their perspective to one of value and respect, then a true social/cultural shift occurs. The legislation helps to protect the endangered sector, whether human or otherwise (as in the case of the Clean Air Act), until individual values shift on a large scale and the endangering behaviour ceases. Legislation is basically remedial.

When I view the world as interconnected, or 'webbed', I realise that *as I change, the planet changes*. My shift in awareness radiates out through the entire network, affecting the whole web. My inner environment (belief systems, conceptual framework, thoughts, knowledge, emotions, etc) helps to create my outer environment.

My relationship with others is a dramatisation of the outer environment that I have created through my inner work. 'Others' includes the realms of mineral, plant and animal. Through relationship I realise that 'I am other', that the other acts as a mirror in which I can, sometimes painfully, see myself.

3. Commitment to service.

Service is the point at which consciousness is put into action. Through service, work on oneself interfaces with the outer world. The scope of a community's service must encompass more than the immediate group of humans if the community desires any sort of longevity. The average life of such groups in the US is six months—most are focused upon the survival needs of the immediate members and never expand their vision to include giving to others in any way.

One of the most important lessons that I learned through living in community is that *service means doing what I love most,* and conversely, *service means loving what I do*. An act of love increases the flow of love in the world. An act of committed drudgery increases the sense of pointless duty and apathy in the world. If I can clean toilets with love, I do more good in one hour of work than a week of dutiful 'community service'. Actually, the comparison of time is meaningless. The point is to instill love into whatever work the individual and/or the community chooses, to strengthen the qualities of love, cooperation and commitment on the planet.

The inner attitude towards work is as important as the work itself. 'Politically correct' actions, for example, performed without love are like trying to play a radio without plugging it in. They lack 'juice' and therefore effectiveness.

One of my favourite quotes (which I cannot, unfortunately, credit) is, 'Don't ask what the world needs. Ask instead what makes you come alive. Because the world needs more people who have come alive.' *Coming alive* is the greatest service that anyone can render.

The communities that embody and demonstrate all three criteria live what I have termed a 'Gaian lifestyle': a way of life that sustains and augments the health, life and diversity of the planet.

This book, then, is a journeying story—and one that is by no means complete. The journey has taken me around the world twice, from intentional to neighbourhood to traditional communities. I have found glimmerings, scraps, pieces and segments of the kind of community I have dreamt of, but nowhere have I found the picture complete. This story of the last five years of that journey is meant to be a point of departure for further exploration into what I have come to call 'Gaian communities'. I haven't found anyone who has unlocked the complete formula yet. And perhaps the 'perfect form' is not the goal of the quest. To live the dream of a Gaian community to the best of our ability, to make our *lives* an expression of love for life and the Earth, of our hunger for a peaceful world, may be reward enough.

The theory of how to live in harmony with the Earth and all of the planet's inhabitants means nothing until it is enacted, until the flesh and bones of our lives clothe it. I offer you the bones of my life, the trail of my journey, in hopes that it will inspire you to enact your own visions of 'how life could be'.

CHAPTER 1
January Beginnings

My journey with the Bear Tribe begins on New Year's Eve, on the cusp between the old year and the new. I, too, am perched on the edge of an indefinable newness, something more than the usual expectant resolve that fills me at this time of year. During the flight from Ohio, excitement and worries and expectations have crescendoed inside me. Now, as we taxi along the snowy runway, I wonder who will meet me. I watch the snowploughs, tireless as ants, moving across the pavement to clear away the snow, and I wonder if *anyone* will be here.

Waiting in Spokane airport, I release some of the vague discomforts into the solid familiarity of words: 'On the precipice, in a liminal state, waiting for a change to grab me and run . . . .' Should I be silent or openly gregarious? Can I add to the vision of this community or will I simply fill a void in space? I want to be able to contribute, to learn, to give, to receive, to become a vital part of this place.

In the end, no one comes to pick me up. "Neemee Mosha called," explains an airline clerk when I answer an announcement over the loudspeaker. He raises his eyebrows as he reads the message—obviously 'Neemee Mosha' (actually Nimimosha, a long-time resident of the Bear Tribe) is not a familiar name to him. "Snowed in on the mountain, she says. You can take a taxi to this address."

By morning the thick waves of snow have stopped, but another couple of days pass before the roads are clear enough to drive into the mountains that rise outside Spokane. During the days in town I learn a lot about the publishing and catalogue business that the community runs out of a small house there, but I am chafing to see Vision Mountain where the Bear Tribe has a mostly self-sufficient farm. When Carl, a long-term visitor, offers a ride out to the farm late one afternoon, I jump at the chance.

Within a few minutes we are driving along the dusky, snowy roads heading north-

1

west. The light soon wanes into darkness, and my vision of the landscape telescopes to the tunnel of brightness cast by the headlights. Although I cannot see very much, I know that we must be heading into a rural area—the road twists and rises and finally dissolves into a series of ruts. The last mile must be covered on foot—without a four-wheel drive, we can't negotiate this section.

The unpaved road that winds up Vision Mountain stretches into the snowy night, lit only by the stars flashing in the sky. I arrive slowly, steps weighted by my backpack as I walk up the mountain road. We talk very little—I need all of my breath to keep up with Carl's easy strides. After nearly a mile, we see bands of light ahead, pouring from the house windows across the snow drifts.

Excitement, that fine-lined perspective just this side of fear, builds and breaks as I step across the threshold of the Long House and into the warmth of the living room. I pause for a moment, blinded by the brilliance of electric lights. Slowly my eyes absorb the details of wooden beams, cooking utensils, decorated Christmas tree, a wooden table and benches. I did not expect electric lights or Beethoven's Sixth Symphony blaring from the stereo. I accept a plate of spaghetti and slide onto one of the benches lining the long table. I have arrived.

After dinner I rummage in my pack for notebooks and pens. I am determined to keep a journal of my time here, to record faithfully my experience as a 'participant observer'. I remember all of the theory carefully digested in last autumn's sociology course, 'Methods of Research'. Tonight I am diligent about writing notes in a memo book, flipping pages with gusto, describing the living room, what I had for dinner, and other invaluable bits of information. I plan to photograph the land and the people and interview each member of the Bear Tribe in order to create an audio-visual with the members describing, in their own words, the experience of living in this community. In addition I will write a paper for the Mellon Foundation. Hence, the obsession with notes.

I turn to my journal for more personal thoughts, mulling over my relationships with two men at Oberlin . . . . *Still churning thoughts of Julian and Eddie in my mind . . . Eddie sent a letter that arrived today, full of vacation doodles, pictures, a smashed flea, love, thoughts. Hmmmm, is he in Oberlin tonight, or is it tomorrow? Must write soon. The stove is hot, makes me want to move or sleep. Probably best to move at the moment.*

I climb upstairs to my room, one of a series of five sleeping rooms. The walls are a bit wider than my outstretched arms. I have just enough space to walk around the built-in bed and store my backpack in the corner. The roof slants steeply on the house, so I can stand up only in the front half of the room. Through the thin floor I can hear every movement and word that passes in the living room and kitchen below. In this small community, though, of eight members and four long-term guests, any private space, no matter how tiny, is a luxury.

Over the next few days I begin to fall in love with the Bear Tribe. I have romanticised heavily about the 'simple life' of self-sufficiency, and I am relieved to find that I enjoy the daily tasks of living, so different from the life of a college student. Callouses develop on my hands as I learn to chop wood for the first time. My fingers, already strong from playing the violin, grow sore and then stronger as I learn to milk the cows.

The hour after dinner is a favourite time when I follow the pool of light cast by the kerosene lantern swinging in Cougar's mittened hand, footsteps crunching in the snow, breath billowing in the freezing air. The cows stand by the barn door, waiting to be let in for the night. I sit on a stool, forehead pressed into a steamy flank for warmth. My hands grasp the teats and gradually fall into a rhythm, sending jets of milk hissing against the sides of the bucket. As we work in the shadowy lantern light of the barn, Cougar, a member of the Bear Tribe, tells me of his early life, his involvement in the Free Speech movement, and the twists and turns that led him eventually to this community.

"When I was a kid," he explains, "I didn't have many friends, not human ones at least. I had a backyard full of animals, ones that I had found and some that people had brought to me, animals that were injured somehow. I used to talk mainly with the postman. He would always come around the back to see what I had. It was like a zoo back there."

During the early sixties Cougar (or Don as he was known then) became active in the Free Speech Movement. "You know, Sun Bear was involved, too. We worked out that we were at the same demonstration one time, standing almost next to each other. I kind of have a memory of him that day. Funny how we end up living together years later."

As well as demonstrating, Don was organising, too, which made him a target for the FBI. "Yeah, they tried to arrest me more than once. One time the FBI detained a couple of us for a few days, separated us so that we couldn't check our stories. We both refused to talk, so they finally had to release us."

"You ever worry about having an FBI record?"

"Naw, although I've thought about trying to get a copy of my records through the Freedom of Information Act. But I didn't want to stir things up again. I thought it was better to let it lie."

In the late sixties and early seventies Don and his (now ex-) partner Hetty joined a couple of 'back to the land' communes, both of which collapsed within a year. "Those people," exclaims Hetty, rolling her eyes, "none of them wanted to work. I would walk into a real mess in the kitchen in the morning and look around for help. 'Oh, I must meditate now,' everyone would say. I was doing lots of work, they were meditating, and nothing ever got done." Her comments confirm my thoughts about a community's purpose. Without vision, one that is larger than the survival needs of the immediate members, the group soon perishes. Most communities from that era lasted only six months. The ones that survived had long-term goals and visions that buoyed them through the initial difficulties.

After the collapse of the second commune, Hetty and Don moved to the mountains of Arkansas to homestead. "I wanted to live without supporting the system in any way," explains Cougar. "We didn't have electricity because the local generator was nuclear-based. We ploughed with horses because I didn't want to use fossil fuel. We helped set up a food co-op in the area to buy anything we couldn't grow. And we taught Simon and Jessie, our two kids, at home."

"Why did you leave?"

"We-e-ell, I had some experiences vision questing on the mountain we lived on. Powerful experiences. I was getting more and more involved in Native American things. I read one of the Bear Tribe books and I knew I had to come. I just knew. I needed a greater purpose for the rest of my life than just living on the land in Arkansas."

Spurred by his sense of knowing, Don sold the house, the land and all of the farm animals. He bought an old car, pocketed the remaining few dollars to pay for gas, and herded the kids into the car (he and Hetty were separated by this time). They set course for Spokane, Washington without any assurance of the outcome of their voyage.

Five years later Don, alias Cougar, still lives at the Tribe along with his son Simon. Jessie, his daughter, lives with Hetty in Arkansas during the school year and

3

with Cougar during the summers. During these dark, quiet evenings in the barn, the two-dimensional first impressions of Cougar—reticent, head bent over a book in the late evenings—take on depth and perspective; he is a man with many facets.

We carry the milk pails across the frozen barnyard to the warmth of the Long House. The mountain is cold at this time of year. Overnight the water trough freezes into a solid chunk of ice over two feet thick. The pine trunks reach tall and straight, but the boughs droop with the weight of accumulated snow.

In the morning I tackle the pile of frozen logs outside the Long House. I have a new appreciation of wood as I learn the skill of splitting logs. "Wood warms you twice, once when you cut it, and again when you burn it," wrote Henry David Thoreau. I would add a third and fourth—when you split it, and when you carry it. Sweat beads on my brow as I flail at the frozen logs. "Use your body," instructs Carl, patiently standing by to teach me the basics. "Your *whole* body. Put your weight into what you're doing."

My education in practical, physical skills is beginning. The Earth does not care how many PhDs I have, but the strength and ability of my physical body is paramount. I am reminded of Wendell Berry's comment that the 'uneducated' South American peasant has an education far superior to that of any Manhattan business-person when it comes to surviving upon the Earth. Bereft of brief case and Rolaids, most city dwellers would be helpless in fulfilling their own survival needs. I am learning the skills of an educated peasant.

Carl is my main instructor, especially during my first few days on the mountain. We fall into a natural rhythm of working together with the animals, completing the morning chores of milking and watering and feeding. Unexpectedly our bonding as student and teacher deepens into affection and later flowers into love. The dance of our courtship is very relaxed, a natural outgrowth of the time spent working side by side.

Intimacy is a mystery I hope I never fully unravel. The magic would disappear if I had a clear-cut formula. Somehow in the process of pulling the four-wheel drive out of a snowy ditch with the tractor, the love blossoms. With the final release of the back wheel comes a cracking of the wall that separates our bodies, and the usual hug is followed by a self-conscious, lingering kiss. We have crossed a barrier, never to retrace our steps.

Carl and his world unfold gradually through our work and play together. One evening we decide to go to Pioneer Pies, a restaurant that makes outrageously rich pies. Carl stops eating for a moment, eyeing me.

"What's up?" I ask.

"It's the first time we've been alone. I'm so used to having twenty people around the table."

I burst into laughter. It's true. Living in a community, especially a small one, means constantly interacting with people. Having worked in a student cooperative of 120 people at Oberlin, I see the strengths and weaknesses of this smaller community. Being small means everyone feels needed, yet it also means that they have no place to hide—they cannot easily run from anyone with whom they have a problem.

Besides the waking world of work and play, Carl and I share our dreams. Before arriving at the Bear Tribe, I read *The Kin of Atta are Waiting for You*, a utopian fantasy about a peaceful people who recount their dreams with a partner in their family immediately upon awaking in the morning. Inspired by the book, Carl and I recall our dreams each morning as we lie in bed. I have never shared my inner life in a love relationship before, and the added dimension strengthens our connection.

Just as a common spiritual practice deepens my relationship with Carl, I find my

4

bonds with the community developing in the shared ceremonial life. On Sunday we rise early, dress and sit around the table downstairs, feeding logs into the woodburning stove, waiting for Raven, a member of the Bear Tribe and the Firekeeper for the sweat lodge today. He has been up since five o'clock preparing the fire and rocks. My stomach growls—no breakfast before the sweat because the energy needed to digest food taxes a body already struggling to adjust to the intense heat. Fasting also tends to sharpen the senses, both the physical and the non-physical, and to open the mind to finer perceptions.

My stomach cramps with nerves as well. I panic in small, enclosed spaces. Just the thought of entering a dark enclosure so cramped that I cannot stretch my arms or legs, much less stand, starts my heart pounding. What if I have a sudden urge to stand up? What if the panic overwhelms me and I try to get out by crawling across the red hot rocks in the centre of the lodge?

"OK, the rocks are hot," calls Raven as he swings open the door. "Carl, will you bring the towels, and Kim can you bring the water bottles?"

Some of the nerves relax as I climb up the mountain to the lodge. The overcast sky hides the sun and diffuses the pale winter light. Just two and a half weeks have passed since the winter solstice, the longest night of the year, and the mountain still slumbers, blanketed with a thick layer of snow.

I crouch in front of the fire, warming my hands and gazing across the frozen pond in front of the sweat lodge. Amongst the coals are rocks glowing red, hot as the molten core of the Earth. Huddled against the sub-freezing cold, I can hardly imagine that those rocks will heat the lodge enough to make me sweat.

Wabun, Sun Bear's 'medicine helper' and partner for several years, joins the circle of people gathered around the fire. She passes around a leather pouch of tobacco. "Take a pinch," she explains, "and divide it into two. With one half, make an offering to the fire for what you want to receive at this time in your life. With the other half, offer what you want to release in the sweat today."

I pause, holding the tobacco in my palm. What do I need now in my life? "Creator," I say inside myself, "I want to give fully of myself in this place. And I want to release my fears and doubts about my abilities, about what I have to give in life. Please help me, Creator, help me to give what I can."

We offer prayers for the Wood Beings that have given of themselves for the fire, and the stones, the bones of the Earth Mother, that have given away to heat the lodge. We leave our clothes and towels in piles around the fire and then move clockwise around the lodge, stopping at each of the four directions to offer prayers and invite the spirit of that direction to join us. We step around a long mound of dirt that points to the east from the lodge door.

"That's the turtle's neck," says Shawnodese, the sub-chief of the Bear Tribe. "Make sure you never step over it. That would be like breaking the turtle's neck. Always walk around it." The lodge itself is low and rounded like the back of a turtle. "North America," explains Shawnodese, "is called Turtle Island. The sweat lodge represents a turtle, which symbolises the land of this continent and the Earth as a whole. The lodge is round. In Native American tradition roundness is sacred. When we enter the lodge it's like entering the womb of the Earth Mother. We go to be cleansed and renewed. When we leave, it's like being born anew. We enter the world humbly, crawling on hands and knees, naked like a newborn baby."

One by one we walk to the left of the turtle's neck, stoop low, and crawl through the two-foot-high opening. We sit silently, knees drawn up and arms wrapped around legs to make room for everyone in the circle. Rocks glow in the firepit dug in the centre of the lodge. Already I can feel the dry heat pressing against my shins.

A reverent quiet fills me, the same feeling that accompanies me when entering a church or joining a circle of friends gathered in an orchard to honour the passing of the seasons in ceremonies based on the wisdom of the ancient Celts. Readied by the portal of ceremony, I prepare to enter myself, to discover and stretch the boundaries of who I think I am, and ultimately to encounter the core of my being, where Self and Spirit merge.

In the sweat lodge my sense of family widens to encompass the Earth and then beyond. I am part of this Earth, but not of it. I know myself as substance within the world of Form, yet I sit on the fence that borders the Formless, mediating between the Seen and the Unseen, glimpsing many worlds. Here, in this fluid world, I speak and move in ways that, Earthbound, I would call 'magic'.

My speech becomes prayer as I focus the power of word for the healing and wholeness of all creation. Sorrow pours from my heart into the Central Fire, the Spirit of Fire transforming the pain into a fine-edged love tempered by the heat. I am melting inside—just as my voice melts and weaves into the chants—melting, releasing, flowing into a new form, to emerge from the lodge newborn, into a winterworld of ice and snow and chattering teeth. Through ceremony I am bonded with Self, community, cosmos and Spirit, and through the union I am conceived and born anew.

Two hours before I could not imagine being too hot, but now I welcome the cold sting of snow as I rub it on my steaming body. I feel stretched and clean and airy as if the winter breeze can move more freely through my cells and molecules. My physical awareness extends so far that I am reluctant to encase myself in clothes again, but as the sweat dries and the heartbeat slows, my body chills. I pull on clothes and lace my boots before walking slowly down the slippery path to the Long House.

After brunch, a feast of eggs, vegetables, salad and homemade bread, we gather in the living room for the weekly Council meeting. Raven, a member since he arrived from Germany five years ago, moves around the circle with an abalone shell filled with smouldering sage, fanning the embers with a wing so that we can draw the smoke into the heart, over the head and down the arms. This act of 'smudging' purifies the body, mind and spirit in preparation for the meeting. We sit in silence for a few moments, then Sun Bear offers a prayer that all that passes be for the greatest good of the whole.

The business of scheduling the busyness of the Tribe begins. 'Mosha needs the car to get into town on these days, Donna is driving from town to the mountain that day. Carl needs to make a dentist appointment, which bleeds into a discussion about covering the cost. A freelance journalist wants to visit the community and write an article for the Spokane newspaper. Wabun approaches this cautiously—the woman has a history of writing searing exposés about other communities. After airing several opinions, the general feeling is that the Bear Tribe has nothing to hide, that she is welcome to come.

I grow sleepy as I nestle into the foam cushions of the old sofa. Someone throws a log in the stove as work reports begin. Matthew talks about how his work in town has grown to such an extent that he can no longer maintain the garden this summer. My ears prick up. After only eight days already I am contemplating returning to the Bear Tribe this summer. I am a passionate gardener, though the size of the garden daunts me . . . . I decide to talk with him after the meeting.

Over the month of attending Council Meetings, I observe the informal roles that people play in the group. People often ask Matt for his opinion on various issues. He is treated with a respect that is commensurate with the load of responsibilities he

6

has shouldered. Although he has lived here for nearly two years and was eligible for membership after one, he chooses to retain visitor status. Despite his official classification, he is a leader within the community. I begin to see that in this community power is gained from the amount of responsibility taken, rather than from delegation, as in a corporate hierarchy.

Wabun listens intently to Matt. My mind plays through Wabun's contribution to the Tribe. As Sun Bear's partner for several years, and one of the three people still remaining from the very beginnings of the Bear Tribe, she fulfils many positions, formal and informal, within the community. She is executive director of the Bear Tribe Press, runs apprentice screening programmes, attends Medicine Wheel Gatherings and lectures throughout the US and Europe—the list goes on and on. Within the Council Meeting she is a peacekeeper, able to identify brewing conflicts and bring them to the surface. She is aware of this role and even asks people to help keep her out of it by taking more responsibility in resolving conflicts when they are small. "I am tired of mothering people," says Wabun, sighing, "but I can't ignore the volcano brewing between you two." She eyes Carl and Cougar. They look down and shift a bit in their seats.

"Yeah, we talked earlier this fall about the tension between us, and I'm aware that it's gotten worse lately," admits Carl.

"This *fall*?! You've let this go for so long? .... Carl, does Cougar remind you of your father?"

Silence. Pause. "Maybe that's part of it." Carl looks up. "I'm willing to meet with Cougar and talk this week." Cougar, arms folded, heels dug in and jaw set, nods his head. "OK. This week."

The tension loosens in my shoulders like the snap of a taut rubber band. Startled, I suddenly realise that I can sense someone else's tension or anger in my own body. I begin to see the importance of working with challenges between people as soon as possible, not only to save my own body tension and peace of mind, but also to keep the atmosphere of the community relaxed.

Around three o'clock we take a twenty-minute break to stretch. The smokers head for the back porch. As I stand puffing smoke in the frosty air, Wabun joins me. We chat for a few moments, then Wabun turns to face me.

"You know when I finished school I wrote that book *The People's Lawyers*. I really believed in what those lawyers were doing."

I nod my head, listening.

"At a certain point, though, someone said to me, 'If you believe in what you are writing about, why don't you *do* it?' I realised people would never trust me unless I lived what I was writing about."

I scuff the snow with my boots and look up. "Yeah, I can understand that." Something is jarring deep inside me. My safety screen of being a 'participant observer' is crumbling. I realise that Wabun is indirectly asking me to put my life where my mouth is.

When the Council resumes, I watch Hilary, a long-term visitor with a gentle Southern drawl. His compact, wiry body often shakes with warm-hearted laughter. Hilary's most frequent role is that of the Clown, the sacred Heyokah of Native American tradition, who teaches deep wisdom through laughter, 'making light' so that others can see themselves in a less painful manner. Today, though, he lies on his back with knees propped up, hands folded across his stomach. Occasionally he hauls himself up to perch on an elbow, draws a breath and makes a slow, carefully weighted statement, usually tinged with humour.

Not everyone appreciates his role, however. During the meeting, after one of

Hilary's comments, Shawnodese yells, "You're lazy, Hilary. And you show disrespect by lying on the floor and not making eye contact with everyone."

Hilary sighs, draws himself up on his elbow and looks around. "I sit like this so that I have to make an *effort* to sit up and speak. It keeps me from spouting my mouth off when it's not necessary." He locks eyes with Shawnodese. Another sigh, and he reclines into his interlaced fingers, this time with head propped up slightly by a cushion. Compromise.

I am stunned by Hilary's wisdom in finding a way to speak only what is necessary, a rare skill in a community heavily dependent on meetings. I'm equally incredulous at how long Shawnodese has misjudged Hilary's behaviour. The understanding of his actions comes only after the eruption of a long-held, carefully nurtured grudge. I wonder what meetings would be like if everyone lay on his or her back and had to make an effort to sit up to speak?

Finances are next on the agenda. We need another used four-wheel-drive vehicle on the farm—Matt agrees to check listings in the local papers. The Long House needs a new roof and Carl needs money to have a tooth repaired. *Many Smokes*, the community's quarterly magazine, is a couple of months late due to layout and printing delays. The distribution seems to operate according to 'Indian time'—it happens when it happens, despite the quarterly designation.

Having spent almost all of my time working at the farm on Vision Mountain, I glimpse the challenges faced by the people working in the publishing and catalogue business in town through these weekly work reports. Not knowing the daily rhythm of another part of the community or not having the glue of informal, daily contact causes a crack to develop in the unity of the Tribe. An hour's drive separates the house in Spokane from Vision Mountain to the north of the city. Without daily interaction, resentment can build between the two groups about who is 'really working'. Everyone in town usually works ten or twelve hours a day, six days a week. On the farm, however, the intense winter cold precludes long hours of outdoor work. The vegetable garden lies frozen under the snow, and the larder is filled from the autumn butchering. Cougar retreats more into his pipe carving, Hilary into his books in the evenings, and the folks in town grow resentful of the winter repose—the winter is one of their busiest times. The Council Meetings include work reports for two reasons, depending on your perspective—to support trust and to undermine it.

When the business is finished, we hold hands for a few moments of silence together. Knowing that Sun Bear will be leaving soon for another lecture tour, I run after him as he retreats up the stairs to his room. "Sun Bear, can I talk with you for a minute?"

"Sure, come on up," he offers. I sit perched on the edge of his bed, glancing at the papers, books and medicine objects crammed into the tiny room. Sun Bear smiles. "I never throw anything away that might be useful. Tell me, what's on your mind?"

"Well, I told 'Mosha a bit about an experience I had, and she suggested I talk with you."

Sun Bear nods and raises his eyebrows, waiting for me to speak. I recount the details of a vision in which a man with long, jet-black braids dressed in a turquoise robe led me to an opening in the Earth. He guided me in a flight down a steep, winding tunnel to an underground cavern.

When I finish, Sun Bear nods his head slowly and then looks up. "Go sit on the Earth," he says simply. "Take some cornmeal or some kind of grain in your pocket. Offer it to the four directions. Then sit. Sit and listen. Spend as much time as you can sitting on the Earth Mother."

During the coming week I follow his advice, escaping from the Long House as often as possible to walk on the mountain. Shasta and Tasha, Sun Bear and Wabun's 'medicine dogs', often accompany me on these walks. When I stop to sit on a snowy ridge, Shasta stalks around me and then lies down, wrapping himself around my back. Although Sun Bear's directions sound simple, after years of filling every available moment with *doing*, the ability to sit still in one place is a skill that requires cultivation. This sort of 'doing', though, sitting in one spot, is work of the deepest order because slowly I become aware of where I am, rooted in place, and eventually, if patience prevails, *who* I am. I sit on the mountain, struggling with my Self, facing doubts and questions, and talking with the Creator—alone. The road to such knowing is long—I begin and begin and begin, making a path as I go.

At dusk I return to the Long House. The people here at the Farm spend most evenings clustered around the warmth of the woodburning stove. The constant contact with other people provides a grit that allows no discomforts to go unnoticed. Uncleared disturbances rub into raw wounds that scar in the healing.

Each person finds his or her own way of coping with the lack of private space. Cougar burrows into a chair, long black braids falling smoothly against his chest, eyes magnetised by the book in his lap. Only a shout or a direct punch in the arm can jar him. The printed pages become protective walls in which he wanders.

Hilary retreats into his room in one of the smaller outlying buildings, studying esoteric books and journeying deep within himself. Only occasionally does he spend an evening in the Long House. Eleven-year-old Casey, daughter of Singing Pipe Woman (Donna), sits at the table absorbed in the world of her Walkman headphones, clicking time with her painted fingernails on the table. Some evenings she unpacks her bottles of seed beads and makes earrings to sell to the girls at school. She patiently teaches me to thread the tiny beading needles, wax the thread and string the little beads into long, dangling earrings. Eventually I graduate to necklaces and mandala designs as well.

Ruth (Blue Camas) and Nimimosha play cribbage with a passion. Their conversation is abbreviated to muttering—"Thirteen . . . I need a two or a . . . hmmm"—and the counting of pegs on the board. Their intense concentration relaxes into groans, smirks, laughs and curses at the end of each round.

Occasionally Medicine Flower, a visitor since the winter solstice, limbers her operatic voice in the evening. When she squares herself in front of the piano, knees flexed like a linebacker prepared to tackle any offending notes, the room quickly clears. The wooden walls, however, are thin, and no one completely escapes the thunder of her voice. Even Hilary comments on her vocal callisthenics the next morning.

Acutely aware of people's response to Medicine Flower's singing, I cloister myself in my tiny room to practise some Joan Baez songs. I know about five guitar chords, just enough to get by accompanying myself, and sometimes I practise the violin. My second major at Oberlin is violin performance, so I need to keep my fingers limber, or at least familiar with the instrument. I'm surprised when 'Mosha calls for me to come downstairs to sing. I guess folksongs blend in more easily than Verdi or Wagner.

Around 8:30 'Mosha settles into the couch with Yarrow, her eight-year-old daughter, to read a story. After the story and a round of kisses from everyone in the living room, Yarrow climbs upstairs to her bedroom. Casey follows soon after. By ten o'clock the house is quiet with everyone asleep or reading in bed. I nestle under a pile of blankets—the house is cold at night when the fire in the stove dies—and read a novel.

9

I look up when Carl walks in my room. He draws a deep breath, nodding his head in contentment as he exhales. I stretch out my arm, inviting him to sit next to me.

"Today's a very good day to die," says Carl, leaning his head against my shoulder, "a very good day to die."

I draw back to look at him, puzzled. "What do you mean, die? Is something wrong?"

"No, no," says Carl, laughing, "I mean I'm really happy. It's been a good day."

"Then why do you say 'good day to *die*'?"

"Well, it means if I would die today, I would die feeling complete. It's a good time to go." Carl pauses, pushing his long, blond hair back from his face. "You know, when the warriors went into battle, they looked at their lives, gave thanks and said to the Creator, 'Today is a very good day to die.' They were happy with their lives. They had lived well. If they had to die, they were ready; they would die willingly, honourably. They didn't look at death as something terrible. They knew they would come back to this Earth again."

"Oh," I say, thoughtfully, "I never looked at death that way." Always I have believed that dying was not final, the end of all things, but I have never thought of death as something to greet gladly, with thanksgiving, as a moment to choose with gratitude. "Yeah, it makes sense." I yawn, tired after a long day. "Come on, let's sleep. We have to be up early to milk the cows." I burrow under the blankets, craving warmth in the cold, dark house.

Morning. Or at least I assume it's morning because I hear movements in the kitchen and the squeak of the stove door opening as someone adds another log. My room has no windows, so I can judge the return of the sun only by the light seeping through the cracks in the floorboards. Carl and I lie back to front, our bodies nestled like teaspoons, savouring the warmth and the dreamy threshold between sleeping and waking.

"Carl, are you milking this morning?" calls Cougar.

"Yeah, I'm coming," yells Carl. We dress in the cold morning air, breath hanging in clouds, and head downstairs to the kitchen.

Milking is a ritual. Each piece of equipment has its home in the bathroom off the kitchen. Each bit of the preparation and clean up are steps in a dance. Even in the fog of early morning fatigue, the dance proceeds unwavering. Put the kettle on the stove, heat, pour boiling water in milk pail, check sieve, clean buckets. Carry the pails to the barn. Fill troughs with grain. Clean the cow's udder with the hot water. Settle onto the milking stool. Draw the milk in clean, white jets into the waiting pail. Enjoy the rhythm of the milk swooshing in the bucket. Rest nose against flank, breathing in the warm animal scent, a mix of hay and earth and sweat. Continue until the udder hangs flaccid, ready to be refilled by evening.

We open the barn door, releasing the cows to wander in the snowy pastures for the day. Back in the Long House we clean and replace buckets, pails and strainers, have a bite to eat, and then repeat the dance with the goats. They are my favourites, these two mama goats. Their big ears flap up and down as they bounce on spring-like legs to greet us as we approach the gate of their pen. Once inside, Carl bends down to butt his head playfully with one of them. "One time," says Carl, laughing, "we were playing, and she butted me so hard I fell over. They have really strong heads." Hard-headed. Stubborn. Stubborn as a goat. These and other sayings have new meaning to me as I come to know the personalities of the animals.

I learn, painfully, that geese are the inspiration for the term 'goosing'. Leave your bum unprotected and your back turned on an alert 'watch goose', and you can soon find yourself in mid-air, struck by a wild-feathered missile projected right into your rear with no warning save a last-minute squawk of indignation. When we leave the goats' pen to walk across the barnyard to the chicken coop, I keep a watchful eye for the gander. Geese are sneaky goosers.

I crane my neck around and make a bee line for the chicken coop (two more animal truths). Inside the coop, just high enough to stand in, I breathe shallowly—the acidic smell of dung and fallen feathers stings my nose. I am wary as I lift the mamas from the nest boxes to retrieve their eggs. Their beaks deliver hard whacks.

As I refill the grain dispenser, I notice one chicken that looks sullen and droopy. "Hey Carl, look at that one. Is something wrong with her?"

Carl gently lifts the chicken and examines her legs. "Oh, looks bad. Her leg froze on the perch last night. It must have been really cold in here." He pauses to stroke the trembling bird. "I guess we'll have fresh chicken for dinner."

"You going to butcher her?" I ask.

"Well, she's not in very good shape."

"Let me see what I can do."

"She'll probably be dead by tomorrow, especially if the cold continues, but you can try."

I fill my hand with grain and squat next to the hen, holding the food below her beak. She pecks timidly at first, but soon finishes the handful of grain and then another. I give her water in the same way. In the evening I return to the chicken coop to check on her and give her more food. So far, so good—she's still alive.

On the third morning I find the hen sitting in the same spot. When I bend down with a handful of grain, her eyes look brighter. She fluffs her feathers, shifting a bit. I catch a glimpse of something white. Sliding my hand underneath, I withdraw an egg. "You must be feeling better," I say, stroking her head.

The next day she pecks at my hand, cheeky little bird, and I know that she is recovered. By the end of a week she is hopping around on one leg, resuming an active chicken life.

Although I love working with the animals and know that they are kept to provide food for the Bear Tribe, I have been a vegetarian since I was eighteen, when I left home and could control my own diet. My parents discouraged me, sure that I would die if I didn't eat meat at least twice a day. I did not become a vegetarian, though, because I objected to the killing of cute, furry animals. Even before arriving at the Bear Tribe I learned how to butcher chickens, and while on the farm I have butchered and skinned rabbits.

I choose not to eat meat because of the wasteful and unhealthy way most animals are raised—pumped full of antibiotics and other chemicals (I read recently that farmers are feeding cement to cows shortly before butchering to boost their weight, a practice that the FDA finds acceptable). They are jammed in battery pens and crowded into pastures to the point that manure runoff is the major source of water pollution in the West (see Francis Moore Lappé, *Diet for a Small Planet*).

Farmers in the western US routinely overgraze fragile semi-desert land, often running cattle and sheep on land supervised by the Bureau of Land Management. Stripped of its sparse natural ground cover, the land quickly erodes, washing into the streams and rivers with the rain or blowing away in the wind.

A good argument for grain-fed cattle, right? Wrong. A cow consumes 20 pounds of grain for each pound of meat it produces—that's a poor return by any accounting method. A chicken yields one pound of meat for every five pounds of grain that it eats—better, but still not as efficient as eating the grain itself. Right now on planet Earth we have enough grain to feed the entire world. Read that again. *Right now*. Enough grain to feed the entire world. That's a figure that every US agricultural

11

agency official or government-sponsored aid programme director would like to cover up—permanently. Because it exposes the terrible opulence of the US population, spoiled by large quantities of meat and sugar, grains and produce.

But we grow all our own food, I hear you say. We don't take anything from the rest of the world—do we?

The answer is most definitely *yes*. Most of the beef served in fast food restaurants comes from cattle raised in Central and South America on ranches created by clearing vast tracts of rainforest. The felled trees are not even sawn for lumber or chipped for paper production—they are simply burned where they fall. These rainforests are the planet's richest ecosystem, populated by two-thirds of the planet's plant and animal species.

The richness is deceptive, though, because the rainforest recycles its nutrients in the canopy of the trees through a complex system of epiphytic plants, not through the soil as is the case in a temperate deciduous forest. Some animals spend their entire life cycle in the trees, never touching the ground. Shallowly rooted in the poor soil, the giant trees have adapted to absorb many nutrients through the rain and air.

When first exposed to a rainforest, any uneducated developer would assume that the soil would be rich in nutrients, exceptionally well-suited to raise grass for cattle grazing. Once stripped of trees, however, the soil bakes into brick-like laterite, so hard that only a crowbar can dent the land. During the first year a few tufts of grass grow. Most ranchers abandon the land after only two years. By the fifth year what was once a forest, teeming with plants and animals, is a desert, unable to sustain any life.

My concern for the rainforest as well as the knowledge of the grain wasted in feeding animals inspired me to become a vegetarian. The choice, along with the decision not to eat bananas or coffee, is a way of making a small stand for a way of life that I believe in—sharing resources equitably, living in a way that does not lean too heavily on the land. It is part of an answer to the questions that plague me about how to *enact* the kind of life I envision.

Always my greatest teachers ask questions, ones that turn me inwards. While here at the Bear Tribe I have come across references to Twylah Nitsch, a teacher of the Wolf Clan. Twylah offers four questions to evaluate one's life: One: Am I happy with what I'm doing? Two: Is what I'm doing adding to the confusion? Three: What am I doing to bring about peace and contentment? Four: How will I be remembered when I am gone?

As I work on the farm, spending a lot of time with the animals, I ponder those questions in relation to my own decision not to eat meat. I love the animals here; the daily work with them fills me with joy. Entering the rhythm of seasonal birth and growth and death brings a satisfaction and contentment that quiets my usual impatience. Here I learn there is no way to hurry a chick from an egg or a calf from its mother's womb. To push the growth, or to overstep any part of the cycle, would be to destroy the rhythm as a whole.

At Vision Mountain the animals are well cared for, and their impact on the land is minimal. After much thought, I decide that if I help to care for an animal and butcher it with respect, I can eat the meat. Before killing any of the animals here, we offer prayers to the Great Spirit, recognising that all things come from the Creator. "Don't get lost in giving thanks for the form of something," warned an elder. "Give thanks for the Creator dwelling in that Being." We thank the animal for giving its life away so that ours might go on.

Rabbit flesh becomes my flesh. Then in a sense I am responsible to give away good things through *my* life so that the circle of giving can continue unbroken. As I nurture the animal's life and then take it away, I experience the circular nature of existence. Like the Goddess Kali, I am both nurturer and destroyer, giver and receiver, participating fully in the dance of life and death.

Any feathers or bones, skin or innards that are not used in the butchering process are returned to the mountain. Late last autumn Cougar and Carl butchered one of the cows on the farm, and they have been waiting for the track up to the mountain to clear so that they can return the leftover bones to a special ridge. Although the snow still lies thick on the ground, one cold afternoon in mid-January five of us pile into the four-wheel drive with two large metal bowls filled with the last remains of the cow. No one has ventured along this track on the southern ridge of the mountain since before the snows began, so we bounce along as fast as the vehicle will go, hoping the momentum will carry us over the worst ruts.

The truck strains up a steep hill, slows, and then holds fast, wheels spinning in the ditch. Cougar stops the engine and rummages in the back for a shovel while Carl hauls the bowls from the back of the truck. Together with Kim, he drags one up the ridge. Cougar and Medicine Flower tackle another, alternately lifting and dragging, slipping and laughing up the ridge. I play Margaret Bourke White, focusing my camera as I jump around in the knee-deep snow, photographing the episode for the audio-visual.

I sidle up behind Cougar as he shovels snow from under the buried wheels. He looks up with a mock scowl. "Why don't you put that camera away and *do* something?" he jibes. I grin, adjusting the shutter speed, and quickly take a couple of pictures. "Come on, Cougar, smile. This is your chance to be a star."

A good photographer is a master of camouflage, artfully blending into any situation. I realise, though, that like the research scientist whose mere presence subtly affects the results of an experiment, my recording through the eye of the camera is far from objective. The sight of a camera alters people's behaviour and freezes bodies and minds into uncomfortable postures. After a few shots I put the camera in the car and join Carl in hauling the last bowl up the ridge.

* * *

Tonight is new moon, a time usually marked by a ceremony held on a plateau called 'The Moon Rocks'. Each time I walk up the steep path that winds between large boulders to the Moon Rocks, I have a sense of moving through a portal into another world. The bare rock plateau stretches all around me, undisturbed by soil or grass or tree, the flatness broken only by large rocks and a few boulders scattered over the surface. "That place is strange," commented Carl one day. "Every time I go up there the rocks seem to be in a different place."

Nimimosha usually organises a ceremony to celebrate the new and full moon, but tonight almost everyone, including 'Mosha, is in town. I decide to walk alone up the southern ridge, in part to honour the full moon, and more importantly to grapple with my fear of the dark.

The first hundred yards are easy, the path illuminated by the light glowing from the Long House windows. As I continue, my eyes adjust to the dim starlight, and I discern the silhouettes of tall trees lining the track. "Keep breathing, keep breathing," I tell myself when the trees obscure the view of the Long House. "No molester would brave this cold to attack me."

I stand breathless. The sudden movement of a formless shape in front of me freezes my feet to the track and ices the air in my lungs to a standstill. I am certain

13

of eyes boring into my back, but when I wheel around, intent on catching them off guard, I see nothing. Paralysed by the fear of shadow giants, my knees melt into unstable putty, and I pour with sweat. I hear the moan of wind-stroked trees—ah, not the sound of footsteps—and find the courage to draw another breath.

I walk past the dip in the snow where the four-wheel drive was stuck, willing my body to reach the mountain top. Here on this flat, open ridge where the bones of slaughtered animals are returned to the Earth, I lie on my back, gazing at the stars overhead. The place is not gruesome; instead, it is infused with peace, capped by the velvet dome of sky and stars.

I close my eyes, whispering prayers into space. "Where am I going, Creator, and what is the purpose of my life? What am I doing here . . . . And Creator, what do I need to know about relationships? I'm so confused about the men in my life . . . ." I try to compare two lovers from Oberlin, both so uniquely special, with the painful goal of deciding with whom my heart (or just body?) will lie. Heart and body, though, can't be divided without splitting the soul.

Both men have expressed the need for an either/or choice, unwilling to be caught on the ends of an emotional tug-of-war. I don't blame them. I am not interested in being ripped and swayed by opposing forces either, but the reality of choosing one or the other repulses me.

Perhaps I will be with no one. Neither one has completely captured my heart or consumed my interest as John, my ex-fiancé, once did. Perhaps no one ever will again, for my heart, as my friend Eddie describes it, has learned to keep a secret cloistered part, revealed to no one, not even my closest lover, for fear of losing myself, and submerging once again in an uncontrollable flood of emotions.

And what about Carl? I love you more deeply and honestly than I have anyone for a long time, but I am afraid of putting any pressure of expectation on our relationship, still so new and tender, like the first shoots of spring. Besides, to add another factor to the web of relationships in my life is more than I can handle right now. For the moment I am simply grateful for the beauty of your being and all that we share.

The whispers continue into thankfulness and finally into silence. I am cleansed by the stillness and renewed, ready for the shadow-pocked descent to the Long House. As I walk I see the glow of light from the Long House below me, but I am no longer eager to return. I am learning to walk in darkness and make my own light.

* * *

In late December the Bear Tribe acquired what was a small neighbourhood church with an adjoining rectory. The former church now houses the catalogue and publishing business and provides workshop space in town. The house next to the church is a great bonus, because the people working in town can live away from the clutter and bustle of the business. In the old house everything took place under one small roof.

The first community function in the new 'Circle Center' is a celebration of Donna's (Singing Pipe Woman) marriage to Bob (Golden Bear). Ruth, the grandma of the Tribe and a whiz in the kitchen, begins the food preparations days ahead. In the late afternoon before the party, I drive into town with Carl in his old white Chevy van, winding slowly along the dark, snowy mountain roads. We arrive in time to help unfurl tin foil from bowls of salad and platters of cheeses and meats. The crowning glory is the stack of boxes labelled 'Pioneer Pies'. I surreptitiously lift a corner of one of the boxes. "Leave those alone," calls Ruth, grinning and shaking a finger at me. "They're for dessert."

Donna and Bob pose for a pie-cutting picture and then stand in line to receive blessings from everyone. For the first time in the Bear Tribe's history, the spread of food and drink includes beer. Sun Bear took a long time deliberating this decision, knowing how alcohol has poisoned so many native communities, destroying the souls as well as the bodies of the People. At this time, though, aside from Sun Bear, all of the members of the Bear Tribe are of European descent, brought up in a culture that has had some small success in handling alcohol responsibly. He decided to ease the restriction for special celebrations as long as no drunkenness occurs.

Shawnodese eyes a guitar leaning against a wall and then my violin case. After a few whispers in my ear he announces, "How about some dancing?" Almost everyone in the Tribe goes to square dancing lessons given by a local couple in their basement. It is a fun way of exercising as well as making local contacts.

General whoops of approval, and soon everyone is lined up for a version of the Virginia Reel. Shawno keeps time on the guitar and sings out directions while I play all the fiddle tunes in D Major that I know. After a couple of dances, the lines collapse into a jumble of laughter and squashed toes. I am radiant, happy to have some music to share, and grateful for being included in this family celebration.

By the end of the second week of January, I decide to return during the summer to work in the garden. I begin planning the garden, poring over companion planting charts, descriptions of helpful herbs, and catalogues specialising in northern seed varieties. Through the work, a new appreciation of seeds siezes me. Seeds dance from their coats, never to return to a clothed state of decency. They spring from earth propelled by a song as ancient as creation, as limitless as sunlight, and as common as sand beneath a boulder. They dance into my heart, awakening signs of spring.

Reading these catalogues I am smitten with the impatience of springtime, the push of life that bursts boundaries and floods the heart in that season of renewal. I look up, flushed and eager, and feel my prematurely unfurled petals retracting in the January frost. I know why gardeners need winter—to dream, to imagine and to procure a winter seed coat woven by memories and half-spun expectations.

As if prompted by my longing for Spring, a January thaw teases the land, turning the snow into a sodden sponge. It drips from the trees, tap- tap- tapping sweet rhythms on the roof. Wearing only a turtleneck and a wool sweater with my jeans, I walk up the mountain, boots growing soggy as I climb. In the valley below the warm air hangs above the wet snow, breeding a lazy fog that wreathes the basin. I find a rock exposed by the receding snow and sit down, chin resting on cupped hands. My hands, calloused by the tools that they have known—the handle of axe and pail, knife and hammer—and swollen from kneading bread and washing dishes, are a map of the skills that they have learned.

Fragments of a conversation with Hilary last night flit through my mind. He mentioned the Seth books by Jane Roberts, wondering if I had ever read them.

"No, Hilary, what are they about?" I ask.

"Well, basically Seth talks about creating your own reality."

"You mean like the world I live in is different from the world anyone else lives in?" Hilary nods his head in agreement. "Yeah, I believe in that. But don't you think that some things are beyond your control? Like a tree falling on you, or another car running into you or having cancer?"

Hilary smiles, folds his arms, and peruses the ceiling, searching for words. "I believe I create those experiences in my life, too, usually to teach myself something."

15

"But what about fate? Don't you think some things are unavoidable?"

"I don't know," says Hilary thoughtfully, stroking his moustache. "Some teachers say the rate of karma, the law of cause and effect, is speeding up to the point that every action has an immediate reaction. You resolve things right away, not in some other lifetime. Instant karma. Just add water. That's what the Swami Rama Dingdong types say." He roars with laughter.

As I sit on the rock, absorbing the scent of pines and softening earth, I know that I still live within the walls that I call fate and childhood conditioning. But the mortar is crumbling, the tentative cracks widening, and the beams sagging, ready as the melting snow to give way to more fluid forms. Hilary, you have taught me so many things. You show me how to live lightly—not too heavily, too seriously—so that I can see the humour, the irony and the learning in a situation. My thoughts continue as I plod down the mountain, sunset orange flaming in a pale sky. In the late evening, alone by the woodburning stove while others sleep, I write a poem, trying to distil this month's sojourn as I prepare to return to Oberlin.

Raindrops tap rhythmically
Upon the heavy sponge of snow
A pine frond releases its cargo
The echo reverberating
through my watchful body.
Smoke tendrils curl luxuriously,
Dissipating in the moist cold,
My breath billowing gently from my out-turned face.
Mountain, you have taught me,
Brushed me clean and then filled the gaping void
With quiet repose, expectant watchfulness.

Immeasurable gratitude
For the gift of being:
Being allowed,
Being loved,
Being kind,
Being needy,
Being filled,
Being given.

The Giveaway,
Greatest of all treasures,
A piece of my being,
Some fabric of my heart,
Forever embedded in this moment,
In the moment of this place.
The mountain slowly reveals the magnitude of its strength,
The immediate revelation too great for comprehension.

I walk in dark,
I walk alone,
Learning, groping
Searching for footprints in the snow.
The path curves,

I sink in the bank
Unable to distinguish the crested roadway.
I look back,
My tracks already covered
This moonless night.
I search backwards and forwards,
Find no clear carving,
And realise that I must forge my own.

* * *

January 28th. Too soon my departure date arrives. I hoist my backpack into the back of the four-wheel drive and ride with Carl to the lower farmhouse where his van is parked. As we come around the last curve, a huge flock of ravens rises from the field and wheels in the sky overhead.

"Wow, I've never seen so many ravens," exclaims Carl as we turn into the driveway. "Must be a good omen for your return."

I smile and reach out to hug him. "I hope you're right, Carl." I sigh, leaning back against the seat. "I'm not very happy about leaving."

During the drive to the airport we are mostly silent. As we sit waiting in the terminal, I grope for words to express my love and respect, but every phrase sits hollow in my throat, too superficial to express the richness of emotion that I feel.

After the boarding announcement is made, we hold each other close and then lean back, looking deeply in each other's eyes.

"I'll see you again," I say quietly.

"Yeah, I feel that, too. No goodbyes, right?" he asks, smiling.

"No goodbyes," I agree. One last kiss and then I stand in line, turning around only once to wave as I pass the last security check.

I find my seat, snap the buckle on the seatbelt, and then stare out the window as the plane taxis into position. As we roar down the runway, accelerating for takeoff, I see a hawk sitting on a fencepost at the end of the runway. As the plane skims over the fence, the hawk sits unruffled, unconcerned about the jet overhead or the white Chevy van that halts on the roadway in front of it. "Thank you, Creator, for that hawk, and for Carl seeing it, too." As I watch, the hawk leaves its perch and soars to the left of the plane.

In that moment I know that my journey is blessed, that my life will continue on course, as unshakable as the hawk despite the questions and doubts that plague me. I know, too, that Carl will share this journey with me, even if he is not always physically by my side. Although our perspectives are different, with Carl rooted firmly on the ground and me soaring above, we share the same focal point, an unending search for Spirit.

CHAPTER 2
Summer's Bitter Fruits

Back at Oberlin I have a few days of quiet before classes begin, a time to regroup and set my goals for the last few months of school. As I suspected when I lay on the snowy mountain top whispering to the stars, I spend the semester alone—both lovers decide to follow different paths, one with another woman, one alone. Besides completing a heavy course load of classes and preparing a 90-minute senior recital, I help organise demonstrations and discussions with the Women's Center, co-anchor a weekly women's radio show with my friend Zoe called 'Wild Women Don't Get the Blues', and swim a mile each day. I am aware, too, that friends with whom I have shared dreams and heady discussions, tears and quiet walks, stories read aloud and group bubble baths in the co-op showers, will soon disperse around the planet, so at times I leave the papers and books and classes to dangle willy-nilly to enjoy just being with people.

Every couple of weeks I phone the Bear Tribe, talking with Carl and whomever else is around. Although we are separated by over 2,000 miles, I feel close to them, more in touch than with my biological family. "Members of the same family," writes Richard Bach, "rarely live under the same roof." During these months I know the truth of his writing.

After graduation I return to Dayton to visit my parents and buy my first car, a used Mazda GLC, bright yellow with a black interior. I name her Sunflower and christen her with a prayer plume that hangs over the rear view mirror to bless our journeys together. Within a week we are on the road, venturing first to the east coast to visit my sister living north of New York City, then retracing our path to Ohio and on through the Midwest, stopping to visit a couple of friends from Oberlin along the way.

At the airport in Denver I meet Carl for a two-week vacation. We drive to Aspen,

Colorado where I spent three summers at the Music Festival, then head south for Utah, Arizona and Nevada before turning north to skirt the eastern border of California.

During the night we drive from Las Vegas, Nevada to the southeastern border of California, arriving in Independence early in the morning. After consulting a few maps, we decide to camp in John Muir wilderness and explore the mountains and lakes in the area.

A side street in the tiny town of Independence narrows to a dirt track that climbs the mountain, clinging to the steep incline of rocky hills. The musty-sweet scent of sage, released by the warmth of the returning sun, lingers in the morning air.

The campsite is simple, just a few portable toilets and water faucets scattered along a loop road. We pitch the tent under the sheltering branches of a bristlecone pine tree, a long-time resident of planet Earth. Its ancestry is so ancient that biologists have found fossil remains of this tree side-by-side with species that have long since gone the way of the sabre-toothed tiger and the Tyrannosaurus rex. This tree is a survivor, its spiralling trunk supporting branches that twist and curl towards the sun, defying the strong mountain winds that scour its bark and lash its limbs into contorted shapes.

Although today is the the summer solstice, patches of snow surround the camp. Higher up the ridge we can see deep snow fields. The calendar may say 'summer', but the air here is as chill as early spring.

We finish setting up camp around noon and then crawl into our sleeping bags. Although I am exhausted after our marathon drive, an intense longing fills me as I lay down next to Carl. He wraps his arm over my curled back, preparing for a nap. I feel the longing press into my groin, harden my nipples and arch my lower back. I turn to face Carl, my knee sliding between his legs, curling close to him as my hands follow the hard muscles up the curve of his leg, buttocks, back, lingering in his long hair, stroking his neck. With an eager tongue, I taste the salty richness of his neck, lick his tiny nipples and circle his navel.

Carl opens a sleepy eye. "I thought you said you wanted to sleep," he murmurs.

"I did," I say giggling, "but now I'm hungry."

Carl smiles, yawns and stretches his body, relaxing against me. Slowly, with the play of hand and tongue and lip and long-held meetings of the eye our bodies grow taut, hard and wet with longing until we flow, one with the other, moving in a rhythm as ancient as the seasonal dance of the bristlecone pine, rooting and growing and casting its seeds into the wind. Perhaps the power of the solstice is in me, or the raw beauty of the mountain; whatever the source of this longing, I dance again and again, aching to feel Carl with me, in me, surging and pushing and growing within me.

"What's gotten into you?" asks Carl, laughing.

"I just can't get enough of you, I guess. You're so irresistible."

Finally, after over an hour of making love, we lie nestled back to front. Carl's belly, warm against my back, matches the rise and fall of my own breath.

Before falling asleep I need to pee, so I unwrap myself from the sleeping bag, pull on shirt and pants, and head for the toilet. I take a moment to check my cervical cap, fingers searching . . . the cap is low, and I realise with a start that it is dislodged, no longer protecting my cervix. Numb silence. "Oooh, Creator, I may have really done it this time." I sit frozen, willing myself to think of other times that I have worried over false alarms.

I take a few minutes to sit alone in the car before returning to the tent. "Carl," I murmur as I slide into my sleeping bag, "I think we had an accident. My cervical cap slipped, and I'm in the middle of my cycle."

"What?" mumbles Carl, half asleep. "Let's not worry about it right now, OK?"

My mind is sharp and clear and empty as I lie in the tent, watching pine frond shadows dancing on the orange tent wall, dancing in the wind to some half-remembered music, dancing with the magic of a mid-summer's night.

The following days are filled with hiking, exploring, lounging in hot springs and eating ice cream. While in Yosemite I call my parents to say hello, remembering the time we had visited this valley ten years before. Mom clears her throat and pauses during the conversation. "Now, we'd like to *suggest*," she says, words hanging like curve balls, "that you call more often because since you last called we could have died and been buried and no one would have known where to reach you to tell you."

"You planning to die, Mom?" I ask earnestly, trying not to giggle.

"No, honey. You know what I mean," she replies curtly. End of topic. When do parents ever quit worrying? Perhaps it is part of the territory, curbed only by the forgetfulness of old age. I've heard, though, that congenital worry can be fatal. I decide not to worry about their worrying.

More hiking, exploring and driving, driving, driving bring us finally to the Washington border and not long after the Circle Center.

I spend a day working in the office with Ruth, stealing onto the porch whenever I can to drink in sunshine. I am longing for the mountain, wondering what is happening in the garden, with the goats and chickens, who is living in the Long House, and how Cougar and 'Mosha and Hilary and Yarrow are.

In the late afternoon Carl and I load our things into the car. In our month together Sunflower and I have covered over 4,000 miles. She's a good trail companion, asking for nothing more than regular fuel stops and one quart of oil in all those miles. When I ease behind the wheel, I pat the dashboard in appreciation. "She's a good car, isn't she?" I remark as I start the engine. "Yep," says Carl, leaning back in his seat, "she sure is."

We drive on the highway rolling west out of town, soon curving to the north. Stores and houses give way to pine forests and mullein-studded meadows filled with summer wildflowers. The roads narrow, telescoping in size until we reach the rocky, rutted road that leads to the Farm.

The land feels different without the winter blanket of snow. A new sort of blanket holds the land, an oppressive heat that builds into a mid-day climax that slowly unravels through the evening. This 'high desert' country has very little humidity to hold the day's warmth into the night, so the dark hours are cold.

The farmhouse, too, is different, no longer the quiet, secluded haven of the winter, but rather a bustling centre for the visitors who have come for the apprentice screening programme. Sun Bear, weary from years of being on the road, wants to spend the summer at home, so the programmes were scheduled on Vision Mountain.

Arriving too late to set up our tent on the mountain, Carl and I sleep upstairs in the Long House. I awake in the morning, eager to work in the garden, but the weather daunts me, alternating between mist and heavy downpours. Sun Bear sits in the living room lecturing about sexual energy. The room erupts frequently in nervous laughter. He also gives his perspective on world situations and offers his ideas about how individuals can help. He seems to have moved from directly enacting visions, the work of his younger years, to becoming a seed disperser, dropping visionary seed-thoughts into eager, fertile minds, hoping that they will take hold and become reality through these seekers.

My thoughts turn to Marion, a beautiful woman from Germany who arrived with her son Denis, aptly named as he reminds me of Denis the Menace, careening around the house and yelling at the top of his lungs. I watched this morning as Sun Bear began his usual approach that signals his interest in a woman. First and foremost is the 'Medicine Man Hug', a close bear hug with hands held firmly, to the point of trembling, on the behind. Innocent talk and questions follow, with a lot of wandering gazes.

Most women who come to the Tribe are both flattered and embarrassed by the attention, flustered by sexual advances when they expected a 'spiritual' man. For Sun Bear, though, sexuality is not separated from spirituality. He breathes a quick prayer, 'Thank you, Creator, everything is good' and then hustles in pursuit. The members of the Bear Tribe have confronted him a few times about his sexual advances and declared that they would warn incoming females about his licentious behaviour. "All right," says Sun Bear, grinning sheepishly, "but you know it goes both ways. It takes two to tango."

So the members warn the new arrivals, but the women continue to flock. Some even offer themselves without solicitation. I feel sad about these women. They revel in strutting from Sun Bear's room in the morning and smile knowingly when people ask how they slept. "I was very warm with a Bear in my bed," one declares, arching an eyebrow. They seem to love the status brought by being in close quarters with a man of power more than they actually love the man himself. I'm sad that Sun Bear either does not see the game or else desires the company enough to ignore the ruse.

Marion, on the other hand, declares that she is on her 'moon time' (menstruation), thwarting Sun Bear's first attempts. In a couple of days she laughs and says, "Vee are good friends, Sun Bear and I, not lovers." Good. Sun Bear needs more friends and fewer status seekers.

Marion and I work in the garden one day, harvesting lambs-quarter in an overgrown field, a task that requires several hours' work to feed 45 people. She asks about the sweat lodge ceremony and its meaning. Practising my German, I try to explain in a foreign language responses that run deep within me, almost beyond the grasp of words. Meanwhile Denis charges around the garden, pulling out half-grown onions, sinking deep footprints into the raised bed, and jabbing sticks down animal holes.

We take buckets of lambs-quarter tops to Hetty and Bill, Cougar's former partner and her new 'husband'. "Vee aren't married in some court," says Hetty. "Dat just makes money for some lawyer if you decide not to be together later. But he is my husband just the same." They are hired to cook for two of the apprentice screening programmes. We find them scurrying among steaming pots, half-wilted in the gruelling late afternoon heat.

"Oh, we don't have time for dose," says Hetty, waving a wooden spoon at us. "I don't have time to clean dem."

I sit down on a bench nearby and grin. "They are ready for steaming. You don't have to clean them." Despite over twenty years of living in the US, Hetty's German accent still shows like an errant slip peeking from under a skirt. Some people chafe at her brusqueness, but I find the grit endearing. She loves as strongly as she blusters, and I respect her for that.

Five minutes before dinner time someone rings the bell outside, and a large crowd of apprentices, members and visitors squeeze into a circle around the 12-foot-long wooden table. We hold hands, close eyes and stand quietly as Raven offers thanks. "Creator, Great Spirit, Grandmothers and Grandfathers, Spirit

21

Helpers and Spirit Keepers of this land—thank you for this food, for these gifts from the Earth, for the plants and animals that have given away so that we might eat today. Thank you for the Earth and the Water Beings that nourished them, the sun and air that has sustained them. Thank you, Creator, for this time to be together in this place. May we use this food in a good way. Ho!"

"Ho!" echoes around the circle. People fill their plates and disperse to seats around another wooden table in the Long House or to chairs and benches outside. In the winter we did not have the luxury of eating outside, but we also did not need the extra space. With around 25 people participating in the apprentice screening pro-gramme, plus another five to ten visitors in addition to the majority of the Bear Tribe membership, the Long House is full to the brim and overflows to the circle of chairs and benches arranged on a small area of cleared ground outside.

Everyone takes a turn at washing the dishes sometime during their stay. Only the cooks are excused from the rota—they have enough pots and pans to wash to make up for many kitchen clean-ups. I add my plate to the growing pile next to the sink inside and join Carl for the evening milking.

In the last hour of sunlight, already flaring gold among the tops of the pine trees, we gather in Hilary's room—Hilary and his friend Connie, Hetty and Bill, and Carl and I. We lean against the unpainted wood walls, rolling Drum tobacco cigarettes and puffing smoke into the still air. We swap stories about travels and family and inner journeys, interrupted with laughs and questions and 'oh-that-reminds-me's'.

"I wish I had some photos to show you," I muse at one point, "but I hardly used my camera this trip."

"Oh, I've never had a camera," says Hetty, her face puckering in disdain.

"Never? I think they're nice to help remember things."

"Ach, I have pictures dat I carry in my mind. Whenever I have time, when I'm not doing anyting, I can sit down and close my eyes and see dose pictures. I don't need some special photo album. I carry dem with me. When I see something beauti-ful, I concentrate on it, using my mind like a camera, and den I have dat picture with me always."

The next day when I am working in the garden, I look up at the aspen tree grow-ing above the spring. The breeze shimmies through the branches, twirling the shiny leaves that glint in the sun. "I wish I had my camera with me," I mutter, and then recall Hetty's words. I put down the weed bucket and open the shutter of my mind to absorb this tree. The details include the smell of the warm earth beneath my feet, the honey fragrance of wildflowers blooming around the spring, the touch of breeze playing on my cheek, and the sound of wind whispering among the leaves. The pic-ture fixes in my mind, much richer than the two-dimensional world of Kodachrome, a treasure available for enjoyment at any time within the vault of my mind.

* * *

6:30 a.m. The sun is rising over the far ridge. The alarm beeps insistently next to my sleeping-bag-cushioned head. Carl rolls over for a quick morning kiss before pulling on pants and shirt in the chill air. I idle for a few moments, watching the pale dawn light strengthening in the summer sky before crawling out of my sleep-ing bag.

We prepare the buckets and hot water in the Long House. Already Hetty is mix-ing eggs and Bill shaping biscuits for breakfast. Carl and I load the gear into the back of the four-wheel drive and begin the bumpy descent down the mountain to where Twiggy, a newly purchased Swiss milk cow, lives. Cougar traded the other

22

two cows for this pedigreed matron, knowing that the milk from this one cow would equal the output of the other two combined. Initially I missed the other cows, the former reigning queen of the barnyard and her obedient princess-daughter, but I grow to love Twiggy, despite some of her cantakerous ways. Her patience is like an hour-glass, determined by the amount of grain left in her trough. As the last grains disappear, the fidgeting begins. She also has developed a passion for human food.

During the summer Cougar moves the grazing animals down to the lower barn where they have more pasture land to roam. Often, though, the gates between fields are left open, and frequently I find Twiggy with her nose buried in a tuft of long grass growing near the porch of the lower farmhouse. I discovered her one day poking her head into an open door of a car just returned from town, her wet nose plastered with dusty white powder, munching happily from the fifty-pound bag of white flour that she had ripped open.

Carl's hands work in counter-rhythm to mine, two teats each, the 'swoosh, swoosh' of milk streaming into the pail punctuating the silence. When the udder hands flaccid, we weigh the bucket of milk, record the amount in a diary that gathers dust on a cross support of the barn, and then open the door for Twiggy to return to her grassy pastures. And they are most decidedly *her* pastures, although 'Mosha's horse shares the space. Twiggy skips and dances, she never simply walks (unless being called for milking time); her stiff legs pop her straight into the air as if propelled on unseen springs.

We clank up the road to the Long House and perform the cleaning ritual, washing pails, buckets and strainer. A quick bite to eat, and then we repeat the dance with the goats who live in the upper barnyard. Both mamas are giving milk. One gave birth to a kid just one month before, and the baby frisks in a pen next door, bleating for the coke bottle of warm mama's milk set aside for it. Initially I am upset by the separation of mother and kid. Brought up in the suburbs and foreign to the ways of a farm, this seems cruel to me. Through talks with Carl and Cougar, though, I learn that the goat kids adapt more easily to human contact if they receive milk from a bottle. The kids are easier to handle because they are not as strongly bonded with the mama goat. I balance my love for these animals with the realisation that my daily food, and thus my very *existence*, is dependent upon their gifts. They are not pets but rather partners in my bid for survival. The practical application of caring brings harmony into the cycle of production—still following the basics of good animal husbandry, but adding the glue of love to the process.

After feeding the chickens and checking on the new litter of bunnies in the rabbit hutch, I walk down the mountain towards the lower farmhouse. Dust rises in small clouds around my feet. No rain has fallen for several weeks. A few days ago we prayed and danced for the Thunderbeings to bring rain. The sky darkened and a few forks of lightning glimmered in the evening sky, but only a few drops of rain fell. In this 'high desert' region water is vital to the survival of the vegetable garden. With this in mind, the garden was located next to a spring that flows throughout the year. The water collects in a pool dug below the spring, just deep enough to jump into on hot summer days. A couple of years ago someone installed a pump. Annette, the Danish visitor who has taken on the vegetable garden since my departure in January, has rigged a series of hoses to water the garden with sprinklers—much more convenient than watering by hand.

I join Annette, kneeling in the path beside the bean bed, and begin to weed. We talk a bit about her planting schedule and her challenges with unfamiliar vegetable varieties. In addition to lecturing in a university, Annette and her husband cultivated an organic vegetable farm in Denmark. Some of the North American vegetables, such as winter squash and some of the beans, do not grow in the north of Europe, but Annette's native sense with the soil and plants overcomes her unfamiliarity with the new varieties. Under her care, the garden is immaculate—the beds are double dug, seedlings transplanted and the paths mulched.

Knowing that Annette arrived on the bus in Spokane this past March, unable to speak a word of English, I ask her how she heard about the Bear Tribe and decided to come here.

"One night," explains Annette, "I had a dream. This man told me he needed someone to care for a garden. I knew he was a Native American man, but I had never seen him before. Later I found a book from the Bear Tribe with his picture on it, and I knew it was him. I knew him from my dream. So I quit my job and came."

"Just like that? You just arrived without contacting anyone first?"

"Yes, I just knew I had to come. So I did. That was all."

We work for a while in silence. I ponder the strength of this woman who has left her homeland to travel to a country with no knowledge of the language, where no one would greet her by name. Only faith in her dream could sustain her. Her introduction to the Bear Tribe was a phone call from Traveller's Aid at the local bus station explaining that a woman had arrived, able only to say 'Bear Tribe'. Would they please come pick her up?

I wonder, too, at her trust in herself, in her own intuitive knowing. Observing her outward actions, her rigid organisation and stubbornly tenacious way of accomplishing things, I would not peg her as a likely candidate for otherworldly dreams and visions. Perhaps, though, what I perceive as rigidity is only her expression of personal power harnessed to accomplish a task. Undoubtedly these characteristics qualified her for a demanding life experience—adjusting to another culture and language, a cooperative lifestyle, and an unfamiliar landscape to cultivate.

At noon we return our tools to the small shed near the spring and walk along the hot, dusty road to the farmhouse. Beads of sweat streak the dust that settles on my face. After lunch Carl and I retreat into his old Chevy van—the outer metal walls, exposed to the sun, sear any flesh that touches them, but the inside is shady and, with the door left ajar, cooler than our tent baking on the hillside. We snooze for about an hour, until the heat climaxes and then begins to diminish, before resuming our work. I walk up the hill to the outhouse, pee, and glance at the toilet paper—no signs of blood. Mid-July and my moontime is about two weeks late. My breasts are tender, ". . . like they always are before my period begins," I reassure myself aloud, addressing the rough, splintery walls of the latrine. "Stop the drama. I am *not* pregnant."

I resent that Carl, although concerned, does not live moment by moment with this tension. For him pregnancy is a mental possibility, but for me it is a physical reality that can transform my body completely, alter my hormonal balance, rearrange my emotions and change the focus of my life. The thought of the aftermath of a pregnancy—a child—nearly paralyses me. I lie awake at night, hands covering my womb, allowing my mind to wander. "What if . . . what if . . . how would my life change? What would he or she look like . . ." and then I wrestle myself into the moment, angry that I even entertain the possibility of being pregnant.

On Sunday morning I find a couple of small red-brown spots on the toilet paper. "Thank you, Great Spirit," I murmur into the early morning light that burnishes the wooden walls with gold. "Thank you." A woman on her moontime does not enter the sweat lodge, so I walk through the forest to the ridge overlooking the valley and sit for a long, relaxed meditation.

Late afternoon. No more blood has flowed. I am sure tomorrow will bring a heavy flow—my menses often starts slowly.

A day passes. And another day, and another. After chores one morning I call Planned Parenthood, making an appointment 'just to be sure'. It is too late to bring in a first urine sample, but the nurse assures me that a second will probably be all right. I find a clean jar and a cooler in which to store the urine sample, fill it with ice and head for town.

Heat surges in waves from the black-topped pavement. The sun, reflected from mirrored windows, is dazzling. I sweat, not only because of the temperature, but also because of the nervous energy generated by butterflies colliding in my stomach.

The urine spilled en route to town. I'm almost relieved. I salvage what I can and take the remains to the desk.

"Oh, that should be no problem," the nurse reassures me when I explain why the sample may not work. I smile thinly.

"You'll have to wait a couple of hours before someone can see you," she says. "Do you have any other errands in town?"

"Yes, I do. I'll be back in a couple of hours."

I drive to the Public Library, read Carson McCullers, and compliment myself on how calm I have become. The minutes tick by. I look at the clock less and less frequently, my shoulders recede from my ears, my fingers relax on the edges of the book.

I gather my books and drive to Planned Parenthood. Glancing down at the charts, I see 'NO' pencilled after my name. "Good," I comment to myself. "The test results are negative. I'm not pregnant." The receptionist motions me into a chair. I read a pamphlet and catch snippets of conversation from the desk.

A young woman with precisely cut, feathered-back long hair and skin-tight jeans stands at the desk. "Tell the Doctor I want complete anaesthesia."

"But the Doctor usually recommends a local anaesthetic for terminations," replies a nurse matter-of-factly.

"Tell him I want a general. He'll do it. I know, I've been through this four times before."

My heart races. This woman has been through four abortions? How could anyone be so nonchalant about terminating a pregnancy? My fear level skyrockets.

Grace Spotted Eagle's words from a lecture come to mind. When asked by someone in the audience how she, who believed in the sacredness of all life, viewed abortion, Grace replied, "You're asking the wrong question. Ask instead why women in this society would *want* to have an abortion. Why do they feel they do not want to bring new life into this culture?"

I sit pondering the threat of motherhood, wondering why I view it as a threat. I watch a toddler hanging from his mother's knee, head thrown back, pitting all of his weight against her leg in an attempt to dislodge her from the chair. Motherhood. The 'hood' of monks, a hood like blinders on a horse, telescoping the world to the concerns of running noses and rubber balls, pats and kisses, clutching hands and cluttered living rooms. In this culture that 'hood' means isolation.

Cut off from the support of an extended family or a cohesive neighbourhood community in a traditional housewife role ('traditional' in terms of the white culture of the US since the late 1950s), or else fulfilling the role of a single parent who provides both financial support and primary care for the children, no wonder women balk at the prospect of having children. I read recently that less that 20% of the US population fits the stereotyped model of a nuclear family—2.3 children, husband working outside the home, wife working within the home (though the statistician would hardly acknowledge the woman's responsibilities as 'work'). The majority of US households are headed by single mothers. Despite these facts, the Reagan administration has consistently pushed for legislation that supports the mythical all-American family, leaving the majority—households headed by single mothers—in the dust.

The receptionist interrupts my reverie. "Ms Boice, you may go to Room 8." A pleasant woman greets me and leads me into a tiny room, just big enough for a desk piled with papers and two chairs. We relax and chat for a few minutes until she pushes back her chair from the desk. "I'll go get the results from your test," she says, smiling as she closes the door behind her.

I yawn and stretch my arms to the ceiling, pushing away anxiety with the movement. I know the results will be negative, like the last time my period was late. The *worry* about missing my period is what's holding it back. Once I know I'm not pregnant and relax, my moontime will come."

Steps outside the door, wood brushing on carpet as the door opens. File in hand, the woman sits and faces me. Pause. Three heartbeats. "The results are positive." Pause. I must look stunned. "You're pregnant. Is there anything I can do for you?"

At first I feel nothing. Breathing stops completely. The moment hangs timeless, suspended in space. Without moving my eyes I etch the entire scene into my body. The shape of the desk is precious, the chairs gracious, the walls patient.

The magnitude of change sweeping through my life short circuits my mind. Thoughts stop and emotions churn in collisions too quick to follow in a logical, linear fashion. Anger "Why me?" collides with fear "How can I possibly keep this baby?" buffets joy "My body works! I'm carrying a child!" smashes against sadness "Not now, Creator, oh please not now."

"Is there anything I can do for you?"

I stare mutely. I am afraid to surrender to this river of emotions, afraid that every last vestige of strength will wash away in the emotional current. No, I must be strong. I cannot collapse into this sea of feeling, or I will drown.

My mind re-enters to challenge the river with an oar—flimsy against the raging torrent, but familiar and therefore comforting. "Judy, what are you going to do with a baby? You love children, but how could you possibly finish school and raise a child?"

The thoughts fire in quick succession, continuing to explode while outwardly I ask quiet, distant questions about local abortion clinics, fees and schedules. The counsellor hands me a checklist of questions to consider, basics like 'Do I have financial means to support a child at this time?', 'How do I feel about parenting a child alone? With a father?' About twenty questions fill the page. I glance through them. They are more oars to challenge the river. The banks are crumbling, but I hang on to the counsellor's words, a raft that floats me in the present moment, as she describes 'symptoms' that often accompany pregnancy.

I remember nothing of the journey from the room to Sunflower. I pull my dress over my thighs to avoid burning them on the seat that has been baking in the sun. Heat. Penetrating the cool logic, steam rising from the river, rising to envelop me in a cloud that buffers the sharp edges of reality. I am rooted in this moment, and this moment, and this moment, driving to the Circle Center, taking a shower, noting the tenderness of my breasts and belly under the spray of water. Nausea wracks my stomach. I pee every 15 or 20 minutes—all classic 'symptoms' described by the counsellor. Why didn't I notice them before? And why are they called 'symptoms', like a disease, instead of 'signs of potency' or simply 'changes'?

I sit in the living room, knees tucked under my chin, waiting for Carl to return from his appointment with Regina, a Reichian therapist whom nearly everyone at the Tribe visits. She lived in a cabin just below the Long House, but during my months away she moved to Idaho to be near her teacher. Now instead of a three-minute walk to her cabin for a session, Carl drives an hour each way to and from her house in Idaho.

When Carl arrives, we hug for a long time in the kitchen and then lean back, silently locking eyes.

"Well?" he asks.

"Congratulations, you're a daddy."

Silence. "Really?" asks Carl, incredulous.

"Yes, really."

"Oh."

After dinner we walk through the fairgrounds, remnants of a World's Fair, amidst crowds of people riding merry-go-rounds, playing games for prizes, and eating pizza, ice cream and cotton candy. I feel alone in this sea of people, closed within my thoughts.

Originally we planned to join a folk dancing group on an outdoor platform across the river. When the music begins, Carl looks longingly across the river. "You want to go?" he asks expectantly.

"Carl, I just want to talk with you, alone." My mind is unable to grasp much besides the pregnancy.

A couple of minutes pass. "Are you sure you don't want to go? It might take your mind off things."

"Carl, I don't want to jump up and down—I don't want to disturb the baby."

Tears well over, hot on my cheeks. I know I cannot keep this baby. I have so many plans—to study naturopathic medicine, to be a doctor, to travel and write and . . . and . . . and . . . . If I kept the baby now, I know I would resent the loss of my freedom and the disruption of my plans. I want a child, but not now, Creator, please not now.

And Carl—I love you, but could our relationship withstand the strain of having a child and beginning a family when we barely have begun to know each other? I have watched other people stumble into marriage as a result of an unplanned pregnancy. With many the pressures mount for years and finally explode, dissolving the relationship. "It would have been better," one friend confided, "if we had had a chance to live together before the pregnancy. We really only had about seven months together before the baby arrived, and living together was so different from our experience of dating."

We sit on a bench, talking and crying and holding each other until sunset colours fade and the lamps lining the paths cast circles of light along the darkened pavement. As we walk to the car, the Earth feels soft-spun-firm beneath my feet, like the delicate thread of the silkworm wound into a hard-shelled cocoon. I know my feet tread on hard ground, but I can barely feel them. The Earth seems so far away. Everything seems far from my world as I collapse inward, into my womb.

* * *

During the week I talk with two other women in the Tribe about their experiences of abortion. The stories ease my mind about the physical pain involved, but I sense that the emotional pain will be much longer-lived.

Carl and I both talk with Wabun about the child. We have decided that, to help ease the journey of the child, we want to honour its soul with ceremonies both before and after the abortion.

Wabun leans against the rail of the porch, crosses her arms, and eyes us both. "What's up?"

Carl sits on a stool, kneading each finger on one hand, then the other, clasping them, stretching them, kneading again. I sit on an old wooden chair, elbows propped on my knees, hands clasped before me.

"We have something to tell you, Wabun," I begin, "and something to ask."

"Yes?"

"When I went into town this week, I had a pregnancy test. The result was positive. Carl and I are pregnant."

Wabun nods her head. "I noticed that your breasts have grown larger." I feel my sore breasts pushing against my overstuffed bra. Yes, why hadn't I noticed earlier?

"What do you plan to do?"

I explain our decision to abort the baby and how we have wrestled with it, acknowledging our love for children along with the difficulty of parenting a child at this time.

"You know," comments Wabun when I finish, "Cougar and Kate were pregnant with a child last year. They decided not to keep the baby. I think there's a child that's been trying to enter the Tribe for a few years now."

I look down, words catching in my throat. Thoughts of Grandmother Evelyn (Eaton), a teacher and close friend of Wabun's, slip through my mind. Although I never met Grandmother Evelyn, I feel I know her through the books she has written, not her early novels, but her later writing about her personal spiritual journey. Evelyn bought some land just above the Long House, and although her physical body has crossed over, I sense that she has never really left. Her tipi rises amongst the pine trees. The skeleton frame of a sweat lodge stands nearby, rocks still in the fire pit, a cracked glass jar waiting to hold water, waiting as if she has left for a short journey, planning to return.

Her books about her personal journey begin in . . . Independence, California! The memory startles me. Carl and I conceived the baby in the mountains outside Independence, where Evelyn lived in her later years. Could it be . . . was Evelyn's spirit somehow involved in our pregnancy? This connection plus the power of the summer solstice . . . perhaps this baby really is meant to . . . but . . . oh, Creator, I've decided, no not now, not *now*, I can't go through the turmoil of deciding again.

"Wabun, we want to ask you to have a pipe ceremony with us before the abortion to . . ." tears well in my eyes, "to honour the baby, to treat it with respect and bless it. Could you do that with us?"

"Yes, if you come into town the day before we could have a pipe in the evening." She uncrosses her arms and rests them on the rail behind her. "You know, you two have one of the best relationships I've seen here at the Tribe."

Carl and I quickly smile at each other and then look down, a bit embarrassed. Wabun scans our bodies. "It would be a beautiful baby—you are both well built and healthy, fair hair, clear skin . . . ."

"Yes, it would be a beautiful baby," I murmur, reaching for Carl's hand. He draws me onto his lap, and I press my face into his hair. We clasp each other tightly, as if trying to press comfort and support into each other through our bodies.

We decide to have a ceremony following the abortion as well. We want to keep the foetus to bury on the Mountain, on the top of a steep hill that rises sharply like a runway, to help speed the soul's return to the Creator. Inbetween the busyness of daily chores that keeps me nailed to the present, I make phone calls to local abortion clinics.

28

"Can the father be with me during the operation?" I ask the clinic west of Spokane, staffed by a women's collective.

"No problem," says the woman. In the background kids squall and laugh and slap against squeaky vinyl chairs. The place feels good over the phone.

"May I keep the foetus?"

Pause. "Why do you want to keep the foetus?"

"I want to bury it afterwards, like a ritual of release."

"Well, that sounds like a good idea, but as a women's clinic we get so much hassle from the Right-to-Lifers. They watch and check *everything* we do, and I think it would look really bad if they found out we were saving foetuses."

"Yeah, I can understand that."

"You can have the father with you, though."

"Thanks."

I call a local clinic. "Can I help you?" asks the receptionist, her voice as tart as a fresh-picked apple.

I ask about fees and appointments and then about essentials.

"Can the father be with me during the operation?"

"No, the doctor does not allow anyone to accompany the patient."

"May I keep the foetus?"

Silence. "I think the doctor would question your emotional stability."

"I want to bury the foetus, not keep it forever in the refrigerator."

"I'll have to ask the doctor."

She calls back later in the afternoon with the doctor's approval. Now I have a choice between having Carl with me or keeping the foetus. I opt for the foetus.

In the evening, after my usual chores, I walk down the mountain to milk goats for neighbours who have gone away on holiday. Golden light flames on the splintered wood of the gate and the weather-worn walls of the barn. Each farmer has his or her own ritual for milking. I arrange the buckets, shoo the kids into their pen, and place the stool in its appointed place. The repetition soothes me, freeing my mind for deeper thoughts as my body follows familiar patterns.

After milking I join Carl in the living room of the neighbour's house—we are housesitting as well as taking care of the goats. We relax into the sofa, muscles giving way to the softness of the cushions. We decide to have a meditation to connect with the baby's spirit, so we sit side-by-side, Carl resting his hand over my womb.

When I move inside and open to the baby's spirit, I feel like a tiny dinghy riding waves far from shore with no land in sight—the smallness of my being engulfs me. Instead of fearing this smallness, I feel soothed, riding a current of peace that threads through a sea of changing colour and light. My heart defies the boundary of my chest, opening and stretching out and out until it connects with our child's spirit.

"My friend," I say inwardly, "I love you greatly, but the time is not right. Please come back to us later, we are not ready now. We love you. We love you a whole lot."

Coming out of the meditation, I sense that the soul lives in a beautiful world. I cannot feel guilty about leaving it in this realm. I also cannot justify bringing into the world a child for whom I would not be responsible—the pregnancy would drain a lot from my body (already I feel the strain), and I could not endure bearing the child without the reward of keeping it. "I am too busy now," I tell myself and yet realise that the pace of my life will only accelerate in the coming years. Without a father to share the parenting, having a child is unimaginable, and Carl and I still have much to learn and many ways to grow before we could live together permanently and nurture a family.

29

July 24th. Late in the afternoon Carl and I drive to the Circle Center in town to meet Wabun for the pipe ceremony. Evening light softens the stark emptiness of what was once the sanctuary of the church. Wabun draws smudge bowl, fan, crystal and carved black stone turtle from her medicine bag. She asks us to stand and then smudges us from head to toe. The smell of sage smoke curling around my body soothes me. Wabun hands me the turtle, instructing me to hold it over my womb. Carl stands facing me, his hands resting on mine.

The magnets of Carl's wide-open eyes draw me irresistibly through the iris, through the nerves and cells and molecules and atoms into some formless, nameless land where the essence of Carl resides. My Goddess, what a beautiful father you would be.

We call the baby's spirit to be with us. I sense a blackness in my womb as I address the child. "We love you and wish you an easy journey away from us." My voice falters as the sound knocks against the hard, wooden walls of the sanctuary, the words flattening into insignificance as I address these realms behind the physical sensing world. I continue, self-consciously. "We are not ready to bring you into this world at this time, but we invite you to return to us, or another couple, when you are ready."

Carl's voice rises into his eyes and feeds directly into me. "When I was holding my hand over Judy's womb and trying to connect with the baby's spirit, I saw a seagull against the sun. I feel the baby's spirit around us, but not in the womb. I don't think we, or the child, would be happy about it coming into the world right now."

"I don't think the child's spirit has entered the womb either," says Wabun in her weighted, even-paced way. "I sense the spirit swimming in the ocean of life, unbounded and free. Perhaps it is not yet ready for the limitations of physical form."

Wabun picks up the crystal and passes it over my body. It becomes hot in her hand. Carl closes his eyes and sits down, holding his head in his hands. "Whoowph, I feel nauseous and dizzy," he murmurs.

Wabun prepares and fills the pipe, offering each pinch of kinnickinnick (herb mixture for pipe ceremonies) to the four directions, the Earth, the Sky, the Creator. She prays for the cycles of life—birth and growth, maturity and death—and blessings for the child and Carl and I.

This offering of smoke hangs on the rift between the Seen and the Unseen, feeding the Mystery that pervades both the Formed and the Formless. The smoke dispersing in the air provides a bridge to vaster realms, and with each puff I add my own prayers, asking blessings for the child, for Carl, for my own health, and offering deep thanks for the support given to us by Wabun and the rest of the Bear Tribe. I cannot imagine making this difficult passage alone, without the support of a loving, understanding community.

We sing a song of thanksgiving to end the pipe. A blue-grey veil of smoke drifts in the shafts of evening light bending through the windows. Quiet. A car passes on the street outside. A hard-won peace enters our circle.

Carl and I take turns expressing our love and appreciation for each other. We thank Wabun and the Bear Tribe for the support that we have received. Then, the walls of formality softened, Carl curls against my body, resting his head in my lap. I stroke his hair and follow the contours of his finely modelled face.

I look up as Wabun finishes packing her medicine bag. She pauses, then draws out a cloth bag. "Lie down," she says, nodding at the floor.

Wabun kneels beside me, taking pinches of cornmeal from the bag and rubbing it in gritty spirals into my feet. "May these feet be blessed to walk a good path." She moves to my belly. "May this womb be blessed, Creator, able to bring forth new life when the time is right." She touches my breasts. "May these breasts be blessed to nurture." The cornmeal massages my neck. "May this throat be open to express truth and beauty." She rubs my lips with cornmeal. "May these lips be blessed, speaking truth with compassion." She rubs cornmeal over my eyes and into the crown chakra, blessing each part. I sink deeply into my physical body, sensing the life bursting in each cell, feeling smooth and warm and stretched.

Carl and I walk to the old rectory next door, and drag a mattress into the basement for softness and warmth on the hard cement floor. I brought a speculum with me so that I could show Carl my cervix, to give him a sense of what would be happening during the abortion. Viewing the cervix myself, with the aid of a flashlight and a small mirror, I am surprised by its increased length and firmness.

When we crawl into our sleeping bags, I want to touch Carl, to feel him inside me, because I know we won't be able to make love for several weeks after the abortion. I kiss his neck and flick my tongue around his ear. Carl jerks back his head, irritated.

"Come on, I'm exhausted."

"Please?"

"No, I'm really tired."

I turn my back to him, drawing my knees into my chest, my body clenched with anger. I feel abandoned and alone as I sink deep inside myself, my world becoming smaller and smaller and more isolated.

Silence, stiff as a tombstone. Carl draws a slow breath, hissing it out through his lips in exasperation.

He touches my shoulder. When I pull away he presses more firmly and rolls me toward him. "Come on," he demands, "say it."

"What?" I mumble.

"Say it."

"I feel small and lonely, like I have to separate from this baby without your support."

"I'm willing to support you in other ways. I'm just too tired to make love."

I stifle a small, embarrassed smile. He's not playing the 'bad guy' scenario I have running in my head. Am I childish and greedy to want to make love? Deep inside I know that he is willing to support me, but I am expecting the support to come in one way, *my* way. To let go of self-pity means admitting that I was wrong to be angry with him—or does it?

I wait suspended, knowing I can sink deeper into this smallness as a way of hurting Carl (and myself), or I can step out of this collapsing world and meet him on another level. Am I willing to let go of pain I no longer need? Am I willing to let go of my righteous self-pity?

I nestle into Carl's arms, the tension of anger melting from my neck and jaw and back. I will myself outward to meet him. "I am sorry, Carl," I breathe into his shoulder. "I'm sorry for turning away."

Carl reaches for the bag of Runes, ancient Celtic symbols given to the God Odin after he hung for nine nights from Yggdrasil, or World Tree. The Runes, according to author Ralph Blum, are ". . . an ancient alphabetic script each of whose letters possessed a meaningful name as well as a signifying sound. (They) were employed for poetry, for inscriptions and divination, yet never evolved as a spoken language."

Preparing to consult the Runes, I frame questions in my mind. What do I need to know about the abortion? About timing? We both draw a Rune about timing—each

31

of us chooses the Blank Rune. My fingers play over the smooth, featureless surface. Blank—contact with the Unknown, the Unknowable. Are we testing the Creator? Remapping 'fate'? "Blank is the end, blank the beginning," reads the interpretation. ". . . At the same time pregnant and empty, it comprehends the totality of being, all that is to be actualised . . . from the runic perspective, even the very debts of old karma shift and evolve as you shift and evolve. *Nothing is predestined;* there is nothing that cannot be avoided."

Carl turns off the lights and draws me close to him, our bodies warming steadily. We make love, deep and moving, holding each other very close. The tension leaves my body, sweet exhaustion replaces the nerves, and sleep envelops me, comfortable as a well-worn coat.

The following afternoon we drive to the clinic, a simple one-story, L-shaped building, neat and square and sterile. In the car we light some sage in a bowl and smudge, drawing smoke around our bodies to cleanse and purify ourselves before entering the building.

Carl waits in the reception area while a nurse guides me into a 'waiting room', just large enough for two cots. She hands me a white hospital gown and a pair of tube socks. "Here, you can change into these." I slip off my familiar clothes and pull the hospital gown around me.

Knowing that Carl cannot be with me during the operation, we insist that he be present during the explanation and question time. The doctor agrees and invites Carl to sit in a leather chair next to mine. We sit holding hands, listening calmly.

"Any questions?" asks the doctor, eyeing Carl when he completes the presentation.

"Nope."

"And you?"

I shake my head. I have read the section on abortion in *Our Bodies, Ourselves* so many times that I almost have it memorised. On the way out of the office, Carl and I pause for a long hug while the doctor discreetly shuffles papers behind us.

Back in the tiny waiting room, a nurse enters with a paper cup full of pills and some water. "Here, swallow these."

"What are they?"

The nurse taps her foot. "Valium, codeine and an antibiotic."

"I'm allergic to antibiotics, and I don't want to take Valium or codeine."

"The doctor prescribed them," insists the nurse.

Our eyes lock in a battle of wills. I finally compromise. "I'll take the codeine."

Another woman named Sue joins me in the room. We giggle about the tube socks and talk a bit about our lives. The nurse enters again to lead me down the hall.

She glances at my back, the hospital gown swinging freely as I walk. I avoid her eyes. She reaches behind me, holding together the folds of the gown as we walk down the hall. I want to brush aside her hand—haven't these people seen bodies before?—but I restrain myself, ignoring the imposition.

I climb onto the table, propping my knees in the supports. Funny how the nurse worries about my bare bottom in the hall, yet on this table I am expected to open my crotch wide for the doctor.

Alone in the room, waiting for the doctor to arrive, I hold a crystal in my left hand, place my right hand over my abdomen, and visualise energy moving from the crystal, through my arms and into my womb. I talk with my uterus, explaining what will happen, and then consciously relax each part of my body. With my 'inner eye' I see a tunnel before me that plunges deep into the Earth and I fly through the long, deep passage to meet my guide. After a moment of silent acknowledgement, he transforms into a bear and curls around me. The warm, furry presence comforts me.

"Hello, how are you doing?"

"Fine, Doctor, just fine," I reply, opening my eyes.

The nurse smiles. "You want to keep the foetus, correct?"

I nod my head.

"Will this container be all right? she asks, holding up a small specimen jar.

"Yes, that's fine."

"And you know to keep it in the refrigerator until you, ah, need it?"

"OK, that's fine."

The doctor is relaxed, commenting on my freckled skin and red hair. He inserts a speculum to clean the vagina with Betadiene.

"I noticed more mucus than usual. Do you think there's any vaginal infection present?"

The doctor looks up. "No, not unusual. You do self-exams?"

"Yes."

"OK, now I'm going to give you two shots of novocaine in the cervix. You will probably feel a pinch."

I barely notice the injections. So far so good.

"Now I'm going to insert a series of dilators. To size eight, right?" he asks the nurse.

"Right, doctor."

I feel some pressure as the metal instruments open the cervix.

"Now I'm inserting the vacuum."

Pain shoots through my womb. It rises in a wave, cramping my stomach and halting the air in my lungs, so sudden that it freezes screams in my throat. When the wave breaks in my brain, I almost lose consciousness. A high-pitched whine squeals in my ears, and black spots explode before my eyes. The core of my body cools; beads of cold sweat erupt on my upper lip and forehead, and then squeeze from every pore of my body.

"Looks like you're sweating this one out," comments the doctor. He sounds distant, his voice muffled as if talking underwater, reaching me through a sea of pain.

The nurse pushes damp strands of hair from my forehead and pats my arm.

"Twenty more seconds. Now a new sensation."

He inserts another instrument, scraping the walls of the uterus to remove any residue.

"You must have hypnotised yourself not to bleed. There's no blood," says the doctor.

I smile wanly, clenching the crystal in my hand, too weak to respond. The visualisation must have helped.

The nurse administers an injection to make the uterus contract. Cramps, worse than any menstrual pain, grip my womb.

"Do you know what a four- or five-week-old foetus looks like?" asks the doctor.

"Yes, I think so."

"Well, it's mostly placenta and fluids. You won't really see the foetus because it's so tiny, and the vacuuming pulls apart the placenta anyway."

I nod mutely. All of my energy is focused on staying conscious.

The doctor stands beside me, looking down, his eyes soft and brown and steady as a priest's. He pauses, forehead creased with compassion. "It's always a hard decision."

Hot tears sting my eyes, and I nod. "Yes, it is a hard decision, one I hope I never have to make again."

33

Rest. Nausea. Wheeling back to the recovery room. Vomiting. Sue comes back looking pale, ghostly, obviously pained. "You OK?" we ask each other. No light-hearted chattering, just cramps and more pills to make the uterus contract, and sleep. If an abortion is this painful, childbirth must be excruciating. I don't know if I could live through it.

The nurse gives us a lecture about not having 'sex' until our next menstrual cycle. "Is it OK to have orgasms?" I ask.

The nurse stares for a moment. "Yes, orgasms are permissible." I wonder if she has ever had one.

"But no intercourse, right?"

"That's correct."

Gingerly I pull on my clothes, glad for the soft cotton pants and shirt. I go to the toilet and find bright red spots on the toilet paper, the first blood I have seen for almost two months. As I leave, the nurse hands me a small round specimen jar with a few tablespoons of hamburger-like placenta floating in a watery red fluid—our baby.

Carl is waiting for me in the reception area, and he holds me for a long, long time. His arms encircling me are an island of comfort in this reception room. I watch Sue leave the clinic with her husband. She walks slowly, head bowed. He never touches Sue except when he brushes her to open the car door. He glances quickly around the parking lot as if checking for onlookers.

I close my eyes and hold Carl tighter, grateful for his deeply rooted strength and his arms, supple as spring green boughs, wrapped around me.

Dark clouds gather as we drive home to Vision Mountain. The meteorologist on the radio explains that the long hot dry spell this summer was caused by southerly ocean currents, unusual for this season. Now the currents have changed and rain, blessed rain, is coming.

I open the car window wide, breathing in the sharp-sweet air, acrid with the smell of static electricity. My body is taut, expectant as the clouds preparing to birth rain from their swollen bellies.

When we arrive on Vision Mountain, Carl does the evening chores while I lie on the couch in the neighbour's house, watching the clouds and the dying sun, crying. We drive to the pond in front of the sweat lodge and climb the long, steep ridge, the 'runway' to speed our child's spirit to the Creator. My womb is tender and my legs watery. My feet seem to belong to some other body, though I hear footfalls crunching in last autumn's fallen leaves below me. Like a puppeteer guiding a marionette, I will my legs to carry me up the slope.

A tree grows at the top of the ridge. Among its roots we dig a hole with our bare hands—a grave in which to bury the foetus. Pain rises from my heart, backwaters in my throat until I can no longer contain it, and then overflows as sobs that pierce the thick, storm-charged air.

Four times we yell to release the child to the four directions. We chant for the child, for the Creator and for ourselves. Carl sits behind me, gently rocking me while more tears flow. In the deepening dusk the forest dims to tree silhouettes outlined with darkening shades of grey. Mosquitoes swarm in the heavy, humid night air. Heat lightning flickers, and groans of thunder rumble around the mountain.

We stand to tie a prayer plume on a branch of the tree growing above our baby's grave. When the feathers disintegrate, dispersed by wind and rain, the soul will be completely free. Our ritual complete, we stand for a few moments watching the flashes of heat-lightning glowing on the far ridge. Carl turns on his flashlight and takes my hand. Slowly we make our way down the steep ridge.

That night we awake to booms of thunder that reverberate through the house, rattling pictures on the walls and shaking the bed on which we lie. Rain, driven by gusts of wind, lashes against the walls and hammers on the roof, in its fury releasing the tension of the drought-stricken mountain. The storm breaks something within me as well—the grip of emotional turmoil with which I have wrestled since the summer solstice.

For the next couple of days I rest quietly, writing in my journal and reading long-neglected books. One afternoon I hear a knock at the door—Hilary strides into the room, clothes dusty and spattered with paint, and plants a kiss on my cheek.

"Hey, how come you didn't tell me you were having an abortion? I mean I knew you were down here housesitting, but I had no idea what was up."

"Hey, Hil', take a seat. Thanks for coming to visit. You want something to drink?"

"Naw, I can't stay very long. I just wanted to come down to see how you were doing and give you some support," he says, winking. "What's up?"

"Well," I begin, searching for words, "it's been a difficult, um, *challenging* time." I describe our struggles in choosing to abort the child, finding a helpful clinic, and enduring the terrible sense of loss I feel now that the 'termination' is complete. "I've just wanted a quiet space to rest for a few days. I'm really glad to be here. You know, it's funny, when Mrs Waldemyer came asking for someone to look after the house, I knew I had to say 'yes'. I didn't know why, I had no idea I was pregnant at the time, but I had a sense of rightness."

Hilary smiles and leans forward, uncrossing one arm to point a finger at me. "Remember how that feels," he says, emphasising the words with jabs of his finger. "If you remember that feeling, that sense of rightness that helped you create this situation, you can create it again. I try to do that in my life. You know, notice when things go right. Then I can learn how I do it, and I can repeat it when I need to."

We chat for a while longer, then walk outside together, Hilary following the road up the mountain while I head for the outhouse. I like leaving outhouse doors open, especially when they overlook a beautiful view, but any scene will do. The experience of looking from the outside in, viewing the world through the frame of a doorway, remoulds my perspective on many things.

I turn my gaze to the house. Canning jars and cement-crusted buckets lie in a jumble under the house. Discarded wood and insulating scraps poke out from the far corner. Sun-bleached clothes lie heaped in random piles or hang from a rope strung between two trees. Nails and sandpaper and broken plastic forks and a baby doll without a head snag my eye as I survey the yard.

I return to the house to fish wet laundry out of the washing machine and feed it through the electric wringer. This machine is of the same vintage as our 1947 farm tractor, a short-lived species, the kind stalked by biologists searching fossil records for a 'link' between vaguely related species. The washer resembles the hand wringer that gathered dust for years in my grandmother's cellar, yet the shiny enamel of the wash tub reminds me of the Maytag washer that stood in the basement of my mother's house. Ivan Illich once commented that our technological society rarely retains the intermediaries of its evolution. I can, for example, find a horse-drawn plough and a two-ton combine tractor, but few, if any, manufacturers still produce the tractors that were spawned in the movement from simple plough to harvesting giants. Like the biologist's elusive 'link species', these tractors fade into the fossil records of old farm journals or enjoy a second life in agricultural museums.

So what enabled this washing machine to survive extinction? I look around the house and find my answer. Poverty. Or, more accurately, relative poverty. If installing plumbing themselves would save some money, the Waldemyers would do it. If buying a particular model of washing machine would save money, they would buy it. But they *do* have money. Some. And 'some' is more than most people in the Third World will ever see. And while this family might lack material wealth, the children are well fed from the vegetable garden growing below the house and the goats that graze in the accompanying field. They have a whole wilderness outside their front door to explore. Their greatest asset, though, is loving parents who, despite the cluttered disarray of a house under construction, provide a secure home for the kids.

A car strains up the mountain. Peering out the door I glimpse a white van rounding the curve of the road. It's Carl, returning from his appointment with Regina. Running down the steps, arms outstretched, I meet the van as it comes to a dusty halt in the front yard.

Carl looks down as I approach, slamming the car door with a jerk of his arm. "I need space," he says, warding off my approach with his raised hand. "I nearly had an accident on the way home."

The words affect me like a hard freeze during apple blossom time. I wither into myself. Arms fall to my side. "I'm going for a walk," I tell Carl, and stride angrily along the road. Muffin, the Waldemyers' dog, starts yapping, disturbed by the tension between Carl and me. "Come on, Muffin," I yell, "stop it." But she is inconsolable, her barks echoing in the valley as I climb the mountain.

Marching towards my power spot, I slow when I reach Grandmother Evelyn's Medicine Wheel and veer off the road. Although I have passed this spot many times, I have never stopped to savour it. Immediately I feel at home, the tension in my body relaxing as I collapse in front of the western arm of the Wheel. Gently I touch the large, smooth black stone before me—its warmth surprises me. The stones still hold the heat of mid-day. Although the sun has not set, the ridge to the west shades this spot. Only the tall pines, standing like sentinels guarding the eastern and western quarters of the wheel, still catch sunlight in their upper branches. A row of pine cones hems the outer circle.

I close my eyes, sending roots from the bottom of my spine deep into the Earth, right to the very core, drawing calming strength up into my body. Inwardly I move to the centre of the Wheel, to the Creator stone, bringing with me all of the people with whom I feel anger or hurt. Carl, Sun Bear, past lovers and childhood bullies join me in the centre, all of us sitting in a circle holding hands.

"Why am I here?" bitches someone. "What negative effect could I possibly have had on your life?" John, my ex-fiancé, looks up innocently. "I love you, Bear (our pet name), really I do." His voice weaves with Julian's—"God, will you please leave me fucking *alone*?"—and Sun Bear's—"Be happy. Everything is good."

I feel indignant, knowing that we are gathered here as equal souls. They could just as easily be called by someone else—or request my presence—to resolve some aspect of a relationship. I stand before each one in turn, asking for peace between us, praying for the ability to see their good qualities, and asking that we release the need to dwell upon each other's worst points. Standing before Julian, I begin to sob, overwhelmed by the resentment and disdain still welling from him towards me.

The circuit complete, we stand and hug each other; then, turning sunwise, we revolve faster and faster until we spin out of the centre of the Wheel.

I open my eyes to the beauty of the mountain. Soft evening light outlines the trees, both the straight-spined trunks growing around the circle and the ones that curve in relief against the ridge. Boulders rest resolutely among their twisting roots. I circle the Wheel, admiring the rocks, then return to the road, ambling now, savouring the cool evening shadows and my hard-won peace of mind.

Yarrow joins me as I stroll down the mountain, eager to help milk the goats. We take turns sitting on the stool and kneading milk from the mama goat's teats.

Yarrow tugs my arm as I walk to the house. "Tell me a story, Judy, *please*. I give her a 'some-other-time' look, but she persists. "Come on, please, please, *pleeeease*."

"OK, all right." I, too, love stories, and she knows it.

"Well, once there was a rich man who lived in a house way up on a hill, far from where anyone could see him. This man was lonely, so he sent a message into the village that he wanted a bride, but not just any bride . . . ." As she listens to 'The Bride Killer', Yarrow's eyes grow wide, just wide enough to tell me that she's scared—but won't admit it.

She cuddles next to me on the sofa when I'm finished, reluctant to leave, but I crave some quiet time. "Come on, Yarrow, it's time for you to be on your way home. They'll be wondering what happened to you . . . ."

"No they won't. I said I was coming to milk goats with you."

You can't fool kids. They have X-ray ears. "I've got things to do. I'll see you tomorrow."

"Will you tell me another story?"

"Maybe."

As I walk out the front door with Yarrow, I notice a slip of paper tucked in the frame. "I love you. I'm sorry for being mean. I'd like to talk when I get back. Love, Carl."

I jam the note in my pocket and head for the clothesline to gather the last of the laundry. As I fold the clothes, it dawns on me—Carl could have been killed on the way home. No wonder he was shaken and needed some quiet time. Instead of being angry with him, I could have given thanks that he was still alive. Perspective. I have lost perspective on what is most important—Carl's life or my bruised emotions. "Geez," I scold myself, "and it only took me three hours to realise."

* * *

The Waldemyers arrive home after 12 days away, about 120 days too soon for me. I have grown to love this quiet, cluttered space. Carl and I pack our things and reinstate ourselves in the two tents pitched on the bluff beside the Long House.

Kim approaches me not long after unpacking. "Can I ask you something?" she says, looking earnest.

"Uh-oh, it sounds serious. Let's go outside, away from the noise." The Long House is crammed with people and feathers—the apprentices are making prayer plumes.

"What's on your mind, Kim?"

"Well, my mom isn't doing too well, and she's asked me to go back to New Jersey for a while. I've talked with Wabun and Shawno and some others about being gone for the month of August. That means . . . ."

". . . that you need someone to be the household manager," I finish for her.

"Right. How did you guess?" she jokes. "Would you be able to do it?"

"Tell me what's involved," I reply, "before I say yes."

Kim lists a series of responsibilities, jobs ranging from vacuuming the carpets to cleaning the outhouse, from ordering and picking up food to organising the root cellar.

"And you take care of canning food, too, right?"

"Yes," says Kim, smiling quickly as she looks down. "It's the busiest month of the year for picking and canning."

"But I don't know anything about canning."

"Neither did I when I started. I can show you what I know in the next couple of days, and there are plenty of books around. *The Joy of Cooking* is the best. And Thundy (Thunderbird Woman) is around to ask. She canned hundreds of jars of jam and fruit and veggies last year. She was the one who refurbished the summer kitchen so she had space to can away from the house."

"Hmm . . . there really isn't anyone else to ask, is there?"

"Nope," says Kim. We smile at each other.

"I'll do it."

"Great," says Kim, face relaxing into a grin. "It's great how everything is falling into place. I just have a few more details to take care of before I go."

After she swings through the Long House door, I stand alone outside, momentarily stunned by my own decision. This pause, and the accompanying hollow stomach, often follow a major commitment as inner priorities shift and change. The shift is as subtle as the turn of a dial on a ship's control panel, but the effect of the movement is enough to completely re-orient its course. Doubts and worries bob in the wake of changing wave patterns. Do I have the skills? Will I be able to do a good job? And I'm not even an official member of the Tribe—what am I doing?

But I have said yes, and that commitment opens a floodgate that pours energy into my being. While moments before I ran on an internal battery, subject to winter freezes and the drain of daily use, in this moment I touch a switch, triggering a charge that surges without waning, oblivious of season or place or destination. Life force. A reservoir far greater than my own individual resources, an ocean where once a pond existed. And the password to this vast supply is a small, ordinary word—'yes', yes to something greater than myself. Ironically, in this act of giving myself to fulfil the needs of the whole, I experience my own empowerment.

Leaving doubts in the backwater, I put my energy into forging ahead. Opening the screen door of the summer kitchen, I survey piles of paper, butchering tools and blood vats jumbled on the counters. Dusty Mason jars and lids and metal rings lie heaped on top of gas heating rings. Boxes and discarded papers clutter the floor. Obviously no one has worked here since last summer.

The spirit of the Household Manager takes full possession. Tapping a source of inspiration with *teeth*—so ferocious that I am certain I can chew through the best that any mess-maker can throw before me—I sharpen my claws and pounce.

The initial pounce only increases the damage. After an hour, with my hair capped with cobwebs, face smudged and hands grimy, the clutter spills out the door as I empty drawers and boxes, unearthing forgotten treasures—an orgone energy collector and a carefully kept record of weather patterns, mousetraps, kitchen utensils, bars of soap, bags of canning salt, a pressure cooker, two gas rings, a half-empty gas cylinder, and rubber tubes to connect them.

Within two days the summer kitchen is transformed, ready to process beans and other vegetables that require the pressure cooker for canning. Dusting shelves and cleaning jars, vacuuming floors and ordering food, snapping beans and pitting cherries—the endless round of daily tasks refills me, just as movement recharges a car battery. Movement breeds energy breeds more movement—when I say yes. Movement breeds strain breeds exhaustion when I say no, or even maybe.

As I immerse myself in work on the farm, I am more aware of those who are not fully integrated. Most short-term visitors arriving at the height of the summer's activity drift aimlessly, unable to match the pace of the community as it surges ahead with its load of summer work.

38

One sunny hot day in early August a guest joins me in the lower garden to harvest Sugar Ann snap peas—great for freezing, better for eating. I rarely eat lunch after working in the garden. During the mornings I graze among the beds, leisurely munching juicy peas and fresh-pulled radishes, lettuce leaves and trellis beans. I matter-of-factly revel in my food, content as a cow in clover.

As we ferret out peas artfully camouflaged among the leaves, the visitor asks questions about the garden. "How come you don't rig up a drip irrigation system in the garden? The sprinkler system shocks the leaves, and water sitting on the leaves can sunburn the plants, too, because it reflects the sunlight."

My chewing becomes less leisurely. I'm irritated, like a cow chasing flies with its tail. I sigh, recognising the enthusiasm of the uninitiated, untainted by the drag of history or the status quo. Their eye pierces methods long engrained by convenience or, even worse, by habit.

"Cougar rigged a drip irrigation system last summer for the fruit tree seedlings. I haven't been able to find it in the long grass this summer. I'm not even sure where the hoses are or the spigots to connect them with the pump. You see, Matt was tending the garden last year, and he barely had time to keep it weeded and watered with all of his other work." When in doubt, blame the *last* supervisor. "Now Annette is using a sprinkler system that she turns on in the morning and the late afternoon, when the sun won't evaporate the water right away or burn the leaves."

"Oh, but it's bad to water plants in the late afternoon. They can mildew overnight. It's not good for them to be damp when it's cool at night."

I'm beyond irritated. I'm beginning to snort as I flick my tail.

"And the tool shed. I was noticing you don't brush dirt off the tools before you put them away. How come?"

"We're lucky the tools are even *in* the garden shed. They used to be in a shed next to the pig pen (a mile up the road), but Annette organised having them down here for the summer."

"But it's a mess in there. I had a hard time finding a trowel."

"Maybe you would like to clean the shed and organise it."

"Oh, but I'm only here for a few days. It was just a suggestion."

Despite my irritation, in this moment I recognise myself, six months earlier, mirrored in this guest. Upon arrival I enthusiastically identified 'junk' areas that needed reorganising, shelves that needed dusting and organising systems that buckled under the weight of an expanding membership. I made suggestions that were received with comments like "We do it this way because. . ." or "Wait until you've been here a while, you'll see why . . . ."

Today I realise that I have moved from enthusiastic suggester to defensive protector of 'the way things are'. "Wait until you've been here a while, then you'll understand how things work," I want to say, but I check myself. This man is right about the irrigation system and the tool shed—I agree with him completely. But *who* is going to do the work, and *when*? Already my work day begins at 6:30 a.m. and continues until around 10 p.m. When can I possibly find time to clean the shed or install a new irrigation system, never mind the time to research a method and make a trip into town to buy the materials. Besides, I have a hunch that someone else *has* thought of this possibility and opted for the present system for a variety of reasons I am unaware of. I make a mental note to talk with Cougar this afternoon.

Ruminating these thoughts, I walk the mile up the mountain to the Long House. These short-term visitors have a lot of enthusiasm and ideas but few outlets to apply them. They usually connect with a particular person and work with him or her for the duration of their visit, which can give a skewed impression of how the Bear

Tribe functions and what it's about. Ideally each visitor would experience all aspects of work on the farm and spend a day in town working in the Circle Center before focusing on a particular area.

Maybe I'm being too organised, though. Often the person with the perfect skills for a particular job shows up at just the right time. I think of Guenther who arrived last week, not long after Hilary began work on clearing the dead, burned trees on the mountain above the Long House. Razed by a forest fire several years ago, the dead trees could fuel a wildfire set by lightning or a spark from an open fire, especially during this summer drought.

At Sun Bear's suggestion, Hilary began cutting down the burned trees, chainsawing them into segments, and hauling them down the mountain to the Long House. In addition to reducing the risk of summer wildfires, the cut trees will provide our winter wood supply for the Long House's woodburning stove.

The day the chainsaw began to dull and the machine whine in protest, Guenther arrived. He lilted (he never walks) up the mountain, examined the chainsaw, and quickly applied his mechanical wizardry. He repaired the machine, sharpened the chain and then ensconced himself in the garage at the bottom of the mountain, casting spells of regeneration over the ailing farm vehicles. Eyes twinkling and hands covered with grease, he wields his wrench with the grace of a magician using a wand. He even *looks* like an elf, and he lives his life with the same whimsical aliveness, blowing like a wind-loosed leaf to his next destination, resting gracefully where he is needed until a fresh gust carries him onwards.

But what about the visitors who arrive confused and ruffled by the winds? They drift about the farm, working a bit, going for walks, eating meals. They sit on benches outside the Long House, watching the ebb and flow of movement around them. When they do have an opportunity to become a part of something, they usually spark with enthusiasm and bristle with helpful suggestions. They move from critical bench warmers to participants in that stream of activity flowing around them. They get wet. They sputter. And, for the most part, they swim.

What can we do to support people in making that initial plunge? How can we draw out skills from people a bit too shy to dabble a toe in the waters? And, from the Tribe's point of view, how can we willingly, even gladly, receive suggestions to improve things without defending ourselves or 'the way things are'? And once we accept those suggestions, how can we inspire people, visitors *or* members, to fulfil them?

I perceive the short-term visitors as an untapped resource, but trying to integrate new people only increases the irritation. Our organism has no clear channel in its membrane to absorb them. They stick like burrs on the hem of the community instead of joining the internal structure. How can we make our group membrane more permeable?

In the aftenoon heat I sit in Carl's van, scribbling notes—too hot to work outside. Sweat beads on my forehead and rolls down my cheeks. Within an hour I have a fully fledged job description for a 'visitor co-ordinator', complete with a list of responsibilities and an outline of the personal qualities needed to fill the position.

On Sunday I read the proposal in the Council Meeting. "Can I have a copy to enter in the computer with our other job descriptions?" asks Shawnodese.

Wabun smiles. "You've outlined all of your own qualities in that job description." I look up, surprised. "Why don't you fill the job?"

Like the visitor in the garden who catalysed this process, I am offered the opportunity to remedy a situation. Writing a job description and outlining a possible programme was a positive response, but now I realise that visioning is only the *first* step. Enacting is another. Am I ready for more toddling steps?

"Well, uh, yeah, I guess I can, at least for the rest of the time I'm here."

"Great. Thanks for the work you put into writing this down. Now, who has more new business?"

I sink into the chair, wondering what I have said yes to. Doubts wrack me briefly, soon replaced by enthusiasm. During the break I corner Cougar.

"Shall we start meeting in the mornings to sort out who will work with whom?"

Cougar yawns and stretches his arms above him. He's seen crusading reformists before. "Naw, mornings are no good. Too many details with the animals and chores."

"How about the night before? I can meet with you briefly, and you can tell me what you're doing and how many people you need."

"OK."

"After dinner tonight?"

"Yeah. That's fine." He yawns again. I punch him playfully on the arm. He grins.

I corner Hilary and Carl and everyone else working on the farm. We work out a system to plan the next day's work, allocating visitors according to the needs of the day.

Great. The members are organised. Now I just need to be sure the visitors want to participate.

In the evening we sit in a circle—the short-term visitors, Hetty and Bill, Carl and I. We hold hands for a few moments of silence and then settle into the grass. So far, so good. Expectant eyes turn towards me.

"I thought we could go around the circle and briefly say how we are and then share any expectations we have for the week."

We move slowly around the circle, each new speaker opening a bit deeper into him- or herself. This simple ritual of expressing feelings, being vulnerable and sharing expectations weaves a web of kinship among this group of individuals. The composition of that web is a mystery to me, but I know the power of its action. When the last speaker finishes, shadows lie long on the grass, and a comfortable quiet fills the circle. It hangs without hurry, content with itself, needing nothing to fill its measure. It is a quiet bursting with itself, leaving no room for further sounds.

Someone shifts a leg in the grass. The silence, like a grey-bellied cloud, disperses slowly. "Thank you," says Bill. "I didn't know what to expect, but this was nice. I'm glad I came."

"Hmm . . ." I murmur, nodding. That's why it's nice. Anticipating the unknown and then finding it agreeable is what makes the tasting sweet.

We continue to meet at the beginning of each week to say goodbye to people who are leaving and to welcome new visitors. I feel myself stretching emotionally and mentally with each new influx of people. The boundaries of my heart surprise me. With some visitors I feel an immediate sense of kinship. Other relationships require slow, careful cultivation. With some the gaps are never bridged, and we remain acquaintances on distant piers, separated by an expanse of silence.

41

CHAPTER 3
Vision Quest

Despite my disdain of workshops—the ultimate 'quick fix' in learning—I decide to participate in the Vision Quest workshop scheduled for mid-August. Questions about my future still plague me. The Naturopathic College of Medicine has accepted me for their four-year programme, but I have deferred admission for a year, wanting a break after the pressures of undergraduate studies. I also want a hiatus from academic work to evaluate the direction of my life. The academic track is magnetic for me—I could easily move from degree to degree, lost in the all-consuming tasks of notetaking, memorising and churning out papers on command. The immediacy of the demands in an academic life narrow my vision to the moment. Focused on short-term goals, I lose sight of how my daily efforts contribute to a long-term vision. I am expert at filling time, but is the activity fulfilling some larger purpose? Without a vision for my life, how can I act effectively in this moment? Within a traditional Native American society, no one is considered an adult until she has a vision for her life—how would she know how to act responsibly without the larger context of a life vision? And besides the uncertainty about my future, I crave solitary time for myself after a summer of frenetic activity.

During the first day of the workshop Sun Bear, Raven and Shawnodese share their own experiences of vision questing. The power of their stories alters my initial view of the four-day vigil on the mountain. Instead of a quiet, restful reprieve after a demanding summer, I realise that the Vision Quest could transform the direction of my life. I am still doubtful, though, and contemplate the possibility of not receiving a vision. Perhaps I am not yet worthy. Or what if a vision presents itself and I miss it? And what if I *am* guided to follow a path—could I live up to the vision? Even if the guidance contradicts my plans? I know, too, that I must clear the voices of parents, family, teachers and friends that clamour within me before I can realise *my own* vision. I must find my own path and the courage to walk it.

They send us from the circle to find a power spot on the mountain, to accustom ourselves to listening to the Earth. I walk slowly along the road crossing Evelyn's land and climb the rock escarpment that leads to my spot. I sit for a while on the rock ledge, sun baking the surrounding granite. My freckled skin tightens, the first sign of sunburn, so I move into the shade of a pine tree, wrapping my arms around its trunk. I nuzzle the crevasses of layered bark, inhaling the antiseptic-sweet smell of pine tar. For several minutes I focus on the terraced bark, the inner colours of golden orange and soft pink partially exposed by the peeling outer layers. As I explore the surface with my hands and eyes, I realise that as the tree exfoliates, shedding its hard outer layer, it exposes the beauty of its inner core. This tree teaches me, for I, too, am working to peel away unnecessary layers of protection and to discard outdated material, hoping to dis-cover the wisdom within me. I learn that such weathering can expose great beauty.

Another day passes, filled with more preparations for the Quest. We will begin at dawn with a men's, followed by a women's, sweat lodge to purify ourselves before the vigil on the mountain.

"Remember," says Wabun before we return to our tents for the night, "no talking when you get up in the morning. Silence is a way of honouring a sacred space, so don't talk on the way to the sweat tomorrow."

I lie next to Carl, curled in my sleeping bag, staring at the walls of the tent. My mind is crackling with nervous excitement, wondering what the Quest will bring.

Restless sleep, then the greyness of first light. Carl lies inert. I pull on clothes, stuff sleeping bag into its sack, and gather poncho and Ensolite pad. I collect crystal and topaz necklace, sunscreen and sage-filled smudgebowl, a flicker wing and the soapstone Goddess that Carl carved for me and place them in a pouch.

I walk up the hill to the sweat lodge with the same expectancy as on those September mornings when I returned to school, freshly bathed outside and whisked clean inside by a sweep of good intentions. I place my crystal and Goddess on the mound in front of the lodge and join the circle of women standing or squatting around the fire. The sweat is hot and deep and moving. I pray hard for vision and the strength to accept whatever I receive.

After the sweat we move to the Medicine Wheel for a final blessing. Sun Bear stands in the centre of the Wheel, holding a large shell with sage smouldering in it, greeting each one as she enters the Wheel from the East (new beginnings, illumination), smudging and blessing her before she passes to the West (experience, introspection). This ritual roots me in the importance of the moment, preparing both me and the community for radical newness. Ultimately I must quest alone and find my vision through a solitary link with the Creator, but I know that the community supports me. The Tribe holds each vision quester in their awareness, including the seekers in the community's pipe ceremonies as well as in personal prayers.

Within the Tribe my duties will remain the same, but after the Vision Quest my attitudes and actions can alter without comment. This ritualised questing provides a safety valve for change in a culture with tight family bonds. In the culture in which I grew up, the two-week stay at summer camp provided a safe environment for change—I allowed myself to be different when I returned, and my family accepted the changes more readily than if they came overnight within our home. A camper at Farm and Wilderness crystallised this awareness for me: "I like coming to camp because I'm allowed to be different when I go home. I change a lot every summer."

In a culture without rituals to prepare itself for life passages, no wonder so many people have to physically remove themselves from a situation in order to change.

'Children' leave home to go to college or get a job—the American culture's equivalent of passage into adulthood. After a year or two away, different behaviours and values are accepted more easily by one's family. Without a safety valve for change, family bonds become boundaries that either stunt any growth or contain the need to change until it finally explodes in unpredictable behaviour. A mid-life crisis is, in one review, a long-postponed cry for inner transformation that goes unrecognised in the individual, the family and the community. Desperate lunges—a new relationship, house or job—do not address the fundamental urge to transform internally, to alter one's ground of being according to the season of one's life. I want to transform and have that newness recognised within my community. Nothing is more outlandish than a butterfly eternally classified as a caterpillar.

So, at this time I enter the cocoon of my inner being, searching for the key of vision to unlock the potential of new life as an adult within a society. The gestation period also gives those around me time to adjust to transformation.

Wabun and 'Mosha silently lead half a dozen of us along the track through Evelyn's land. I wait as Wabun places each person in a site. Finally only Wabun, 'Mosha and I remain. We climb the rock escarpment. I smile quietly as we walk directly through my power spot. Wabun directs me to a hollow just south of my usual place. When they leave, I am still for a few moments, not wanting to break the calm with any movement.

"Crawk, crawk." The rasping cry of ravens draws my attention upwards. Four black birds circle slowly, coursing higher and higher, weaving in and out amongst each other. Two fly in tandem to the south, two wheel to the north. Four more birds appear, circling up, and then disappear. "Thank you, Creator," I murmur. "Good beginnings."

I busy myself with small things—coaxing sleeping bag from its sack, unrolling Ensolite pad, arranging beading materials. When I settle my back against a rock, viewing the valley below and the far ridge, my shoulders hunch with tension, as if to hold back unseen walls that keep me confined in this space. Time moves imperceptibly. The sun seems to be anchored in position. If I think too hard, I will go mad. Several times I resist urges to spring up, cross the bluff and run . . . run anywhere. To a book. To a conversation. To a radio programme. To a counter full of canning jars. Anywhere that I don't have to face myself.

The walls are composed of my past, hemming me in my present, tense and unable to move. Which bricks in this wall can I discard? What do I want to leave behind me? A parade of lovers march through my mind—can I forgive you all and set you (and myself) free? Parental expectations of greatness, teachers' demands for perfection and my inability to fulfil their dreams pass before me. For hours I list all of the things, people, lovers, values, plans and desires that I must leave behind. Leaving the baby is the hardest, along with Carl.

What do I choose to carry with me? I search for a long time and find only three things—love of family, self-assurance and equality. A small amount of baggage compared to what I am discarding.

I watch clouds, scanning them for some visionary message. A lion's head stretches into a feathered wing followed by a curly lamb. I strain to find significance in the bank of clouds sliding to the east, but their meaning, if any, escapes me. Shadows roll languidly over the trees, although patches of sky still reflects bright sunlight. Wind stirs, bringing a slight chill, most welcome after the heat of the day. I smudge myself and roll a tobacco offering. Having no pipe, I offer prayers with a simple roll-up—simple method, deep prayers, praying for vision, for myself, for the Bear Tribe, for all life around me. I crawl into my sleeping bag, staring into the tree above me.

As I focus on one branch, the body of the tree begins to vibrate. I blink a few times, and the movement stops. As long as I hold still, the tree pulsates with a thrumming of tiny lights, points of colour that pop in and out of sight. I wonder if the lights are significant—am I seeing the 'aura' or the life force of the tree? Finally I relax into my pillow, close my eyes and fall asleep.

I awake to an orange-red moon threading through clouds on the horizon. Will the Vision come now? I prop myself on an elbow, taut with watchfulness. An owl hoots in the distance. Heat lightning backlights the clouds rimming the horizon. No thunder yet. I doze and awake again. The moon hangs overhead, partly shrouded by dark rain-sodden clouds. Thunder rumbles, and the rain begins. I gather everything close to me and try to cover it with a poncho. Rain drums hard on the plastic above me. It seeps into the bottom of the bag, soaking my feet. I feel raw and vulnerable, exposed to the power of the mountain without the usual comfort of shelter.

Finally I fall asleep in the soaked bag. I dream of bicycling along a country road fringed with evergreen trees. I stop at a small store with a garage and gas pumps. Two boys run outside and jeer at me, calling me names. I'm not sure why they do it. On the return ride, I meet Ruth (Blue Camas). Somehow we exchange vehicles and I am driving a huge green car. It steers like a boat. This time when I stop for gas, the boys smile respectfully. I awake with the first streaks of dawn, then doze again.

I am walking through the high-vaulted halls of Oberlin Conservatory. I talk with my chamber music coach, who studied with Schoenburg (somehow that's important) about scheduling a private reading in violin improvisation.

The dream fades. The sun climbs behind a cloud on the horizon, emerging as I stretch in my sleeping bag. Thunder rumbles to the south—more storms later?

I shake my head as I record the dreams in my diary—seeking the safety of an academic environment to learn how to improvise, to ask a composer, who *writes* music, to teach me how to play spontaneously without written notes. I get the message, though, that it's time for me to make my own music, in essence to create my own life, not to perform other people's compositions.

I am anxious. No visionary creatures have appeared. No vivid, life-changing dreams. Will I fail? I wrap my arms around my knees, rocking in a tight ball. Please, Creator, please, give me vision. Please.

I am distracted by my body—scratching spots and blisters, squeezing splinters, scraping dead skin from the bottom of my feet. And when will my mind be still? I fight between staying rigidly alert and allowing my mind to wander or even doze. Which way is best, the clenched-jaw 'give it all you've got', or the relaxed acceptance of whatever does (or doesn't) come?

I move to the rock outcropping facing south. A nuthatch lands on the tree to the east, pauses, and darts a few inches up the trunk. He turns to stare at me. I admire the precisely drawn black and white stripes on his head, the rosy breast and his sleek blue-black back. A raven flies overhead, so close that I can hear the muffled 'woosh' of its wing flaps.

A squirrel runs up the tree, its claws clacking on the rough bark as it skitters in nervous spurts. Standing on a branch, its front paws resting one on top of the other, the squirrel eyes me and begins a mad chattering, scolding me for invading his territory. The indignant scolding continues for several minutes until a thought comes to me. "Your mind is like this." The squirrel shakes a paw at me and twitches its tail. "Your *mind* is like this." Then the squirrel bounds across the branch, dive bombs head first down the tree, scurries over the rock face beside me and into the jumble of boulders and trees in the knoll below.

Gradually my shoulders unknot, my forehead smooths and my mind relaxes. I contemplate the trees growing below me in the valley, straight-limbed pines with tinges of blue at the end of their branches. I have had difficulty sitting in this circle for one day, yet they have endured this view for decades. My mind takes on tree form, looking through their eyes. I watch the banks of clouds billowing over the ridge and dispersing after storms. I observe the mountain transformed from season to season. Colours burst and fade among the broad-leaved trees. Sun cycles pop and flash from day to night to light again. I realise with a start that the tree will outlive me. Its sense of time rolls at a much more leisurely pace. What I endure, the tree glimpses. My long days are savoured moments in its life. "To live long," says Cicero, "it is necessary to live slowly." And I would add to that *broadly*. By that measure, the tree will certainly outlive me.

I feel the rock beneath me and ponder its age. It has endured for millennia in this spot, weathering slowly while generation upon generation of tree has risen from and then returned to the soil upon this mountain top. This rock has probably even watched changes in the *species* of tree that populate this mountain. It tells me, in its slow, timeless way, of patience. How to sit like a rock. How to *watch* with patience. How to endure. The rock speaks of stillness, a rootedness that comes from knowing this place for millions of years. From this stance, my vigil upon the mountain is fleeting, a short-lived interlude in the life of this mountainside community of tree and rock and soil and bird.

As my mind quiets, my thoughts are fewer and more significant. During the heat of the afternoon, cowering in the thin shade cast by the twisted branches of the pine tree above me, a thought about speech comes to me. I have not spoken for nearly two days, except for a few short prayers, and as my energy dwindles with the fasting, I realise how much energy I usually expend through talking. I realise how powerful words are—they drain energy because their utterance is a projection of power. The less I speak, the more power each word has. I resolve to talk less, listen more and place my words carefully, to use their power wisely.

In the afternoon I lie quietly on my belly under the tree, sifting pine needles through my fingers. My hands begin to tremble. I watch, fascinated. My arms begin to vibrate against the ground in front of me.

I pick up my crystal, move outside the circle to pee, and then settle on my pillow in the southwest of the circle. As I gaze at the crystal, the face of an old woman alternates with the head of a cougar. The scene shifts to a tiny figure traversing a yellow sand desert flanked on the left by a bald eagle and a hand arching over to reach the eagle from the right. I close my eyes and place the crystal on my forehead, over the third eye. My arms beat hard against the side of my body, then settle outstretched at my sides. The drumming returns, then settles into a gentle flapping.

As I move I see a hook-beaked bird from the side and then head on. I stare into its eyes and then view the whole bird. The eagle lands at my feet and pecks at my toes. She moves to my head, hammering through my skull and eating my brains, emptying the cavity.

"Come with me," commands the eagle. My wings/arms (I can no longer tell the difference) pump hard and then slow to a gentle flapping. We fly over large expanses of forest dotted with lakes and bisected by rivers that thread among the hills. We pause to rest in the branches of a tall tree. I wait, hopping from one taloned foot to the other. "What is the purpose of my life?" I ask the eagle.

"Be patient," she replies.

"Will I know tonight?"

"Perhaps."

46

I ride the wind currents over the lakes and forest, back to my rock ledge over-looking the valley. Gradually I sense the wind pushing against my body. I open my eyes and watch clouds drifting across the late afternoon sky.

Minutes pass. A few hours spill through my awareness. I ponder how I have spent most of my life screened from the natural cycle of light and dark. With electric lights, I am not obliged to plan my day according to the passing of the sun.

On the other hand, a bear, like other forest creatures, knows the sun's pattern and heads for a winter den when the light lapses into autumn. I once pitied a bear for spending so long in unconscious slumber, but now I wonder . . . . What do bears dream during those long winter nights? Do they dream the land awake? Do they dream the spring wildflowers, do they swim the fish and gather the honey and grow the tree? I ponder the cycling of day and night, rolling one over the other, tumbling like clowns in the circus gripping hand to hand, pulled by the other's forward drive. The cycle rolls on and on, a drama unfolding outside my window, on a stage foreign to most housedwellers—the theatre called Earth.

I decide to watch the whole drama —the passage of the darkness as well as the light. I resolve to stay up for a whole night to observe the complete cycle of a day, so I lie down for a brief nap in the late afternoon.

I awake, immediately at full attention. Shadows stretch across the valley below and up the far ridge. I lie on my stomach, peering over the rock ledge into the hollow, watching the shadows deepen into darkness. The first star appears in the pale lavender-grey sky. In the twilight, the trees dance as they did last night. If I stare at something, the edges pulsate with waves of light. The stars enter one by one, then in clusters, filling the dome above. A star shoots across, etching a trail of light that streaks half the length of the sky before it fades.

I doze, despite my best efforts to stay awake. The moon is overhead when I open my eyes. Foosteps crunch in the pine needles to the west. Slowly I sit up, peering through the silvery light. Is it an animal? I hear a car and then two doors slamming. I have to pee badly—as much from fright as from a full bladder. I stand up. The 'animal'—that's what I tell myself it is—scurries away. The stream of pee sounds like a river in the stillness. When I sit down I hear the 'animal' waddling in the clearing below.

To the southeast red lights glow in huge columns. Light pulses from the bottom upwards, dies, then repeats. The columns to the left glow steadily, but the right side of the structure pulses only occasionally. Probably the electricity generating plant. I am happy to see the lights. Though distant, they comfort me, like the street lamp of early childhood glowing silver-grey into my bedroom at night. I return to my sleeping bag, watching the moon.

I imagine all of the ways vision could come, based upon others' stories—awakening to four baby eagles in a row, a rattlesnake coiled nearby, or a satellite writing my name in the night sky. I feel discouraged. Nothing has happened as I imagined it would . . . and perhaps the weight of expectation, doubled by comparison with other people's experience, has slowed the process.

"Come on, Judy," I scold myself angrily, "I want my *own* vision, not someone else's." The anger dissolves some of my discouragement about the Vision Quest. I lie, eyes wandering among the stars overhead, relaxing.

My mind relives the journey that brought me to this place. I have been stretched and pulled in so many directions, yet the pieces of the journey seem to follow smoothly enough. In retrospect, the pattern is even graceful, each step overlapping the one behind it. What I perceived at the time as great leaps become simple steps when looking back with a view of the whole pattern.

I need to open to this larger plan. I need, quite simply, openness. I balk and retract a bit. "No, not total openness. I don't want to be hurt." Another thought passes through, "No pain, no gain." Insightful poet or masochist?

"OK, Creator, I would like to know with whom to be open, to best give my energy. I need a centre so that I will not be pulled all over the place by whomever needs my energy. That centre, that information about people and my purpose, would come *from my vision.*"

Aha, why I need vision! So let's have it, Creator. I'm tired. I'm starving. I'm cold and weak and pitiful. Have pity on me, Creator, and give me vision. Damn it, *give me vision.*

I awake at dawn and sit with my back against the stone. Time slides by, greased by my empty mind. There's nothing inside to snag it, so it slips by unnoticed.

Mid morning. Thought enters. "No one has the same perspective I do." I have a unique angle from which to view that far ridge, different from any other creature on this mountain.

I move to the rock face rising in the north of the circle and lean against it. My belly, cheek and outstretched arms press against the gritty, cool surface. My feet feel large as if they are stretching into the ground. Stillness.

"All plants take their life from me," says the rock. The voice enters after a feeling-sense pulses through my heart. "That is why a tree can live on a rock. It draws its nourishment from me. Always leave some large rocks in a garden to remind the plants of their true source of nourishment."

I rest for a while, leaning aginst the rock face, and then turn to the boulder sitting in the centre of the circle. Yesterday I made plans to spend part of the day on this rock. I find my pillow resting on top of it—did I put it there?

I sit down. My shoulders ease. My jaw relaxes. My face softens. My mind stills. Time, like an airborne glider, banks and then stalls. I hang suspended, enjoying the feeling of weightlessness.

I'm curious about the lights I saw last night. If it was an electricity generating plant, or a radio tower, I wonder why I've never seen it before, although my night-time walks usually skirt the southern ridge, not this eastern-facing side of the mountain. I write a note to 'Mosha and slip it under the empty water bottle just out of sight of the circle. Each day she makes the trek up here to fill my empty bottle with water. She is my lifeline to the world beyond this circle.

Mid day. The sun burns heat into the rocks. I retreat under the tree, lying on top of my sleeping bag to nap, sleepy after the night watch.

A grasshopper flies against my third eye. The impact awakens me.

"Wake up and *look*," he seems to say.

I lie still, waiting expectantly.

"You're not scared of me—that's a good sign."

He crawls across my back and onto my left shoulder. I can feel the weight of his body resting there, but when I turn to look, I see nothing. Drawing up on my knees, I look to the left and spot the grasshopper calmly walking under the arch of a fallen pine frond on the boulder next to me.

"Look under, look *under*," he commands.

A lizard darts from under a rock just an arm's length in front of me. A wide brown stripe runs down his back flanked by a thick black line, a wide yellow band and then a wide black stripe. The head and body are beautifully formed, sleek as a torpedo. He darts a couple of inches forward, revealing an iridescent blue tail.

We stare at each other for a long time, frozen in wonder and fear. Spontaneously he jerks his head up and then scurries along the rock to the north, footfalls too quick to decipher, a fluid flurry of movement propelling him missile-like, leaving no trail.

Stunned, kneeling motionless, I wait. No more movement under the rock. Quietly I reach for my waterbottle, unscrew the lid, fill it with water, and place it carefully near the rocks. As I sit back, a second lizard appears in the same spot. He crawls out to reveal his full body, as if to tell me, "Yes, indeed, you did see a six-inch iridescent blue-tailed lizard." He curls his head to meet his tail, tiny feet relaxing on his back. Suddenly he torpedoes between the rocks and under the boulder against which I have been resting for two days.

How could I spend two days in this place and not notice these lizards within reach of an outstretched arm? 'Look under, look under' runs through my mind. In order to look under something, I must first be awake. Fully conscious. And I need to perceive small things. Quietly. To look under rocks and into cracks. To hunch small and humble on my knees to see the details. To look *under* something. Stand under it. Stand under it.

A switch snaps in my awareness. To stand under. To under-stand. To understand. I must learn to *look under* things in order to understand. I feel an unaccustomed openness, a calm eagerness that I have not experienced before on this mountain.

Did the circled body of the lizard mean completion—coming full-circle? Late afternoon; I feel weak and dizzy, seeking shelter from the blazing sun. A butterfly swoops across the circle, landing briefly on my nose. Dragonflies drone, hovering on helicopter wings, eyeing me. The animals seem to sense my inner quiet and approach without fear.

Moving my legs is an effort. When I stand, the scene before me blazes white and then blurs out of sight. Deep breaths restore my vision and steady my legs. I give myself landmarks to keep me present in the circle. Just hold on until the sun reaches that tree. OK, until it reaches that branch. Now, prepare the smudge bowl and tobacco. Wait until that shadow reaches the rock. Now the next rock. Good. Keep breathing. Light the sage. Draw the smoke into my body. Light the tobacco. Prayers . . . prayers, Creator, thanking you for this day and this mountain and this life. Prayers . . . the words escape through fissures in my mind, replaced by images. I pray in picture-words, more eloquent and precise than the words of language.

When the tobacco embers die, I make myself a promise. When darkness comes, if I do not see the towers with pulsing red lights on the far ridge, I may leave. I wrap my sleeping bag around me, leaning against the rock, watching the tree-lights shimmer in the twilight, waiting. Waiting.

Darkness wraps itself slowly around the mountain, beginning in the hollows and then leisurely spiralling to the peaks. In the darkness I scan the far ridge. No lights glimmer. No electricity generators. No radio towers.

I grin. The only structure of that magnitude that could appear and disappear from that ridge in one short day is a UFO.

I gather my things and move slowly down the mountain. My legs feel rubbery as if I had spent days in bed. Stopping to rest along the way, even my sleeping bag feels heavy in my arms.

Electric lights blaze from the Long House windows, harsh to my eyes accustomed to moon and starlight. I stand in the doorway clutching my sleeping bag, wordless.

"Do you want some tea?" someone asks.

I nod mutely and stare around me. Like an anthill the house throbs with people moving in set patterns around the furniture. They stop in various places to perform various functions. Their chatter melds into a drone, the words colliding too quickly for me to differentiate.

Wabun stands beside me and touches my arm. "You're very open and sensitive right now. You might want to go somewhere quiet for a while. Cougar and I can talk with you about your experiences in a few minutes—we need to finish with someone else first. Save the power of your experience. Don't talk to anybody else." She squeezes my arm gently, and I nod.

Carl comes in the door, arms outstretched. "Hey, how are you?" he asks, grinning. We hug for a long time, satisfied with simply touching. Quiet. He feels warm and solid and full of life—he squeezes me and leans back, lifting me off my feet, rocking back and forth like a delighted child with a teddy bear. "I missed you," he says, lips puckered in earnestness, half pouting. "I'm glad you're back."

"Me, too," I reply simply. "Me, too."

Wabun and Cougar help me to interpret my experiences on the mountain. When I describe the shimmering tree lights, Wabun nods her head in understanding. "Yes, you were seeing the life force of the tree." And when I described the trembling of my hands and arms, she nods again, recalling how her own arms trembled before she had visionary experiences or began to channel information. The description of the eagle seen in the crystal draws Cougar to attention. He smiles as I describe the four views of the eagle. "That's a power animal for you. They always show themselves from four different angles. That's good." We discuss the dreams and different ways of understanding them. I also describe my encounter with the lizard, teaching me to look under things, and the columns of red light on the far ridge.

"Hmmm . . . ." says Wabun, pausing for a moment. "Lots of people have reported seeing lights and different kinds of ships over the last few years. Donna and I saw something when we drove back to the farm from Spokane one night. They seem to be attracted to this area of the country."

When we finish I make my way along the path outside the Long House, carrying my bundle up the ridge to our tent. Carl's breathing is deep and slow, already verging on sleep, but he reaches out to hold me when I slip into my sleeping bag.

We awake early the next morning to milk the cows. Carl and I load the pails and paraphernalia into the four-wheel drive and trundle down the mountain.

As we crouch on either side of Twiggy, drawing jets of milk from her udder, thoughts begin to pop in my mind. "Today I need to (long list) . . . . And she said this to so-and-so . . . . I wonder what's for lunch. I'm still so hungry . . . . Carl and I talked about canoeing next week . . . . What day could that be? . . . ."

I push back on my heels, snorting in exasperation.

"What's wrong?" asks Carl.

"My mind. It's full of thoughts again. So many thoughts." Somehow I hoped that the silence attained on the mountain would travel with me, but already within an hour of waking the mind is chattering and gossiping with itself to keep itself entertained. Frustrating.

Fourth morning. All of the vision questers have returned from the mountain. The women gather after the men for a sweat lodge of completion and thanksgiving, to thank the Creator for vision and a safe return. Inside the lodge I sit next to the door, pulling down the flap behind me. Darkness. The early morning light does not penetrate this womb, closed to gestate these vision-infused souls before birthing them into a new life.

Wabun offers sage and sweet grass, sifting them over the rocks glowing in the centre. I draw the sweet, pungent smoke around me, breathing deeply. Although this lodge is dark and contained, a situation that normally would ignite my claustrophobia into panic, I find this space expansive. The darkness rolls endlessly all around me. I could be floating in boundless space, weaving among stars and planets except for the cool moist earth beneath me, reminding me of my central rooting to

50

this planet Earth.

As the first water hisses on the rocks, we welcome the spirits into the lodge with a chant. More water on the rocks; steam fills the lodge. The first beads of sweat break on my skin.

At Wabun's direction I open the flap a crack. "We welcome Wabun, Spiritkeeper of the East," she begins. "Wabun is the Eagle who sees far with clear Vision. Wabun's time of day is dawn, when light first returns to the Earth. The season is spring when life begins to stir again after the Long Cold of Winter. Wabun's time of life is birth and childhood, when we first begin this Earthwalk. The qualities that Wabun brings are wisdom, clarity and illumination. We welcome Wabun in the lodge at this time. Welcome, Wabun, Spiritkeeper of the East. *Ho!*"

Steam hisses from the rocks, pushing out from the centre in waves of heat. "Does anyone have a chant to offer Wabun, Spiritkeeper of the East?"

Silence. My heart beats with the memory of Eagle revealed to me on the mountain. I want to honour you, Eagle, I want to sing for you, sing you, become you as a way of honouring your being. Sounds rise in my throat, pushing aside reserve. I hear myself speak into the darkness. "This one would."

"Ho," responds Wabun.

"Fly like an Eagle," I begin, the women echoing in response. "Flying so high (Flying so high), circling the universe (circling the universe) on wings of pure Light (on wings of pure Light)."

The sound greets me, reverberating like an echo across a still lake. Rising, rising, the world of forest and lake revealed in the darkness before me. Rising, flying, wings pushing against the air currents, riding, coasting on the draughts. My shoulders tense in sympathy with the wingbeats, soaring, soaring on currents of sound.

After four rounds, the sound quiets. My shoulders relax. I return to the lodge, sitting quietly on the cool earth, breathing the steamy air that presses hot as an iron into my nose. Prayers begin, prayers for myself, of thanks for the Vision Quest, for all the aspects of myself that I have Seen, thanks for the Eagle's presence and the gift of learning to under-stand.

"And Creator, I pray for the strength and courage to live my life according to my heart, according to your will. May I have the courage to See the Vision for my life and the strength to fulfil it. Creator, please help me in this. Please help me."

The rounds continue. Like a heat-blasted flower, I wilt into the Earth, relaxing into limpness.

Second round, honouring Shawnodese, Spiritkeeper of the South, whose qualities are love and trust and innocence. One of the women begins to cry, her jagged gasps filling the lodge.

"Let go," says Wabun. "Let go and cry. Keep breathing. Don't hold back. Just let go."

Sobs and wordless anguish push from her heart. I feel the sounds reverberating in the centre of my chest, yet I am at peace, sharing her pain and holding her supportively in the same moment. We are joined by pain but bonded by the love that pushes behind the anguish. That love, corked by pain and anger and mistrust, is as persistent as a mountain stream welling from its source, pushing against all obstacles until they yield to its soft, steady strength.

End of third round. "We'll take a break now," says Wabun. "Everyone can rest outside."

"Can we stay inside if we want to?" I ask. I am reluctant to leave the lodge, wanting only to lie on my belly on this cool earth.

"You need to learn flexibility as well as endurance. Everyone outside."

Fourth round. For the Earth Mother. Through the women's prayers I glimpse the visions that they have received. The heat is strong, the prayers are strong, the love is strong. My chest tightens, expands and then bursts with love for this Earth. "Please, Creator, please, use me. I want to serve this Earth, to be part of the answer, not the problems that fill this planet. Please, show me. Use me. Guide me in serving this planet."

When the round ends, we crawl outside. I collapse in a clump of jewelweed, spent. Without thought. Quiet. Death-like.

Slowly life returns. New life. My Being cools into a new shape, like the lava poured from the core of the earth, cooling into new forms of land. I am emerging, lava-like, into a new life.

* * *

The last weeks at the Bear Tribe are both a completion and a beginning. I plan to return here after four years of study as a Naturopath, joining the community in its vision of establishing a clinic of holistic practitioners, but I realise both my life and the lives of the people here at the Tribe will change, probably drastically, in the space of four years. Time seems to move here at an accelerated rate, catalysed by the demands of fulfilling a vision of a better world. Questing is, in a sense, continuous in this place, and since form follows thought, the focus upon bettering life on the planet and within oneself breeds constant change.

That search for improvement strikes the collective from time to time as well. Sometimes the need for change swamps the daily round of details in which most of us swim, face down, oblivious of the larger picture. Where are we going? Collectively and as individuals? The gap between where we are and where we want to be is, once again, too wide for comfort, and we need to reassess our commitment and our direction.

This dance between what is and where we want to be is the tension that moves a community forward. Like an elastic band stretched taut between the present and a future vision, we are drawn irresistibly towards that vision, sometimes balking and stumbling, but always moving, drawing nearer, finally reaching. Part of the challenge of a visionary group is facing disparity without despair, viewing the gap as a catalyst rather than a roadblock.

We gather in the evening in the lower farmhouse for the first of a series of meetings. The smudge bowl passes around the circle, the smoke of sweetgrass and sage curling into the corners. We sit silently for a few moments.

"Creator," says Sun Bear, "may we be guided in this time together. Ho!"

Sun Bear props his elbows on the arm rests of his chair and laces his fingers below his smooth brown chin. He fidgets a bit, always uneasy in this contentious world of words. "I'll let Shawnodese start. That's why I named him Subchief. So he could do all the talking and I wouldn't have to." Sun Bear grins and turns to Shawno, nodding. "It's all yours."

Shawno sighs. "Thanks, Sun Bear, thanks a lot. Well, the issue that we want to discuss tonight is the farm. We've been looking at the finances and seeing that the farm is losing money, has been for a few years. We simply haven't been able to attract people who are willing to work hard and are skilled in making this place self-sufficient."

Already a few hackles rise. The gap between the farm and the town workers is the first to show.

"The publishing business and the catalogue show some profit, but most of our funds still come from Sun Bear's talks and workshops. We simply don't have the resources to support people who are not willing to work hard on the farm. Carl, now I notice you have not been doing as much as when you first arrived . . . . And Hilary, you are still spending most of your evenings out in your room."

Carl fidgets, irritated. "What do you mean, I haven't been doing enough? I've completely cleared out and organised two sheds this summer *and* I've taken care of the animals and helped with the wood."

Hilary lies on his back, fingers laced over his belly, his softly drumming fingers betraying his agitation. He draws himself to a sitting position and folds his legs underneath him. "Shawno, this is an old myth I want to put to rest right now. I know you think I stay up all night reading . . . ."

"Yeah, and you get up at 11 o'clock in the morning."

"Well, look, in the winter I got up later simply because there wasn't so much to do on the farm. Now I'm getting my ass out of bed early every morning to work on the wood. And maybe you haven't noticed that with Guenther's help I've repaired all the chainsaws and other equipment in the toolshed. Come on, Shawno, can you let go of this grudge you've held against me for so long and see me as I am?"

Shawnodese sits fuming. Wabun takes over, noticing my distress. I have been shaking my head and pursing my lips, puckering my chin in anger.

"Judy, do you want to say something?"

"Yeah," I burst out, "I want to say something about the farm. I think the people in town don't know how hard it is to work out here—chopping wood, teaching people how to do things, taking care of the animals and the garden. I'm working as hard as I can. I'm giving my full energy from early in the morning until late at night. I can't work any harder."

"We're not upset with you," responds Wabun. "We know you've been working hard."

"But the other thing," I continue, "is that Sun Bear's vision includes teaching people to walk in balance on the Earth. The farm is meant to be the living demonstration of that vision. How can we give up the farm and be true to Sun Bear's vision?

The steam spent, I sit back, listening.

Sun Bear leans forward, opening his hands to gesture. "You're right about the farm fulfilling the vision, teaching people to live on this Earth. Now, Wabun here," he says, pointing in her direciton with his outstretched palm, "is the kind of person I know I can depend on to survive. The first winter we were together I remember we drove by a cow that had just been hit on the road. A whole bunch of people were standing around looking at it, wondering what to do. Well, we didn't have any meat for the coming winter, so we stopped the car and hopped out and said, 'Here, we'll take care of this.' We hauled the cow into the back of the car and took it home before anyone could say anything. That's how we had food to eat that winter. That's the kind of person I want to live with, someone I know can survive, can get in there and work."

Wabun's face softens. I see the love, honed by struggles and mellowed by the years, resting quietly between them.

Cougar shifts in his chair. "You have anything to add?" asks Wabun.

"Ye-e-es," begins Cougar in his slow-paced gait, stroking his moustache as he ponders. "I've been noticing we went to all the trouble of getting this special hybrid cow and now everyone's allergic to cow's milk. It's OK in the summer when all the apprentices are around to drink it, but in the winter we'll have gallons of extra milk. It's an example of poor planning. I wanted to reduce the number of cows from two small producers to one cow that gives as much if not more than the other two combined. But now I see we won't use all that milk in the winter, it'll just go to waste. I think we can do without the animals. It's cheaper to buy eggs and milk in town. And we've put away enough meat in the frozen meat lockers in town from our butchering to last for a couple of years."

The discussion vacillates between accusations and conciliatory suggestions. At the end of the meeting Wabun turns to David, an actor from London and one of Sun Bear's apprentices who has had a lot of experience working with groups.

"Can you give us some feedback on what you see going on in this group?" asks Wabun.

David shifts to cross his legs and lean forward, hands clasped around his knee. "To begin with, you've got to be aware of what you're *doing*. You start this meeting by smudging. Do you know what you're saying by doing that? Smudging means you need to clear negativity. Is that what you really want to say to each other, we have a lot of negativity to release?

"Also, be aware that this community has a planetary purpose, so you also attract planetary problems. You work in microcosm to solve the problems of the macrocosm. They come right here, right into this group, for you to solve or succumb to. You work not just with personality issues, but also with archetypal patterns. No wonder you all feel tired and burnt out. You process the world's problems day in and day out, and you also carry the weight of expectations. So many people look to this place as an example, they expect great things from the community. You must be aware that you carry these weights day-to-day. And don't take the conflicts too personally. They serve a larger purpose."

A kernel of truth in David's comments roots in me. I recognise the weight of expectation and how it plays a double-edged role in my life—as a burden that weights my daily acts with undue importance and as a catalyst that gives my life of mundane tasks a deeper meaning.

After the meeting I slip into my sleeping bag, my mind as full of thoughts as the sky is peppered with stars. Late August—the nights are chilly. I can see my breath in the flashlight's beam.

Two nights later we meet in Donna's cabin just below the Long House. Tonight instead of confrontations we share visions—for the Tribe and for our own lives. The vision for the Tribe runs in a similar vein through each person's description—the importance of work with the land, the ceremonies, the teaching with apprentices. Some have specific visions for the long-term physical development of the farm—building Vision Mountain Center, a round structure to hold courses on the mountain and serve as a nexus point for visitors. The long-term members recognise a need for more private space, envisioning small self-contained sleeping and cooking units for the future. All of these structures could be built through the Building School—a programme for long-term visitors to learn construction skills—proposed by Golden Bear, a friend of the Tribe.

Instead of sitting at rigid attention, nerves jangling with an onslaught of emotions, I relax into my chair, revelling in this unexpected glimpse into each other's lives. In the hectic day-to-day schedule, I take these people for granted in certain ways. I assume they share the same vision for this community (why else would they be here?), and that their presence here is permanent, a given. Especially among the long-term members I imagine their role stretching unendingly through the history of the Tribe.

During the meeting I approach a door within myself, a room rarely visited, where my dreams are stored. I seldom enter this room, much less share its contents, for fear that the gossamer images, not yet clothed with bone and flesh, might escape into thin air, never to be captured again.

Listening to the people in the circle, I enter their sacred gardens, long protected from prying eyes and the measuring stick of logic, where they reveal their greatest desires. How I wish we always spoke on this level, or at least indulged in it more often.

Raven begins, his face puckered in earnestness. "I see so many things that need to be done here at the Tribe, but I know I don't physically have the skills or the ability to do them. When I first came here I worked with the animals. Coming from Germany I had never worked on a farm before. I did the best I could, but every day I prayed with the Pipe that someone would come to the Tribe who really could take care of the animals. About a year later Cougar arrived, and I was very thankful for his work on the farm. Now I am working in town, putting in long days with the catalogue business, and I see so much that has to be done, but I can't work any harder. When I push too hard, my liver acts up. I damaged it when I was young—I was an alcoholic by 14. I used to wear a hip flask to school to drink between classes . . . . So now I have to live with that, and every time I try to push too much, I get sick. It's really frustrating, because I see so much that needs to be done." He pauses to rest his chin on his upturned hands, looking down at the floor as he draws a deep breath.

"And what is your vision for yourself?" asks Wabun gently.

Raven looks up. "My greatest dream," he says, arms and hands animated as if the words were pouring through them, "has always been to return to the ocean, to learn navigation by the stars, and sail in a ship." His face is alight, forehead creased with expressive wrinkles. "I want to sail in the North Sea, near the town where I grew up. The sea there is always changing, oh, sometimes really wild . . . . Yes, that is my personal vision, what I really want to do." He sinks into the sofa, curling his arm around Kim, face radiant and relaxed.

Thunderbird Woman describes her concern that children begin their lives in a loving environment and her desire to help them as a nurse. Already she has begun courses at the local university.

"I still have books that I want to write," says Wabun, "and with all of the administrative work with the publishing business, I just haven't had time. I would like to have a year or two just to write. Also," she adds, glancing towards Shawnodese, "if I'm going to have a child, I need to do something about it soon. I'm already 38. I want to lose weight and be in really good physical condition to carry a baby."

I wince momentarily. Our baby's presence still lingers just within reach, almost tangible.

Sun Bear grins when asked about his vision for himself and the Bear Tribe. "It's the same thing," he says chuckling. "I want to teach people to live with respect on the Earth Mother. I want them to learn practical skills so they can survive on this Earth and not be so dependent on the government and other things that want to suck them dry."

For Sun Bear, reverence for the Earth means little unless it is actually applied in life. Actively applied. "If it doesn't grow corn, I'm not interested," he says.

The ceremonial life of prayer, thanksgiving and inner contemplation feeds the daily work of application. The fruits of labour nourish the wellspring of thanksgiving and prayer. Picking peas becomes an act of gratitude, milking cows an act of contemplation. Prayer in the sweat lodge is an act of power, calling forth wholeness for all of creation.

The inner and outer world distinctions crumble. I see myself reflected in the raven's wingbeat. I feel myself rooted with the tree. I glean knowledge from the flowing of a river. Where is 'inside', and where is 'out'? They meld in an expanse that stretches around the whole earth and beyond. The cords of connection run deep and far.

"Now, as for specifics," continues Sun Bear, "I'd like to see the Vision Mountain Center completed. I'm not sure how that will continue now that Golden Bear is out of the picture, but I want to see the Building Programme go ahead. We've got the plans, now we just need the people to make it go. See, we teach people how to build and they build the Center for us in return. Golden Bear also had plans to start members' housing. Now, these things are important, especially for people who have been around a long time."

Several heads nod. After only a few months living in and around the Long House, I know the premium placed on privacy. Every square inch of aloneness has great value. Walks on the mountain and trips to the outhouse are among the only ensured moments of privacy. In summer, though, even the outhouse often has a waiting line.

Shawnodese mentions the health clinic envisioned at the Circle Center in town. "We already have a couple of apprentices preparing to move their practices into this area," says Shawnodese. "Within a couple of years, the Healing Center should be a reality."

The atmosphere of this meeting is so different from the one earlier in the week. People speak openly. Their eyes sparkle. Their body posture is open, arms and legs uncrossed. A sense of warmth and acceptance fills the room.

The circle complete, Wabun looks around. "Great. Now we know everyone's vision, and they almost all lead away from the Bear Tribe. What do we do now? The vision exercise is nice, but what do we *do* with it?"

"Well," says Shawno, "at least we know where people are coming from and what we can expect from them. That's a start. And we do mostly agree on a vision for the Bear Tribe."

While the basic vision for the community varies little from person to person, the emphasis on details changes. The core purpose comes from Sun Bear's vision, so the basic foundation for people entering the Tribe is clear. Tonight, though, as people express their own visions, I realise that the *personal* reasons for entering the community are as many as there are people. Sometimes the individual does not know consciously why s/he came. I had the excuse of a research project to arrive here, but in retrospect I see that I came to learn and transform. I had a conscious reason (the research) to come, and inner reasons (not fully conscious) to stay.

Balancing personal and group vision is an art. Few people make a lifetime commitment to the community. This means the group lacks long-term continuity, but the movement of people in and out of the group allows for the arrival of people with the right skills or qualities at the right time and the exit of those who have completed their service and are ready to progress to other things. The difficulty, though, is that projects championed by a departing member lapse unless someone with equal enthusiasm picks up the ball and runs. Most folks have their arms filled with so many other projects that they have no room for additions. Visitors promise to complete the new shed by autumn. In November it stands half finished, without a roof. Someone promises to rebuild the wood shed and chop and stack the wood before they leave. The axe rusts amidst a clutter of unsplit logs. "Better not to start," sighs Wabun, "than to leave something half finished. Now there's another job to do, and no one to complete it."

After the meeting Carl and I walk to the Long House kitchen to rummage a midnight snack. As we munch sandwiches, Raven comes into the darkened house, searching for something on the table.

"Raven," I say, reaching to touch his arm, "each time I hear you speak about your life, I have more and more respect for you. You've lived through so much. You are a wonderful being."

We stand for a few moments, beaming at each other, then Raven steps back, bows his head and clasps his hands behind his back. He stretches his neck forward, eyebrows raised, eyes searching for mine like a raptor viewing the sky above for signs of movement. "I feel the same way about you."

My heart bursts tonight. I live among so many treasures, yet I have not recognised their beauty, or I've discovered it late, just as I prepare to leave. How many facets of other people are yet to be revealed and appreciated? Already I regret my departure, looming only a couple of weeks away.

Now that Kim has returned from New Jersey, I spend most of my days weeding the garden, planting late season crops, and canning in the summer kitchen. Deborah, a German girl here with her mother, often joins me on the steps of the summer kitchen to snap beans and talk and giggle.

One afternoon I look up at the sky, piercing blue glazed by late summer gold around the horizon. "Deborah, do you like blackberry pie?" I ask in German.

She drops the beans and glances up, eyes wide. "Ja-a-a. Sicher." Of course.

"Then let's go pick blackberries. I know where we can find a patch of them."

We gather bowls from the kitchen and head up the dirt track towards a neighbour's cabin. The two brothers who own the property return periodically to live and work on the land, but this summer they are away. The cleared land around the cabin, uncut for several years, is a hot bed for berry canes. We move gingerly among the prickly arching stems, easing into the centre of four-foot-diameter clumps, pulling juicy blackberries as we go. As the bowls fill with berries, our fingers stain a reddish-purple, and our lips blossom purple with berry juice. The sun glares. Sweat trickles down my forehead and erupts on my arms, stinging the scratches made by the berry thorns. Cicadas and crickets drone in the grass, their choruses rippling across the meadow. Bees hover over the open blossoms, and wasps circle around the ripe fruit.

We return to the Long House, picking thorns from our fingers and rubbing itchy scratches on our legs and arms as we walk. We drink some water from the spring under the tamarack tree and relax in the shade of the porch.

Soon I set about making pie crusts. When I go into the root cellar in search of lard, I lift the lid on the central fruit and vegetable bin. Damn, the cooks forgot to use yesterday's swiss chard. Annette, the gardener, will be angry. And the strawberries I brought from town yesterday are already moulding.

I gather the greens, strawberries and lard and head for the kitchen.

"Tom, can you please use these?" I ask, holding out the box of limp chard.

"Well, I'm already cooking red cabbage. I think that would be too much."

"OK," I reply, sighing. We've had this discussion before. "Please look in the fruit and veggie bin before you decide what to cook, and use what will go bad first."

"Right, right," says Tom, smiling. "I forgot to look."

I make the pie crusts and fill the pastry with blackberries laced with honey and butter. When the pies are in the oven, I turn to the strawberries. Half an hour until dinner—what can I do with 12 pints of moulding strawberries?

Fruit salad. That's it. Cut out the bad parts and mix the good with some other fruit. I hate seeing food go to waste, and experience has taught me that I can't rely on the busy cook to brainstorm uses for food on the verge of spoiling. Within half an hour, along with Deborah and a couple of hungry apprentices, I salvage the strawberries and incorporate them in a fruit salad. This work of making something out of nothing satisfies me deeply. Whoever coined that phrase, though, must not have counted sweat and time when they zeroed the balance at 'nothing'. So many items easily disposed of become treasures to those who have time. Time to transform them into something useful.

I collapse onto the sofa, resting for a few minutes before milking time. So many projects begin like this—I see something that needs to be done but the time or the materials or the people power simply are not available. Once I begin, though, determined to finish, all the required help arrives, the inspiration ignites and we finish the project on time.

Tonight Heike, a new visitor, joins us to milk the cow. Am I imagining it, or does Carl sound especially eager and friendly as he talks to this woman? I feel an unaccustomed pull of jealousy and find some detail in the milking ritual to dispute with Carl. By the time we finish, I have transformed jealousy into anger.

"Look, Carl, why don't you two drive back alone. I want to walk up to the Long House."

"You sure?" asks Carl.

"Yeah, I'm sure."

I dig my hands into my pockets and walk quickly, my feet stirring clouds of dust into the still evening air. I think about Carl's comments after his last appointment with Regina, how she recommended that he remain sexually active while I'm away in Europe. My stomach drops out when I think of him with another woman. I can not imagine returning here to find him sleeping with someone else. I bend my head towards the swirling dust, my chest aching with loneliness, trying to talk myself out of being jealous.

The woods smell of autumn. Early morning crispness prickles my nose. Frost patterns lie in the shadows of the summer kitchen steps.

New visitors arrive including two hardworking young sisters from Canada. I teach one of them how to use the pressure cooker to can the beans—one job that I know will continue after I leave.

Leaving. I am so fully rooted in the daily rhythm here that I can hardly imagine a morning when I do not wake to the pine trees outside the tent. And when I leave, this glimpse of the Bear Tribe will freeze into my permanent reference point for explaining the community and my experience here, yet I know things and people will change. In some ways drastically. But for now, in this moment, the memories coalesce and begin to crystallise, organising the loose fragments—a conversation, a tree on the mountain, the fragrance of a cow at sunset—into a transparent cluster, so much a part of me that I can barely discern where it ends and I begin.

The days slip by, filled with the usual round of chores. Only a self-conscious tenderness with Carl belies my awareness of the fast-approaching departure. Each moment we are alone I want to touch him—his face, his hands, his hair—I want to store the memories of him, like the jars of jam and beans lining the root cellar shelves, in an accessible space in my mind, to be lingered over in the aloneness of the coming months.

This autumn I will journey with my parents to Britain and then set off on my own to explore Europe. Alone, which makes me a bit nervous, but it's a challenge I have chosen for myself. I want to conquer alone so that Europe becomes mine, absorbed on my own terms without the filter of someone else's reactions or experiences.

One of the more painful aspects of my personality is stubbornness. Once I decide to do something, my soul drags me through the most ingenious sorts of resistance —illness, heartsickness, grief, doubts. Souls have little patience for the trivial disruptions that bob in the wake of fate. Especially when the fate is self-created.

So now, despite pangs of homesickness (in advance), long-lingering goodbyes with the mountain and passionate moments with Carl, I prepare to go. My car is packed. The animals are fed. Carl and I have lingered a long while in each other's arms. I have wandered through the Long House three times searching for any forgotten odds and ends. I have said goodbye to everyone. Twice. And it's almost lunchtime. So I stay for a last meal with friends.

When I roll Sunflower from her parking spot on the mountain and point her down the road, a shiver shakes my shoulders. I stop at the curve of the road just before the Long House passes out of sight and turn around to look. To imprint a memory of this moment, like the internal photographs that Hetty taught me to take, to carry with me. Always. Because somehow I sense that I will not return, not to this place, although in my life I usually do return to old haunts, overlapping new experiences with the familiarity of the old. The intuition surprises me, and I dismiss it. Of course I'll return, after I finish school if not before.

CHAPTER 4
Findhorn Foundations

The train lumbers out of Inverness station, headed east towards Aberdeen. I settle into the blue and green plaid seats, threadbare after years of use, carefully noting the names of villages as we pass. 'Forres' is the name I'm searching for, where I will be staying for a week at Cluny Hill College for the Findhorn Foundation's 'Experience Week' programme. A *whole week,* I remind myself, as I gaze across the autumn-brown fields, the stubble of barley stalks bristling from the rocky ground. After a month of almost constant movement travelling throughout Britain, a week in one place is a welcome luxury. I'm curious about what I'll find in the community. So much has been written about the Foundation, so many larger-than-life stories passed by word of mouth, that I wonder if I will be disappointed in the day-to-day reality of the place. During my travels I have met people who lambasted the community as a high-priced rip-off and advised me to steer clear of it. Others gave dewy-eyed reports, declaring that anything the Foundation did was wonderful. So today, sitting on the train, I approach with a healthy dose of scepticism, intrigued by the contradictory reports.

Traces of forest separate the fields, burnished pale amber and brown and brilliant yellow where the larches still hold their needles. The autumn colours, like the stone houses of the villages and the people who move among them, are muted, reticent, reluctant to speak aloud and break the stony silence. Even on this sunny Saturday morning in late October, grey and brown predominate in the landscape. No garish colours intrude upon the cultivated calm. I sense a reined-in serenity, like a horse held in sharp check, a restraint that borders on suppression. I feel it even in my own body, almost as if I am collapsing in on myself, my shoulders curling into my neck and chest, shrinking from the barren landscape.

Just thirty minutes from Inverness the train stops in the town of Forres. I eye the disembarking passengers and single out two other women who look slightly out of place among the weathered Scots.

A tall, lanky man approaches from a bus—by American standards really an over-sized van—asking "Are you going to the Findhorn Foundation?"

"Yes," I reply, hoisting my backpack onto my shoulder. I smile, knowing that I, too, appear out of step among the local passengers.

"Come on, you can put your pack in the back of the bus." I settle into the seat, quiet during the short ride through the narrow streets lined by stone houses with sharply sloping slate roofs. I recall a photograph from the book *Faces of Findhorn* that shows guests arriving for Experience Week unloading their suitcases and back-packs in front of Cluny Hill College. Now I am about to enter that picture, to breathe the life of my own experience into the flat image. Already the world that I have tentatively built around that central image is crumbling, contradicted by the grandeur of the stone buildings cum elegant mansions that line this road away from the centre of town.

We turn onto a steep, curving driveway, passing through a tunnel of holly trees and Scots pines that finally opens to a view of a yellow sandstone building with high windows topped with stained glass. As we round the last corner, the building seems to stretch on and on, ending with a long dining room that rests on the precipice of a steep hill. The steep drop flattens to form a lawn and herbacious bor-der before rolling across a single track road into a vast expanse of manicured green—the local golf course. As I glance up to the top of a knoll where the golfers tee-off, I am reminded that the sport of golfing was born in Scotland among the heather moors. On the tiny green middle-aged men and young boys and stout white-haired ladies stand side-by-side. The passion for golf cuts through all ages and social ranks in this country, a love that withstands rain and snow and the fierce winds that rage across the northern Atlantic.

Inside I push through swinging glass doors etched with pastoral scenes into the lounge where upholstered chairs are arranged in a semi-circle in front of a fireplace. I sink into a chair and smile at the two women who shared the bus journey.

"Welcome," says a man sitting to my left. "My name is Alan, and I'll be your focaliser for Experience Week. Did you have a good trip?" As the others respond, I note our 'focaliser's' (is that the same as 'facilitator'?) shoulder-length hair neatly tucked behind his ears, full beard and moustache precisely trimmed, and delicate, almost pointed fingers resting along his jawbone. Most prominent are his blue eyes, intently focused on each woman as she speaks. His compact, sturdy frame, gently rounded at the shoulders and hips, completes my image of a Scottish elemental—either a dwarf or elf. Elf, I decide, noting his easy smile and laugh. Dwarfs are a sombre lot.

Our conversation is interrupted by someone 'hoovering' (vacuuming) the lounge. "Sorry," says Alan, "Saturday morning we have Housecare. Everyone helps to clean the whole building and prepare the rooms for the new guests. It's the most hectic time of the week as people are leaving and arriving at the same time."

"Do you need any help?" I ask, eager to immerse myself in the doings of the community right away.

"No, thanks for offering, but we've got enough people for this morning. You can take some time to relax and settle in here."

I return to the entrance hallway, noting the high ceiling and six-foot-wide carpet-ed stairway rising before me, lush houseplants in the alcove opposite the reception desk, and the round 'mail wheel' with alphabetised slots for letters. I peer inside the 'B' slot and find a letter addressed to me from my parents, a welcome surprise. I have been travelling without definite destination or address for nearly two months. Knowing that I would be here for a week I have given friends and relatives this address. The sense of stability in having an address, even if only temporary, is somehow reassuring, as is the act of unpacking clothes and arranging them in a chest of drawers. Although small, these are defiant acts of permanency for an itinerant traveller.

After emptying my pack and storing it on top of the wardrobe, I escape into the woods behind Cluny Hill College. My body feels heavy after a week of sitting on trains and buses, subsisting mainly on 'digestive biscuits', the standard British 'cookie'. I stride along the wide paths cut through a pine plantation, the slender trunks marching in unwavering rows, the monotony broken only by the autumn-gold leaves of a few run-away beech saplings. Completing the loop, I walk along a track that skirts a large hill with a tower on top—'Nelson's Tower' reads a sign pointing up the hill. I stand on a platform built against the northern face of the tower, opening my arms to greet the expanse of bay and ocean and mountains beyond. I realise now that I glimpsed this tower from the train; it must be a landmark for miles around. Beyond the thin rows of houses in the town below are carefully kept stone-walled fields intersected by meandering streams. Autumn-hued trees pepper the rises, black ribbons of road outline the fields, and pine plantations stretch to the west of the bay. Most commanding, though, is the outline of mountains thrusting and falling behind the haze that rings the northern horizon, the view spanning far to the north of Scotland.

When I arrive back in my room at Cluny, I feel a bit chilly—a common state in Britain where most houses were built before the advent of central heating—and pull on a thick wool sweater purchased on the west coast of Scotland. I walk downstairs to the dining room in Cluny Hill, pushing through the heavy swinging doors that open into what was once the centrepiece of the building when it operated as a four-star hotel managed by Peter and Eileen Caddy, the founders of the Findhorn Foundation. A long table filled with bowls of steamed and fresh vegetables and mixed salads of all sorts stands at the front of the room. A side table with a heating tray supports two large pots, one filled with rice, the other with vegetarian goulash. Against the opposite wall is a table with homebaked bread and cheese and butter.

I revel in the spread of food. As a vegetarian travelling in Britain, this is an oasis in a land of beef, potatoes and greasy fried food. I fill my plate and search for a seat among the rows of tables, settling for one near the front illuminated by the pale autumn sunshine. Tall windows, stretching nearly to the top of the twenty-foot ceiling, line both sides of the dining room, culminating in a curved bay window at the southern end of the room. Chandeliers hang at regular intervals above the tables. The high ceiling, the raised designs in the woodwork and the overall symmetry of the room are typical of the mid-nineteenth century when Cluny Hill was built. Everything seems to be highly polished and neatly arranged, right down to the silverware tray in which the spoons and forks rest back to front in neat rows.

The table soon fills with other Experience Week guests—we seem to gravitate towards each other, magnetised by our common unfamiliarity with the territory. The conversation runs along lines that soon become entrenched: "What's your name?" "What programme are you in?" "Where are you from?" and the most searching, commonly asked opener, "What brought you here?" Some have an epic adventure story about the journey that led them to this place, others respond simply, "I don't know. I just knew I had to come, so I did." The conversation turns to books read and workshops and courses undertaken in the quest for 'spiritual growth' and 'self-improvement'.

"Oh, this is vonderful," exclaims one woman, an exuberant middle-aged Swede wearing bright red lipstick. "I haven't been able to talk about these things with anyone for years and . . . well, maybe *never* before with total strangers."

I smile and excuse myself, wanting a few minutes of quiet before the first session of Experience Week, scheduled to begin at 2 p.m. I, too, am glad to be surrounded by people who openly speak of their dreams, ideas and spiritual striving. Having lived in other communities, I consider this behaviour the norm, and after a few months of travel I am glad for the homecoming.

About 1:50 I walk through the hallways to our meeting room—the details of the woodwork, the creaky spots in the old wooden floor, the colour of the carpet and the worn handle on the doorway stand out sharply. Everything seems more vivid, more significant when I am expectantly awaiting . . . I'm not sure exactly what, but I sense that this week, like all group encounters, will reveal things about myself and others normally overlooked when I am alone or living in a familiar routine.

Our meeting space, the Beechtree Room, is named in honour of the four large beeches growing on the hill below and the delicate strips of bark used to paper the walls. A fig tree stands before a bay window that curves out towards the golf course, and a fire blazes in the fireplace opposite the door. I find a seat among the circle of chairs arranged around a lighted candle surrounded by fresh flowers.

After a short welcome and a quick outline of the week (filled with activities from early morning until 9:30 p.m. each day), Alan and Angela, our 'co-focalisers' for the week, list the rules in the community.

"We have only two rules," explains Alan, "and we ask you to follow them. If you can't, we will have to ask you to leave. The first rule is no illegal drugs. This is not because we have some judgement against drugs or people who use them, but simply because they are illegal and we abide by the laws of the land. We also expect that people will not abuse legal drugs, like alcohol. Can everyone agree to that?"

Silent nods. "OK, the second rule is no smoking in public places. You can smoke outside or in the smokers' lounge downstairs and in your room if your roommate agrees. We try to accommodate smokers together, but please check with your roommate before smoking in your room. Got it?" he asks, smiling. "It's pretty simple and straightforward."

We move on to 'group agreements'. "These are agreements we make," explains Angela, "to make our group life together easier. We work a lot in groups in the community, and we find these basic agreements make things much easier. So, we'll go through them and see if everyone can agree to them. I'll explain each one and then we'll have a circle check—you put your thumb up if you agree, down if you don't, and to the side if you have a question."

Everyone gives a 'thumbs up' to the three basic agreements—beginning and ending sessions on time, giving full attention to the speaker and making 'I' statements. The last one is new to me, intended to focus people on speaking from direct, personal experience. "We are here this week to learn about each other, not to discuss ideas or theories," says Angela. "When someone uses the word 'we', I may not necessarily feel included in the collective 'we', my experience may be different. So this week we, ach, I mean *I*, can practise speaking from my own experience. I just showed you what *not* to do," she adds, laughing.

"And we, I mean *I*," continues Alan, "want to say a word about the term focaliser." He explains that as focalisers he and Angela hold a larger awareness of the group, but they are still part of it. "We're not like bosses to tell you what to do. We are part of the group, and, yes, we have a role to help direct or *focus* the group's process. You may be familiar with the term facilitator, and the role of a focaliser is similar except that we're not separate from the group, we're members of the group as well."

After a brief loo (toilet) break, we stand in a circle massaging each others' shoulders. Some of the stiffness in the group, the formality of beginnings, loosens along with the shoulder muscles. When we sit again, Alan guides us in a visualisation, focusing on the journey that brought us to this place, any expectations that we might have about the week, and anything about ourselves that we want to 'share' with the group.

Moving around the circle, each person recounts the path that led them here—spurred by a book, a conversation, a prophetic dream—and the sorrows and joys of a lifetime usually bared only to the most intimate friend or the most casual acquaintance. The increasing vulnerability of each person widens the boundaries of safety for the next until the walls separating hearts are paper thin. When the session ends I remain in my seat, enwrapped by the sense of warmth and acceptance still lingering in the room.

At dinner Hal, an American just arrived from Israel where he was studying in rabbinical school, stops between forkfuls of food. "I never knew a group could get so close just by talking about themselves," he says, smiling. I laugh, nodding in agreement. My critical detachment begins to soften. After only one three-hour session I can see the magic of this place working through the people in my group in their open smiles, eager conversation and intent eye contact.

Saturday evening is our only free evening. I retreat into my room shared with Brigitte, the red-lipsticked Swede, to read and then fall asleep. I open the book and read a page, reading and re-reading each sentence. After a couple of paragraphs my mind is exhausted, already filled with so many new experiences that I have no internal space to assimilate more. The book lies in my lap, unnoticed as I stare blankly out the window. Thoughts spin through the week of travel in Britain and then jump to the summer and Vision Mountain. My heart shrinks with loneliness when I think of Carl. I think of you often, so very often, but I sense a distance in our connection. A few weeks ago I dreamt that you were sleeping with Heike; I awoke crying in my pillow, my heart aching. When I called you on the phone, feeding ten pences in the machine as fast as it could swallow, we had time only to say a few sentences before the money ran out. Another time when I called Kim said, "Oh, they're out canoeing today." They. Two people. Carl and someone else, most likely Heike. Ninety percent confirmation of my dream, but I want to hear it from Carl himself.

I go downstairs and find Alan in the lounge, asking him to open the meter phone so that I can call the States. I sit in the tiny phone booth, just wide enough for the door to open into, heart beating as I dial the number for the Bear Tribe. I simultaneously dread and long for Carl's voice greeting me at the other end of the line.

Carl does answer the phone. "Hey, Judy, how are you?" he asks. I tell him a bit about my travels and my impressions of the Foundation. "And I had this dream, Carl . . . ." I'm uncertain of how to approach the emotions roiling inside me. "It was about . . . well . . . ."

"Yeah, I know. I had a dream, too, and I knew how you would respond."

"What did you dream?" I ask, shoulders clenched, bracing myself for the response.

"I dreamt that I met you and Hilary in a roadside cafeteria, like a rest stop. We sat at the table, and I told you about Heike and me. I told you I was afraid someone else would tell you about us before I could, that they would talk shit about me. I wanted to be the first to tell you."

"And what did I say?" I ask quietly.

"You said you already knew, and it was all right."

Tears sting my eyes. "It's true. I dreamt about you being together. Are you happy?"

"Yeah, Heike and I have a real strong connection. It's good."

"Then I'm happy for you." I pause, fighting back tears. "I had a sense you were together . . . I hurt a lot, wanting to talk with you, missing you . . . ."

"I'm sorry about that. I wanted to tell you sooner, but the phone is so damned expensive and we only talked for a couple of minutes."

We talk a bit about what's happening at the Bear Tribe, the comings and goings of the people who formed the daily fabric of my life just two months before. My heart aches. I feel hollow and lonely in the centre of my being. Our plans to meet in January and possibly move to Portland, Oregon, together, where I will study naturopathic medicine, dissolve in that moment. I feel tender and soft and loving and lonely all at once.

"I love you, Carl," I say finally, aware of the expense mounting on the meter and the pain that threatens to rise through my carefully controlled voice. I always have to be the strong one, I tell myself with an ironic smile, not wanting the other person to carry the knowledge of my pain as a burden.

"I love you, too. A lot. I'll be praying for you in the sweat."

"Thanks, Carl. Take care."

I sit in the phone box, gently pulling my lower lip, tears rolling onto my cheeks and wetting the open phone book.

"Thank you, Creator," I murmur to the voiceless walls, "that I found out here, in a supportive place, not off by myself somewhere."

I step gingerly off the stool and open the door. Alan is waiting in the hall.

"Finished?" he asks.

"Yes. And I'm feeling very emotional. Can I have a hug?"

"Sure," he says wrapping his arms around me.

I feel paper thin as sobs push up from my aching chest. They emerge from my throat as silently as stillborn children, exhaled in long sighs. I gently stroke Alan's back. Anything I touch feels precious when I am in great pain.

"You have a very gentle energy about you," says Alan, leaning back to brush the tears from my cheeks with his handkerchief.

"Thank you," I sputter, smiling despite myself.

"You want to talk?"

"Yes, if you have time."

"Sure, I have time. Let's sit in the lounge."

We talk for a few minutes, sharing our experiences with ending relationships. Talking helps some. If there is anyone here I feel close to, it is Alan—I sense a kinship between us. But what I really want is some time alone, to cry and remember and let go. I return to my room, slide under the covers and curl into a tight ball, staring into the moonless, starless night.

In the morning our group meets at 9:30 in the ballroom. Tall windows topped with stained glass designs rise behind wooden benches built into the thick walls. I leave my shoes by the door and walk barefoot across the cold, wooden floor. The room is unheated except for one free-standing propane heater that has little impact on the chill.

"This morning," explains Alan, "we will do some Sacred Dance, which is a non-verbal way of experiencing ourselves as a group." The dances, brought to the community by Bernhard Wosien, come mostly from the European folk tradition, collected by Bernhard during his travels. He tried to uncover their deeper meanings by talking with the villagers who performed them and by studying sacred geometry. Over the years he came to believe that the most sacred aspects of the Western mystery tradition were hidden in the patterns of the vernacular songs and dances until the deeper truths could once again be openly revealed. Along with the basic steps, Bernhard taught what he could discern of the deeper meanings in the dances.

During the dances I feel the loneliness easing inside me. The steps free the knots in my emotional as well as physical body. The joyous movements combined with steady eye contact strengthen my sense of connection with the people in the group. The last dance is a slow, meditative circle dance choreographed to Pachelbel's Canon. "We move two steps forward then one back," explains Alan, "rocking on the foot behind you. It's like life. What's the saying? 'Two steps forward, one step back'—progressing forward and then stepping back, forward and back, over and over again."

Scenes of the chamber orchestra with which I performed this piece run through my mind along with images of life in the conservatory, my relationships with friends and lovers and family. I cannot see the future, but I know that I have so many things from my past to leave behind, to let go of, before I can begin anew. As we move around the circle, I am surprised to feel tears rolling down my cheeks. I do not feel pain, only a quiet sense of release. Never before have I cried so gently, so easily, without tightness in my throat or agony in my heart.

After brunch we pile into one of the community buses—'Hamish' reads the name plate. Nearly everything here has a name—the hoovers (e.g. J. Edgar), the mop sink in the kitchen, the washing machine in the basement. "It's a way that we recognise the life of inanimate 'things'," explains Alan when someone questions why the bus has a name. "It's a way of showing them respect and reminding us that we need to take care of them with the same respect that we do humans—or maybe more in some cases!"

The bus moves through the town—mostly deserted this Sunday morning except for the rows of cars parked along the street outside the churches. The road winds through fields and meadows until we reach the village of Kinloss where we turn north to skirt the eastern side of Findhorn Bay. The tide is out, leaving the sand at the back end of the bay exposed. Shore birds peck at the creatures in the sand. Seagulls wheel above.

We turn into the caravan park, marked by a large sign that reads 'WELCOME TO THE FINDHORN FOUNDATION' with a listing of items sold in the community's store, the Phoenix Shop. "Great," I mutter to myself, "another New Age venture bent on selling itself and other New Age doo-dahs."

A woman named Willa, our tour guide for the afternoon, meets the bus. Her eyes are the clearest blue I have ever seen. They are wide open and sparkling with mischievous joy. She, too, reminds me of an elfen spirit.

We begin the tour with the 'original caravan', made of green-painted metal, the corners rounded like a 1960 Chevy Airstream. The whole affair, including a tiny extension built on the back, is about 20 feet long and 6 feet wide and housed Peter and Eileen Caddy, their three young boys and co-worker Dorthy Maclean.

"Someone wanted to scrap the caravan a couple of years ago," says Willa, "to make space for another one, but the community reacted strongly. Sentimental value, you know, and guests are always asking to see the caravan where Peter and Eileen lived. It was so old we couldn't move it without it falling apart, so we made it into the Communications Centre. This is where we keep in touch with people and groups all over the world. Somehow it's very appropriate that the communication comes right out of the original site."

Our herd moves into the central garden located just behind the 'original caravan', a series of raised beds supported by low stone walls and wooden boards. Splayed apple trees line two pathways. A cold frame sits in front of another ancient caravan named 'The Hollow' surrounded by gorse and broom and nestled in the lowest spot to the west of the garden. To the east is a path that leads to the Community Centre, referred to simply as the 'CC', visible through an arched trellis adorned with a climbing rose bush. Roses still bloom on the trellis, and the brassica family—mainly kale and cabbages—stand in the beds, seemingly oblivious of the autumn chill.

"Where are the large cabbages?" someone asks.

The question sparks a whole history of how Peter and Eileen Caddy came to live in the caravan park. They came here 'temporarily' in the autumn of 1962 after Peter lost his job with the company who managed a chain of hotels that included Cluny Hill Hydro, run at that time as a summer hotel that serviced bus tours of Scotland. Although he had improved the hotel from a two-star to a four-star rating, the company chose to fire him, in part because of his failure to salvage another failing hotel farther south where he and Eileen were transferred for one summer season. Perhaps the company also was irked by Peter's declaration that he worked for God, not for them. He ran the hotel according to guidance that Eileen received during meditation. Peter followed the directives without question, and, combined with immediate action on any of his own intuitive flashes, the hotel thrived.

The dismissal notice came as a shock. When the hotel closed for the winter, Peter and Eileen moved with their three children to the caravan park, certain that they would be living there only temporarily until the management came to their senses and reinstated them at Cluny Hill. In guidance Eileen heard "You will return to Cluny Hill." Reassured, Eileen set about making the caravan tolerable for the coming winter.

Their friend Dorothy Maclean, met through their mutual involvement with a spiritual teacher, joined them for daily meditations in the cramped caravan. Towards spring Peter began to plan a garden in the area behind the caravan, a neglected spot once used as a refuse tip. Although he had no previous gardening experience, Peter hoped that his efforts would supplement the meagre unemployment benefit that the family relied on to survive.

Soon after the work in the garden began, Dorothy communicated in meditation with what she termed a 'Deva', Sanskrit for 'Shining One'. She understood this Being as the essence or blueprint for a particular manifestation on Earth. In the first contact, it was the Deva of the Sweet Pea. The communion with the devic realm deepened in the coming months and years. The guidance ranged from specific directives for the garden (i.e. how to make compost or not to replant the lettuce thinnings) to more general insights from the Landscape Deva.

The tiny garden flourished. Each year Dorothy and the Caddys reclaimed more of the abandoned dump until every available bit of space was filled with plants. In addition to working from dawn to dusk in the garden (a span of nearly 20 hours at midsummer in the north of Scotland) Peter continued to send out job applications and go for interviews. Although he was well qualified, each employer found some reason not to hire him. After five years an unemployment benefit officer came to visit Peter at the caravan.

"Do you think you are being prevented from obtaining employment?" asked the officer.

"Well, yes, perhaps God does not want me to have a job."

"God?"

"Yes, God is in charge of our lives. He always provides whatever we need."

"Well, if God provides all of your needs, do you suppose He would take care of you if we discontinued the unemployment benefit?"

"Yes . . . yes, I suppose He would."

So the government cut off the unemployment benefit, leaving the Caddys without a regular income. Miraculously, the needed funds did come. And so did more and more people as word got out about enormous vegetables growing in the sandy soil. First the agricultural extension agent came, then others who were attracted by the unexplained vigour of the garden.

Some were drawn through booklets of Eileen's guidance, printed on an old hand-cranked press bought for a small sum. In need of quiet space away from the cramped and noisy caravan, Eileen made a nightly pilgrimage to the public toilet block in the caravan park to record 'the still small voice within', which she identified as the voice of God. The guidance gave directives for the budding collective as well as inspiration for inner growth. Always the guidance stressed the importance of each person listening to the voice of Spirit within themselves, of looking *within*, not to a dogmatic religion or guru, for answers and direction.

"And where do you keep all of the forty pound cabbages?" A chuckle ripples through the group.

"Well," says Willa, smiling, "you can see there aren't any here. We don't grow large vegetables any more. At a certain point Eileen received guidance that the community no longer needed the large vegetables to have faith that the work with the nature spirits was working. We've shifted our focus from growing vegetables to growing people."

"And what about the wild area? I read that you set aside a place for the nature spirits to live undisturbed."

"Yes, that area is over in that corner," says Willa, pointing to a clump of gorse and weeds. "That was actually ROC's idea."

"Who's Rock?" asks someone.

"It's actually the initials for R. Ogilvie Crombie. I can't remember what the 'R' stands for. He was a Professor of Physics at Edinburgh University and had an astounding connection with the nature spirits. He met Peter Caddy at a meeting, and after that he would come to visit. During one of his stays, he suggested leaving an area for the Devas and Elementals to live undisturbed—ROC said they like wild areas best. If you want to know more about the specifics of the garden, I recommend reading *The Findhorn Garden*. You can buy it at the Phoenix Shop."

I wander a bit among the rows of raised beds, crouching down by some of the late-blooming flowers. I have a sense of a garden in recline, not just because of the autumn season. Like perfume lingering in a room after the wearer has departed, I have an impression of the magic that catalysed this piece of the Earth into its moment of glory. But the moment has passed, and the soil is simply soil, and a cabbage undeniably a cabbage. Perhaps the success in the garden was meant only to draw attention to this spot on the Earth and the community's work. Once this was accomplished, the community's relationship with the nature kingdoms could fade into a secondary interest. I linger by the cabbages, disappointed by their ordinariness, wondering if I have arrived too late.

We move to the sanctuary, one of the first semi-permanent buildings in the caravan park. To meet the local building codes for a caravan park, any structures had to be capable of being dismantled and moved within 24 hours—certainly not solid ground for a growing community

We sit for a few moments on the gold upholstered chairs arranged in concentric circles around a single pillar candle in the centre of the sanctuary. The only decoration on the walls is a Sunrise Panel, a pastel rainbow-coloured weaving produced in the Findhorn Weaving Studio.

"Eileen heard in guidance that the Sanctuary should have no symbols or adornment," explains Willa. "The community was to be a place where people of all religions and spiritual traditions could live together with respect for one another. So the Sanctuary is a place where we can all meet together, in the Silence. We don't have any outer rituals or forms of practice as a community. Each person finds his or her own way of listening to the God within."

A note strikes deep within me. As we sit silently for a few minutes, I close my eyes and feel a deep sense of peace. The strain of absorbing all of the newness eases. I feel gratitude for Peter and Eileen and their unswerving trust in their own inner guidance that formed the foundation of this community. And of all the communities that I have visited, this is the first to open its arms to *all* traditions, to honour the many ways of connecting with Spirit. For that I am grateful.

We walk from the Sanctuary to the Universal Hall, a five-sided building that was the first permanent structure built by the community. Stained-glass windows designed by James Hubbell flow in wave-like designs across the front entranceway. The outer walls are local sandstone inlaid with increasing beauty if you follow the sequence of construction as the workers refined their craft.

The roof is covered with smooth, round stones hauled from Findhorn beach. As I look at them I am reminded of the movie *My Dinner with André* in which André describes the 'magical' construction of the Universal Hall's roof. The roof, he explained, is not nailed down. Instead it is held in place by the weight of the rocks resting on it and at certain special times the roof actually levitates and hovers over the Hall. I am too self-conscious to ask if the story is true. I begin to wonder about *all* of the stories I have heard about the Foundation, not so much the information read in the community's books, but rather the word-of-mouth descriptions that are ripe for embellishment and exaggeration. Having lived at the Bear Tribe, I take rave reviews of other communities with a grain of salt. Usually uttered by passing visitors who have not stayed long enough to experience the shortcomings of a place, the stories are adorned beyond recognition as they pass from person to person.

Still, though, even the community's books hint at the extra-ordinary at work amidst the daily work of living. Again, moving through the Hall, I brush something almost palpable, the vision that inspired this building and the guiding power that drew the resources necessary for its completion. As Willa recounts some of the examples of manifestation that contributed to the construction of the place—such as a donation for the exact amount of money needed to buy the land, or the people with necessary skills appearing on the right day—the massive accomplishment of building this Hall dawns on me. It was constructed by a crew of unskilled amateurs working on total faith with no budget. The fruits of the extra-ordinary surround me in this building.

We walk around Pineridge, a loop road lined with caravans and bungalows, the residential section for the Foundation members in the caravan park. In addition to the tiny dwellings, one section of the loop is dedicated to craft studios—weaving, pottery and art. Willa explains that the studios were built in the 70s, when the community's membership soared to over 300. With more members than were needed to cover the basic running of the community, Peter agreed to have a group of artisans working full time in the studios to help develop the emerging 'New Age culture'.

In the early days Peter's decisions on all matters were final, accepted without question. This benevolent dictatorship continued more or less until Peter left the community in 1980. Fortunately he did establish a group to take on the visionary and decision-making tasks that he alone had carried through the years of the community's growth. In many communities leaders leave abruptly without preparing another individual or a group to shoulder vital tasks, creating turmoil that often leads to the dissolution of a collective. Others prepare to leave but never actually make the final break—the community drifts on 'hold', guided by a tired leader who is unable or unwilling to hand the reins of control to fresh leadership. Peter accomplished both—he prepared and then he exited. The Foundation did falter for the space of a couple of years, crippled by a large debt incurred through property acquisitions in the 70s, such as the purchase of Cluny Hill Hydro (renamed Cluny Hill College) and Cullerne House, as well as the restoration of Drumduan House, a large private home not far from Cluny Hill that was donated to the Foundation. The community also agreed to steward the Isle of Erraid off the west coast of Scotland for a Dutch family who purchased the island for summer holidays.

Along with the financial strain came a mass exodus of over 100 members within the space of a few months. The remaining members struggled to fill all of the work positions needed to keep the basic services running. 'Frills' such as dessert maker in the kitchen or full time work in the arts—including a community string quartet, a theatre group and the craft studios—were scratched from the work rota. Four years later the community population has stabilised at around 220 members, but the personnel department still struggles to keep the basic departments (kitchen, garden, dining room, maintenance and housecare) staffed. The dusty windowsills of the weaving studio leave me with the same impression as the garden—the arts have bloomed and faded in this community, pigeonholed as leisure pursuits after the more pressing demands of daily living.

The tour ends in front of the bookshop where I browse through the shelves upon shelves of books on metaphysics, meditation, dreams, earth mysteries and psychic phenomena. Travelling with a backpack means that I can carry only one book at a time, giving away one before buying another—good training for a book packrat like me. I climb on the bus empty-handed.

After dinner we meet to 'attune' to work departments. "Most of our community decisions are made through attunement," explains Alan. "It means 'tuning into' something greater than myself. In the community that usually means aligning myself with what we call the Angel of Findhorn, the Being or essence that overlights this centre. I acknowledge my personal desire, let it go, and then I can tune in, like resetting a radio dial, to the wisdom of the greater whole. Tonight, instead of just talking about attunement, we will actually use it to choose work departments. You may be surprised by what you get from the attunement—it may be something completely different from what you originally wanted to do. You may find yourself raising your hand for some work department you never thought of. OK, any questions? All right, make yourself comfortable and close your eyes . . . ."

Before I close my eyes I know where I want to work—the Cluny Hill garden. Cullerne garden, which we visited earlier on our tour of the caravan park, seems tired and featureless. The Central garden seems to be finished for the year, and besides I am not eager to get up half an hour earlier to be on the bus that shuttles from Cluny to the Park in the morning.

When I open my eyes, I still know where I want to work—Cluny Hill garden, but two other people raise their hand for the same work position.

"OK, folks, someone is going to have to move to another work department. Park Housecare and Cluny Kitchen still need one person."

The group sits in silence for a few moments. "Damn," I think to myself, "I'm always the one to give in, always the peacemaker."

70

I raise my hand. "I'll work in the Cluny kitchen," I say, choosing familiar territory. Having worked in a vegetarian cooperative with 120 people, I am comfortable in large kitchens. "Well," I muse inwardly, "at least I will be warm and dry if it rains or snows."

A 'sharing' fills the balance of the evening, a time for anyone to speak about insights, problems and/or experiences. "I'll remind you again," says Angela, "that people often feel things more strongly while they are here. This is a chance to support each other by listening and giving our full attention to whomever is speaking. No one offers suggestions or advice to anyone unless they ask for it. Our role as a group is simply to listen."

"And the more you give out this week, the more you will receive from the experience, so I encourage you all to really share yourselves, perhaps take some risks that you haven't before," adds Alan.

The response is slow, weighted. The silences are long. Somehow the easy conversation of bus rides or dinner table becomes strained under the spotlight of attentive listeners. The structure of the circle and the self-conscious awareness of the group agreements add a ritual element for me. I come to regard these times during the week as a 'sacred space', similar to the circle formed through the invocation of the directions in a Celtic ritual or the circular frame of the sweat lodge in Native American tradition. Here, the 'space' is marked by nothing more outstanding or esoterically significant than a circle of straight-backed chairs, yet the sense of a time and space 'set apart', on the Earth but not of it, is palpable. The community claims not to have rituals or ceremonies, but even without any particular physical structures or invocations, the circle of listening minds and hearts is a powerful bonding ritual.

My heart is beating faster, my signal to speak, to take action. The pulse quickens, crescendoing until I take a sharp breath, ready to speak. Someone else shifts in their chair. "Well, I can share next." The wave washes back inside me, building to another peak when that person finishes.

"I have something to share," I begin. "Wow, my heart is beating really hard, so I know I need to speak." I describe my experience during Pachelbel's Canon, the sense of leaving things behind, including my relationship with Carl, that released the stream of tears without any tearing or hesitation in the throat. "I've never cried like that before, just gently releasing something. I really enjoyed the dances and was grateful for the chance to connect with all of you that way."

Quiet nods. The circle sinks into silence. The candle wavers. The atmosphere builds and thickens, each passing moment making the deepening silence harder to penetrate. Finally Wim, a Danish man, shifts his legs, tucking his hands underneath his thighs, and looks up.

"I am full of questions," begins Wim. "My background is science. I'm working on my doctorate. You know, all of my friends are curious about this place. They think about it, but none of them would come with me when I decided to come. They like to think about it, but maybe the experience is too . . . scary is the word? too different. I realise most of my life I have thought about things and never experienced them." Silence. "I am changing that by coming here." Nods. Clasped hands. More silence.

Pete, born in Somerset and a refugee from the world of wealth and travel and years of cocaine and other drugs, sighs heavily, stands up, turns his chair around, and sits down, resting his elbow on the back of the chair. Agitated, he runs his fingers through his hair.

"Come on, people," he fumes, pushing up from the chair and striding around the

71

room. "Let's get real." He pauses to perch an elbow on the mantlepiece above the fireplace, rapping the knuckle of his thumb, clenched inside his fist, against his lower lip. "I haven't heard anyone really speak from their guts. I'm bored. Very bored. And I would like to leave this session."

Stunned by his statements and unsure of how to respond, I sit with waves of agitation surging through me and, from what I can see, through the group.

"I feel like you've discounted what other people have shared," says Alan. "Their experience is just as valid as yours, and I haven't heard you give anything of yourself."

Wim nods. "I was trying my best to share what I was thinking and experiencing."

"Well, look," says Pete, hand falling to his hip, "I'm bored and I want to leave. Does anyone have a problem with that?" He eyes Alan and Angela.

"Don't ask me," Angela replies. "Ask the group."

"Does anyone mind if I leave?" he asks, glancing around the circle.

"I'm not very comfortable with you leaving the group," says Jim, a tall, lanky, bearded Californian in his late fifties, recently retired from a successful business career. His quiet, gentle voice soothes my jangling emotions. "We're just beginning to build a sense of the group, and I'd miss your presence. But if you really want to go, I can support you doing that."

Most people in the group nod in silent agreement.

"Does everyone agree with that?" asks Pete, fist tapping against his lip.

"Yes," comes the verbal response. Nods. "Go ahead."

Pete plucks his jumper from the back of his chair and swings it over his shoulder, draping it from a crooked finger. Other hand dug into his pocket, shoulders hunched around his ears, he saunters across the room and out the door.

Someone else picks up the thread, sharing her response to touring the caravan park and the morning of Sacred Dance. Stephen, an Australian man whom I met while hiking in the Lake District, finishes the sharing. "I'm amazed at how together this group feels. I mean, we've danced a bit together and talked a couple of times, and already I feel as if I have known most of you for a long time." He sniffs, shrugs his shoulders and shakes his head, admiring the improbability of the situation.

"OK," says Alan, "before we have a closing attunement, I remind all of you that tomorrow morning you will go to the work department you attuned to tonight. We next meet as a group at 1:50 tomorrow in front of Reception for a group photo. See you then."

* * *

Morning. Dawn grey peeks through the slits in the curtains. 7:30 and the sun has not yet pushed over the eastern rim of hills. Although I have not slept very long, I am eager to get up, spurred by anticipation for what this day will bring.

After breakfast I wander into the kitchen. A slender man with precisely combed hair, his movements as neat and exact as his appearance, greets me in midstride.

"Good morning," he says, cocking his head to the side in an abbreviated sort of bow. "Are you working with us in the kitchen this week?"

"Yes."

"Right. Good. Welcome. My name is Ian." His words are as neatly pressed as his trousers.

"Can I help you with anything?"

"Well, you'll find an apron over there," he says, pointing to the door that swings between the dining room and the 'stillroom' where the dishes are washed. "And

72

then you can start potwash over there," indicating an alcove with two long metal sinks with a series of eight-foot-high drying racks on the wall opposite.

I find the aprons, the sort that chefs wear. Moving back through the kitchen en route to the sink, I note the stainless steel pots resting under the shiny, stainless steel counters. The spice rack is a series of shelves like a bookcase filled with dozens of bottles of spices, all neatly labelled and arranged in alphabetical order. Another set of shelves houses a collection of vegetarian cookbooks. Below them is a table covered with a white table cloth with a brass candleholder in the centre. A variety of chairs and benches surround the table. Another set of sinks says 'For vegetables only—no washing dishes here!' Two bins stand under the sink, one labelled 'Fresh greens only' and the other 'Cooked food'.

"Do you compost the greens?" I ask Ian as he whisks around one of the counters, storing the remains of the morning's breakfast in plastic tubs and placing them on a trolley.

"No, we don't. The gardeners take care of the composting."

"Right." I move to the sink, place a stopper in the drain, and begin filling the sink with hot water. Steam rises from the basin. I revel in the warmth, acutely aware of the chilly draughts in the rest of the building.

As I scrub bowls and cooking utensils from breakfast preparation, I relive memories of the first large community kitchen that I worked in. Then I was overwhelmed by the size of the pots and pans and utensils.

What impresses me most in this kitchen, though, is not the size of the pots and pans, but rather the cleanliness and organisation. Everything shines. Everything has a place. The drawers and shelves are marked to indicate what resides in that space. And from what I can tell, opening drawers to put away the utensils, everything is in its place.

Jim, the Californian from Experience Week, joins me washing pots. At 8:45 another man comes storming through the door, slaps a notebook on the table, drops into a chair and throws himself on the table, head resting in his arms.

"Good morning, Lauren," says Ian, pausing in his work to tilt his head, the visible extent of his concern. "All right, crew, let's gather at the table. It's time to attune."

Six of us gather around the table. "Lauren, you *are* focalising this morning, aren't you?" asks Ian.

"Yeah. OK. Right," says Lauren, clearing his throat as he draws himself upright in the chair. "First let's go around the circle and—ahem—give your name—aaach—where you are from and how you are. Aaach. Briefly. 'Cause I'm a bit nervous about the meal and want all the time we can have to finish it. OK. I'll start." He giggles as he looks over at Ian. "What?" asks Ian innocently, face cracking into a grin.

"Nothing," says Lauren shaking his head. "OK. I'll begin. I'm Lauren. I've been a member here since May, and I work in the kitchen. And I'm going to focalise the meal. How am I? Tired because I was up last night until 2 a.m. doing a co-counselling session and then I came down here to check on a recipe, so I went to bed about 3:30 and now I'm exhausted. I probably should have just stayed awake and gone to sleep after lunch."

Ian is smiling, looking down and shaking his head. Lauren, in his mid-twenties and bursting with nervous energy, is as effusive as Ian is contained, yet I sense a deep affection between them.

We move around the circle, first to Jim and then Ian, then on to two women who are 'DGs', which I learn means 'Departmental Guest'—a one-week short-term guest in a programme that bridges Experience Week and the long-term programme.

73

The emotional barometer varies from exhaustion to 'feeling present' to excited anticipation.

"OK," says Lauren, "let's attune." We settle into our seats, holding hands in a circle—a few moments of fumbling as we get in the proper position, right palm facing up, left facing down. "Why do we hold hands this way?" I ask Lauren.

"It's so you receive energy with your right hand and send it with your left. That forms a clockwise spiral of energy which is the movement of spirit manifesting into matter."

"Aha. At the Bear Tribe we did it the opposite way."

"That would be the movement of matter into spirit."

"Anyway," says Ian, cutting us short, "let's attune."

We close our eyes, taking a deep breath, quieting our minds and bodies.

"Let's take a moment to welcome each other," says Lauren, pausing for a few seconds, "and also the Angel of the kitchen, the being that overlights this part of Cluny Hill. And we welcome the qualities of fun and efficiency to be with us this morning."

After a few moments of silence Lauren begins a hand squeeze that passes around the circle, the signal that the attunement is complete.

We choose jobs and set to work, the six of us weaving among each other on trips to the food shed or the walk-in refrigerator, squeezing around each other in the narrow passage of the potwash area, juggling bowls of chopped and grated and steamed vegetables in various stages of completion.

At 10:30 Ian glances at the clock. "Time for tea break," he announces.

"Tea break?" I ask, incredulous. I am accustomed to working flat out until a job is finished.

"This is Britain, you know," replies Ian, smiling impishly. "The troops would rebel if we didn't stop for tea."

"Oh." I pause, looking at the bowl of uncut onions in front of me. "Do we have to take a break?"

"Of course not. You can continue working if you choose to," he replies, raising an eyebrow.

I slip into the lounge for a quick cup of tea when I have finished chopping the onions. Almost all of the chairs in the lounge are filled with people, some drinking tea and talking, others hidden behind newspapers. Someone in the far corner is playing a guitar, one of the half dozen instruments leaning against the wall available for anyone to play.

Back to the kitchen. The meal still has not gelled into its final form. The illusion of a vast expanse of time, viewed in the early morning, contracts to a narrow race track with a red-tape finish at high noon. Everything is 'near completion' in various states of disarray. I am sure that we accomplish three times as much in one hour as in the preceding two.

The clock races to noon—it's a thoroughbred, intent on winning. Five minutes to twelve. Lauren is pulling trays of vegetable pie from the oven, the salad crew is sprinkling garnishes of parsley, and the potwash crew is churning pots and bowls and knives through the soapy water.

Noon. The trays of veggie pie rest on a heating tray in the dining room, the salads stand in artful arrangement on the long central table, and the crew of cooks, white aprons smudged with the fruits of our labour (except for Ian, of course), stand around the table with hands entwined and eyes closed. After the clatter of bowls, the roar of blender, the buzz of timer and the hiss of steam from the pressure cooker, my ears ring in the sudden silence.

"Let's give thanks for this abundance of food and see it blessed," says Lauren, pausing to clear his throat, "nourishing those who eat it on all levels . . . . Thank you."

I hang my apron in the stillroom and head for Sanctuary which begins at 12:10. I am hungrier for quiet time than for food right now.

In the hallway outside the Cluny Sanctuary I kick off my shoes, grab a neatly folded gold wool blanket from a pile behind me, and walk barefoot across the plush carpet of the inner passageway. I settle onto a cushion, leaning against the wood-panelled wall, taking a moment to admire the elegant simplicity of this room with its wood-beamed vaulted ceiling rising to a peak high above. In the centre of the room is a long plate of glass balanced on thin sections of a birch log, decorated with a simple arrangement of flowers and a white pillar candle. The meditation begins precisely at 12:10 with a few words of Eileen's guidance followed by a long stretch of silence. As my mind quiets, my awareness moves further and further inwards, perched in the region between sleep and wakefulness. As is the case with some dreams, the contents of those insights evades my grasp when I am jarred into wakefulness by the words of the woman guiding the meditation.

"And now . . . keeping this sense of inner peace and alignment . . . we visualise love and light pouring from this circle, moving around the planet, blessing and uniting all of mankind . . . . Thank you."

Slowly my awareness returns to my body, the breath deepens, and the usual jangle of thoughts resumes. *'Mankind'* blares in my mind. The New Age still has a lot to learn about sexist language. And 'Love and Light'—what about honouring the darkness, the fertile realm of the Goddess, as well? And why just blessing *humanity,* one aspect of the whole Earth? I thought this place professed to be *planetary* in its outlook.

The thoughts continue through lunch and the group photo session, and follow me into the ballroom where we meet for Group Discovery. "Like Sacred Dance," begins Sandy, a member of the community who will lead this afternoon's session, "this is another way to experience yourselves and the group in a non-verbal way, with a sense of fun and childlike play. Even though we are 'playing', be aware that some of these games can bring up strong emotions and deep insights. So just stay in touch with yourself and your feelings through the afternoon."

The games move from boisterous, laughter-filled 'Hug Tag' to slower-paced trust games and finally to quiet, vulnerable interactions. During one 'game', I lie on the ground, curled in a foetal position, while a partner unfolds my body ever so slowly until I lie on my back, open to the world, reassured by my partner's hands resting quietly on my shoulders. By the end of the afternoon I am stretched and flexed and opened, full of love for this group of people and the world in general.

"Be aware," says Anne, Sandy's wife and co-focaliser in presenting the games, "that you are very open and sensitive right now. You may find you have some strong feelings, perhaps ones you haven't had before or haven't had for a long time, so just be gentle with yourself."

The initial connection that I felt with Alan is growing and today, my heart stretched open by the games and the exploration of feelings, I overflow with love for him. As the group disperses, I skip across the ballroom floor to the bench where Alan is pulling on socks and shoes. I sit beside him, throwing my arms around his neck.

"I just want to tell you," I say, emboldened by the childlike openness of the moment, "that I think you are beautiful."

"Thank you, I think you're beautiful, too."

We sit for a few moments, eyes fixed, breathing deeply, smiling. After a quick hug, I skip across the floor to Gillian, a Scottish woman recently returned from seven years in South America, with whom I already feel a strong sisterly bond.

"Want to walk in the woods?" she asks.

I nod, delighted. We float into the woods, accompanied by Armando, a one-time millionaire who lost all his wealth after a coup in Argentina; he now lives in Hawaii near his son, piecing together his life on new foundations. Wim, the Belgian scientist, joins us, too. We walk silently through the woods, joined arm to arm, pausing to bow our heads into a circle with arms wrapped over each other's backs, then leaning back to drink in the starry sky above. My heart is bursting, in love with these companions from the far corners of the Earth, with humanity as a whole, with the planet, with love itself.

As the week passes, the group grows more cohesive and more understanding. Our sharings range from descriptions of joyous discovery to painful internal re-enactments of past tragedies. Anything that blocks the full expression of the heart bubbles and eventually surfaces for expulsion. On Thursday night we have a session called 'Personal and Planetary Transformation', the first attempt to turn the group outward, away from the strong bonds that we have forged, to view the experience in terms of how we can apply it to the rest of our lives. 'As I change, the planet changes' is the basic premise. And the work of change can proceed anywhere on the planet. Learn to change myself instead of trying to change the world around me.

Caroline, a member living at the Park (caravan park) has come to 'share' with us. No one ever comes just to 'talk' here, like a lecturer at a university. Earlier in the week those people who were primed by various New Age courses and workshops sat with notebooks in their laps, pens poised to record the crumbs of wisdom dropped by all-knowing souls. Now notebooks sit under chairs or lie closed on laps. When people *share*, directly from the heart, the information lands in the heart instead of on an intellectual level. The practice of making 'I' statements means there is really nothing to discuss in the analytical, intellectual sense. People simply present their own view of their lives and the world, without attempts at conversion or coercion. The statements stand on their own, without need of contradiction or agreement. They simply are.

Caroline's recounting of the challenges, pain and occasional madness of her personal journey moves me deeply. Agitated when the session ends, I quickly leave the room, not wanting this fluttering, flopping disquiet within me to escape before I have confronted it.

I move into the entrance hallway, pull open the heavy door and wander into the night, pain engulfing me before I reach the first turn in the driveway. I sit on a ledge built around one of the garden beds, pull my knees up to my chest and wrap my arms around them, gently rocking back and forth on my stony perch. I close my eyes and immediately see the image of a little girl, about three years old, blond-haired and smiling, running across an expanse of grass. I know she is my child, our child, Carl's and mine, as she would have looked at three. I unfold my legs and sit upright, tears pouring as I sense within my body how I would feel if I were pregnant, precisely five months pregnant, my belly gently rounded and full with the growing foetus.

I bless you, child. I release you once again back to the Creator. You are beautiful, so very beautiful, and I miss you, terribly. I miss the life in my womb tonight, and I grieve.

The chill of late autumn finally presses through my wool sweater. The demands of the body pull me back to the moment. I push open the front door and move through the lounge to the stillroom to make a cup of tea. The agitation of an hour earlier is replaced by a deep calm.

Friday. Our morning kitchen crew completes the meal by 11:15. Each day we have finished a bit earlier as we perfect a way of working together. We sit at the table, Ian and Jim and I, laughing and talking about our lives. Ian, I learn, was a solicitor for the British Army. The precision of the army is imprinted in his actions, but this morning he laughs deeply and his stern face twinkles—he could easily pass for a woodland elemental. He would probably disapprove of the description, but I harbour it anyway, delighted by the contradictions in this man.

In the afternoon our Experience Week has a 'completion session', a final sharing time to bring our group to a close. And this afternoon we are indeed a group, far removed from the awkward collection of individuals that entered this room last Saturday afternoon. After a brief meditation to recall the events of the week, Alan places a stone in the centre of the circle. "Today we will be using this stone during the sharing, in a ritual inspired by American Indians. We call this a 'talking stone' (I groan inwardly, recognising a well-intentioned bastardisation of the 'talking stick' of the Council Meetings), and whoever holds this stone has the power of speech, and we give them our full attention. When they finish, they take a moment to tune in and then give the rock to someone else—the next person they sense is ready to speak. So it's also a chance to practise using your intuition. All right," he says, placing the stone in the centre next to the candle, "anyone can pick up the stone to begin."

The stone passes slowly among us, releasing floods of tears and laughter and deep reflection. Magically by 5 p.m. the stone stops, resting once again in the centre, and with its repose I feel the same weighty quiet within me, a rounded fullness that requires nothing more to fill its measure. I regret leaving these new-found friends, but I also am eager to move more deeply into the community. The transition is eased by the fact that nearly half the group will remain for at least another week with a few planning to stay for three months in the Essence of Findhorn programme that begins tomorrow. When I first considered coming to the Foundation while writing an unsuccessful grant application for the Watson Fellowship, I had planned to take part in the Essence programme. Now, though, I am content to stay for a month—already an extension of my original plans to stay for one week.

In the evening our group meets for an informal sharing of song and poetry and any other inspiration of the moment. Britte wears a theatrical red dress and belts out an operatic aria, flinging a fur boa as she struts around the room. Gillian sings quiet, soulful songs from South America, and Hal reads a favourite poem. For me the crowning glory of the evening is Alan's audio-visual about trees. As I watch his photographs of tree and leaf and bark, I think to myself, "Now this is a man I could fall in love with—a man who understands the Earth."

Alan and I have acknowledged our mutual attraction, but Guest Department rules forbid the involvement of focalisers with the guests in their programme. "I usually need a day to myself after Experience Week," explains Alan after the sharing, "but then I look forward to getting to know you a bit more."

CHAPTER 5
First Footing in Scotland

Our courtship begins with a walk in the woods and an evening of conversation with many silent spaces. I am tongue-tied and giddy as a 15-year-old in Alan's presence. I trip over unseen branches as we walk, breathe shallowly, and tingle when our hands touch and swing together.

Alan tells me immediately that he is in love with a woman who was in an Experience Week he focalised two weeks before mine. Although she was not interested in pursuing a sexual romantic relationship, Alan describes the deep heart connection he felt with her.

My logical mind steps in momentarily, cutting through the giddiness that floats me about two inches above the Earth. "What the hell are you doing," I ask myself sternly, "entering a relationship with a man who is in love with someone else?" My heart, though, has moved beyond the reach of reason, and I pursue the relationship anyway.

The honeymoon with the community and with Alan lasts another week as I enter the daily rhythm, working three hours in the kitchen in the morning and three hours in the Phoenix bookstore in the afternoon. The second week I move into full-time work in the kitchen. By the third week I begin to see cracks in the perfection of the collective endeavour; by week four I am terribly distraught to find oranges from South Africa and bananas from Chile in the food shed. I am sick with the flu and disillusioned with Alan. I stumble in and out of a horrible depression, feeling that if I fell off the face of the Earth no one would notice. The real work is beginning.

During one of these bouts of depression, I enter the kitchen for my afternoon work shift. During the attunement I briefly share my distress. Late in the afternoon, after spending a few hours in my own little world chopping vegetables and arranging salads, Lauren streaks by, asking if I still feel like no one cares. "Yes," I say, turning to face him. "I still do."

"Oh," says Lauren, laughing nervously as he dances across the kitchen. His face shows embarrassment, and I sense that he is so deeply immersed in his own painful process of untangling his past that he has no room to spare for anyone else's distress, or 'stuff' according to Findhorn Foundation jargon.

Not long after, Joy Drake approaches me about typing and doing some secretarial work for the Game of Transformation work department. Joy developed the board game in the late seventies as a tool for people to clarify life issues, examine points of strength and weakness, and further their path of self-development. First used only within the community, the Game grew and became part of the guest programme and eventually travelled throughout Europe and North America.

Now Joy and her partner Kathy, who helped to develop the workshop after its inception, are working to create a 'game-in-a-box', a version of the complex workshop that can be marketed commercially to reach more people. And the Game, far removed from the realm of Monopoly or any other similar production, is *powerful*. I have heard people speak about it with a respect that borders on fear. "It's so *clear*," said someone, "that it can be painful. Some things I just don't like seeing in myself, and the Game points them out in such a way that I *have* to look at them."

"I warn you," says Joy when I agree to work on the manual for the game-in-a-box, "that you will be working directly with the energies of transformation. That energy will move through all of your life, and that can be uncomfortable at times."

How could it be any more intense than what I have already experienced since I arrived? And besides I am impatient, as always, to speed the rate of my growth.

In mid-November each year the community has an 'Internal Conference', a week-long series of meetings dedicated to evaluating the past year and setting priorities for the next. The Bear Tribe never felt they had the luxury of time to dedicate a whole week to themselves, but Nimimosha writes that this January they will be having a week-long retreat, the first in their more than ten-year history. The Findhorn Community invites only Living in Community Guests (LCGs, those committed to stay and work for at least one month) and the Essence programme guests to stay during the closed week. We are welcome to attend the meetings as 'silent observers'.

The highlight of the week is the signing of the deed to purchase the caravan park, performed on the community's 22nd birthday. The purchase of the caravan park is the culmination of several years of fundraising efforts and the end of a 22-year state of impermanency. Accustomed to likening the development of the collective to that of a human being, the community parallels the purchase of the land with a coming of age: at twenty-two years of age, the Foundation is establishing a solid base for the work of mature adulthood ahead.

To prepare for this work of adulthood, the community chooses 'consolidation' as its theme for the coming year—regrouping inner resources for a coming period of growth. In practical terms 'consolidation' translates into focusing on inner work as individuals and as a collective. It also means accepting no new members for one year. I interpret the decision as a harking back to the 'good old days', a mistaken belief that the excitement and sense of purpose that was so obvious during the years of pioneering growth can be recaptured by stopping and consciously concentrating on it.

The theme for the year usually ties in with the topic for the following autumn's 'October Conference', the most carefully planned and widely attended event of the year. For 1985 the conference is 'The Spiritual Work of Our Times', which falls directly in line with the desire to strengthen the inner work of the community.

The week also includes a gala celebration of the community's birthday with a dinner and cabaret staged in Cluny's dining room. I plan to go to the noon Sanctuary before the big event, but the orange light is glowing above the door—I have arrived too late.

In the lounge downstairs I hear the beginnings of a ferment that festers and finally bursts among the LCGs over the next couple of weeks. An unidentified member taped a notice on the Sanctuary door announcing that the noon meditation would be open to *members only* to celebrate the community's birthday. The LCGs, the backbone of much of the daily work in the community, are incensed. Another member saw the notice and tore it down, also angry that anyone would be blocked from the Sanctuary, meant for all who live in the community.

In reaction, the LCGs draw closer together, strengthening as a group. With the reluctant consent of the LCG focaliser, we decide to plan and run our own twice-weekly meetings and organise extra support evenings for sharing, poetry, reading or whatever people want to do together. Open to members. *Of course.* We weren't going to make the same mistake of exclusion. During our quiet, well-organised insurrection I realise that the community has few channels to absorb the suggestions of its guests—the members are too busy trying to maintain themselves and 'educate' the guests. A few members, though, usually the newer ones unjaded by the 'I've seen it all before' attitude, listen with interest and even attend some of the evening gatherings.

Despite the strong bonds that develop in the group, the sharing of deep feelings and insights is still challenging for me. I do it, but with difficulty. The stony silence of the group after sharing pain or joy or anger can be unnerving—I am so used to judging the quality or 'rightness' of my statements according to other people's responses. Here, though, the point is to say what is true for *me*—there is no outside point of reference. The silence forces me to turn inside myself for affirmation. After one meeting I sit before the typewriter, banging on the keys.

"Thank you for sharing", yes, my guts tasted sweet
I spew them into the indifferent vacuum of people,
mildly interested on-lookers.
What can I say that could shock you,
oh you who sit in judgement and yet offer no sentence.
Can't you see that these things rip my soul, that I feel
naked and cold and angry at my vulnerability.
I try to learn not to want or value your response
and find myself harbouring bitterness at the silence that greets me.

. . . i hide so much inside myself. i have to feel safe before i can show my vulnerability, my need for love and sharing. i create a crisis to be able to have my needs met—sickness, depression, and the edgy, giddy feeling of just-under-the-surface anger.

Our strong cohesion as a group, unusual for LCGs, lasts until the holiday season when many guests return to their homes in other countries. A few make plane reservations to leave after the New Year's Peace Conference, but I have no definite plans for departure, and the lack of clarity makes me squeamish. "Part of my anxiety about leaving," I write in my journal, "is feeling that I have not consciously invoked a purpose here—I don't know what I've got because I don't know why I came . . . . Yes, I did have some purpose in coming here—to learn more about how communities function, are led, how they connect with the Earth here. I come away with the purpose of finding my inner strength to benefit myself and the people whom I am to serve."

One day in Sanctuary as I focus on knowing a definite departure date, I hear 'December 16th'. But December is nearly a full year away.

"*December* 16th?" I ask quietly.

"Yes. December 16th, 1986."

1986?! That's *two* years away.

Coming out of meditation I dismiss the date as outrageous. I will be studying medicine, not here in Scotland. During the next couple of days, though, the date persists in my meditations. Finally I decide to talk with the LCG focaliser about next steps in becoming a member, 'just to explore the possibilities' I tell myself.

Late December. Despite the inward draw of the long, dark nights, the community lumbers into action after a brief closed week for Christmas to prepare for the New Year's Peace Event. I choose to usher for the event as my work rota for the week. The first evening I am delighted when I feel a tap on my shoulder and look up to find Brigitte, the mother of Deborah with whom I spent much time this summer at the Bear Tribe. We chat excitedly about the changes in her life and mine before she scurries into a seat at the beginning of the session. I glow inside, knowing in this moment that I have entered yet another world, the overlapping circles of 'New Age' (for lack of a better word) centres. Music was another such world for me—a new acquaintance would almost certainly know another musician whom I knew. I expect that I will be seeing more familiar faces here as time moves on.

New Year's Eve. Unlike the years spent at drunken parties or babysitting and watching Guy Lombardo on the television, I observe the passing of the old and the beginning of the new year in sanctuary. Quietly. Re-living the events of the past year—was it only a year ago this very night that I stepped off the plane in Spokane, Washington to visit the Bear Tribe? And now my footing is in another culture, another land, another continent.

At midnight I hear a swell, like a distant roar, from the centre of Forres a mile below. Bagpipes whine and people shout. Now begins the ritual, more important to most Scots than Christmas or any other holiday, of 'first footing'. People pass from house to house, stepping over the threshold for the first time in the new year, placing their foot in the door to receive a dram of whisky before moving on to the next home. The visiting continues until quite late; it's sometimes past sunrise before people take to their beds.

Tonight, sitting silently in Sanctuary, I step over the threshold of the passing year and into the new, firmly planting my foot in the land of Scotland—for how long? If the coming year holds as many changes as the past one, I could be in Tahiti by next January. Teaching scuba diving or spraying suntan oil on lazy tourists (as my friend Stephen from Australia writes that he is doing in Italy.)

Just after midnight Joy leads a meditation to choose an Angel card for the coming year. This tiny deck of cards, each with a quality like Hope or Surrender or Power inscribed on it, is part of the Game of Transformation and is widely used in the community. I reach for a card, placed face down on a tray in the centre of the Sanctuary, my heart beating as I turn it over—the Angel of Anticipation. I slump into my chair, sure that the coming year will be spent with a tip-of-the-tongue, never-quite-arriving quality to it. Damn. I want to know where I'm going and what I'm supposed to be doing and start *going* there, instead of *anticipating* going there. I look more closely at the card and notice the Angel of Anticipation untying a bow on a big present. When I tune in with the Angel, I sense the excitement and joy that

81

accompany Anticipation, the breathless quality of eagerness that spurs me from one moment to the next. I can choose to greet the coming changes joyously instead of dragging through them—I can anticipate the best.

The next morning a group of about twenty of us drive to the Findhorn beach for a polar bear swim. We leave our clothes on the warm bus seats, slip into bathing suits (the local villagers would be offended by naked pink bodies) and run screaming into the icy waters of the North Sea. The 'swim' consists of running in and sprinting out. We pile into the bus, struggle into dry clothes, and drive to the Station House Cosmic Thermos, the sauna on the Park side of the community.

In the afternoon the conference lectures resume and continue for a few more days. Most thought-provoking of the speakers for me is Willis Harman, a scientist who saw the mind used as a new weapon in the US Defense Department. He had the revelation that it could be used just as powerfully to create a *peaceful* vision of the future. Willis suggests that the most effective action that a peace activist, or anyone for that matter, can take is to spend time visioning a peaceful world. Nothing is invented, nothing comes into being, until it has been conceived. The idea of a television, for example, preceded its physical creation. A vision of a peaceful world must precede the reality. What I hold in mind produces in kind. What kind of a future do I imagine, anyway?

Inspired by the talk, I sign up for a weekend workshop with him. Much of the workshop is spent in topsy-turvy group process, going round and round about this and that topic. I am alternately bored and on the edge of my seat, reacting to a declaration made or a question posed. Finally on Sunday afternoon the bombshell drops.

Willis talks about fear, how action taken to *avoid* something actually *strengthens* the possibility of that feared event happening. I may, for example, take action to create a more peaceful world, but if the underlying motivation is to *avoid* nuclear destruction, I actually carry a vision of nuclear war with a big 'NO' pasted over it. The mind, though, proceeds in creating the *vision,* not the NO. Consciously or unconsciously that vision gets a lot of attention in my mind. The more energy I give to that fear in my life (i.e. doing things to avoid, eradicate or 'fix' that fear), the more energy that thought/fear has to become *reality,* to become real in my life and the life of the planet.

We take a moment to find inside ourselves our greatest fear, and then we move around the circle to name and thereby release this fear from our lives.

I do not need to look far—the fear comes screaming to my attention. "I fear that the Earth will be destroyed in a nuclear holocaust, and that I have no time—no time to waste in saving the world before it blows up." The words come out in a breathless, hurried flow.

The realisation shatters me. I escape to the forest and cry and cry, howling my anguish to the trees and the cold, starry night. I have been living a lie, doing all kinds of wonderful, 'politically correct' things to save the world, but the impetus for these acts was *fear.* All of those actions actually empowered the possibility of the Earth's destruction. The picture I held as I acted was 'I have to hurry, no time, must do before the bomb drops . . . .' All of those correct outward actions were actually harmful because they were matched with a vision of future destruction.

What would I do with my life if I was not driven by this fear? What I have labelled as 'impatience' I now see as a fear-driven need to save the world. Even my decision to study naturopathic medicine was based on the need to be trained and working before I was thirty—who knows if the planet would continue beyond my thirtieth year? Assuming that I *can* construct a new vision, what would I do with my life if I acted on the belief that the world would survive, even flourish?

Roger, a mutual friend of Alan's and mine with whom I have had many impassioned ideological discussions, is talking with Alan when I arrive in his room. Roger pauses to ask how I am, and gives me a big hug when I explain my soul-searching walk. "It's good," he says, stroking my face. "You have so much passion in you, and I see your desire to really serve. You're asking important questions, ones you'll have to answer."

I nod, and the tears flow again. "Yeah, I feel like I have to re-think my whole life."

Alan and I talk for a while and then crawl into bed, huddled together for warmth under the covers. Our relationship has grown in fits and starts. Over Christmas and New Year a relaxed intimacy, deeper than at any time during the autumn, bloomed and then closed by turn.

I am threatened by Alan's descriptions of past lovers—both guests and members—and jealous of their presence as they move in and out of the community. One of Alan's former lovers lives in the room next door to him, another works with me in the kitchen. He often stops to hug them affectionately and talk with them about what is happening in their lives. None of them harbour ill feelings towards me—the woman in the kitchen, in fact, is now a close friend—but I am jealous when I see Alan with other women, even when the affection is purely platonic. And part of the reality of living in a community is that former lovers live among us. The ideal I aspire to is to maintain a solid friendship with past lovers and to accept my partner's former lovers as friends. The constant struggle is to overcome the primal jealousy that comes with sexual intimacy, to learn a new way of relating, to love without conditions. I berate myself for being jealous, knowing it is a sign of my own insecurity, but it continues anyway.

When I feel most vulnerable, I plot an escape to the Isle of Erraid, an island off the west coast of Scotland that the community stewards for a Dutch family. I have watched other LCGs and members visit the island—they return relaxed and rested. From what I can recall of the Erraid audio-visual that we watched during Experience Week, the life there is much simpler than here and more directly concerned with the land. In my mind I have planned to visit after Alan leaves at the end of January for a trip to India and the community of Auroville, but when our relationship becomes strained, I contemplate leaving earlier.

In the evenings we often sit reading in Alan's room. I sit with my back propped against a chair, wrapped in a woollen blanket to insulate me from the chilly draughts. I am reading *Seth Speaks*, one of several books channelled by Jane Roberts. These are the books that Hilary referred to; Alan finds them inspiring as well. As I read, my sense of space and time and possibility expand. If all time is now, as Seth suggests, if linear time is an illusion, the expanse of the world widens, outstripping my present conceptual grasp. The 16th century is happening now and so is the 27th. The Stone Age overlaps the Nuclear in an eternal now. Worlds of which I cannot even conceive run parallel to this one. Only my acquiescence to the common belief in linear time keeps me rooted in this time frame and hinders me from slipping between centuries.

After reading a section about dreams, described as a source of teaching and a way of travelling between times and visiting dimensions other than the physical, my dream life becomes more vivid. Or perhaps I am just more aware of it. One night I dream that I am walking along a corridor of cut stone, wearing a long black cape that swishes over the smooth floor. Ahead is an open doorway that sends light streaming into the dim hall. Information is running through my head—it seems quite ordinary to me, yet I am to enter this room in order to 'channel' this information. But it's so obvious. Will they call me a charlatan?

Just then we pass under a bell tower. The huge clapper sways and hits the bell. The reverberations ring through my own body as well, blotting out any other awareness. The buzzing sensation terrifies me, and I pull myself into wakefulness, sitting bolt upright in bed, but the sound of the bell and the vibrations in my body continue. Eyes open or closed, I see the hallway. The sound and the sensations continue for a few minutes according to the clock, but internally it feels endless, frightening, inescapable. Finally the sound fades, and I return to sleep.

Initially I interpret the dream as a warning against 'channelling' or trusting the voices that I hear inside. Later that week a woman named Pat works with me, guiding me in 'gestalting' the dream, becoming different aspects of it. When I move up the rope that swings the bell, I feel constrained and frightened, but once I reach the bell and stand astride it, I have a tremendous sense of freedom. I can view the whole countryside. I feel as if I could jump from the tower and fly. "Why don't you?" asks Pat. After hesitating for a moment, I spread my arms and push off from the tower, soaring birdlike over the fields below. My sense of terror associated with the dream lessens.

Steve, a friend with a long history of experiences in the 'unseen worlds' offers another interpretation. "The bell," explains Steve, "is a symbol for the call to worship the Spirit, or Godhead." The dream, according to him, symbolises the universe calling me to open to spirit, to recognise my own spirit within, to let my inner light and divine wisdom shine. Steve, eternally positive in his interpretation of events and persistent in drawing forth the best in anyone or anything he touches, suggests that the ringing bell was a signal of validation, encouraging me to trust my inner voice. Although the sound terrified me, Steve describes the divine message as a very mild display of fireworks. "Believe me," he says, "they can be—how shall I say it—yes, more *dramatic* I guess would be the best description." After having heard some of his inner experiences, I am inclined to agree with him.

As Alan's departure date nears, we grow more tender and gentle, partly because I am uncertain whether I will still be here when he returns. The parting may be permanent. Alan plans to spend six weeks in Auroville, an international spiritual community in the south of India. He started having dreams about Auroville last autumn after he found a brochure in the lounge. Taking this as a 'sign' to visit the community, he began to make plans even though he didn't have enough money to pay for the trip.

A month before he was due in Auroville, Alan sat talking with a friend, encouraging her to trust the community, and the universe in general, to supply what she needed to complete a project. "Look," said Alan, "I trust that if what I'm doing is for the benefit of the *whole*, I'll be provided with everything I need." His friend was sceptical, convinced that she needed to look after her own interests. Someone interrupted the conversation with a message. "Telephone call, Alan—at the payphone."

Nick Galloway, president of Greenpeace in Britain, was on the line. "I have good news for you, Alan," said Nick. "You've won first prize in our Christmas raffle."

"First prize?"

"Yes, £1,000."

Alan returned to his friend, beaming. "The universe just paid for my trip to India," he said, smiling. "You see, it works! If I'm working for the good of the whole, the whole supports me."

On the day of his departure, I walk with Alan to the train station. The sun barely skirts the horizon on this pale winter morning. Dark clouds hang in the west, the aftermath of a heavy snowstorm down in England. This winter is one of the coldest in recent European history. Rome, unequipped with snow removal equipment, is paralysed by a few inches of snow.

Here on the Moray Firth we have had little snow, although the mountains visible across the bay are deeply blanketed. The Firth is blessed with a microclimate radically different from areas only a few miles further inland. The Gulf Stream skirts the west coast of Britain, curves around the top between the mainland and the Orkney Islands, and then flows south, ending in the Moray Firth. The land, sea currents and sky conspire to make this one of the sunniest places in Britain. This strange phenomenon is what attracted two major air force bases to this area before World War II. Often the only hole in the cloud cover over Britain was on this Firth, making it a safe passageway for the returning bomber pilots.

Alan and I sit quietly together in the train station, pressed side to side. Our goodbye is a classic movie scene, Alan leaning out the train window to kiss me goodbye and then waving until the train clacks out of sight. I walk through the streets of Forres alone, feeling hollow and lonely inside.

When I return to Cluny Hill, the halls are dark—the electricity board has temporarily shut off the current to work on one of the power stations. In the gloomy hallway I peer at the noticeboard and find a note with my name.

"No bus to Erraid next week," says the message from the focaliser of Transport. The bus usually runs every other week in the winter and every week in the summer, leaving Cluny Hill at 5 a.m. on Saturday morning and arriving at Erraid, on the southwestern tip of Mull, around 11 a.m. "Christine Harris from Newbold is going to Iona. Perhaps you can arrange a ride with her. Love (heart) Transport."

Great. More details to arrange. I call Christine at Newbold, an independent project closely associated with the Foundation. Newbold House is a smaller community only a fifteen-minute walk up the road from Cluny Hill that runs its own guest programmes. We arrange to travel together on public transport to the Isle of Mull, a two-day trip by bus and ferry.

On the Thursday after Alan's departure is the introduction to the three-day version of the Game of Transformation. Although I have played the 'game-in-a-box' a couple of times, this will be my first experience of the full-blown workshop. On the way to the meeting room, I notice a small package beneath the mailwheel with familiar handwriting—my mother's. While waiting for the demonstration to begin, I open the package and find small things that I have requested as well as mail—postmarked *October*. The package has been delayed nearly three months in the mail. Among the letters is a note from the Naturopathic College of Medicine saying that registration fees have increased, please send the balance by February 5th.

I sit for a moment, staring blankly. The box arrived just one week before the deadline to reply. The universe seems to be asking me to decide—will I study medicine next autumn or open myself to new possibilities? The choices are school or the world, not school or Findhorn. What would it be like to live without the firm anchor of my life plan as a Naturopath? The possibilities seem endless without that reference point.

I could simply pay the additional fee and leave my possibilities open . . . . No, for too long I have tried to keep all options free to avoid making a final decision. I decide to use the Game of Transformation to clarify my direction.

My Angel for the Game is Education—perfect for exploring my attitudes about school and learning. In the Physical realm I use my intuition to move to the Earth Blessing Square and receive positive feedback for my action. My movements continue smoothly until I enter the Intuitive realm. Here, I enter the Dark Night of the

Soul, a depression so deep that I am unable to continue moving on the board. Within the circle of players I am a bit defiant, flaunting the reflector sunglasses I must wear, crossing my arms in mock toughness. But internally I am crumbling, the sensitive interior raw with pain. During the next half-day (until my next turn) I relive all the major traumas in my life—childhood illnesses and hospitalisation, separation from my fiancé, my limitations as a musician, the abortion, leaving Carl, and the terrible aching aloneness inside me that no one ever quite fills.

As I relive the experiences, I understand suddenly that they have been my greatest teachers—the pain has aged me and brought wisdom far beyond my physical years. Those lonely, dark passages brought me more than Algebra or English Lit. or Music Theory ever did. They shaped the expression of my soul, not the knowledge of my personality.

When I emerge from the Dark Night of the Soul, my notebook is filled with scrawled realisations, chief among them the knowing that *life* and its living is my greatest source of teaching—the true grit of education. For so long I have relied upon formal institutions to educate me, but I'm beginning to recognise the teaching available in daily living. I am long on theory and short on experience, and I decide to rectify the balance. By the end of the weekend, suspending the agonising drama of my usual decision-making process, I decide to become a member of the Findhorn Foundation.

After verbalising this decision I feel strangely calm. Perhaps knowing that I *can* change my mind lessens the trauma. Or perhaps, a likelihood I rarely allow myself, the decision is so obvious a next step that it does not ruffle my inner composure.

I am reminded of a talk given by Joyce Pearson during the Peace Conference —say 'yes' to something and then watch one's life change because of it. Part of me hesitates. What about school? Am I avoiding a career, postponing it out of fear? I answer myself that I can pursue a career later. For now I can 'save the world' by saving myself first .

Tonight, relaxing after the workshop, I read *The Wise Virgin*, a collection of stories about transformation within individual women's lives. The words seem to affirm my decision. "If I can be whole myself," says Isobel, "then I am already helping society by producing one individual less to worry about. And it is as if by being as whole as possible in myself I can influence other people to be whole. Unless you change the basic underlying attitude of the people, you cannot change the forms in which a society operates. If you are working towards becoming responsible as an individual, society will automatically change."

Responsibility—the Angel that I drew to complete the Game. Bingo. Part of the 'responsibility' comes from being response-able. Able to respond for decisions that I make in my life. All during the Game I was waiting to hear, "Yes, you should do such and such." But no voice can do that for me. The knowing has to come from within me, and then I (the inner self) always *chooses,* using will to say 'yes' or 'no' to the opportunity.

The following Friday Christine and I leave for the west coast. I am looking forward to the more relaxed pace of the island to digest all the insights from the Game. Christina and Patrick, members from the caravan park, join us Saturday morning on the ferry from Oban. On the Isle of Mull we board another bus that takes us through the barren mountains of Mull to the town of Fionnphort. Here Christine leaves us for the short ferry ride to the Isle of Iona, only about a mile away across a narrow channel of the sea.

Christina and Patrick and I set off towards Erraid on foot, walking along a bitumen road that climbs from the tiny village of white-washed stone crofts. We cross grassy hills dotted with rocks and pools of water caught in boggy depressions that glint in the brilliant sunlight of this cloudless day. On the horizon the blue of sky merges with a deeper blue of sea—their exact line of union is hazy. Sheep bleat and bah and skitter on rigid legs, frightened by our approach. Those legs look ridiculously thin and fragile compared to the round barrel of their bodies, plumped by the thick matting of winter wool.

Also conspicuous on the island, though conspicuous from lack, are trees. In protected glens or in a few select pine plantations, the trees cling tenaciously, struggling against the sea-borne winds that blow uninterrupted from Ireland to this west coast of Scotland. Once the island was covered with trees and the brunt of the wind dispersed among many branches. If you have ever been sheltered in a forest during a strong gale, you may have noticed the cooperative effort of the trees. Together, through the combined swaying of their woody bodies, they absorb much of the wind's energy. Trees are like the nerves of the planet, sensing the movement of wind and rain and then transmitting that information through the fibres of their bodies into the crust of the Earth.

Now, though, sheep have replaced trees, and the new victors assure their dominance through the humble act of grazing. They nip the young seedlings which never grow beyond about four inches if they survive at all. If you look among the heather near an aging copse of birch, you may find tiny seedlings with stems as large as your little finger. Like bonsaied trees they grow in width but not in height.

Ahead of us the road curves around a barn and dwindles into a dirt track that crosses a boggy meadow. As we round the curve, I see the jumble of stones and boulders of the rocky shoreline, the narrow expanse of sea, and the cliffs of Erraid beyond.

"See the houses?" asks Christina.

"No, where?"

"There's a row of eight houses—stone cottages. That's Main Street on Erraid."

Wisps of smoke slant in the breeze, and I follow them to their source. Suddenly the line of cottages jumps out in relief—they are well camouflaged among the surrounding rock faces.

We watch an orange-suited figure moving along the pier, a natural outcropping shaped and smoothed by cut blocks and cement. In the sea below a rowboat bobs, straining against its mooring. The figure clambers down a stairway on the side of the pier, steps into the boat and starts the engine. We wait at the top of the landing, a line of flat stones cemented together, slicked by moss and covered with seaweed at the lower end.

When the boat chugs to the landing, we pile our packs into the bow and then lurch into the bobbing craft. I revel in the smell of salt and seaweed and the froth that splashes my face when we slap against a swell. We rock and sway, the flat sides of the wooden boat bobbing awkwardly over the undulating body of the sea.

A small knot of people is waiting on the pier to greet us new arrivals: Janet, the focaliser of Erraid; Chris and her three children Holly, Ivy and Sky; and Dick Quartel, an ex-member at Cluny Hill now spending six months on Erraid as a gentle transition out of the community. We put our gear into wheelbarrows and push them up the hill to 'Main Street', the wide, flat avenue that runs between the row of cottages on one side and a series of walled gardens on the other. I stop to admire the rows of cabbages, cauliflower, kale and broccoli.

"Those are beautiful," I comment to Chris. "I'm surprised they can stand the cold."

"Well, the brassicas are hardy, and on the west coast the winters are relatively mild, so they do well almost year round," says Chris.

"Do you grow all of your own vegetables?"

"Yes, or at least close to it. Sometimes we have a few things sent from Findhorn in the winter, and we always have to bring in fruit, but for the most part we grow our own vegetables, including potatoes—*lots* of potatoes. And we have Mouska the cow for milk and the chickens for eggs."

"Do you have goats?" I ask eagerly; they were always my favourites at the Bear Tribe.

"No, I'm afraid not. When the community first moved onto Erraid, they tried having goats, but they weren't very successful."

"Why not?"

"Oh, they kept getting loose and rooting in the garden and generally raising hell," says Chris, smiling.

I move down the row of cottages, standing in pairs with alleyways inbetween, to No. 2 where Dick Quartel is staying. Guests live with members in the houses, sharing a communal living room and a tiny kitchen where breakfast and the ever-important 'hot drinks' are prepared. Mid-day and evening meals are served in the dining room at the far end of the street, in Cottage No. 8.

I greet Renate, the German woman staying in the front guest bedroom, and pass into the back bedroom where I drop my pack on one of the cots. Through the back window I look across a stone-walled yard, shared with the cottage next door, outfitted with a privy on either side.

The sun is brilliant, pouring through the window and heating the room. I close my eyes and bask in the sunlight for a few minutes, inhaling deeply, breathing prayers of thanksgiving for the journey, for the sun, for the wild freshness of the elements, and for the active work with the Earth in this place.

I pull on a pair of rubber Wellington boots, the premier British footwear for anyone who steps beyond the boundaries of citified pavement, and walk along the main street, admiring the sweep of mountains to the northeast, the blue, blue sea sparkling in the sun, and the Isle of Iona across the narrow channel to the west. On this clear day, the details of houses and streets and figures on the pier of Iona stand out like a perfect made-to-scale miniature.

Holly, coat flapping and child-sized Wellies slapping on the smoothed earth, runs down the street, swinging a bell as he goes. "Five minutes to Sanctuary and half an hour until lunch!"

Patrick joins me, hands crammed into his pockets, shoulders hunched around his neck as we push through the wrought iron gate and climb the steep path to the Sanctuary. We leave our boots outside and push open the door. Simple jute woven mats cover the floor, and a few wicker chairs line the back wall. A semi-circle of cushions faces the front wall made of glass, opening like an eye onto the Isle of Iona and the vast stretch of ocean beyond. I settle on a cushion and sit gazing across the landscape, feeling inner boundaries ease in response to the open sweep of space and light and water before me.

Sunlight dances in patterns, like a kaleidoscope of shattered mirror, the water reflecting the brilliance of sun above. I am raw and small sitting upon my pillow, surveying expanses of space and time that challenge my dreams of self-importance. What do dates and degrees and struggles mean against such a large backdrop?

I close my eyes, entering the deep silence of unbounded space, relaxing into places of my Self that have been cramped within walls of human construction. When I leave the world of human shaping, I no longer have the padding against space and time and the raw power of the Earth that comes with living in enclosed structures. I enter a world much larger, more subtle and infinitely more powerful.

When I open my eyes at the end of the meditation, the horizon already has changed. The eastern sky, piercing blue at noon, is now wrapped with a front of clouds that is moving steadily over the eastern peaks of Mull. The wind is rising, buffeting the eastern wall and whistling around the corner of the Sanctuary. I walk down the path to the gate, wind tugging at my hair, and into Cottage No. 8 where lunch is being served.

The kitchen and dining room floors are being painted, so the sitting room becomes the temporary dining room with two long tables stretched along the front. Bowls of buttered potatoes and an urn of broccoli soup steam on the table. Cabbage and carrot salad, fresh from the garden, stands alongside freshly baked bread. I slide into a chair beside Renate as she ladles a bowl of soup from the urn. "You vant some?" she asks.

"Please."

Linda, a member of the Erraid community, chuckles. "Renate was going to fast when she came, but she took one look at the food at Saturday lunch when she arrived and never talked about fasting again."

"It's too good," says Renate, mouth filled with freshly cut bread. "I can fast some other time when the food isn't so good."

"You'll *have* to, to make up for the amount you ate last week," jokes Ivy, giggling as she reaches for the potatoes.

"Hey, Ivy, don't *you* eat too much or you won't have room for cake when your friends come," warns Chris.

"Is it your birthday?" asks Patrick.

Holly, Ivy's twin brother, jabs a finger into her side. Ivy shrieks and wriggles with laughter. "It was *both* our birthdays on Thursday, but we decided to wait until today to have a party so everyone could come over."

"Yep, the house will be full of noisy kids this afternoon," says John matter-of-factly. He cups his chin on his hand, calloused and stained by work with the boats and fishing nets and axe, and surveys the kids as they begin a tickling fight. "Probably best to go out for a walk this afternoon," he says nodding towards Renate and me, the only guests on the island.

Through snatches of conversation I form basic sketches of everyone's lives. Linda, shoulder-length brown hair neatly tucked behind her ears, eyes calm in her fine-featured face, was an artist and teacher before she arrived on Erraid. Since then she has revived the work with crafts on Erraid to provide some income for the group. Having focalised the huge vegetable garden for three years, she now works with spinning and weaving wool, most of which comes from the sheep that the Dutch family keeps on the island.

Chris lived with her former husband on the Isle of Mull, not far from Erraid, working an organic farm. They separated when the children were small, and Chris came with the kids to visit Erraid. They never left. After a couple of years John, an English solicitor with a passion for boats and sailing, arrived, fell in love with Chris and became a father to the three children.

"I got my family ready-made," he says, glancing out the window. "I didn't have the bother of the birthing and infant stage."

I laugh, thinking he is joking.

"I mean it," he says, eyebrows cocked above his stern, bearded face. John talks and acts and lives straight, with no energy wasted on idle words.

Dick speaks only occasionally throughout the meal. His strokes his soft brown beard and asks in his Dutch accent (he sounds like he's swallowing marbles) for bread or another helping of soup. I sense that our house, too, will be quiet.

In the afternoon I begin my explorations of the island, walking up the track behind the Sanctuary, past the ruins of an old croft, and up to a round building perched on the crest of a hill—the observatory. As I lean against the rusting structure, protected from the wind, I contemplate the lives of the people who first settled this island. Dick told me that the cottages were built for the families of the lighthouse keepers who took turns tending the lamps of far-flung lighthouses among the islands, living alone for a week at a time on a rock among the waves before returning to their families on this island. Robert Louis Stevenson was among the children raised here. His early experiences and fantasies spun while wandering the island became the inspiration for the book *Kidnapped*.

Erraid has not changed much since those days. Cows and chickens still sigh and cluck in the barns, smoke still curls from the chimneys, vegetables arrive fresh from the garden along with fish from the sea. Sheep bleat among the hills and seals lounge on the rocks on the western shore. As in the mid-1800s, no cars whine upon the island. Only the hum of electricity along wires stretched from Mull betrays the century. The simple introduction of electricity has altered the way of life here. The long winter evenings, once defied by candle and lantern, are now held back by the blaze of electric lights. And slowly the gadgets of civilisation have made their way to the island—the hoover, the blender, the refrigerator, the washing machine. Electricity transformed the world within the walls of stone, the realm of daily tasks once dominated by woman. But the padding it provided against the harshness of the elements was thin—except in the case of darkness.

Electricity also replaced the fires of the lighthouses, once tended by solitary men, with electric lamps that made their labours obsolete. The families left the island and the shells of their cottages weathered for decades until the property was bought by the present Dutch owners.

I move from the observatory, leaving behind the firmness of the track. The hills are tangled with winter-green heather accented only by the dry, brown fronds of bracken fern. I pick my way through the woody shin-deep vegetation along narrow paths forged by sheep. I walk among the hills, ambling down gentle slopes to the sea (where my boot sticks in an unseen bog while my stockinged foot carries on) and scrambling up narrow, almost vertical ravines. My eyes focused on the highest point, I climb to a high plateau marked by a pile of stones and view the silhouette of mountains on the hazy south-eastern horizon, the unbroken stretch of ocean to the south, Iona to the west and Mull to the north and east.

My breath hangs heavy in the late afternoon chill. My body has grown soft with weeks of indoor living and plentiful food. As I slosh towards the row of cottages that I know lies beneath a distant ridge, I realise that at Cluny Hill several days can pass without my venturing beyond the doorstep. The water arrives in pipes from an unnamed source, electricity flows from a distant hydroelectric plant, the water is hot, the food is served—I am freed from the details of daily maintenance for 'greater things'. But why are those details necessarily burdens? They root me in place and simultaneously expand my awareness of a larger whole. I know what the weather is doing, even without a radio report. I know it when I push open the front door to wheel the barrow to the pier to collect a load of firewood.

Here, on an island on the edge of a larger island ('Erraid' is Gaelic for 'the bit at the end'—it's really a tidal island to the Isle of Mull) on the coast of the British Isles, the practice of weather watching has been perfected to an art. People talk about the weather because it has *meaning* here. It changes quickly, passionately, in a land dominated by its relationship with the sea. Unlike a large land mass that subdues and paces the movement of clouds above it, a sea-dominated landscape is unpredictable. Clouds can form from the vast belly of the sea and race across the ocean with no barrier to curb their flight. On an island, wind and water overshadow the balancing, calming quality of land.

As I move down the hill, the salt air is tinged with the scent of human dwellings and wood smoke. I descend slowly, both reluctant and relieved to rejoin the indoor world.

* * *

Through the week the temperature drops until first the grass and then the soil and finally even the edges of the sea are frozen. The supply of running water, connected from a tank to the cottages by a series of shallowly buried plastic pipes, halts when the pipes harden in the frozen soil. Any water needed for cooking or drinking comes from rain water cisterns next to the back door of each cottage. Showers, previously rationed according to the amount of hot water available in the back boiler of our woodburning stove in Cottage No. 2, are now non-existent. I wear my long underwear to bed, crawl inside my sleeping bag, and then bury myself under feather coverlets. Just before sleeping I allow myself the luxury of turning on the electric bar heater which takes the edge off the cold air of the unheated bedroom.

One morning I turn on the heater to warm the room before getting up and then roll over to snooze. After a few minutes I notice a raw sensation in my throat. Yawn, stretch, open eyes—the room is filled with thick blue-grey smoke. I catapult out of bed and discover the feather comforter smouldering on the electric heater. It must have slid off the bed and onto the heater when I rolled over. Thank Goddess I did not sleep soundly when I turned over.

Embarrassed and apologetic, I join the morning meeting at 9 a.m. Everyone gathers on a circle of chairs and threadbare sofas in the sitting room cum temporary dining room. Each member announces his or her intended work for the day and how many people they need to help with the project. After a few cloudy days the sun is brilliant, so I offer to help Chris with digging Jerusalem artichokes in the afternoon, but for the morning I will be mending the quilt with scraps of fabric. I learn later that the members decide to take the electric heaters out of the bedrooms as a safety precaution—with some accompanying grumbles, as the heaters were one small source of comfort on icy winter nights.

After lunch Chris leads me to a long bed of Jerusalem artichokes next to one of the walls of the gardens, explaining that she wants to put something else in this row, and it has to be carefully cleared. Jerusalem artichokes are persistent; any remnants of the bulbous tubers sprout in the spring. Dressed in borrowed rain pants and slicker to protect me from the wind, wool-stockinged feet crammed into Wellington boots, and hands protected by holey leather gloves, I begin digging with the flat garden fork. Every few minutes I pause, straighten my back and gaze across the sea, the mountains, the Isle of Iona, absorbing the stillness of the winter islands bereft of tourists and pilgrims bound for the rebuilt ruins of the Abbey on Iona. How could anyone tire of this place?

The meeting of the elements here evokes feelings so ancient they nearly escape my conscious detection. The act of digging, of bringing up roots from the earth that I know will be cooked and then consumed to become part of my body, becomes a deeply satisfying act of union with the life cycle of the planet. I am not alone, disengaged from the wheel of life. Instead I grasp a spoke of the circling universe, this fork that kneads the Earth, and revolve through the mysteries of life. Here within the confined wall of the Garden, the full song of Creation is sung.

5 p.m. My fingers are white with cold under the holes in the gloves. The sky is darkening to pink. The sun shoots flames of warm red across the rim of clouds to the west. In the garden shed I brush the dirt from the fork, rub it with a dry cloth, and then wipe the prongs with an oil-soaked rag. The tools hang or rest neatly against the walls, blades shining, wooden handles well oiled, each carefully placed in its proper spot. Even the brushes to clean the tools have their own wooden box.

I join Janet in the kitchen where she is gathering buckets to milk the cows and food scraps to feed the chickens. We carry pails and buckets down the track towards the pier, stopping at the barn door to call the cows. They slog reluctantly across the muddy barnyard, torn between the desire for food and the freedom of roaming the island. The chickens are much quieter than the ones at the Bear Tribe, and less prone to whacking outstretched hands. Janet coos and talks quietly, stroking the hens as she moves the grain and water troughs and empties the food scraps for them to eat.

Janet waits patiently while I draw milk from Mouska's teats. With equal patience she answers my questions about her life before she arrived on Erraid. Her brown eyes, large and round like Mouska's, soften as she tells of her work as an artist and her unplanned stay of several years working in a healing centre. Originally she came to Erraid to teach the members how to make stained glass and to help establish a studio to generate another craft business. Erraid depends for its income upon crafts—primarily candlemaking plus weaving and stained glass—and guest fees. Most of its food is supplied by the land and the sea. Although the community of Erraid does not preach self-sufficiency or living closely with the land, in a matter-of-fact way they live these principles and fulfil them more successfully than the Bear Tribe does, with all of its workshops and books and lectures.

Looking around the barn, I am aware of neatness and the respect for 'objects' that permeates the community. I learn that 'roughing it' does not mean slovenliness, but rather a heightened awareness and appreciation for the implements that make life easier. So different from the Bear Tribe where tools were thrown in a shed still caked with mud or left to rust in the rain. Perhaps I exaggerate in memory, but I certainly did not experience the tidiness that I have come to respect here.

The Bear Tribe, though, lives on a piece of land that is still mostly wild, unworked by humans. The land, as well as the people, exudes a brashness, a freshness that I have never experienced in Britain. The land here feels older, somehow deeper. I notice a difference here, too, in the way people act and relate with one another, a difference that seems to be nurtured by the environment. The Bear Tribe is still struggling through its adolescence, young and fresh like the land. Here the people are older, generally more mature, or perhaps *subdued* is the correct word, tamed and controlled like the land cultivated for countless generations.

We return to Cottage No. 8, climbing along the track with full pail of milk and basket of eggs. The moon is rising in the east, casting a silver path across the inlet, illuminating the row of cottages in ghostly whiteness. We stop to lean against the gate, quiet as we wonder at the familiar view metamorphosed by moonlight.

Dinner. Shepherd's pie and steamed kale. I eat beyond pleasantly full, absorbed in listening to conversations and somehow feeling that I need to continue eating to justify my presence at the table. Rationally I know this is not true. Looking around the table tonight I feel the strength and maturity of the group. I am humbled in this community, feeling young and shy and quiet.

Disgusted with myself for having eaten so much and also eager to walk under the full moon, I swing through the gate and head up the track towards the observatory.

The wind is calm and the rush of waves against the shore is smoothed by the swollen tides of full moon. I stop often to listen to the silence. Yes, I can *hear* something in the absence of sound, a vibration, a hum in my inner ear that is sweet and harmonious and unexpectedly rich. I sit on a boulder just beyond the observatory, noting the speckle of electric lights glowing from the cottages scattered over Iona and even more widely dispersed on Mull. The churning of my mind during the day—self-analysis, thoughts of Alan, endless comparisons of this and that—stands suspended, lingering on the edges of the silvered stillness of this night.

The cold finally seeps through the layers of clothing, and I reluctantly retrace my steps, once again pausing to lean against the gate, noting the change in the angle of the moonlight pouring across the sea. Cottage 2 is dark and quiet when I return. Renate has moved to Iona this week and Dick is out visiting elsewhere. I throw a log in the stove and then settle into a chair, resuming my embroidery work on a shirt for Alan. Although I think of him often, I do not miss him. I sense our love will remain whether or not we are together when he returns from India.

I am sharply aware of how a shepherd must feel in mid-winter, alone with the wind howling outside. I can understand also coming to love such solitude fiercely and begrudging anything that disturbed it.

* * *

I awake to another sunny morning and decide to continue working in the artichoke bed. Blue sky, hazy horizon, bright sun. The air is cold, but my body warms with the movement of working with the soil. Today I dig in compost, giving life to the Earth in a gentle way.

Instead of eating lunch I walk across the island, the usual boggy bits frozen and crackling beneath my boots. When I walk over the crest of a hill and spot the sweep of sand that marks Balfour Bay, I see a figure moving across the strand. I meet Linda on her way back and follow her barefoot tracks across the beach. In a nook among the rocks sheltered from the cutting wind, the sun warms my skin like midsummer. I peel off my shirt and enjoy the feeling of sunbathing in February on a North Atlantic beach while Italy is frosted with snow.

In contrast to a morning of nurturing the Earth, I have chosen to spend the afternoon slaughtering chickens. As I walk, I think about ways in which I am giving away in my life and how I would feel about being slaughtered for someone's food. In dreams, each time I come close to death, I am afraid to take the final step. I am horrified by thoughts of my own death. My belief is that I will return to this Earth, but I am not eager to repeat the work of growing up again.

Mick, a long-term visitor preparing to become a member of the Erraid community, is already down at the barn. When I arrive he is holding by its legs a decapitated chicken still flapping its wings. He looks pale and slightly greenish, his mouth hard and his lip bent down to hold his emotions.

"How are you doing?" I ask, noting the spatter of blood on his slicker and pants.

"It's not easy killing my girls," he says, wiping his nose on the sleeve of his free hand.

I nod. "What can I do?"

"You can hold their legs until they quit flapping. The first one," he says with controlled calmness, staring blankly at the horizon, "got away from me and ran down to the pier and jumped into the sea."

I have a clear image of the headless bird catapulting away from the scene of its own death, and I laugh aloud.

Mick eyes me morosely. "I do not find it humorous," he says, cocking an eye-brow at me.

He hands me the still-gyrating chicken, and I stifle a smile. Standing quietly I offer prayers of thanks for these birds and the gift of their bodies for our food. Calmness spreads through me. I am a midwife for their journey out of this world, quietly celebrating the round of death that precedes rebirth in a new form.

When the bodies lie quiet, we take them to the coatroom on the side of No. 8. John and Jonathon, another member on Erraid who focalises the candlemaking studio, join us with stools and black plastic bags. We set to work plucking feathers, telling jokes and drinking tea. John tells me I'm the only guest who has ever helped slaughter the chickens, and Mick glances at me, puckering his forehead as if to say "Yes, she's a queer duck, all right," playing at sarcasm —perhaps. With Mick I have a hard time separating teasing from disdain.

In the evening I pack my things. Tomorrow I go to Iona to stay for five days in Traigh Bhan, a retreat house maintained by the Findhorn Foundation since the early 70s. Renate will return to Erraid the day after tomorrow, leaving me alone in Traigh Bhan for three days.

In the morning a strong wind blusters, fierce enough to make the short crossing from here to the mainland risky. So many activities here, even the simple coming and going to and from the island, depend upon the mood of the tides, the winds and the weather. The howling wind blusters down the chimney and seeps into unseen cracks. It buffets me off balance as I walk with full pack down to the pier where John is untying one of the boats from its mooring. Each weekday morning he ferries the children across the channel. The postman meets them on the far shore and drives the kids along his route to the village of Bunessan where they attend school with around thirty other children from the southwest of Mull. The waves were so rough yesterday morning that John chose not to make the crossing, but this morning he decides the sea is calmer. Still, the journey is rough. Waves break over the bow of the ten-foot dinghy and hammer against its sides. Sky and Holly and Ivy sit like fluorescent orange rocks, sealed in their rubber rain gear. They are accustomed to the fickle moods of the sea.

When the boat reaches the far shore, the children jump out and run along the slippery stones. I follow more slowly, ungainly with the added weight of my pack. I ride with the children in the post van to the town of Fionnphort where they leave me to wait for the ferry to Iona.

This boat is much larger than the rowboat 'ferry' from Erraid, big enough to carry a half dozen cars—easily 10% of all the cars on Iona. With 100 residents and one main street, cars are not in great demand on this island.

The street stretches north and south from the ferry landing. To the south is the only grocery store on the island. I stop to buy a pint of milk but find the door locked—lunch hour. The variety shop across the street is open, though, and I stop to chat with the shopkeeper, commenting on how quiet the island is.

"Aye, most tourists come in the summer, not the winter," she says, nodding. "Too cold for them."

I nod as I pull my wool hat over my ears and head north along the narrow bitumen road. The map I looked at in the variety store says this is the 'Avenue of the Kings', used for generations to transport the deceased Kings of Scotland to the graveyard outside the Abbey. The road winds around the ruins of the nunnery destroyed by the order of Henry VIII. I pause underneath one of the southern windows noting the carving on the lintel—Sheila Nagig, the Celtic Goddess of Life and Death, spreading her vulva for all to admire the source of Life and Fertility.

The nuns, I decide, were not limpid, weeping figures as the Virgin Mary has become in the hands of the Catholic Church. These women, at least some of them, actually chose to live among sisters as a positive alternative to the demands of being a medieval 'wifman'—old English for 'wife or *appendage* of man'. True, the noblemen were expected to sacrifice one daughter as a 'bride of Christ' to the Church. But standing under this window I sense that this nunnery, the only woman-dominated realm in a patriarchal, medieval world, echoed with laughter and bloomed with herbs, flowers and a quiet regard for the strength of woman.

Although the nunnery stands in partially restored ruins, the Abbey, domain of the monks, has been fully and gloriously restored, revived for a new type of Christian community living within its centuries-old walls. The winter winds howl through the churchyard, whistling through the Celtic lattice work in the 20-foot-high crosses. The taut wires of the fences lining the track hum in eerie half-tone harmonies. The road winds among farmhouses spaced farther and farther apart until it reaches the tip of the island. At the top of the last rise I turn to the east, walking along the fence line of a farmyard. Nearly at the edge of the sea stands Traigh Bhan, its upper windows like unblinking eyes gazing across the sea to the shores of Mull.

Renate is in the kitchen, poking at the remnants of yesterday's fire. The house is cold, the air chill enough to crystallise our breath into clouds as we speak. I am living my imagined Scottish horror—no escape from the winter cold, not even inside the house, because of the lack of fireplaces and fuel and the high cost of electricity.

Somehow, though, the imagined panic never materialises. To be alone, or almost alone, for Renate soon leaves for a walk across the frozen island, is a welcome luxury after months of community living. I realise suddenly that I have not been alone for more than a few hours since my Vision Quest last August. I am hungry for this kind of contemplative space. Having scattered myself all over the globe in the last year, I have no desire to rouse myself to go to Ireland or Germany or even a warm, exotic place (easily spoken with my legs slowly roasting before an electric fire).

My days are filled with walks across the rocky hills of the island and long meditations in the Sanctuary at Traigh Bhan. The intense cold continues, freezing the edges of the sea and the small rock pools along the coast. The cold bites more deeply, too, because I fast for the three days that I am alone in the house.

I establish a rhythm of awaking at sunrise, climbing the stairs to the Sanctuary, and watching the orange glow of the sun spread over the mountains of Mull and onto the sea. After an hour in Sanctuary, I pull on coat and Wellies and walk along the 'White Strand of the Monks' in front of the house. The fresh air and brilliant light intensify the outline of each surface. I find myself drawn into the realm of beauty hidden in tiny forms.

I discover spiralling shells among the rocks on the north side of the island. The spiral, so precisely formed, is the movement of life itself, spreading in ever-widening circles. The beauty of the shell is obvious—why don't I see the same perfection amongst the larger patterns of life on this planet, within my own life as well? Perhaps I stand too close to life to see the intricate, overall design. My vision is blurred by the immensity of force right in front of me.

I am calmed and inspired and strengthened by the great play of rhythms around me. They are more than sound patterns—there is rhythm in the bird tracks, in the shape of the fissured rocks, in the movement of the waves and foam surging and then receding on the shore. The sun and the moon cycle rhythmically. All pulse joyously to their own beat, yet they make one great whole, a symphony of *patterns* .

My meditations deepen through the days as my mind quiets. In Sanctuary I ask why I am at the Findhorn Foundation, what lessons I am to learn in this place. The answer is simple and direct: to connect with myself, to learn how to live and work with other people, and to deepen my link with the Earth and indirectly with my inner self. As I prepare to leave the island, I am reaching some sort of inner completion as well, experiencing a deep purging. Does that mean letting go of Alan, my parents, the past, future plans? I only know that I can feel the molecules shifting, somehow completing an old form and preparing for the new.

The greatest gift that I have received by living here these few days is a rediscovery of my independence, my inward strength. Ultimately I can stand alone, and simultaneously I can merge with the world. I find my love for the Earth will fill me, my inner spirit, no matter who comes in or out of my life. I am almost afraid to write this, dreading that the declaration may draw a testing to me, the loss of everything that I hold dear. But I am only finding wholeness, not negating my connections with the world.

I am ambivalent about returning to Cluny Hill. I look forward to connecting with friends and returning to Alan's room, but I dread the uproar of renovations in the Cluny Kitchen, the effort of commuting to the Park to eat, and the stifling indoor work of typing all day. These last two weeks have reconfirmed my desire to work with the Earth. I decide to initiate the transition from working with the Game of Transformation to the Cluny Garden.

On Saturday morning, after a final flurry of packing, I meet the Findhorn bus in Fionnphort. During the long ride, I ponder thoughts from the morning meditation. 'Celebrate the talents of other people. Realise that these gifts do not detract from your own but rather strengthen the whole. Celebrate, moreover *appreciate,* the gifts in others. This appreciation will help you to work in unity.'

This ability to appreciate others without need to compare them with myself reminds me of Paul Solomon's statement, "God is a being who can recognise good without a point of reference." For too long I have used other people's abilities as my reference point. Gradually I am learning that I can do things that are not on a 'professional' level and still bring joy to other people and myself. During the autumn I was reluctant to use my camera because Alan is such a good photographer. In the last two weeks I have begun to photograph again and appreciate how much more artistically I view the world with camera in hand, seeing so many patterns and colours that I would otherwise overlook.

The meditation emphasised giving as well. 'Share all that you can. The journey is the destination. Don't put off living, don't delay doing and giving because you think your destiny or purpose in life is somehow in the future. The moment for making a life is *now*—live well on the journey, for it will continue forever. You will *never* reach a final resting point. Quit looking for an answer in the future and live in the *now*. Always.'

For so many years I have prayed desperately for a purpose—which in this moment I realise was a desire to know my destination. And without a destination, what is purpose? Simply an orientation to life, to living fully and deeply and well in this moment? Could the answer to my quest be so evasively, eloquently simple?

Early evening. The bus rolls into Cluny Hill, and friends greet me with hugs. After depositing my backpack in Alan's room, I make some herb tea in the still-room and then wander into the front hallway to read the noticeboard.

'EarthLove' catches my eye. The word and the triskelion design spark my interest. 'A board game to explore your relationship with the Kingdoms of Nature and to experience Oneness. Introduction TONIGHT, Cluny Lounge, 8 p.m.'

The clock says 7:50. I amble into the lounge and join the circle of chairs arranged in front of the fireplace.

The game's creator, Phoebe Reeve, explains its principles and history. The workshop evolved out of her experience of living at the Foundation for four years, working in the garden at Marcassie (no longer a part of the community) that was run strictly through attunement. Phoebe leads a meditation with 'Allies' which she describes as the essences of the beings of the Earth. In the meditation we actually *become* the plant or animal or environment depicted on the card. I choose the Elephant and revel in the quiet, massive strength of this creature as I move within it.

Over the next three weeks I play the EarthLove boardgame several times. The mechanics are similar to those of the Game of Transformation, but the purpose is vastly different. The EarthLove game serves as a mirror in which people can explore their relationship with the different kingdoms of life—mineral, plant, animal, human and Oneness. Instead of focusing solely on personal issues, EarthLove highlights the interaction *between* the players as well, reflecting the planetary nature of the game. Deeply moved by the power of the workshop, I offer to help Phoebe in any way that I can, either here or in the United States.

By the end of the week after my return from Iona, I notice that in Alan's absence a lot of the energy that went into our relationship is now dispersed into the community as a whole. The time without him is actually an important evaluation period. I have a stubborn independent streak that says "I'll be damned if I stay anywhere for a man." I want to be sure that I'm here because this is where I need to be, not because I'm in love with someone.

On Thursday evenings I join Onda, a delicate, softspoken German woman, making tofu in the kitchen. For years Alan has been the constant in a stream of people who volunteer to make tofu, and I take his place during his holiday in India. We work among the steaming vats, pressing the liquid from the soya beans, and then curdling the hot milk. One evening everything seems to take longer than usual. The clock reaches midnight before we begin to ladle the curds into the wooden pressing boxes. David Earl pokes his head in the kitchen door, up late to complete his rounds as 'night porter'. This job, shared on a weekly rota, includes checking that the doors are locked, the lights turned off and the back hallways mopped. "You're up late," he comments.

"Yeah," I say, pushing a strand of hair from my steam-moistened face, "we're a bit slow tonight. The milk took a long time coming up to temperature."

"Well," he says, in a mock-fatherly tone, "make sure you don't get to bed too late or you'll be tired for work in the morning." He turns to leave, and then changes his mind. "And besides, you're not getting *paid*, you're an *LCG*. You don't *have* to work so hard."

David Earl is the LCG focaliser, so he's intimately aware of the issues we long-term guests face. I laugh with him, and jibe in return, "And what do they pay you for pushing a mop around? £10.00 a week? Besides, I don't care what they call me; I feel like a member, so I don't mind doing extra work."

"Well, sleep well. Hope you finish soon."

Although the statement about feeling like a member was a bit off-hand, I realise that I *do* feel fully involved in the community. After the initial months of adjustment, I even begin to consider organising events. During tea break the following morning I talk with Robin, a member living at Cluny Hill, about creating a celebration for International Women's Day. Our brainstorming overflows into ideas about beginning a women's group here to *do* things, not just talk and 'process' issues —we have enough of that in the rest of our lives. I miss the strong community of aware, alive women who were a vital part of my life at Oberlin and am painfully conscious of the general lack of awareness about women's issues at the Foundation.

97

Where awareness exists in the community, it is stifled or left unspoken, or worst of all it becomes a stigma used to label and then quickly dismiss someone's observation as their 'personal stuff'. This morning, though, I hear in another woman the desire to connect as sisters, simply to enjoy the company of women.

Moments later Phoebe joins me. During our conversation Phoebe offers to have me live with her in Washington, DC this summer to train as a 'Game Deva'. Her generosity surprises me—although I feel a strong sense of kinship with her, we have spent little time together, so the offer is unexpected. "Let's see how things go," I say, wanting to give her space to change her mind. "We can decide before you leave."

This morning two important parts of my life—relationship with the Earth and with women—have come together in one sitting. I giggle internally, appreciating the way the universe streamlines its messages. On Iona I heard that my purpose was to explore my connection with the Earth, and thereby indirectly with my Self. Sure that this meant working in the garden, I find myself presented with another scenario, one that was beyond my ability to plan—to guide the EarthLove Game, a vehicle to help humans explore their relationship with the Earth.

Organising the International Women's Day celebration is a challenge—so many details to arrange, a host of other small but important duties to oversee. I also learn that nothing moves in this community unless intentions are very clear. Robin and I decide to encourage people to dress as their favourite woman character for the special dinner on March 8th. When a member named Carol reads the sign announcing the event, she is enraged, not wanting men to show up in 'drag'. The possibility of men dressing up as women hadn't entered my mind. I stand quietly as Carol rages at me in the hall. Upset by her reaction, we have a quick discussion and decide to take down the signs and reword them, editing the bit about dressing up.

Somehow, though, I am still in touch with that unshakable centre that I discovered on Iona. That central core is quiet enough to act as a mirror that reflects other people's behaviour, and they often stop in mid-sentence, embarrassed by the clarity of their own reflection. Carol returns a few hours later to apologise, realising that she over-reacted.

Sunday night my inner equilibrium tilts once again, when I argue with David Earl about changing work departments. After the fiasco in early December—waiting for the interim LCG focaliser to arrange my move from the Kitchen to the Game work department—I decided to facilitate the transition from the Game department to the Garden myself and inform David Earl afterwards. I patiently explain why I took the actions I did, drawing on my past experience and the lessons I learned from it.

"Well, you learned the wrong lesson," yells David Earl. His vehemence surprises me—we have been friends for the last few months, often joking and teasing one another. He holds his line, and I hold mine. Neither one of us blames or accuses, we simply continue to restate our positions—passionately—and finally end at an uneasy draw. Although my sense of centre is jarred, I do not lose it.

The next day when I see David Earl, he gives me a hug and appreciates me for our clear communication. I appreciate him, too, because we were able to disagree without making each other wrong. And our friendship wasn't lost in the process, either.

March 8th, International Women's Day. The sherry hour from 5-6 p.m. and the dinner following are a success judging by the applause after dinner is served. Soon after the dishes are cleared we head for the Universal Hall in the caravan park where Del Calcroft, an LCG for the last four months, is giving a one-woman sharing, an outpouring of her creativity and her special brand of humour.

Her arrival at the Foundation is a classic 'my life was changed completely' story. A native of Australia in her late forties, she had never heard of the community until she travelled in Britain. Within a month of hearing the name she was on the doorstep, enrolled in the Experience Week programme. "Crikey, I'd never heard of past lives or spirit guides or 'metaphysical' before—it was all new to me."

While waiting for the first Experience Week session to begin, Del sat watching her travelling companion, a young artist, paint. Intrigued, Del asked to borrow some water colours and paper—her first attempt at painting. The result was stunning—the pine knoll on the rolling hill of the golf course was sensitively captured on paper.

Something uncorked in Del. During the following weeks she produced 'heaps' of paintings and poems. She laughed and joked and 'ear-bashed' the customers at the Phoenix Shop where she worked and increased the sales considerably. With her upfront Aussie outgoingness and lack of pretension, she won many people's hearts.

This evening's performance includes songs like 'They're Looney at Cluny' and sombre poems about her work as a midwife in Saudi Arabia. She recounts some of her visionary experiences and then welcomes a raucous chorus line of prancing men in pink tutus. We sigh and cry and laugh, celebrating the creativity of this woman. The performance has a bittersweet tinge to it: in addition to celebrating, we are preparing to say goodbye. Tomorrow she is leaving for the United States with only the barest outline of a plan. Knowing Del, though, she will adapt, armed with her resilient sense of humour and matter-of-fact acceptance of the challenges in her life.

Over the weekend I join Phoebe and four members in a preliminary training to guide the EarthLove game. As we play and discuss some of the moves, I gain an inkling of the amount of skill and wisdom needed to evoke the depths of this game. As part of my completion at the end of the weekend, I roll the die to see where I will land as an indication of my 'next steps'. I land on Planetary Transformation, symbolised by the Volcano. Just as the molten core of the Earth erupts to create new land, the space represents an experience of one person transforming so radically that everyone around is transformed as well. Their life orientation is forever altered.

During a break for dinner, I walk by the sea and stop to raise my arms, to offer myself to the Creator. Use me. Guide me in how to serve. I want to help the planet, and I offer my Self to be of use in any way. Guide and protect me as I let Your Will flow through me. The volcano is beginning to boil. The molten rock is swirling and twisting within me. I stand on the brink of the cone, waiting expectantly for the rush of liquid rock and the searing heat of change to overflow into my life. I am unsure of the timing but convinced of the inevitability of the eruption.

During the following week I have my first interview for membership with the guest department. Stan and David Earl and I talk for about an hour, exploring why I want to be a member in the community, my understanding of the Foundation's purpose, and my expectations for living here. After talking we attune to the Angel of Findhorn, visualising a column of white light that represents the community. When I visualise myself stepping into the light, I feel at home, clear that I belong in this place at this time. David Earl and Stan have similar images.

"Great," says David Earl. "I'll leave a note with Personnel to schedule an interview with them later this week."

The second interview also lasts about an hour. The questions are similar, though some are more pointed, especially from Roger. We have had long, heated debates while sitting in the sauna about life philosophies and some of my difficulties with the hierarchical language and concepts used within the community. During the hour both he and Maria help me to clarify my purpose in becoming a member of the

Foundation—to bring my awareness of the Earth into the community and to learn how to bring about change within myself and the community as a precursor to enacting change for the planet as a whole.

Again, the final decision rests on the outcome of the attunement. I see myself entering the column of light and am at ease with the movement. Roger and Maria also attune to the appropriateness of membership and report the impression that different potentials within me will be activated according to my focus during the time I am in the community.

I leave the room with a quiet sense of balance, relieved that the series of interviews is complete, but unsurprised by the outcome. The interviews are anti-climactic after my internal struggles—I have had over four months to ponder every angle both for and against the decision.

Because the Foundation has decided to close membership for a year, I must wait until November to begin Orientation, the programme that precedes membership. Along with about a dozen other LCGs, I am in an unnamed category. We are more than LCGs, having lived here longer than the usual one or two month stint, but less than members. In an effort to open spaces in the LCG programme, usually vacated as people move through the Orientation programme and into membership, Personnel asks that the people accepted for the autumn Orientation leave for a few months. The request melds perfectly with my plan to live with Phoebe for the summer, but I am still reluctant to leave the community.

After a brief trip to London to meet Alan on his return to India, I travel north to the Orkney Islands with Catherine, a friend from Oberlin studying in London this semester. During our journey I see in her the black/white differentiations and criticisms I acquired at Oberlin. Against the backdrop of our conversations, I recognise how I have been struggling to accept the shades of grey in between. The grey is part of the territory that comes with enacting my idealistic visions of how I think the world could or, in my passionate moments, *should* be. In my life the good and the bad blend, neither one obliterating the other. Instead they co-exist in amiable, lacklustre hues of grey.

A couple of days after my 23rd birthday I draw an Ally and an Angel card to guide me during the year. The Angel—Surrender. The gift I receive is an image of chains loosening around my wrists that are completely freed as spirit begins to flow through my arms. Surrender does not mean being chained, it means losing shackles so that I can become an effective channel for the Creator.

My Ally is the Butterfly, and when I move inside the form I experience the cocoon, cut off from outside stimulus. Contemplative. A space set apart to allow the transformation from larva to winged butterfly. I know that I cannot move from one stage to another without a time of isolation in between.

When I view the Angel and the Ally together, their connection strikes me—Surrender to the Butterfly, which I experience as Change. Certainly the last year has been filled with change—what more lies before me? I sense that this transition, like that of the butterfly, will be an internal one instead of the dramatic outer leaps of the past year.

When I return to the Findhorn Foundation at the end of March I am excited, even ecstatic. As I walk among the beeches and pines of Cluny Hill after my first days of work in the vegetable garden, I wonder how I could ever be anything but happy here. By the end of the week, though, *boom*, the roller coaster starts and I would rather be anywhere else in the world.

In the garden I work with Penny, the focaliser of the vegetable garden. This morning, a glorious sunny day with the first hints of summer warmth, I work in one

100

of the raised beds, digging cooked food into the soil. Since my arrival, I have been dismayed at the amount of cooked food that is dumped with the rest of the garbage. When I asked why the food was not composted, Penny told me that the cooked food had to decompose anaerobically (without oxygen) which means that it needs to be dug into the soil, and she didn't have time to do it. Eager to take on some responsibility in the garden, no matter how small, I offer to take care of this task. Penny agrees, so I invite Alan, who focalised the vegetable garden for four years, to show me his technique for digging in the food.

This morning Penny calls me over to the bed where she is planting parsnips. "Look," she says, "I realise I have been trying to share the power of creating the vegetable garden with you. I've really been struggling, though, because I've never worked in a garden before, and I really want this garden to be my own. I talked with Marion (the overall focaliser of the Cluny Garden) and she supports me in doing things in my own way."

I nod, listening quietly, waiting for the punchline.

"When I was growing up, I never had a room that was really my own. My mom always invited people to stay with us, and she would put them in my room, and I would have to sleep somewhere else. Just for once, I want to have something that is my own."

"Hmmmm . . . how can I support you?" I ask. Like a child expecting to be hit, I endure the long explanation. I can't imagine what I've done wrong—I haven't done anything without consulting her first.

"Well, I approach the garden in an emotional-intuitive way. I have to because I have no previous experience. I've been reading some gardening books, but I'm trying to rely more on attunement."

I nod, waiting.

"Your approach is intellectual, like wanting to dig in the cooked food because of some ideal you have about recycling and planet-sustainable agriculture and whatnot. I don't think politics belong in the garden. That doesn't fit in with my plans."

I sit dazed, wondering with whom I discussed the whole idea of digging in cooked food.

"This garden has had a lot of masculine energy put into it—Alan, and then Roger. I hear the garden crying out for a more feminine approach. I'm trying to dig as little as possible. I want the soil to have a chance to rest and recover after all of the male energy that has been put into it."

Sure that any attempts to explain my position would be interpreted as masculine intellectualisation, I don't even try. "So you're asking me to do whatever I'm told in the garden and not make any suggestions?"

"Basically yes, I want to make my own mistakes and learn by my own intuition."

During tea break I sit in the garden, struggling to regain my inner equilibrium. Hurt surfaces first—I feel unwelcome in the garden. My enthusiasm has been misinterpreted as manipulation. Anger follows—the frustration of being an LCG, working hard within the community without any clear-cut place to apply my own inspiration. I condemn myself for repeating the same scenario as in my work in the Game department. There I was helping to fulfil Joy's vision of the game-in-a-box. Here I am asked to carry out Penny's plans for the garden, whether I agree with them or not. My joy in being in the garden evaporates in the morning sun. The honeymoon with the garden is over.

I close my eyes to meditate, trying to still my emotions and find some understanding in this situation. My initial enthusiasm, I realise, has to be replaced by a love for the garden that transcends human bullshit. The garden is a place for humans as well as plants to grow, and I am willing to stay to participate in that cycle of growth.

I finish my work for the morning and make my way to the dining room for lunch. As I fill my plate, Marion, the over-all garden focaliser, plants herself next to me and begins to yell. She rages about how I should have brought the issue of saving cooked food to the whole garden group instead of just talking to the dining room focaliser about it. Then *she,* as garden focaliser, could talk with the dining room focaliser about saving cooked food. Any fabric of composure that I regained this morning shreds under her knife-like words.

Rather than endure a long tirade, I escape from the dining room and into the sunshine, sitting at the top of the stairway that leads down to the beech grove. I clasp my arms around my knees, bury my head in my lap, and sob. Why are things so difficult here? No one told me I had to go through some hierarchy just to dig in cooked food. Why are people so threatened by these simple actions? I must have done something terribly wrong to be verbally abused that way. Am I really too aggressive, too intellectual, too domineering in my approach to the garden?

I feel arms circling my shoulders. I lift my head to find David Earl sitting next to me. Gratefully I bury my head in his shoulder. He sits patiently, stroking my hair until the flow of tears diminishes.

"What's up?" he asks, clear blue eyes puzzled and concerned.

Between tearful gasps I recount my experiences of the morning and the encounter with Marion. David listens quietly.

"Marion's a very angry person, you know."

"Yeah, several people tried to warn me before I joined the garden, but I never had any problems with her before."

"It sounds like she dumped some of her own 'stuff' on you."

Slowly I gain some perspective on the situation. Always I am ready to accept the blame for someone else's anger. As we talk, though, I glimpse the pent-up hurt and frustration in Marion's life which triggered a reaction far out of proportion to the actual incident.

"Something I've learned with Psychosynthesis," offers David Earl as we focus on my feelings of hurt and rejection, "is that I am more than my emotions."

I pause, puzzled by the statement. Through the months of living at the Foundation I have struggled to come to know my emotions, to be able to describe them moment by moment. Without identifying with emotions, who would 'I' be? "What do you mean?" I ask.

"Your Self is greater than your emotions," he says in his carefully hybridised British-American accent. His eyes pierce into mine, adding weight to the words. "Try saying it—I am more than my emotions."

I repeat the words, but I'm still unconvinced. What is this 'I' that is more than my emotional reactions?

"You are also more than your mind or your physical body. Your emotions are not 'you', they are just reactions to the situation . . . . And you're doing a good job of riding the roller coaster here."

"Roller coaster?"

"You know, the ups and downs."

"You think I'm doing a 'good job'? I don't know; some days I'd rather be anywhere else than here. I wonder if I really want to be a member or not."

"I know how you feel. I have my days, too, when I'd like to pack up and go. But I'm still here, and so are you. You haven't jumped off."

"You question being here?" I ask, incredulous. Somehow I have assumed that all of the members know beyond doubt that they belong here and fulfil their stay without inner questioning.

"We all question from time to time. I try to take it one day at a time, and I've been here over eight years."

As the day continues, I gain some perspective. In the evening my roommate Annette, unaware of my traumatic day, reports that she had dinner with Penny and Marion. "I didn't recognise you from their description," she explains. She got a picture of a 'young upstart' who had not acknowledged their authority as focalisers. "Perhaps your strength threatens them somehow," suggests Annette. "Maybe that's why they feel you have invaded their territory."

"Perhaps," I reply absently, staring out the window into the evening clouds. I am willing to let go of some of my enthusiasm and try to be more contemplative in the garden, but I cannot accept that I have communicated incorrectly or that I have been trying to impose my will on the garden.

Before the garden group attunement on Friday, I talk briefly with Marion and share with her my distress about how she interacted with me earlier in the week. She listens and nods, her long thin arms crossed, resting on her willowy knees. I am relieved to have finally spoken directly with her about my reaction to her yelling, and we join the rest of the garden group in Sanctuary for our weekly meditation .

Afterwards we move into a room downstairs for business and then tea. During the sharing that follows, I recount my struggles through the week. Although I do not ask for suggestions or feedback when I finish, each one in the group offers her interpretation of why I was wrong in how I acted. I am stunned by the group's response and forget that according to the 'rules' of sharing they have no right to comment unless I ask for feedback. Having struggled to overcome my usual pattern of withdrawing when hurt or threatened, the 'attack' is doubly painful. "See," I tell myself, "it's better not to show your feelings than to be crucified for them."

Over the coming weeks I draw more and more inward in the garden group. I say little and volunteer few suggestions, taking on small responsibilities only when asked. The withdrawal is not without side effects, though. Over the next couple of months I am often sick in bed, stricken with sore throats and bronchitis, a personal sign that I am holding back words and suffocating myself. Finally, in desperation I go to Roger to talk through my difficulties.

"Why do you want to stay in the Cluny Garden?" asks Roger after listening to my grievances. "Why don't you move to Cullerne or some other garden?"

"I only have a month left before I go to the States," I say sighing, "and I'm not eager to go through changing work departments again. Besides, if I don't learn the lessons in the Cluny Garden, I'll just repeat them somewhere else."

"Right," agrees Roger, "you would learn the same lessons, but you *do* have the freedom to choose the *quality* of the lessons. They don't *have* to be painful."

A line from the *Book of Runes* flashes to mind. "Are you suffering over your suffering? The quality of the passage is up to you." I realise I have a choice—either to change my approach to the garden, emerging from my inner chrysalis, or to move to another work department in the community.

"I hate giving up on anything," I tell Roger. "I'm going to stick it out in the garden."

I draw an Angel card on Sunday night to help me in healing my relationship with the garden group. The Angel is Healing. I smile quietly; yes, welcome, I need all the help I can get.

The following week I take part in a week-long workshop on herbalism with David Hoffmann, author of *The Holistic Herbal* and a friend of the Foundation. The study renews my interest in natural medicine and my excitement about working with herbs in the garden, but the additional strain of attending classes precipitates another bout of bronchitis.

Trying to uncover the cause of the malaise, I delve into my frequent illnesses as a child, reliving the pain and frustration of those times. I consult the Runes which tell me that 'What is happening is timely in your process. If the well is clogged, this is the moment for cleaning out the old . . . Control of the emotions is at issue here. During times of transition, shifts in life course, and accelerated change, it is important not to collapse yourself into your emotions—the highs as well as the lows." I *know* that I discharge a lot of energy during my emotional upheavals, but to make these words part of my daily life is difficult.

Cleaning out the well . . . what needs to go? A lot of attitudes . . . like my conception of criticism. I have been preparing a concert of Baroque music with a young Austrian pianist and recorder player along with the organist at a local church. During the rehearsals my ego bruises easily; I have not yet learned to respond egolessly to criticism.

Barbara and I talk afterwards, something I never would have done while in the Conservatory. I admit my feelings of being looked down upon and my anger over being criticised.

"I look at it this way," says Barbara, smiling. "Either the person is right, and you should listen to the criticism *or* the person is ridiculous, totally off, and it's doubly silly for you to get angry over ridiculous criticism. Either way, there is no reason to get upset." Wise words, but again difficult to follow.

As I walk through the front hallway en route to my room, the phone rings. The telephone angel is with me—Phoebe is on the line. We finalise plans for my arrival in Washington, DC. I feel a rush of love for her and gratitude for having a purpose in returning to the US this summer. And something niggles, too, a feeling that the summer will be completely different from anything I can imagine.

A week before my departure date we give two chamber music concerts—one in the front room of Drumduan House and another in the local church. Afterwards the separation pains begin in earnest. Alan tells me that Patricia, the woman he fell in love with shortly before my arrival, wrote saying that she will return to the community a week after my departure. Oh, universe, your sense of timing is glorious. The bottom of my stomach disintegrates, and my heart clenches. I know that Alan, as always, will follow his heart, and I'm afraid that will mean falling deeply in love with Patricia while I am gone.

For two days I sink into a deep depression, knowing that I must release Alan and everything I love about the Findhorn Community. I have no idea if I will really come back here to live. Already my life plans have flip-flopped several times in the last year. Knowing how much I have changed in the last eight months, I cannot predict what the next four months will bring. I could be anywhere. Gulp. *Anywhere.*

The second night of my depression Alan dreams that I am dying, and no one else is around. He holds me, hugs me and cries. Through my death he gets in touch with feelings for me that he has kept hidden even from himself. The family stands around my coffin, throwing dirt and leaves into the hole.

Alan shouts, "But she's still alive!"

"Yes," they answer, "but she has surrendered."

Alan holds me as he recalls the dream, tears flowing again. I am touched and feel a lot of love for him. I wonder, though, why he seems to need a loss to access his deepest feelings.

America—what will you feel like? Now comes culture shock in reverse, returning to my native land. While in Britain I have learned that the America I love can never be seen on television or read about in the papers. America lives in the land, the people and my own experiences of living. Often I am embarrassed by American isolation and our collective ignorance of world situations. The country believes in the naive power of Uncle Sam, the image of Big Brother aiding the rest of the world. For a month after Ronald Reagan's re-election I told people that I was North American or Canadian, reluctant to associate myself with a population so engrossed with appearances and blatantly unconcerned about quality or substance.

Now, though, as I face returning to the US, I recall my deep love for the land and for the goodness of common people. Where else in the world could I meet a woman forty years my elder on a Greyhound bus, strike up a conversation about social justice, and start a correspondence that has lasted several years?

When I arrive in London, having taken the 13-hour overnight bus from Scotland, I call my friend in New York with whom I'll be staying. Before he can give me his work number where I can reach him when I arrive, the money runs out and the phone line buzzes mercilessly. Standing in a London phone box, surrounded by scrawled advertisements for prostitutes specialising in tying and fancy dress, I panic momentarily. Where can I stay when I arrive in New York? Whom else do I know?

I wander into one of the nearby parks, discard shoes and dig my toes into the spring-green grass. "Creator," I pray, "you'll have to help me with this one. I don't know what's next." As I sit relaxing under the tree, a thought comes to me. I will meet someone I know in London today. Who could that be? I can think of some people I would love to see and others I would rather avoid.

Moving through the streets of London I watch for familiar faces. Nothing. I scan the train carriage en route to the airport. No one. Still no sign of a familiar face as I pass through the maze of corridors and escalators to the concourse. The waiting room at the gate is overflowing with passengers. As I approach, I glimpse a shock of long, wavy dark hair—Sun Bear.

I smile and drop my bags in a chair next to him, circling him in a bear hug. We talk of his travels in Europe, the challenge of his gruelling schedule and the latest news about people at the Bear Tribe.

The boarding announcement blares on the PA system. We part with a quick hug. I spend most of the flight in meditation, inwardly calming myself and asking to be guided in what to do when I arrive in North America. I could try to book a flight to Dayton where my parents live, but I'm not sure if there are any this late in the evening. Or I could take the train north of New York City to where my sister lives, but I haven't been able to contact her on the phone—perhaps she is away.

When the plane lands, I unexpectedly burst into tears. Something moves deep inside me. After months of being a foreigner, I am at home, or at least as close to a home as I have ever known, where I intimately know the customs and unspoken expectations.

After waiting in line for a passport check, still intoning silent prayers for inspiration about what to do, I walk down the ramp to the baggage belt. Sun Bear is waiting for me at the bottom.

"Hello, dear," he says, patting my arm. "My flight out West is cancelled because the airline is on strike, so I have to stay overnight in an airport hotel. Do you need a place to stay?"

I stare for a moment, wondering if he heard my internal struggles on the plane. "Uh, well," I stutter, "yes, I do need a place to stay."

"Good. Let's get your bags and go."

Within 15 minutes we are en route to a hotel. The weariness of nearly 30 hours of travel and two nights without sleep overtakes me as I begin to relax.

"Thank you, Great Spirit," I murmur, looking out the window at the lines of street lamps stretching through the maze of airport exchanges. How appropriate that Sun Bear serves as a bridge for my re-entry to North America. This man and the tradition he embodies is a large part of that unnamable love that I have for this continent, and part of what I hold to be good and true among the human species that I often criticise for its behaviour upon the planet at this time. I am grateful for Sun Bear and other Keepers of the Bridges of communication and respect between cultures. They tread back and forth, not fully accepted by either side, weaving bonds across the gap with the fabric of their own bodies and lives and dedication.

CHAPTER 6
Kindergarten Years

The summer is more and less than I expected—more adventurous and affirming and less focused upon the details of the EarthLove game. For a month I backpack and visit friends in New England. In early July I arrive in Annandale, Virginia, a suburb of Washington, DC, to live with Phoebe and her parents. In addition to working with EarthLove, I help Phoebe with her work establishing a Findhorn Foundation resource centre for North America, and together we organise a national gathering for the end of August, designed to compress the contents of Experience Week into a weekend. For ex-members of the Foundation, we also plan a day-long reunion before the start of the gathering.

About a week before the event we get a call from a man who has just seen *My Dinner with André*, a film that includes a brief, mythologised reference to the community. Although the details were skewed, the film-maker had captured the essence of the place as one where the extraordinary is enacted by ordinary people.

"Well, I'd like to come to the gathering, but I don't know if I can," says the man on the phone.

"Why?" asks Phoebe.

"Well," he says, hesitating, "I smoke."

"So do I," says Phoebe.

"I drink," continues the man.

"Me, too."

"But I eat meat."

"So do I," replies Phoebe.

"And I'm gay."

"That's fine with me," says Phoebe matter-of-factly. "Anything else?"

"No," says the man slowly. "I guess there's no reason why . . . I can't . . . ah, well

. . . ." With every conceivable obstacle to a 'spiritual experience' dissolved, the man registers and arrives on schedule for the gathering.

Around eighty people attend the Findhorn Gathering at Massannetta Springs, a Methodist conference centre in central Virginia. Former members, short and long-term guests, and people who have only heard the name or read the community's books arrive. Even an Air Force family who lived in the village of Findhorn before being transferred to the US visit on reunion day.

During the three-day weekend we experience the Angel of Findhorn, the essence of the community, through our sharings and activities. In a Christian conference centre in the American Bible Belt, we create the spirit of community together. After the participants have packed their bags and returned to their lives across the US and Canada, we chat with the folks who run the centre as we pay the bills.

"You know," says one man, stroking his shaven chin with a work-worn hand, "we have a lot of groups come here that call themselves 'Christian'. Now, I know you don't call yourselves 'Christian', but you're the most Christian group we've ever had here."

Phoebe and I glance at each other, smiling quickly. 'The Christ', the spirit of tranformation and unconditional love, was obvious even to an outside observer, and a biased one at that.

After the gathering, people in the Washington DC area are hungry for more contact, so we arrange a potluck dinner and meditation a month later. Knowing the amount of energy that will be required to sustain the fledgling resource centre, I am torn between working with the spirit of the Findhorn Foundation here in North America and returning to the community in Scotland. I decide to retreat for a few days to an island off the coast of Maryland to make a decision.

For three days I wander the beaches or swelter in my orange tent, the only protection from the sun and ferocious biting flies. I record dreams, meditate and scry the stones and waves and star constellations for messages. Despite my efforts, I have no revelations.

On the last morning of my retreat, I awaken quickly, without any lingering dream state. Details are tumbling through my mind—everything that needs to be arranged for my journey to Scotland. The stream of information continues for a few minutes until I suddenly sit up, prop myself on a sandy elbow and smile quietly. Here is my 'answer', given without fanfare or great drama.

So I am going. Within three weeks I have returned to my parents' house in Ohio, packed and said goodbye to the community growing up around the resource centre. Phoebe and Lloyd, a faithful friend and support through the summer, accompany me to the airport. We talk of this and that and complete a few last-minute details of EarthLove business (I am by this time a certified 'Game Deva'). During the stretches of silence I sit in semi-shock, torn internally by the separation from so many people whom I have come to love.

As I stand in line to board the plane, a funny look crosses Phoebe's face. "What's up, Phoeb?" I ask.

She reaches down to the floor and picks up something from under her foot. "I don't know. I think it's for you," she says handing me a plastic housefly, so realistic that Lloyd raises a hand to swat it.

"A fly, to accompany me on my flight, right?" I say, laughing. "Here we go, manifesting again." Our summer has been filled with many such magical moments, and I am heartsick about going. The parting is as difficult as leaving a lover.

Alan meets me at the airport in London. My worries about Patricia were unfounded—within a week of arriving in the community she fell in love with one man and by the end of the summer she left to marry another. Alan and I spend a few days together in the city, enjoying our reunion. Once I have adjusted to the time difference, we travel north, stopping to visit Alan's parents along the way.

I have about one month between my return to the community and the beginning of the Orientation programme. During the first week I am a dispassionate observer, sharply aware of my impressions. I vow to maintain my links with the world beyond the community, the 'outside world' as people refer to it. I abhor this distinction of 'inside' and 'outside', finding it quite arrogant.

In an LCG meeting someone describes how ". . . no one understands me out there. I am so glad to have people here to talk to." I am exasperated. The world I know is *full* of conscious, loving people of all ages and races and nationalities. I have found them hiking in the Adirondacks, in bus stations, on planes, on the road hitch-hiking, in university classes, in other communities. The Findhorn Foundation certainly does not have a corner on the market of conscious, alive people.

My stance is based on the knowledge that a supportive, loving community can be created *anywhere*. Transformation and unconditional love can sprout and flourish in the most unlikely places; in fact, they seem to seek out and favour the forgotten cracks. My experience with the resource centre allowed me to *choose* whether or not I wanted to return to the community in Scotland—I know that the Angel of Findhorn is not constrained by geographical location. The Angel can be invoked anywhere.

For a week I work in a self-created 'odds and ends' department, filling in the cracks in various work areas still strained with the end-of-summer guest load. Usually the flow of guests diminishes after the October Conference. Only the hardy ones remain to endure the diminishing light and the Scottish winter wet.

For another three weeks I work in the Cluny kitchen. Despite my intentions to keep abreast of the events occurring in the wider world, my focus gradually telescopes to the immediate concerns of the community. Immersed once again in the daily flow of work and friends and meetings, I prepare for the beginning of the Orientation programme.

First weekend in November. I move to the Park into a caravan named 'Rainbow' nestled among birch trees and a small flower garden. When I arrive, Rachel, my room-mate, already has her books and clothes immaculately arranged. I toss my bags and boxes on the bed in a jumble, and turn to retrieve another load. I catch Rachel's eye—her eyebrow is raised at a half-concerned, half-amused angle. As I hurry to the car, I wonder if we will be like the 'Odd Couple', one meticulous, the other incorrigibly sloppy. I resolve to keep my half of the room as neat as possible.

I need not have worried. When all of the bags are inside, Rachel gives me a warm hug. After the flurry of unpacking, we settle into chairs on either side of the kitchen table, drinking tea and smoking Marlboros. The kitchen, about two-thirds the size of our bedroom, is just wide enough to skirt around the table, with another couple of feet of space near the sink and stove. Behind me is the door to another bedroom, half again as large as the one in the back, where David and Damien, also part of the Orientation programme, will live. The luxury of space, though, is offset by the location of the only bathroom in the caravan—in the back corner of their bedroom. Any time Rachel or I want to use the toilet, we have to walk through their bedroom.

Over the weeks this arrangement of chairs and teacups and elbows propped on the table becomes a point of friendship, a sharing of life stories and soul-searching exposés of the moment. David and Damien sometimes join us, adding the stories of their lives as well. The path of self-discovery, recently embarked upon in my life, is a well-worn track in Rachel's, over 20 years long. This difference, though, is no barrier to our friendship. I find in her a sister-spirit whom I love and admire deeply. With the amount of time we spend sitting at the table, gradually revealing our lives, I sometimes wonder if one day we will sit in silence, having exhausted our stock of stories and insights and carefully kept secrets. So far, we never have.

The Orientation programme is the most disorienting experience of my life in the community. For eight weeks we meet daily, the group of twenty orientees plus two focalisers who have volunteered to guide us through our passage into the core of the community. We meet every afternoon and a few evenings each week. We learn the history of the Foundation and its present structure and listen to presentations about group life. Once a week we have a sharing with various community members who tell us about their own experience of different aspects of community life. Both Eileen and Peter Caddy come to talk with us (Peter is visiting the community for about a month, his longest stay since he left in 1980). We also visit the different parts of the community, including the Isle of Erraid.

During the mornings we work in various work departments—just enough time to provide a sense of grounding in the daily life of the community, but not enough to overcome the intense self-involvement of the Orientation group. The traumas and joys and general drama of our group outstrip any other concerns.

I work with a woman named Jennifer in the Kindergarten of the newly established Steiner School within the community. The school plans to move out from under the protective umbrella of the Foundation and into independent status in the larger community of Forres and Morayshire within a few years, but for now it is staffed by members of the Foundation.

My first experience with the children is the daily challenge of gaining acceptance—loving the first trusting touch of a tiny hand within my own, enjoying the activities of painting and bread baking and storytelling. Even though I have worked with children before, I am nervous spending first an hour and later a whole morning alone with the children.

When Orientation ends just before Christmas, we endure a final round of interviews to attune to our decision to become members. In my attunement with Personnel, I see myself approaching the column of light. Initially, instead of stepping into the column, I spin away. I realise that the column is revolving like a merry-go-round, but I approached as if it were still. The second time I approach more cautiously and enter the light with ease. Maria has a similar image along with the information that she sees me swimming through mud and standing on water and walking through fire ". . . and you will be asked to do this because you have the strength to do it." I groan inwardly. I know that I have invoked a great lesson in deciding to become a member; I want to learn to bring about change within myself, the community and eventually the planet. But I am not eager for more difficult, painful lessons.

After the final attunement, I escape to Alan's room and begin to sob, shaken by the finality of the decision and the likelihood of a difficult time ahead. I don't know which would have been more painful, being accepted or being rejected. Later in the day, David Earl wraps his arm around me. "I know when I was accepted as a member, I went through a period of questioning. You know that saying, 'I don't know if I want to be part of a club that would accept me as a member'? That's how I felt."

The first traumas surface as illness. On Christmas Eve my throat is sore and my head feverish; within a couple of days it develops into a raging bout of bronchitis. I quit smoking, drink pots of herb tea and lie in bed, but the fever continues for quite a while. Desperate to discover the cause of the illness and release it, I use my inner vision to return to the site where I joined Eagle in my vision quest, hoping to regain strength and perspective through the journey.

Eagle and I fly over the lakes and mountains of eastern Washington state. At one point, I swoop down to a tree that I visited before with Eagle, where she pecked a hole in my head and fed the contents to four baby eagles who were nesting there. I had nearly forgotten this part of the vision, and remember now that Wabun suggested I spend some time talking with these babies to find out who they are and what they are about. As I sit on the branch, the mother Eagle once again pecks away the top of my head and feeds my brains to the baby eagles.

"Who are you, babies?" I ask.

"Wisdom." "Love." "Peace." "Justice."

"What do you have to tell me?"

"Know thyself," says the first baby.

"Love thyself," says the second.

"Be at peace with yourself," says the third.

"Be just with yourself," commands the fourth.

"What does 'being just' mean?" I ask, perplexed. Eternally I am full of questions.

"*Balance*. Right action. Always pursue right action within yourself."

Inspired by the words, I relax a bit. I wonder how much more I have to learn from that 'simple' revelation during my vision quest. The flight with Eagle was perhaps the most powerful point in my vision quest, yet at the time I almost overlooked it, expecting the power of vision to come through some complex revelation. I sense that the Eagle has much more to teach me in the years to come.

Eventually the cold passes, but other traumas take its place. The next upheaval comes with work department assignments. Although Jennifer needs help in the Kindergarten, Cluny Housecare is desperate for someone to work full-time and eventually take on focalising the department. For a few days I agonise over whether or not to work in Housecare. I vacillate back and forth and finally decide to work part-time in the Kindergarten and part-time in the Cluny Garden. I also ask for one shift each week to continue training the people who are interested in guiding the EarthLove game.

Personnel, though, feels I am too stretched between working part-time in the Kindergarten and part-time in Cluny Garden. They refuse to allow even one work shift (a morning or an afternoon) to be devoted to EarthLove work. I understand that they are trying to protect me from scattering myself too much as I first move into membership, but the refusal actually increases the pressure. I have to offer the EarthLove training on my own time.

Through the winter and into spring, I continue to work with the children, but each day I dread more and more the bus ride to the Park and the walk to the Kindergarten. These children unwittingly bring out every trauma from my own childhood. Through our interactions, I relive the most painful patterns of growing up. One day one of the boys pauses during snack time to point at each of us around the table. "I love you," he says, beginning with Jennifer. They both look adoringly at each other. "And sometimes I love you and sometimes I hate you," he says looking at me. "Right now I love you." And he continues around the table, "I love *you* and I love *you* and I love *you* . . . . "

I can't fool the children. He mirrors back to me exactly how I feel about him —sometimes I love him and sometimes I hate him. These children teach me so many lessons.

On one hand I hate setting limits for the children, but gradually I learn that the limits are not meant to squelch the children, but rather to provide clear boundaries of expectation. Once I have begun with sloppy boundaries, though, they are hard to recover. A couple of the kids re-enact one of the most painful scenarios of my childhood—creating silly names, initially not meant to hurt. The action, though, recalls my brother who *did* create names to hurt, to put me in my place when he felt mean or insecure. The children sense my reaction and pursue the game. For days and weeks. They begin it when I am at my weakest, when my tolerance is almost nil. I hate getting out of bed in the morning to go to school.

Gradually the long nights of winter shorten until they near the balance of day and night, the spring equinox, which also happens to be my birthday. I was born 16 minutes before the passing of winter into spring, so this solar holiday has special significance for me. And as the years go by, I notice that the gifts of this day, the really important ones, are less tangible and more powerful.

For weeks I have been agonising over what unconditional love really is. I struggle to find it in my relationship with Alan. He lies quietly next to me at night, telling me that he cannot force his heart to open. I lie still, quiet, sure that I will never know this love, this love without bounds, without conditions. It is reserved for the realm of saints.

But this day, oh, this day of birth, something uncorks inside me. After a meal in the Community Centre to celebrate the equinox, we move into the Universal Hall for a Sharing followed by a meditation. I have decided that for my birthday I want to give away something, to share a gift of myself with the community. So I arrange my slides according to the kingdoms of life and add music of the Earth and human instruments—the sea, river, frogs, loons, owls and wolves meld with saxophone and violin and tabla. As the images roll before my eyes, my heart begins to swell. These are the things of the Earth that I love. This is what I want to share, my gift to humans and back to the Earth; I want to share the gift of love for this planet.

Following the Sharing is a meditation that begins with Celtic harp music, performed by Judith Pintar, a friend of the community. As I sit with eyes closed in the darkened Hall, listening, the strings seem to pull something in my heart. In the silence that follows an inner door unhinges. My heart swells to the boundaries it has known and then beyond. I am cocooned in love. My thoughts still continue, but they seem to live about three feet outside the core of my body. Even if I *think* of things that usually make me angry or jealous, in this moment I know only love. I *am* only love. My chest is unfurled, stretching beyond the bounds of my physical body. When the meditation ends, I have no words to describe the experience. I am afraid that if I talk the love will fade away. On the way back to Cluny love pumps through me. I lie in bed and love is surging through me. I am reluctant to go to sleep, wondering if this blissful, open heart will be closed when I awake.

In the morning I awake as usual, but the memory is strong within me. Two days later I sit in the greenhouse alone, transplanting tiny cabbage seedlings. Again something uncorks inside. The love wells out of my heart and creates a thick blanket of silence all around me, almost touchable. I feel I can reach out my arm and identify the place where the blanket of love ends and the thoughts and feelings begin. They seem so far away, these thoughts, and so insignificant. My chest aches with the stretching, but it is a blissful ache, a sign that the love in me is blooming—not for one person or one thing but all things, all beings. It is a love for the cosmos and for Spirit itself. It is a passionate love for the tiny cabbages poised between my fingers and the chair on which I sit and the hills that roll across the golf course and the mountains beyond and, and, and, and . . . it is boundless.

Over the coming weeks my heart continues to pop open at odd times, sometimes in moments that I would normally greet with anger or jealousy. This heart has a mind of its own; it does not follow the 'logical' emotional responses that I have come to know. And it is an experience that transcends emotion; thoughts and feelings continue outside this cocoon of love. I don't know what to call it or how to describe it. Could it be an experience of unconditional love?

The roller coaster that David Earl identified for me, however, is in full swing. While the highs are higher (this experience of blissful love), the lows are also lower. From these ecstatic experiences of my heart opening, I sink into the mire of past patterns that are evoked through working with the children.

Wave upon wave of cold and flu decreases my resistance. I cannot seem to regain my strength. I am caught in a dilemma, attempting to reconcile my needs with those of the community, trying to define what service means to me. I long to work in the garden and interact more with adults but feel obligated to help in the school as it struggles to establish itself in the local area. Service at this point means doing what is needed, and true service is doing what I detest most. I can learn the most, I tell myself, from seeing and eliminating my resistance to doing a certain job. No pain, no gain. Service is synonymous with struggle. Holding that belief, I do create struggle in my life. The children are pushing me into areas that I would rather leave untouched, re-opening wounds that I would rather ignore. I try everything to ease the situation, including visualising better scenarios, connecting with the children's Higher Selves before I go to sleep, discussing options with Jennifer, and sending healing to the Kindergarten before I arrive.

I take a few days away from the community to rest and try to shake off a lingering bout of bronchitis. When Alan comes to pick me up, I tell him how much I missed him. "Well, actually," replies Alan, "I was glad to have some time to myself. It's been really draining for me to support you when you've been sick so much."

By the time we arrive back at Cluny Hill, I am so hurt and angered by his comment that the equilibrium regained by being away is lost completely. I lie in bed sobbing, wanting to be anywhere but this community, feeling trapped and desperate to be healthy again. I rest all day Sunday and return to the Kindergarten on Monday morning. By mid-afternoon the fatigue and fever have returned. I lie in a bathtub of warm water, unable to move. Something has to give, I decide, or I am going to snap.

The following day I talk with the school group, telling them that I cannot complete the last month of the school year. I expect disapproval at my inability to persevere, but I am beyond worrying about their reaction at this point. Instead, they seem to have expected my decision and offer to assist me in any way they can. My struggles must have been quite obvious; perhaps I have hidden them only from myself.

Although the immediate mental and emotional stress lessens, my physical body is still weak, so I decide to take another break from the community. This time I give myself a week instead of a couple of days to recover. I stay with John, a friend of the community, in his stone cottage on a farm about ten miles from Forres. Sleeping, eating, reading and walking by the ocean fill my days. Each day I can walk a bit further. John and I talk long into the evenings, and his tough, Cockney humour and insightful wisdom help me to gain some perspective on my struggles. My strength begins to return.

John's cottage is part of a local estate, and the farmer keeps all of the expectant mother cows in a neighbouring field. One morning one of the cows begins to moo and groan. Off and on I sit watching the straining cow, tail arched, legs planted firmly on the earth. I go inside to make some lunch and return to my patch of grass next to the field to watch the birth. Everything is quiet. I sense that something is wrong but ignore the inner prompting, not sure what to do. Half an hour later the farmer strides into the field, and John jumps over the fence. They stalk over to the area where the cow has been straining and pushing. I hold my breath. The farmer reaches down and jerks the legs of a newborn calf. No response. A stillborn baby.

John walks over and tells me how sometimes a calf can be saved by jerking its legs soon after birth—the shock activates the lungs. My heart is heavy. My intuition about the difficult birth was right, and I didn't act.

A couple of days later another mother begins to moo and snort. I take up my waiting position again, wondering what this birth will bring. I can see the contractions rippling along the mother's underbelly. I go inside for a hot drink and return to find the mother licking a still-wet calf, the umbilical cord swaying, the calf just beginning to struggle up on its dizzy legs. I breathe a sigh of relief.

Later in the day I find a larger meaning for myself in these two births. I realise that my relationship with the community up to this point has been like a still birth. The projects I have initiated and the work that I have done are like embryos that emerged without life. I feel dead inside. The second birth gives me hope, though, a possibility that I can begin again and give birth to something that will continue to grow and develop.

At the summer solstice four women friends come out to John's house to join me in a sweat lodge. He has built a lodge in the tall grass just beyond the stone walls of his garden and created a fire pit nearby. The day is warm, bordering on hot, and the sweat is very hot. Love flows hot and molten in the lodge, clearing and healing all that blocks its path.

When we return to Cluny Hill, I reluctantly say goodbye to John and carry my backpack to my room. Already I can feel the unnamed fatigue returning, so I climb the hill behind the car park, known as the 'power point'. A spiral path winds up the hill to a smooth flat patch on the top. I lie on my back, looking up into the branches of a birch tree, relaxing in the patches of sunshine dappled on the earth. The branches and leaves seem to spark with tiny lights, just as during my Vision Quest.

The more I focus on the tiny, perfectly shaped leaves, the more my heart opens. After about an hour, I am filled to bursting, and the surge within my heart presses into my mind in the form of words. Unable to stop the flow, I run to my room and grab a notebook, scrawling the words that press insistently from my heart:

I am a miracle. I am a **miracle**. *Each year I am new, completely new. I transform the soil into this tiny, perfect leaf, emerging, growing, dying. Yes, you saw me bare, seemingly barren, in the winter, and yet I changed. I change without fear. I press out from my centre with these leaves, each year reaching a bit further, and each fall I die, completely changing once again. I grow, burst forth, fade, die, rest over and over within the same 'life'. You, too, change and grow and die and rest and change and grow and die and rest, all within the same life. Don't fear change. The growing is worth any 'mishap'—being blown over, whatever. We grow anew each year with perfect faith, with joy in this burst of quick growth, summer. I am a miracle, I am a miracle, and so are you, for we are one, of Oneness, of the same spirit.*

After my period of rest, I know that within a few days I must choose a new work department. Reception needs a focaliser; Housecare is still short on staff. But my heart is still pulled towards the garden, and that is where I finally decide to go.

The Cluny garden group is in transition again. No one remains from the crew that worked there the year before. Marion has left the community, and Penny has moved into the Guest Department. Christa, the current focaliser, wants to move into the Guest Department as well. Only one other member is working full time in the garden, and neither of us is eager to take on focalising the whole department. When Rory, a member recently returned from a long stay in Auroville, steps forward to take on the position, I am relieved. He focalised the gardens at Cullerne for several

114

years and has a lot of knowledge. Over the years he has weathered many fluctuations in group process, and he's developed a philosophical attitude about the community in general.

In fact, Rory is a bit of a self-styled philosopher. He can rave about esoteric dream interpretation, shift into a discussion of jazz styles, and then throw in a few comments about O'Carolan, the great 18th-century Irish composer. When he speaks in meetings, people really listen. "I usually try to throw in some sort of a cross current, you know, like a good jazz musician. I like to shake people up a bit and get them thinking."

During the first weeks in the garden Rory and I have lots of long discussions, as we plant seeds in the vegetable garden, about poetry and styles of gardening and Earth Mysteries and Scottish music. At the weekly attunements, though, we lock horns over how to go about some of the work. Rory vacillates between laid-back Californian cool and army drill seargant style. One week he forgets to request guests for the coming week (in mid-summer we get them anyway—Cluny Hill is overflowing with people) and the next decides that something needs immediate attention and asks for two or three group projects in addition to the regular guests. Cora, the other member in the group, and I react when Rory's army sergeant personality takes control.

When he declares that he is going to 'hit the hedges' and 'clear the banks' during the coming week, we have heated discussions about leaving *some* wild areas and keeping *some* indigenous species. In the end, though, I realise that the details we argue over are a cover for my underlying distress about his militant approach. And after a few weeks of sparring, I finally verbalise my feelings. Rory smiles. "Yeah, the folks at Cullerne used to tell me I would overdo it at times. I'll try to be more consistent. I know I can get too laid back and then I over-compensate by trying to do a blitz to catch up."

"And let us know if we can support you in some ways. You don't have to do everything yourself," I remind him. After that, we do share more of the responsibility with the guests, and Rory asks eventually if I would like to focalise the vegetable garden.

Although I was sure I could take on the whole garden when I was an LCG, now, just over a year later, I doubt my ability to do almost anything. I have allowed difficulties with the children and struggles with the EarthLove game to erode my confidence. Peter Caddy once said that the community is a 'graveyard for egos'. Well, mine seems to have rolled over and died and taken my sense of self-worth with it.

When Roger returns from an extended trip to the States where he was nursing his mother through a series of operations, he spends some time talking with me. After a few minutes of patient listening, he stops me. "You're very clear about what you don't want; that's all I've been hearing. What *do* you want in your life now?"

I pause, dumbfounded. No one has ever asked me what I want. Not really. Maybe whether I wanted chocolate or strawberry icecream, but not what I *really* wanted in my life. Slowly I warm up and find that I do have a clear idea of what I want—the kind of work situation, relationships, living situation. "You say you want a place to work where you can express your own creativity, instead of doing someone else's work, right?" asks Roger. I nod. "Well, do you realise you've been offered the opportunity to focalise the veggie garden, to do it any way you want?"

I blush. "Yeah, but I'm not sure that I can do it."

"Look, it's there for you. If you could have it, would you take it?"

I pause for a few moments, feeling absurd. "Well, sure I would . . . . Yes, I *do* want to focalise the veggie garden. I will."

Next we talk about relationships. Roger leads me in an exercise to visualise what I have now and then what kind of relationship I want to have. "Roger," I say when we finish, "what I want is a long way from where Alan and I are now, and I'm afraid that means ending our relationship."

"It might, and it might not. You've made some choices, and set something very powerful in motion. It's like a stretched rubber band drawing you towards what you truly want in your life. So be prepared for things to change."

Within a couple of weeks, the wheels of change do begin to grind. I take on focalising the vegetable garden and set to work reclaiming the area. The last focaliser left the garden in a state of disarray at the height of the planting season. The time has passed to transplant most of the spring crops, and the seedlings for the summer were never planted. Weeds grow two feet high in some of the beds as well as on the paths. I enter the garden half-way through the season, in mid-stride, in a mess.

And my relationship with Alan is deteriorating. He is facilitating a workshop this week, so I see him very little, but tonight is the end of the week. I tell him that I will be planting spinach down in the vegetable garden if he wants to come and spend some time with me.

At first I am content to work, enjoying the long sunlight of the summer evening. But as the sky begins to darken and there is no sign of Alan, my heart grows heavy. I know in this moment that our relationship is of little concern to him. In fact, I think he views it as a burden. I gather my tools, still hoping to see Alan walking down the path, and carry them to the greenhouse. I return to my room alone.

Just before I am ready to fall asleep, Alan comes into my room to say goodnight. I tell him how hurt I am that he never came down to the garden. "Well, I said I *might,* not that I would. I wanted some space to myself after the week."

"Yeah, and you've been having your space all week long, too. That tells me you really aren't interested in our relationship."

Alan is silent, brooding for a while. "Look, I really don't have energy for this right now. It's late, and I'm tired."

"OK, then how about talking tomorrow? I'm really on the edge of deciding to end our relationship."

"I have to do my laundry tomorrow."

"Your *laundry?!* That tells me a lot, Alan, when your laundry is more important than our relationship."

We finally agree to meet the following afternoon. All night and through the morning I feel nauseous, as if my stomach has sunk three feet. I cry as my friend Dianne and I make beds, part of the Saturday morning Housecare rota. Dianne is a good friend to both Alan and me, and she is filled with compassion for both of us.

In the afternoon Alan and I have a long discussion, filled with tears and angry words and love. We decide to take three days for each of us to meditate and decide what we want to do.

Internally I have decided that we will separate. I show up for a Sunday cooking shift—my body is there, but my mind and heart are collapsed inward. I feel soft and sensitive and depressed. David is in the kitchen, too, a good friend with whom I share the inner details of my life as well as bouts of laughter as we imitate our favourite imaginary mid-town American couple together. Towards the end of the afternoon he strolls by, placing a hand on my shoulder. "Euuunice . . ." he drawls, "how's them beans a'cookin'?" I giggle despite myself. "Now, you knowuh I caan't work with you *hangin'* on me like that," I jibe. "Git along, now, afore I *suhwat* you."

Roger looks up from the sink. "Now how do you feel?" he asks. I feel like a child

116

caught with my hand in a cookie jar. I'm supposed to be depressed, not laughing. "Um, I'm OK right now."

"See," says Roger, smiling, "your feelings can change from moment to moment. It's OK. You'll make it."

Over the next couple of days I spend a lot of time meditating. Dianne and I have been following the exercises in *Joy's Way*, a book by Brugh Joy, that focus on the heart chakra. We already have a strong sister-love for each other, and the work with the heart deepens that love even more. Dianne is the most love-filled, heart-centred person I have ever known. She can sit in rapture in a bed of spring crocuses or stand for hours revelling in the night sky. A single note from a song can transfix her. She approaches everything with a child-like wonder, with true enthusiasm that is infectious. Children love her. She knows how to meet them as fellow human beings.

Dianne is one of very few people with whom I can wrestle like a bear and roll and laugh and snort on the floor. And she is wise. Often in a meeting she will start out by saying, "Well, I'm not very good at putting things in words, but . . ." and that heart of hers takes over and she says just the right thing that shifts the group to another level of understanding. Usually she can't remember afterwards what she said—it was an offering of inspiration for that moment.

While reading *Love Medicine*, a book about a Native American community, I read a section that perfectly describes Dianne. I knock on her door, just across the hall from mine. It's always open to allow the wind to circulate through the room, but I don't want to disturb her if she's doing something. "Dianne, this book reminds me of you. You may not like it, but can I read it to you?"

The book describes a young boy who has healing in his hands. He lives purely out of his heart. Like a turtle, says his grandmother. If you cut a turtle's head off, he would still keep living because his brain is in his heart.

"That's you, Dianne. Your mind is in your heart."

"Why did you think I wouldn't like it?" asks Dianne, sitting on the floor amidst scraps of felt and ribbon and beads. She's always making something, something beautiful. Colour and shape and scent are her domain. In her hands the scraps of this and that become magical little gnomes or satin-starred wands for the children in the playgroup.

"You always say your brain doesn't work, that you don't know how to say things. But it's just that your brain is in your heart . . . . I don't know. I just wanted to tell you that I love you."

I can see that Dianne is absorbed in what she's doing, so I return to my room to meditate, hoping to gain some clarity about my relationship with Alan. When I reach a certain point in the meditation, I find myself flying head first down a tunnel, going deep into the Earth until I reach a hole to my left, dimly lit by a fire in the centre of the cavern.

"Come," says an old man standing near the opening. He motions for me to sit down on the sandy floor. People of all ages and races sit around the fire. They gaze quietly at me, some nodding as I sit down.

"Who are all of you?" I ask the old man.

"We're your family. Your spirit family. We are with you always."

For the last few days, my greatest fear about leaving Alan has been loneliness. Some relationship, no matter how bad, is better than being lonely.

"We love you," says the old man.

I know in my heart it is true; I can feel the love. "But I want someone to keep my bed warm and go to the movies with me," I tell him. "I'm grateful to have a family, but I also want someone in my *physical* life, too."

"Remember, we are *always* with you."

At the end of the meditation, my heart is flooded with love. I walk downstairs and run into Alan in the hall. We pause to hug each other. "How are you doing?" he asks.

"I just had this experience of, well, I guess you could say meeting my family. My true family. And, you know, suddenly it doesn't matter whether or not we're together. I know that I'm loved."

In that moment, all of the trauma about our separation disappears. Ironically, as I release the desire to continue our relationship, a door simultaneously opens that allows me to meet Alan on a new level. I've let go of all expectations, and suddenly everything is possible.

The next evening we meet in the Sanctuary to make a final decision about our relationship. During the meditation I have an image of Alan and I as eagles, flying together, working together. After the meditation, I share the image with him, interpreting it to mean that we continue our working relationship whether or not we continue as lovers. Alan has a sense that our relationship is not complete, that we still have more to do together. "And I felt all of the love that you have for me and realised that I haven't let it in. I want to acknowledge you for all of the ways that you have shown your love to me over the past couple of years. And I feel my heart really open to you right now."

So after the trauma of separating for the last few days, unexpectedly we are back together again. The relationship begins to look more and more like the picture that I chose with Roger's help. Although it still isn't perfect, we are at least working at it and growing in love for each other.

A couple of weeks later Roger and Maria announce that they will be giving a course called 'Technologies for Creating'. Although I rarely take workshops, this one appeals to me. Since his return from the States, everyone has noticed a change in Roger. He knows what he wants and is effective in moving towards it. He has worked with a lot of people as he did with me, helping them to clarify what they really want in their life. Roger attributes the changes to the 'Technologies for Creating' course which helped him to clarify his life direction and gave him tools to realise that vision. Knowing how the simple exercise I did with Roger rearranged my life within a couple of weeks, I wonder what the whole course would do? At the last minute I sign up for the workshop.

At the end of the five-week course, I am sure that I have missed the point. Nothing seems to have changed. Gradually, though, over the following weeks and months, I begin to notice the things that I have chosen coming into my life. I have chosen, for example, to work with people whom I love and respect and who love and respect me.

In the autumn I realise that I work in such a group. I didn't have to change work departments, the love simply evolved in the Cluny garden group. Our weekly attunements are filled with laughter and caring and support for one another. Sometimes we discard business altogether and go for a walk on the beach or visit a local garden. Our friendships overflow the boundaries of work hours as well. Most of the garden crew join a couple of other community members to form a ceilidh band to play traditional Scottish dance music and sacred dance tunes. I realise one day that I actually look forward to going to work.

Earlier in the summer I would roll out of bed around 8:15, stagger into the garden shed about 8:50 (five minutes late) and have to think quickly on my feet about what to do in the garden that day. This morning, though, I awake and sit with my back against the wall, meditating for about 30 minutes. Then I reach for my notebook, asking inside how I can best use my energy in the garden that day, and then I simply write what I hear:

The vegetables need more water. They need more personal attention, like picking off the caterpillars, weeding, touching. A lot of greens need much more love—hence, so little swiss chard and cress. No one particular fertiliser or 'booster' will be most beneficial. A gardener needs to be persistent and flexible. When you plant a seed, bless it, water it immediately, sing prayers, watch it a bit, love it a lot. The leeks need more compost. The strawberries as well. Lots of compost on the celery patch. Attention to the kale. Lots of care for the new seedlings going in.

I dress and walk out to the greenhouse. Before me is an assortment of international guests, in peak summer season about eight or so, with varying levels of proficiency in the English language, usually from primitive to barely understandable. "I like that you should these pointy plants have me to water." (All forty of the cacti could be watered in 10 minutes and only need attention every couple of weeks. She has *decided* that this is her vocation for the coming week. This is going to be a great week.) Rory and Cora are already seated in the circle of benches and chairs outside the greenhouse. We each explain what we will be doing this morning and allow the guests to choose what they want to do. Then the fun begins.

We have an attunement, a time of holding hands and joining outwardly as well as coming together on an inner level, bringing our individual notes into harmony. Sometimes the person leading the attunement says a few words, other times we attune in silence. We fumble hands up and down and giggle—"Thumbs to the right, you know, like hitchhiking." When the time of silence is complete, the guests are expectant. "Where are the cabbages and big vegetables?"

I begin to organise tools in the garden shed. One woman asks incessantly what she can carry. "This, this? You need this?" I finally stop and look her full in the eye. "Just breathe deeply. Just stand there and breathe." She laughs nervously, thinking I'm joking. By the third time she begins to get the idea.

I trundle down the path with a wheelbarrow full of tools. One woman tells me I should have Gunther push the wheelbarrow. I look at her, perplexed. "Oh, you know, he's a man; he needs to feel useful." That's not the world I know and understand, I think to myself, nor one I want to support. I decide to ignore her definitions of Gunther's insecurities and continue pushing the wheelbarrow down the path.

We reach the vegetable garden with its raised double-dug beds. I work with the French intensive gardening method and companion planting. This year I'm using the bio-dynamic astronomical planting guide as well. I explain and demonstrate the work to be done and then start people on their task.

Work. Some guests come here grumbling that they paid for their programme, so why do they have to work? After living in a few communities, I realise that the quickest and deepest way to know the heart of a community is to know how its members approach work. For a disgruntled airline personnel manager from Holland, this is hard to understand. Even harder to understand is the sometimes paradoxical message that guests (and members) receive about work. 'Work is love in action' is the community's motto about work. 'Work is my spiritual practice, where I bring into actuality all of my spiritual knowledge.' Intertwined with this work ethic is an understanding that sometimes people's personal distress demands more attention than weeding the rhubarb bed. Two messages come across: work is an important expression of my spritual path *and* if I am in distress I don't have to show up for work, and other people will understand.

Guests often use the opportunity to work out past patterns about over-responsibility in their life. 'Working out' means learning how to skip work and not feel guilty about it. As a member in the garden, I am caught in a double bind. On one side I am trying to live and experientially teach people about a different way of working, i.e. doing things because I want to do them in the most loving and conscious way possible. On the other hand, 'the most loving and conscious way possible' means taking other human beings and their personal state into account. Where's the line between being supportive of someone in their learning process and supporting each other in making excuses and being irresponsible? And what about doing things efficiently?

One older man working in the garden during his Experience Week took me aside at the end of the week. "Are you someone official here?"

"Well, I work in the garden just like the other members of the garden group," I said, wiping a shovel blade.

"I want to make a suggestion about how you can work more efficiently," he continued. "I used to be an executive, so I know. See, you should have people write in and tell you their skills before they arrive and then you can just assign them to the appropriate place." He beamed a radiant smile, very pleased with himself.

I wanted to ask him where he had been all week. In every guest programme we use a process of attunement to choose work departments. Perhaps the most appropriate place for me to be is the Maintenance department, not because I am a whiz at fixing toilets, but rather because I have a fear of tools that I would like to overcome, or perhaps I have always had a longing to work with tools and never had a chance before. Someone who has worked in an office for twenty years might need the healing power of the garden to balance them again.

This morning I turn my attention to one of the rows at the centre of the spiral beds. This area of the garden is arranged into four sections of four rows each, to honour the four elements—Earth, Air, Fire and Water. Remembering the words from this morning's written meditation, I scan the row of Italian cabbage greens barely visible among the weeds. This is one bed that I have not really taken into my heart since moving into the garden; I still harbour resentment towards the last gardener for leaving the garden in such a mess, and somehow the resentment has focused on this bed.

I kneel down and begin pulling the foot-high weeds. Caterpillars have ravaged the fleshy leaves of the greens; only stick-like skeletons of the stems remain. I wonder if I should simply pull everything out and replant. After considering for a moment, I decide to give the plants a chance. One older man, a guest who was a long-time gardener, left the garden with these words of advice: "Keep a plant that you think is dead for one year. You'd be amazed at how many of them come back." So I pull out the weeds and pick off the caterpillars. I bring several loads of compost to the bed, spreading it thickly to nourish the soil as well as to provide a layer of mulch. Then I sit back on my heels, arms wrapped around my knees, and sing "You are so beautiful . . . to me . . . ." I usually sing this as I harvest the plants, to thank them for growing and giving themselves for food. In this moment, singing to these mutilated cabbages, I imagine them growing strong and healthy.

For the next week I stop at this bed each day as I move through the garden, sometimes singing, other times simply nodding and acknowledging their presence. Within two weeks the plants are flourishing. By the end of a month, they are the biggest, healthiest plants in the garden. The leaves are huge, like elephant ears. And juicy. Just a thinning of the leaves fills the wheelbarrow.

To me, this is a miracle. It may not be a forty-pound cabbage, but in my books the return of these plants from half-dead sticks to luxurious, three-foot-high specimens is a miracle. Those plants teach me about the power of love. Not a sticky sweet, gushy sort of love, but the love of care and attention consciously applied. It's the same sort of love that humans thrive on. And in the garden, the power of that kind of love is cleary demonstrated to me.

During the summer and into the autumn I begin to share my experiences with the Earth, both the wild and the cultivated, with guest groups. I also give Ally workshops and EarthLove games again. These times of sharing help reconnect me with my love of the Earth, Love in general and my purpose for being in the community. My health, though better than last spring, is still fragile, and at times I ask during my writing guidance time for insight on how to strengthen my body. Most of the messages have to do with joy and trust:

Much of the process depends upon trust. Trust in yourself, believe in yourself, trust in the unfolding of life and your place in it. You see everything as taking away from what you really want to do, yet you are not sure exactly what you want to do. Silly, eh? A lot of your load could lighten with a dose of joyous humour, a sense of wonder at the unfolding of things. Open to the little surprises, like the micro-world under a flower pot or dew at the centre of a flower or the curve of a lover's smile. These are works of art, as much as any symphony or epic poem. You are surrounded by masterpieces. Seek out and appreciate them. Wholeness will come in the process . . . . Find joy in the things that you are now, expect joy in the being you will become. Joy can fill your body as easily as sorrow. Love can teach as much or **more** *than pain. Let the details of the world slide. You are blessed with the beauty of the Universe.*

The summer passes into autumn; I plant the late-season crops of lettuce and cabbage and begin to prepare for winter. The frost comes early, freezing the runner bean blossoms before they set. October comes, and with it the influx of visitors for the 'One Earth: A Call to Action' conference. Alan is focalising the conference this year, and I help a bit on the planning committee, so I get a front-seat view of the amount of time and energy required to pull off such an event. Over 250 guests participate; it is the largest conference ever hosted in the community. It stretches the community's facilities, and it also stretches the participants, calling on them to make a commitment, or to deepen one already made, in their work for the planet.

When the conference is finished, Alan and I talk about taking a break together after the beginning of the year. We decide on a trip to Australia to visit the rainforest and to connect personally with some of the people Alan has contacted in his work on an international tree calendar. I have been longing for such a break, wanting desperately to have some time away from the community, but as the date nears I have less and less desire to leave.

Part of the reason for my change of heart is a workshop called 'The Next Step' given by Hargrove Associates. Vita, a flamboyant Italian woman who is a member of the Foundation, attended the workshop in Switzerland and was so impressed that she arranged to bring it to the community. Having given the workshop for major corporations and national governments, the workshop leaders are used to working with organisations. The community does a lot of manoeuvring of the schedule, carefully designed to facilitate guest groups, so that a large number of community members can take part in the five-day course. I have been wanting to participate more in the centre of the community, and this workshop is aimed at moving the community as a whole, so I decide to sign up.

Shortly after their arrival, Robert Hargrove and his associates begin to wreak havoc in the carefully ordered surroundings of the Foundation. They smoke in the members' kitchen in the basement. They make a fuss about arranging meals when it suits *their* schedule. They reinforce the label 'loud-mouthed Americans' and alienate a lot of people. The morning before the first session, they rearrange most of the plants in the rooms, leaving some of them crushed together in dark corners of the hallways. I am incensed—my garden work includes caring for the houseplants, and they are like children to me. I have enough trouble with guests who hang their underwear from the pots in their rooms or use the plants as incense holders, and now someone has invaded the meeting rooms as well.

When the session starts, Robert Hargrove spends most of the afternoon lambasting us. "Last night I went into the lounge downstairs and I sat looking around, and you know, if I didn't know this was a community, I could have sworn I was in a geriatric centre. God, this place is *dead*. What has happened to you? When I knew Paul Hawken and sent him over here to write the book *The Magic of Findhorn*—I was editing *East West Journal* at the time—this place was *alive*. Things were happening. And you know a lot of it had to do with Peter Caddy. That man didn't bullshit. He just talked vision. He was outrageous and demanding, and he had *vision*. That's what made this place tick. And I don't see anybody around here with that kind of vision any more. You're just resting on the past. Not going anyplace. I'm interested in people with vision, who are willing to *champion* something."

Robert also rages about how people relate to responsibility in the community. We all make a commitment to show up for all the sessions, but the second morning one person doesn't show up because his wife has had an epileptic seizure during the night. Robert insists that he should be present. Most of us are horrified—people come first, not some commitment to a workshop. "How do you support each other here?" he asks. "Do you support each other in making excuses or in doing what you say you'll do? Think how you relate to each other; is that the kind of place you want to live and work in, where people don't have to be responsible, where they aren't held accountable?"

Each morning we listen to his tirades. During the afternoon and evening we sit in small groups with the sole purpose of looking at our relationship to power, authority and responsibility. In each group we have a 'consultant', whom we eventually rename 'insultant', who makes brief, pithy statements that reflect the group's interaction. With all our usual group agreements gone out the window, we flounder this way and that. I experience the whole gamut of emotions, from disdain to utter rejection to intense love. And through the days I begin to see that I know a lot about the outer *structuring* of groups, but little about their *innards*. What does it mean to support a group leader? How do I respond to authority? To power? Am I empowered in and of myself, or only in relation to how much 'power' someone else does or doesn't have? I realise that I have not learned the inner skills to support someone without feeling threatened myself. How can I, and the group as a whole, support someone with a vision, who is willing to 'champion' something, without feeling threatened?

Robert uses the IBM corporation as an example. The creative chaos involved in the production of the first personal computer threatened the new president so much that he established rules to make sure that such disorder never occurred again. He succeeded in halting the chaos, but he also eliminated the climate for the creation of any new inventions. When the next president took over, he trashed all of the restrictions, and the creative juices started flowing again. He knew that creativity breeds chaos. It's part of the creative process.

The Findhorn Foundation is so neatly organised that there is little room for chaos. Most innovations are greeted with reasons 'why not', chief among them being lack of time, money or personnel. The resistance within the community is so great that only the strongest individuals persist in trying to create something new within the collective, and in the end they are often labelled a 'nuisance'. Many people retract after their first attempts and eventually leave the community or become 'independent members' who live on the periphery, associated with the Foundation but involved with their own projects.

We have a practice session of sorts when people stand up to 'champion' their creative ideas and then invite people to join them in the project. The energy in the room is electric. People are *full* of inspiring ideas for the community, and most of them have been hidden on back shelves for years. The 'juice' spills over into skits that we create to enact our relationship to power, authority and responsibility. They are irreverent and hysterically funny—a living, breathing example of the satirical dramas that marked the heyday of Peter and Eileen's leadership in the community.

When the workshop ends, I am exhausted and inspired. In the community meetings a lot of people speak about the need for change, for taking risks and living once again on the 'cutting edge' that was characteristic of the community in its early days. We know that we need to expand our work, but into what? And how? We have become good at what we do. The guest programmes serve as vehicles of transformation for people (it doesn't really matter what workshop you take, the essence of love and transformation runs through all of them—you just choose the flavour). We could easily continue to do 'more of the same' while the world around us forges ahead, *or* we could reach out and risk new directions. Although we make no conclusive decisions, we know that things need to change *and* that we need to make room for chaos.

One evening soon after the workshop ends I sit in my room, wrapped in blankets on my bed, peering into the starry winter sky. Inspired by the wildness of the wind, I reach for my journal to record my thoughts:

The wind howls and growls outside the window, scouring the last remnants of leaves from the naked trees. Cool, now cold, the air bites my cheeks and chills my lungs as I walk along High Street in Forres. The winter has come, unnoticed, under the crack of my bedroom door, into the lining of my Wellington boots, into the cold chill of my bedsheets. We must remain neighbours, in some semblance of courtesy, until spring returns and warm winds once again soften the land.

I know in this moment why the hedgehog sleeps, why the bear curls into its winter den. I close my eyes and find the black peace of a winter night's sky inside the closed lids. I do not want to return even to the soft lamplight of this room. The peace that pervades me in this moment of nothing is elusive. I want to wrap myself in it as in a quilt before a blazing fire, lost in the dance of flickering flames and raw, pervasive heat.

In the last few days I have been feeling the edges of some great mystery, as a child might hang on the skirt of a beloved aunt or mother. The skirt moves and shifts while my tiny hand clutches at the hemline. This mystery is large, big enough that I cannot pretend to wrap my mind around it. It moves too quickly and looms too large for me to grasp it.

*Sensing into this mystery, I know that I am dancing with **meaning**—the substance of this form of my body, the shape of my life, the reason for the planet Earth and snails and stars and friends and love and houseplants and cars and whales and 'indoors' and 'outdoors'. Who is creating and who is created? If everyone is creating his/her/its reality, then who am 'I' to this teacup of herb tea and its creation? In a fraction of a second you move through my lips and into 'me' in physical form—who art thou now, rosehip and elder?*

And who am I, for that matter? As the nights lengthen, I am drawn deeper and deeper into the dark mystery of myself. Each year as I become more aware of the turning of the season, this inward draw strengthens. Like the leafless trees outside, I turn inside myself, outwardly resting while dreamy inner seeds are planted.

Something is shifting inside. I feel more at peace with the community and with myself. I remember someone sharing with our Orientation group how he couldn't remember much of his first year in the community. Looking back, it was all a bit hazy, and he couldn't recall any of the details. Reviewing the past year as the winter solstice nears, I have the same sort of amnesia which helps to soften the memory of difficult times. Perhaps all the trauma was simply the scouring of the rough edges of my being, and all the illness a result of my resistance to giving myself fully to a new way of living. According to a Zen saying, 'Many potatoes in a pot wash more quickly'. I know its truth after rolling potatoes together in the kitchen sink—they rub the dirt off each other as they tumble. Within the community, all the guests and members function the same way. We rub up against each other, snap off the rough edges and dislodge the dirt. In the end we are cleaned more quickly than if we lived alone.

Inspired by the relaxed peace that pervades me, I consider cancelling my plane tickets to the US to visit my family and friends. Perhaps I don't really need a holiday after all . . . . I'll sleep on it and decide in the morning.

In the morning I have a strong image in meditation. Standing at the edge of a cliff, I hear a river flowing far below at the bottom of a deep chasm. I know that I could take a running leap and bypass the chasm, but I sense that the river represents Source. For me connection with Source, the Creator, comes most easily in wilderness, and during the last year-and-a-half here in Scotland I have craved wild land. Almost all of the wildness has been pounded out of Britain—it remains only in tiny pockets. I realise that cancelling this trip would be like overstepping the chasm—I would miss an opportunity to enter the wilderness and renew my inner link with Spirit.

CHAPTER 7
Claiming Power

After a month in the States visiting family and friends, in mid-February I board the plane to Sydney, Australia to rendezvous with Alan. We spend the next two weeks backpacking in Tasmania and visiting with photographers and activists in Hobart. These people, the core of the 'Green' community in Tasmania, are combining their inner work—in this case a form of eastern meditation and body work—with their outer activist work. We find the same powerful combination of inner and outer work among the people at the Rainforest Information Centre in Lismore, New South Wales. All along the way, through our explorations of the rainforest and the talks and workshops that we give, we find people who are concerned about the rainforest and are acting on that concern. Who put their lives on the line to stop bulldozers when legal means are exhausted. Who devote their lives to reforesting ravaged farmlands. Who rip out the hot-water heating system in their houses because they saw how people in India did not have running water, much less *hot* running water. Who give their lives to writing and speaking and living for the Earth.

Inspired by the way these people are literally putting their lives on the line, I realise that I need a very good reason to return to the Findhorn Foundation. I need a purpose that will sustain me and transcend the small pettiness that sometimes invades our community meetings. I need a vision that will help me remember the wonder in people's eyes when they hear the name 'Findhorn'. They often jumble the details, but as they speak their faces soften and their eyes sparkle. 'Hope' is the closest word I can find to describe the phenomenon. These people have heard of a place where something positive is working, actually *grounded*, on the planet. Through my journey I have become aware that for many people the Foundation is a model for 'the way life could be'. That knowledge fills me with a growing sense of responsibility because I know this vision can only be fulfilled by ordinary people.

We are it. I am it. And I want to live this life in the best way I can, not just for me, but for all of the people who look to the community as an example.

After the weeks of sun and sea and forest, I return to Britain brown (actually freckled), relaxed and renewed. I stay for a few days with my friend Michael, an ex-member of the community now living in Northampton, who is fathering a new-born baby girl. I sleep a lot to compensate for the 36-hour journey across several time zones. In the mornings I meditate, centring myself in preparation for the return to Findhorn.

Each morning images of a storytelling performance run through my meditation. I try to brush them aside, but each day more details come into the picture—which stories, which slides to accompany them, where the performance will take place. The purpose becomes clear as well—they would be stories from different native people around the world, that depict positive images of humanity interacting with the Earth. Any profit from the performance would go towards a project to regener-ate the Caledonian forest of Scotland.

For a couple of years Alan and I have envisioned a large-scale regeneration pro-ject in the west of Scotland. Alan's focus is on the trees while mine is on the indige-nous animal species, such as the bear and the wolf and the sea eagle.

Plans for the performance are put on a back burner, however, when I return to the community. The garden is at the height of the planting season, and most of my ener-gy is focused on direct seeding and transplanting seedlings from the greenhouse into the beds. This season I decide to work more consciously with the devic king-dom, so I include short meditations with the guests who work in the vegetable gar-den to welcome the deva of each type of plant we seed.

The focus on the devas spills into my morning meditations as well, especially the written section at the end. Much of the information is about *how* to work in the gar-den. When I awake with a cold, for example, I hear: "Finish the work with the strawberries. Stand up often to stretch and breathe—do not clench the body with your concentration on the work. Keep stretching, loosening, then the mucus can flow out uninhibited and the crisis will pass quickly. Breathe and enjoy the air, the sun, this perfect day."

The guidance refers to the larger movements within the garden as well. For the same day I hear: "Peace invades the soul of your being and the land when you least expect it. Notice the pattern of the wind today, watch its effects upon energy—enjoy the surges and passings of this 'unseen element'. It is seen in its effects. You can contact the 'invisible' realm of Spirit more easily through an understanding of and attunement to wind. The elements in general have much to teach in your life journey. Enjoy this perfect day, for it is a gift of creation to you, one of its children, and you are a gift to creation. Focus on this giving and receiv-ing, seeing the giving flowing round and round the Wheel."

When I walk into the garden, I stand watching the wind passing in waves through the newly emerged leaves of the beech hedge, remembering the words I have writ-ten. A guest, an older woman from England, also stops to watch. She comments on her walk this morning, and her revelation that the wind is seen in its effects upon the trees. Like God, the wind is visible through its movement.

I stare at her for a moment, incredulous, then smile and tell her of my thoughts this morning. She nods, nonplussed, and goes about weeding the kale bed. Though small, the incident affects me deeply. I realise how connected our minds become in this place. Similar thoughts and even dreams run through people's lives. And since we often refer to the community as a microcosm of the world as a whole, subject to the same faults and triumphs as the rest of humanity, such thoughts must pass through the body of humanity as a whole, the 'group mind' of which the Transcendentalists spoke.

A couple of weeks after my return from Australia there is a spring conference on healing. Sun Bear is one of the speakers, and I host both him and Tom, an apprentice travelling with Sun Bear.

In addition to giving a talk during the conference, Sun Bear leads a two-day workshop. Most of the sessions are filled with talking as Sun Bear extemporaneously shares some of his wisdom. Some people sit hunched over their notebooks, furiously scribbling notes. When Sun Bear mentions using a crystal for something, one woman raises her hand and asks, "Now, is that an amethyst or a quartz crystal?" Sun Bear looks at her for a moment. "Quartz or amethyst?" she insists. "You'll have to tune in, decide for yourself," he says finally.

A couple of women in the workshop talk with Sun Bear during tea break. Their self-appointed mission is to explain to him how to teach. "This is the New Age, Sun Bear," they tell him graciously. "It's about letting people *experience* things, not just talking. So could you include some more exercises in the workshop?"

Never have I seen Sun Bear angry, but when I bring him a cup of tea, he is fuming. "These white people," he says, shaking his head. "This is when I hate teaching them. They don't understand, they just don't understand."

After the break Sun Bear announces that later in the afternoon we will be "doing an exercise. Finding a power spot." He nods towards the pair of women. They smile, pleased at his enlightened reform. "For my people," explains Sun Bear, "there were several kinds of healing. One way is with herbs or laying on of hands. Another way, also a sacred way, and this is the kind of healing that I practise, is to bring *knowledge*. Knowledge is a kind of healing. It brings you into right relationship with yourself, with your people and with the Creator."

As he talks, the image of the eagle from my Vision Quest, feeding my brains to the four babies, comes into my mind. She was feeding my *brains* to the four baby eagles . . . my brains, my *knowledge*. Four babies . . . the four directions . . . feed my knowledge to . . . the four directions . . . the children of the four directions . . . . Something clicks inside me. My purpose is to feed my brains, my *knowledge*, to the people of the four directions. The connection startles me, yet the image is so simple, so clear—how could I have missed it before? My understanding of that vision, almost dismissed as a non-event during my Vision Quest, is *still* deepening three years afterwards.

Shortly before Sun Bear leaves, I ask him about the bear claws that he mentioned in the workshop. I begin a long explanation about some of the dreams and visions I've had, wanting to explain my interest, but before I can finish, he presses a claw into my hand. I stop in mid-sentence. "But, I, uh . . . ."

"Take it, dear. That's for you," he says simply.

A couple of weeks after Sun Bear's departure I become very ill. My friend Robbie, an acupuncturist from Australia, gives me a couple of treatments, but the symptoms only increase. As is my usual reaction when I am sick, I spend a lot of time imagining other places where I could live and other things that I could be doing. I focus inward as well, trying to identify and then eliminate the root of the illness. I do everything but relax.

One morning I list all the separate 'bundles of energy' in my life that scatter my attention. They seem completely disjointed until I begin to cluster them according to areas. As I sit staring at the clusters, an inspiration dawns. When I place the Earth in the centre of the bundles, suddenly they are all related. My love and concern for the planet is what bonds all of the apparently separate aspects of my being.

When I regain some strength, I climb the hill to the power point, bringing the bear claw that Sun Bear left with me. I hold the curved, sharp claw in my hand and focus on it while I sit resting my back against a birch tree. When my mind quiets, I realise that until now in my life I have *gathered* energy, but now is the time to *focus* it. The claw comes now because I am ready to point and then release that energy.

I feel the power of Bear, melting my heart with love. For so long I have identified power with anger, with the flashes that come from my solar plexus. Those flashes of anger, though, block the expression of true power, and I know that I need to clear this chakra before I can 'point' effectively. I cannot claim power until I befriend it, until I breathe it in with love.

When my back tires, I close my eyes and relax on the earth. As I lie there, I have an image of a wise old man standing above me. "Do what you *love*," he instructs. "The 'courses' that you take don't really matter—it's what happens in between. Do what you *love*!"

I sense that something in me is preparing to die, and something else is growing to take its place. When I ask in meditation how I can support the transition, I hear "Be at peace with the process, open to the possibility of *true change*. Relax. This is an awesome event, the mystery of which no being truly understands. You are watching your *self* birth. And no one knows exactly when the labour pains will finish and the new being emerge, but, again, the baby cannot be born through a clenched fist. Let go of any expectations of how this new being will arrive, look, move, etc. Expect only a greater level of power, peace, beauty, fulfilment. And note that this is a baby, a beginning, not a full-blown adult creature. Do not expect all things at once . . . ."

* * *

In late May Alan and I spend a weekend on Erraid. Alan is going to discuss plans for a reforestation project on the island that could be a model for the rest of the west coast of Scotland. He also envisages the project as a next step for the community in its work with the Earth. My plan is to spend a day alone, like a mini-Vision Quest, hoping to ease this new Self into physical form.

When I awake in the morning and make my way to the outhouse, I find blood on the toilet paper—good. I am most sensitive and aware just at the beginning of my moon time, so the timing is perfect. I gather a notebook, pen and extra sweater in my daypack and then swing through the gate at the end of 'Main Street'. Walking up the hill that leads to Balfour Bay, I am warm enough in the morning sunshine to stop and take off my shirt. Always before I have visited the island in winter. Now, though, the land is alive with wild irises and bluebells and other wild flowers.

When I reach the bay, I find a sheltered spot among the rocks and lean back, praying for vision at this time. Immediately I hear, "Go up the hill." To the left a steep cliff juts up from the sea. I balk. I'm comfortable where I am. "Go up the hill." Knowing that the instructions will persist, I climb up and up, slowed by cramps and the spacey, almost out-of-body feeling that I have at the beginning of menses. As I climb my vision broadens to include Iona, the other islands and the deep turquoise sea. I find a cluster of low rocks, the only shelter on this broad, flat expanse on top of the cliff, to protect me from the wind that is rising after the dead calm of morning.

Now, at the top of the hill, I realise what is being asked of me. I must sweat (make an effort) to reach a broader view. This wider view, from the top of the hill, means that I will be exposed to sun and wind (stick out more). In my life it is no longer OK to stay in a warm, sheltered spot on the sandy beach with only a narrow view of the sea (of life).

I sit watching the rocks off the coast as the waves wash over them again and again, slowly shaping them with its action. "How willing are you to be touched by your environment? To let the wind chill and cleanse your bare back, the sun to caress your bare skin? *How real can you be?* How real? How willing are you to meet these elements *just as you are*? Real. Aim to be real."

The wind blows chill across my back until I submit and pull on my shirt. I consider the power of wind. Power. Power surges through the Earth all the time, without judgement. Why am I afraid of my own power? Perhaps some ancient, guilty memory of misuse? Yet, if I am like Earth, using power without judgement, without right or wrong, how can I hurt? And I realise that the Earth uses power *in connection with* greater rhythms, greater sources of power. When I am 'in connection with', in alignment with Spirit in other words, my power has no right or wrong; it just *is*.

As the day continues, I grow more and more restless. My thoughts wander to other things. Midges appear, biting my face and exposed skin. "Are you able to concentrate when distractions come?" I hear. I turn my focus to the rock before me and concentrate on my breathing. When my mind is still, the insects disappear.

Later in the day, as the sun dips toward the Isle of Iona, my mind quiets and new thoughts enter. "Work from points of strength, like restoration ecology," I hear. For so long I have focused on all that blocks me from actualising my vision; I have forgetten that I have strengths. I have visited some of the areas in Scotland where remnants of the Caledonian forest have been fenced off. This simple act, meant to keep out the grazing animals, was enough protection to allow the land to flourish unaided. No new trees were planted; the old trees still had viable seed, and the ground cover soon rebounded. Trees and plants not originally growing inside the fence arrived through the movement of wind and water until the area was alive with all sorts of creatures that had been absent from the Highlands, or had been hiding in the cracks of steep hills, for years.

"You are being asked to begin life anew, but the seeds for this birth lie in your greatest strengths. Protect the areas of strength, let them flourish, keep broadening the healthy bits until the desolated areas are consumed by the vibrantly alive."

What are these strengths? As I ponder, I identify my relationships with humans and with the Earth, my mind, music and writing. But are these really strengths or just areas that I imagine are useful?

"Be more and more sure of your guidance," I hear. "Do not allow others to sway or entangle the beauty and simplicity of your knowing. Keep *simplicity* in your awareness. Do not over-plant or over-extend those areas of strength. Reassess the direction of the community. Ask, 'Is this my direction?' Make no judgement of your worthiness or the worthiness of the community—forget judgement. Just ask if your aims are aligned. *Be honest.* You may be surprised by the answers . . . .

"*Act* on these answers. You are learning that knowledge is meaningless until put into *action,* grounded. The action stems from a still point of vision. Maintain this centred stillness in action—these two states are *not* contradictory. The still vision is analogous to the right-brain grasp of wholeness, and action is like the linear implementation of the left brain. They need each other. Again, knowing is not visible or effective until acted upon. Know this deep, deep inside. You are frustrated that no one sees your beauty or worthiness, yet you have done little to express and share that beauty . . . . Do not expect this journey to be comfortable, but expect it to be rewarding. Sharing your journey is a gift. Your source of strength is in the sharing of such wisdom, *your own* wisdom.

129

"A poor self-image is reflected in poor work. You do *no one* a service by carrying a poor self-image or nursing fears and doubts. Indulging in doubts is like denying the gift that spirit has given.

"These truths sound simple, and they are. Don't get caught up in fancy, convoluted explanations. Find centre, envision, act. Start small and simple, stay simple, grow larger. These truths work on all levels. The work is joyous; it builds on itself, gaining momentum. Keep moving *and* maintain the still point, your inner ballast."

The sun rests on the belly of Iona when I finally rise and walk over the hill to the cottages. Vibrant red and orange fill the western sky. I pause to rest my arms on the wrought-iron fence of the garden and watch the changing colours. Inside the cottage the clock reads 10 p.m. Despite the day of quiet, I am ready for sleep.

After my sojourn on Erraid, my work with guest groups deepens. I am more in touch with the potential for transformation that is available to all who visit the community. I realise, too, that transformation occurs not just in this place, but everywhere on the planet at this time. And as my own process of growth and change becomes more profound, I am able to speak from a wiser, stronger place in myself.

Despite receiving a lot of positive feedback about my work with guests, I weight any form of criticism much more heavily—I still haven't learned the lesson of focusing on my strengths. One day I have a sharp, abrupt interaction with Satya, one of two members working in Personnel at Cluny Hill, that leaves me with the familiar feeling of being heavily judged by her. The disquiet lasts for a couple of days, and I finally arrange to talk with her during lunch. Satya listens quietly while I explain my distress about our communication and my desire to know her *as a person*. We have never really talked together outside of Personnel meetings, and I realise that I *do* want to know her, as a *person*, not only as a Personnel manager.

Satya rests her chin on her folded hand. Always she is elegantly dressed, precisely groomed, manicured and polished—such a contrast to my usual dirt-stained gardening clothes. "Judy," she says when I'm finished, "you know, to me, you are really invisible here. You just work in your little corner of the garden. I never see you in the community at large."

I am stunned. For the last two months I have worked flat out in the garden during the day and given evening sessions with guests at least once, if not two, three or sometimes *four* times a week, plus worked with the children in the Steiner school doing gardening and nature sessions. I can't imagine what else I could take on.

"We need people to fill Sanctuary slots," she continues. "Have you ever thought of leading Sanctuary? That's one way that you could 'come out' more. Sunday morning, for example. We need someone to do the Peace Meditation."

I have always considered leading Sanctuary a task reserved for the 'spiritual heavies' in the community . . . but why not? "I'd rather do something with the Earth, and the Peace meditation is usually focused just on humanity . . . . Could I make the planet the focus of the meditation?"

"You can guide the meditation however you want to."

"Let me think about it. I'll let you know."

After a couple of days' thought, I decide to lead one of the noon Sanctuaries. Despite my initial hesitation, that twenty-minute session becomes one of my favourite times in the week. The night or the morning before, I meditate about how to guide the meditation and write down what I hear. With minor revisions, this becomes the text for the Sanctuary. The meditations are focused on attuning to the changes in the cycle of the seasons. At the end we bless all the kingdoms of life on Earth. Just after mid-summer, at the peak of the growing season, the meditation focuses on love:

130

"This summer season bursts with the energy of bringing things into their outer form. What is the great force that draws life from a seed, that makes the stars dance and draw towards one another, that causes humans to open and fall in love? In all cases it is the same force, for seed and star and human. A scientist would call it gravitation, a physicist attraction. On a spirit level we could call it allurement, and beyond that *love*. The dance of love binds this universe. You strengthen the fabric of this creation by following the promptings of your true heart, by being drawn by, fascinated by, *love*."

Later that week I see a sign on the noticeboard about a workshop with a Celtic harpist—one of my favourite instruments. As well as playing, she will be speaking about the 'Harmonic Convergence'. For a couple of years I have been reading bits of information about the Harmonic Convergence at the end of August, 1987, mostly from Native American teachers. No one here at the Foundation seems to know about the event, so I am pleased that someone will be speaking about it.

The woman giving the lecture has been on a tour of sacred sites throughout Scotland and Ireland. Wherever she goes, she plays her harp, bringing joy and life into the silent circles of stone. "In the Orkneys," she tells us, "one of the islanders told me that no one had played for generations in those circles. No one had come to wake them up, to bring them to life again. And for me, that is what this 'Harmonic Convergence' is about.

"I do have a lot of astrological information about the unusual planetary movements at that time, but the most important thing is that this will be a point of reawakening—both of places and of ourselves. It is a time of reactivating the circuits of the cosmos and also our *own* bodies, because we are microcosms of the whole. Stones, mountains, trees and our own bodies are like grounding rods for this energy. During meditation, when you visualise your spinal column elongating and growing downward, you begin to resonate with the Earth's energy. We are learning to resonate with each other and with the Earth—this allows us to see and experience the land in a different way."

Afterwards I go for a long walk in the woods, inspired by the talk and wanting quiet time to digest it. As I walk, though, my initial excitement begins to wane. I have seen so many sacred things cheapened in the hands of the 'New Age' movement. Gary Trudeau has been satirising the Harmonic Convergence in his comic strip, 'Doonesbury'. I know that something or someone has 'made it', for better or for worse, when they appear in Doonesbury. Trudeau has a keen eye for detecting America's current trends, both the brilliant and the absurd, and in his hands the 'Moronic Convergence' has a lot to say about the New Age and its current obsession with psychic phenomena.

Trudeau has reinforced my dislike of the term 'new age'. I find it arrogant; every age calls itself new, and in the media the label has become tangled up with the ideas of technocrats who envision space bubbles and human-free factories. Even worse is the riff-raff of psychic phenomena seekers who use the term freely. And these 'psychic tours' to visit sacred sites . . . . I pause along the hill to gaze over the bay, smiling. The 'new age' tourist trade visits the temples of past civilisations with a shaman or two thrown in for entertainment. Just as shallow and flashy as the 'fun in the sun' holidays in Jamaica, except that these tours cater for juice fasters instead of beer drinkers. By the time I reach the path below Nelson's Tower, I have decided to spend that weekend in mid-August quietly, not at some new age bash for the planet.

As I walk up the path, an oak twig falls on my head. I stop to pull it out of my hair; the wind is calm, so it wasn't blown down. I wonder what the message is? I stand for a few moments, focusing on the twig in my hand, but I have no clear insight about its meaning.

When I return to Cluny Hill, I go to the basement to take my laundry from the drying racks. They hang about 20 feet above the ground. These long, heavy, wooden racks require a rope to haul them up and down. After taking down my clothes and pulling the rack back into position, I turn to leave. *Smack*, the clothes rack comes hurtling down, right on top of my head. I involuntarily sit down, stunned by the blow. Somehow the rope must have slipped out of the bracket. "OK, Creator," I mumble. "Please, let me hear what you're trying to hit me over the head with. I know I can be thick-headed. Please make it clear to me." As I sit rubbing my head, I decide that I missed the point with the oak twig. I'm afraid that if I don't get the message this time, I'll lose my head the next.

In the morning I go downstairs for Saturday morning Housecare, pausing in the lounge to glance through the papers. As I go into the dining room for a quick bite of breakfast, I meet the harpist. We sit and talk for a while and discover that we have mutual friends in the Mesa Verde valley of northern Arizona where she lives. Our conversation turns to her work with music and sound in the stone circles, and the importance of the Harmonic Convergence as a time of planetary awakening.

Awakening. The penny finally drops; I am being asked to *wake up*, to become fully alive and awake within myself. And if I miss the point when made *gently*, I will be hit over the head with it. Wake up. *That's* what the Harmonic Convergence is about.

That morning I decide to spend the weekend of the Harmonic Convergence with Alan in one of the remnants of the Caledonian forest. For a few days, though, I wonder if I'm missing the point of the event by avoiding the stone circles. In the end, I decide that it doesn't matter where I am. The point is to go where I can best listen and give my love to the Earth, and for me that place is wilderness.

During July Alan and I go through another period of turmoil. This time I am the one who is more distant, once again feeling that we have strayed from the sort of relationship that I want. We seem to be making a yearly habit of this summertime shake-up.

In between the long talks and tears and pain, the demands of the community continue. The Cluny members are meeting weekly to try to create a vision statement about our purpose at Cluny Hill. The closest we can come to agreeing on something is a statement that Rory wrote in a moment of inspiration: "Cluny Hill is a school that seeks to demonstrate the principles of unconditional love and transformation." We argue for weeks about the exact wording. "I don't like 'school'," declares one person. "And I don't like the term 'seek'," declares someone else. "Either we do it or we don't, but *seeking* is not the point." These declarations spin out into long, heated discussions. As I sit in the meeting, I remember the insight David Earl shared with me soon after I became a member, in answer to my frustration with all the meetings that we seem to need to keep the community running. "One thing that I do," said David, "—and believe me, after eight years of these meetings I get tired of them, too—is listen to what people are saying, and then try to understand *why* they are saying it. That's what makes the meetings interesting."

"You mean someone might say something because they need to be heard at that time, for attention, or because they have 'stuff' on the person who just spoke?"

"Right, things like that. I try to get a sense of the deeper undercurrents, that's all."

At a certain point in this series of meetings, I begin to question why we need a vision statement at all. Eric, the focaliser of Cluny, has decided that we need more cohesion as a group, and he's sure that having an agreed-upon purpose to focus on each day will bring the sense of solidarity that we lack. I'm not convinced that vision statements are the *only* way to bring a group together, but the meetings themselves seem to be filling a need among the members.

At least people are *coming* to the meetings, and the discussions are lively to say the least. We are re-examining our reasons for being together, which is a healthy sign. We can never really take for granted our larger purpose for being together without overlooking the fuel that nourishes our group life. The upshot of the meetings for me is a rekindling of the inspiration I felt when I first came back from Australia, to live and work the best way that I can within the community. And that renewed sense of purpose was the whole point of the meetings; as far as I'm concerned, with or without a vision statement they were a success.

In early July my work with guests expands to include leading a couple of sweat lodges for different guest programmes. As we stand around the fire, making tobacco offerings for what we want to give and receive from the sweat, I am moved by the depth of people's commitment to their own transformation and their desire to work for the planet. When my turn comes, I offer to give my creativity and love to the planet and ask to receive my power, to claim it fully. To claim *all* of myself. And to symbolise this acceptance, I take on my full name, Judith.

It takes a few days to readjust, but people in the community are very supportive; we are accustomed to people changing names. Not that everyone does it, but often periods of transformation and growth warrant it. The personal vibration changes, so why not the name? In a lot of native cultures an individual might have several names during a lifetime. In a Western culture it is more rare. 'Judith', though awkward at first, seems to suit me better.

In mid-July I take part in an Experience Week in preparation for focalising one later in the summer. Immediately following the end of the programme, I board the train to England to show my audio-visual about the Kingdoms of the Earth to a Healing Conference. Although I meet many interesting people, I realise that my days of attending conferences are over. Rarely do I hear new information; I need to *live* all of the things that I have heard and read instead of collecting more.

Riding on the train back to Scotland, I make notes about the EarthLove workshop at Newbold, scheduled to begin the following Saturday. This will be the first week-long EarthLove workshop, and I am both excited and nervous. The final schedule is packed, from 7 a.m. meetings for T'ai Chi to playing the board game until 11 p.m. This is my first attempt at including more experiential exercises to complement the insights that come with playing the game. I have always considered it an irony to sit indoors all day *talking* about relationship with the Earth instead of spending time *doing* it. And yet the game is powerful. Each time I guide it I experience more and more of its depth. Its essence is Gaia, the spirit of Earth itself, and I know I have touched only the surface of what it can reveal.

Three of us are co-focalising the workshop: Michael Swain, my friend from Northampton, Margaret, a member of Newbold, and I. Although we have to work flat out to keep up with the schedule we have created, we also have a lot of fun together. The workshop fulfils a lot of my dreams: working with people whom I love, and sharing my love for the Earth.

It also mirrors my own intense focus on action and commitment. The week ends with a flourish—an overnight vigil (in the cold, drizzling rain) to clarify our vision for our lives and the planet, followed by a sweat lodge in the early morning. Almost everyone has major blockages that they wish to release. Although my approach to the ceremony emphasises prayer and not endurance, many of the participants have heard horror stories of sweat lodges led by other people, most of whom have never sweated with a native person. The moment the flap comes down, a couple of people start to panic.

"I really need to get out," says one person beginning to hyperventilate. The panic is infectious. Several people leave during the first couple of rounds. All the blockages they have invoked releasing come roaring into their experience of the lodge. By the end of the process, though, most of the cleansing is complete, and peace fills the lodge. "Thank you Great Spirit," I pray internally, "for the beauty, strength and courage of these people. May we all live and serve well upon this Earth."

When the week ends, I return to the vegetable garden, grateful for quiet, steady work after the week of intense activity. Alan and I have time again to talk and reconnect, and after our separation we find another level of love for each other.

The following weekend we drive to Glen Strathfarrar, a remnant of the Caledonian forest where some areas have been fenced to allow regeneration. It is here that we will celebrate the Harmonic Convergence. We camp next to a stream in a narrow valley that is filled with bilberries just coming to full ripeness. Each morning we awake at sunrise to meditate, connecting with all of the points around the Earth where people have gathered to observe this time of Awakening. After breakfast—a cupful of bilberries gathered from the bushes along the stream—we hike in the surrounding hills.

As I sit quietly, waiting for Alan to photograph some of the trees, I ask what I can give to the Earth at this time. On this day, supposedly the end of one great cycle before the beginning of a new one, I focus my thoughts on humanity. I realise that I have shunned being a human being. My embarrassment about my middle-class upbringing has extended to my status as a human being as well. How can I be of help in this Awakening?

"Become even *more* human, become all a human can be. Bring *that* to Earth." The answer from my inner voice surprises me. During the past couple of weeks I have been wrestling with issues of Violence and Separation—the EarthLove game that I guided addressed both of these issues head on. At one point, one woman told the group, "I want to go through this pain so that I can really heal and release it. I want this experience, all of this pain, to be *useful*. And it helps to know that as I let go of these blockages, I'm doing it for the Earth. If I can let go of Violence and Separation, I make it easier for the whole planet."

Just that moment was worth the whole workshop. Eventually someone's experience of Magic and a 'Luminous Planet through Creativity' healed the Planetary Clouds of Separation and Violence. And as I sit on this mountain today, thinking about the game, I have a new insight. Violence and Creativity, both part of the game, are really two sides of the same coin. I abhor the violence that rages through humanity, but in this moment I see Violence as Creativity run amok. Stifled creativity leads to frustration and eventually, if suppressed too long, is *forced* to erupt as violence. "It is not for you to reason out all of the purposes of violence," I hear internally. "It is enough to deal with your own. Beginning to use your own creativity will do more to 'unstick' the pattern of violence, to *inspire* others, than anything else you can do."

The following day we decide to hike up to the top of a nearby ridge where we can see what looks like a lone pine tree, about a mile from its nearest neighbour. We plan to meditate on the ridge at the time of the sunrise at El Tule in Mexico, when Quetzacoatl is prophesied to come to life again. Sun Bear will be there to dance one of the masks of Quetzacoatl. People at sacred sites all over the world will be linking with El Tule at this time.

Hiking up towards the ridge, I berate myself for not doing more for this event. I probably should have fasted and gone off by myself somewhere, really dedicated myself to this time of transition. No great visions have come, no major revelations. Perhaps I have missed the point entirely.

Just as these thoughts are passing through my mind, we walk by a smooth eddy in the stream. I glance at the surface and notice a rainbow reflected in the water. Puzzled, I look up at the sky. Nothing. Not even clouds. I glance back and forth between water and sky—the rainbow continues to float on the water. "Good sign," comments Alan, nodding at the water. So he can see it, too. It's not my imagination.

As we walk up the ridge—or more accurately scramble, for the slope is steep and we are close to link-up time—I relax internally. This day is meant to be the awakening of the rainbow warriors, and I take the rainbow reflected in the water to mean "You are doing what you need to do. Everything is fine, right on schedule."

As we near the top of the ridge, we find that what we identified as a tree from below is actually a natural standing-stone sitting in a small pool of water. Resting our backs against a rock ledge nearby, we spend an hour in meditation. Internally I link with friends all over the world whom I know are meditating at this hour—on top of a volcano in Hawaii, at El Tule in Mexico, in South Dakota, at a stone circle in the Outer Hebrides, at the Great Pyramid in Egypt, on Mt Warning in Australia. In my mind I visit each continent, weaving them into my awareness of the whole planet.

For a couple of years I have had great expectations of this day. In the moment, though, I see and feel nothing out of the ordinary. In fact at the end of the meditation I sense laughter, as if the universe is enjoying a great cosmic joke. "This is simply another point of dedication," I hear. "Your *whole life* is dedicated to this work, to the changes that are ahead. Don't expect everything to happen all in this one moment. The effects will continue through your lifetime and beyond."

Alan and I share a bit about our experiences at the end of the meditation. We both have a sense that this moment, although special in that it has strengthened people's sense of planetary wholeness, is yet another *beginning* point, an opportunity to deepen our commitment to working for the Earth. As we walk down the ridge and spend time exploring the forest below, I decide that one way I can give to the Earth at this time is to create the storytelling performance that I envisioned last spring. In the evening I write some notes about a possible format, but I have no idea how I will actually pull together the stories and people and resources needed to complete the performance. When I mention my doubts to Alan, he stops to touch my face and gently kiss my forehead. "The way I look at it," he says, "is that no one receives a vision unless they have the power to enact it. You'll never know until you try."

Within a couple of weeks I have a meeting with three other people about the possibility of creating the storytelling performance together: Chris is an accomplished guitarist and wind instrument player, Naomi is a professional storyteller and a sister spirit in our connection with the Earth, and William is a professional dancer who has worked with EarthLove. We decide that the energy of Gaia is what we want to bring into the performance, to actually become the voice and body and spirit of Gaia, to speak for the Earth. Because the performance will be a benefit for Caledonian forest regeneration, we decide to find stories from traditional cultures that exemplify positive relationship with the Earth, especially with trees.

Our first 'rehearsal' together is an evening spent inside an old oak tree that grows beside the Findhorn River. The base of the tree has eroded into a hollow niche. From the black charring inside the trunk I assume that someone 'cured' the decay by building a fire in the base of the tree. Their efforts seem to have been successful—the old giant supports huge branches covered with healthy leaves. The four of us just barely squeeze into the hollow in the trunk. We sit silently, listening to the creaking of branches in the wind and sensing the almost imperceptible shifting of roots below us.

Over the next two months we continue to meet. William finally decides, not long before the performance, that he does not have time to participate. My tension about the event builds to just short of snapping. Naomi's growing impatience with me adds the final straw. She calls after the first dress rehearsal to say that if we don't make major revisions (mainly in my parts of the performance), she will quit.

I run out to the bicycle shed—what was once the freezer room when this was a hotel—and pull the door closed behind me. Here, enclosed by two-foot-thick walls, I can scream without disturbing anyone. And scream I do, overwhelmed with the challenges of trying to organise this performance. I have no professional background in any of it—I am simply a divine amateur being asked, *demanded,* to do a professional job. Why do I always attract perfectionists in my life? And why do I want to give this performance, anyway? Do I really want to help the Earth, or do I simply want an ego boost, a chance to shine as a performer?

When I emerge from the shed, snotty and tear sodden, Chris wraps his arms around me, and we sit in the garden shed talking. "Come on, Judith," he says when I tell him maybe this is all an ego trip and I should cancel the performance. "Do you really think that's true? I mean, if you want to cancel the performance, it's up to you. But I hate to see you questioning yourself like this. I don't think it's an ego trip; do you really believe that?"

"Well, when I first had the vision for the performance, it felt inspired. But now I don't know . . . . I need to think about it."

After a couple of days I decide that I am willing to give it a go, to work on my parts of the performance with Chris and Naomi's help. "All right," says Naomi, "I want you to channel all of that anger and frustration into this part. Put the power into your diaphragm. Let it come out in your voice. OK. Now start."

I look down at the paper and begin to read. "Put down the paper!" she commands. "And walk in from over there as if you were entering the stage."

I walk to the left and amble back to the centre of the room. "Come on, enter like you *are* this man. Get grounded. This is an aboriginal man, and he's pissed off. Get it together."

I practise and yell and bluster through the afternoon until finally the power of the words swells up from the ground and pushes through my heart and into my voice. For weeks my throat has been tight, but now it opens wide and my voice bellows out stronger than I have ever heard it before. "That's better," says Chris. "Now put your *body* into it." My knees bend and feet sink into the floor. My arms swing and stretch and reach like the branches of a tree. Finally, I am rooted in the land of paper bark eucalyptus and red sand and baramundi. I have become something more than myself.

The night before the performance. Dress rehearsal. Adrenalin pumps as we begin, invoking the four directions. We flow from song to story to dance to story, rooted by the power of the moment. The changes are clean, the nuances graceful, the dance and music powerful, the stories moving. At the end of the run through, we stand stunned. Somehow the power of the vision has translated through us. And from comments in the preview audience, that power is infectious. In one week the programme has altered so much that its earlier form is unrecognisable.

The night of the performance is almost anti-climactic after the dress rehearsal. The major difference, though, is the excitement generated by the audience that fills the Universal Hall. My vision was to speak for Gaia, to become the eyes, hands, heart and voice of the planet, and to offer positive images of humanity interacting with the Earth. Tonight we *do* become Gaia. I feel her as I stand in the Hall, digeridoo droning and slides of Australia moving behind me, as I become that aboriginal man who has a vision for the Earth:

I belong to this Earth
and Earth should stay with us.
This law
this country
this people
no matter what people
red, yellow, black or white
the blood is the same.
Blood, bone
all the same.
This story is important.
It won't change.
It is law.
It is like this Earth
it won't move.
Rock stays, earth stays.
I die and put my bones
in cave or earth . . . .
Soon my bones become Earth
all the same
My spirit has gone back to my country
my mother.
This story,
This is true story.
(Bill Niedje, *Kakadu Man*)

To end the performance, the audience joins us chanting:

Ancient Mother, I heed your calling
Ancient Mother, I hear your sound.
Ancient Mother, I share your laughter,
Ancient Mother, I dry your tears.

When we finish, I am high and elated and exhausted all at once. After all the tension and struggle, we have succeeded in creating a perfomance worthy of the trees.

The triumph is short-lived, though. I still need to pack my things to be ready for the bus that leaves for Iona at 5 a.m. tomorrow. Back at Cluny Hill I long to collapse in bed and sleep for a few days. Why, I ask myself as I wander around my room packing, do I always try to do things all at once? Gathering clothes and books and this and that takes twice as long as usual—the lack of sleep and worry about the performance, overriden only by intense focus on the event, overtake me as I begin to relax.

For a couple of weeks I have been torn between staying for the community's 25th birthday celebration during the coming week or taking the time alone at Traigh Bhan on Iona. In January, just over two months away, I will take an extended leave to evaluate my commitment here in the Foundation as well as to visit other communities in preparation for writing. I plan to visit Auroville in the south of India for six weeks, then join Alan for six weeks of backpacking through Rwanda and Tanzania before flying to Australia for three months to visit communities on the eastern coast.

At the beginning of the year I will be eligible for a 'staff position', which means taking on more responsibility, both in a work department and in inner alignment with the purpose of the community, but I want some time away to gain perspective on my life here. Many ex-members and old friends will be returning for the week-long birthday celebration, but I know that this will be my only opportunity to have a week alone at Traigh Bhan before I leave.

A couple of weeks ago, when I shared in a Garden group attunement that I would be going away and wasn't sure if I would return to live permanently in the commu-nity, Chris hugged me afterwards and then pulled away, shaking his head. "I've been watching you come into your power over the last months, and, damn, I wish you wouldn't go. People are always coming into their power here and then *leaving*. I wish they would stay *here* instead."

Knowing that I have only a couple of months left, much of which will be filled with planning the 'Warriors of the Heart' event scheduled over the coming New Year, I decide that I need the quiet time on Iona more than I need an extended birth-day party. I also want to visit Glastonbury, to complete physically one of the trian-gles of 'power points' in Britain, that linking Glastonbury, Iona and Findhorn.

And when I reach Traigh Bhan and settle into the house, I know that I have made the right decision. Over the past months my inner sensitivity has grown. So much information has been coming through in my written guidance time that I have start-ed using a tape recorder instead. Here in the Sanctuary in Traigh Bhan I can attune without interruption to the essence of the island and other energy streams.

Mid-way through the week I take the bus to Glastonbury to visit Chalice Well where Willa and Leonard Sleath, ex-members of the Foundation, are stewarding the property. Willa, the woman who guided the tour of the caravan park for my Experi-ence Week group, is still as impishly full of life as ever. In fact, even more so. When I ask how she and Leonard are getting along, she smiles and raises her eye-brows, eyes wide with mischief. "We're learning how to play together. *Really* play together. After all these years . . . just relaxing and being *silly* together. It's wonder-ful." She tells me about their experience of deciding to come to Chalice Well and all the wonderful, magical synchronicities that led them here. We also talk about the community and their experience and mine, and how they feel having left.

"You know," says Willa, "now, when I say this, I don't mean to put anyone down, but I realised that the community is like a kindergarten."

I nod my head. "I know what you mean. It's like a starting point, where people come when they are just . . . oh, just *beginning* their journey."

"Yes," agrees Willa.

"And there are other places that are like primary school or secondary school, or even university," adds Leonard. "We've met lots of teachers and attended lots of groups over the years, so we have a pretty wide view. But you know, some of the people who go to the 'university' level don't really understand what's going on because they haven't even been through kindergarten yet."

Hmmmm . . . ." I say, pulling at my lip. "Maybe that's what I've been feeling lately. Like I've graduated. Like I've been to kindergarten and graduated, and I'm ready for other things."

Much of my time in Glastonbury is spent walking through the English country-side, the fields marked with stone walls that march in straight lines over the undu-lating belly of the land. Each day I visit Gog and Magog, two oak trees said to be over 2,000 years old. According to local history, they are remnants of an oak-lined corridor once used by Druid priests. In the late afternoon I sit with my back against one of these ancient, gnarled trees, focusing my attention on its partner about eight feet away.

As I relax against the trunk, my sight grows soft and fuzzy. I begin to see waves of green and purple colour flowing back and forth between the trees. I sit bathed in these emanations, unaware of the autumn chill as the afternoon passes into dusk and then into evening. When full darkness comes, I walk back to Chalice Well. After drinking a cup of tea, I climb the stairs to the Sanctuary where I soon enter a deep meditation. In this quiet inner space, I reconnect with my experience sitting under the trees. I feel my heart opening, and words come into my awareness:

*The great oaks have a lesson for humanity. We speak of a peace and knowingness far beyond most humans' comprehension. When the way within yourself is clear to find such peace, you will find us and seek our wisdom and learning. Truly the oak bursts, in its quiet way, with the love of creation. Be aware of all that you radiate during your day/life in terms of love, discord, union or chaos. The thread upon which we live is strengthened or rent asunder according to the actions and thoughts and **beingness** of the creatures upon the Earth.*

Learning is a life-long pursuit. To this day I, an ancient oak, collect more learning and wisdom with each passing sun and moon cycle. How, you ask? I am not constrained to this physically rooted spot on the Earth. I am able in spirit/consciousness to expand to all parts of Earth and beyond. I do not leave my form, but rather expand to encompass those areas of current learning or interest.

*With care, we can become springboards for you and other humans to visit vaster realms. This must be done from a quiet and true desire to serve and expand for the good of the whole. We **cannot** be manipulated for any other purpose. Come in grace and humbleness. We have much to teach in the quiet inner world of the heart.*

When the flow of words ceases, I sit quietly in the Sanctuary. Recording these words in the notebook is both exhilarating and frightening for me. I have no internal measuring stick to determine the rightness or wrongness of the statements; I only know that they come to me through my heart and then translate into thoughts that I can write as words. My friend Gwydion encourages me simply to write what I hear, without judgement, knowing that in time the ability to listen and decipher will develop. Slowly I am learning to trust in the movements of my inner life. Often I see in retrospect the perfection of the small and large occurrences that shape my life and wish I could trust them in the moment.

Tonight I think back to my arrival at Chalice Well and my surprise at finding a picture of Wellesley Tudor Pole sitting on a table. Someone had recommended that I read his books, but when I went to the Park library at the Findhorn Foundation, I couldn't find any of them. I managed to borrow a short book of his, *A Man Seen from Afar*, about his experiences of actually being present in the Upper Room where the Last Supper took place as well as impressions of Jesus of Nazareth as he appeared in his own time. In the introduction Pole concedes that he cannot offer any logical explanations for the phenomena; the reader is encouraged to read critically and take in only those things that ring true in his or her heart.

When I asked Willa about the picture on the table, she told me that it was indeed Wellesley Tudor Pole. It was through his efforts that Chalice Well was restored and opened to the public—*and* the sanctuary in the house includes a full-scale model of the Upper Room that Pole saw in his 'vision'.

Shivers rippled up my spine. I had not realised that Tudor Pole had anything to do with Chalice Well or that he had created a replica of the Upper Room. The tingle in my spine reminded me that some greater hand was moving me, the movements all perfectly orchestrated, even to the details of the books that I read.

Soon after returning to Findhorn, I attend a meeting scheduled in the Park library. Afterwards, looking at the shelves of books, I suddenly see *all* of Tudor Pole's books standing out on the shelves as if spotlighted. I smile inwardly. Even when I think I am moving without a clear course, when I look in retrospect I see how carefully my life is guided. No coincidences. The universe takes good care of me, especially when my conscious awareness moves out of the way.

Only eight weeks remain before I will travel to the community of Auroville in South India. Much of the last weeks is filled with meetings to organise the 'Warriors of the Heart' event. During it, Danaan Parry, noted for his work in US-Soviet government negotiations and other forms of conflict resolution, will lead a five-day conflict resolution training for guests and members. His work here is part of a new trend in the Education Department to welcome people from outside the Foundation to work with guests in major programmes. Past conferences have included speakers and workshop leaders for one session at a time, but never before has one person given a five-day workshop for both members and guests.

In the mid-70s, the 'look within' philosophy was adhered to so strongly that any sort of a teacher was rejected. Through the late 70s and into the 80s the trend softened until now teaching and (selected) input from outside the community is accepted. Last summer's guest programme, for example, included one workshop led by a long-time friend of the community, co-focalised with a community member. Slowly we are learning that our gift is the *way* that we work with people, and that approach—applying love and building a unified, supportive group—can be used to teach many things that the planet needs at this time.

The demands of servicing a large conference usually keep members from participating fully, so for this event we limit the guest numbers and try to streamline the workload so that as many members as possible can join the sessions. Through the five days we explore conflict and love and power. We listen and laugh and linger over Danaan's stories. We practise Taoist breathing and Aikido moves. We roleplay disintegrating family households—the frontline of all peace work—and mediate disputes. We tell our own stories of warriorship around the fireplace one cold, winter evening. And we create fireworks in the Hall, honest open explosions of truth, when we divide into two groups, one of men and one of women, facing each other to tell the other sex how it really is to be a man or woman.

When the five days end, I feel as I did after the performance in November—tired without the luxury of relaxing. I have two weeks to clear my room and pack or sell three-years-worth of accumulated this and that before leaving on my journey to India, Africa and Australia. And I have a *lot* of this and that. Also, after a couple of years of offering EarthLove games without a very enthusiastic response among the members, suddenly a lot of people want to play before I go, so I schedule as many games as I can squeeze in among goodbyes with friends and filling the daunting stack of empty cartons littering my room. Only the finality of an unchangeable airline ticket catapults me through the loose ends that tangle forward movement. Preparing to leave here for a week is challenging, a month difficult, and a final departure horrific.

Swamped by the demands of packing and the emotional turmoil of leaving friends, my throat tightens and then my chest fills with mucus. Despite the deep cold, though, I also feel joyful and excited about the journey ahead.

In my final interview with Personnel, I recount some of my experiences while living in the community. My friend Roger found a quote somewhere that captures my changing awareness exactly: "Don't ask what you can do for the world. Ask instead what makes you feel alive, and do it. Because the world needs more people who have come alive." And I have learned that what makes me 'come alive' is my relationship with the Earth, with the devic kingdoms, and with anything that makes my heart fly open—dancing, playing fiddle music, singing sad and silly songs, lying with friends in grassy fields or having water-pistol fights in the garden.

I share my pain, too, about my struggles with offering my gifts to the community and feeling that they were rejected, my sense of being stifled creatively, and Satya's comment that I was invisible.

"That sounds like her 'stuff'," comments Michael, the new addition to Personnel since Satya's departure earlier in the autumn. "I've always felt you had a spiritual presence around the place, and that's what's most important to me when I look at members. I also think you probably would have had an easier time at another stage of the community's development, when your skills might have been more valued."

When we have a final attunement, I visualise myself moving away from the column of light. Before me I see pools of colourful lights and dancing earthly and elemental creatures along the path. I sense that the time ahead will be filled with graceful movement, stepping from circle to circle of pastel light accompanied by the love and joy of the 'unseen' worlds.

The following morning during meditation, my heart fills and then overflows with love. In this open, joyous moment, words enter my mind that outline a roadmap for the coming journey:

Choose joy and your life will flow with abundance.
Choose joy and all obstacles shall become as sand.
Choose joy and all partings shall be as breathing spaces before a new beginning.
Choose joy and all currents of change shall be as a joyous adventure.
Choose joy and all distrust shall flow like clouds dispersed in wind.
Choose joy and the Earth shall rejoice.
Choose joy and your soul will reach its perfect form.
Choose joy and the song of the cosmos will fill your daily chores.
Choose joy and the dance of Time and Space will bless your Doing.
Choose joy and your Being will radiate the love of Spirit.
So be it, for Love is made manifest through Joy.
(Live these words. They are a stepping stone into a greater way of being.)

141

CHAPTER 8
Auroville

Bombay. Everywhere I look there are people. Walking out of shacks (made from bits of newspaper, scraps of wood fallen from trucks, tar paper and other gleanings from the street) are men in sparkling white shirts, beaten clean by their wives in the muddy irrigation ditches that run alongside the outer streets of Bombay. These men's immaculate clothes and their patient smiles are so incongruous with the shacks they come from. And everywhere skittering across the road are skinny animals with raw sores. And dust. Everywhere the dust. Its smell mixes with the odours of stale urine and curry, wood smoke, exhaust fumes and animal sweat.

India has its own scent, a pervasive composite of odours that is unmistakable. If blindfolded and flown to some foreign land, I would know India from the smell and the menagerie of sounds—the clatter of hooves and the clank of an oxen's bell; the 'schr-r-r-ring schr-r-r-ring' rattle of a bicycle rickshaw's bell, the electronic 'reemp reemp' of a three-wheeled auto-rickshaw, and the all-pervasive 'ta-ta-t-t-t-TAA-TAA' airhorn of a bus or truck.

The plane from Bombay has landed long after dark. I have no reservation for a hotel and only an outdated traveller's book to guide me. The information booth is closed, but at least half a dozen hawkers wait at the exit, offering to make reservations and find a taxi cab. When I ask for one hotel, I am told it has closed. "But, Madam, I can find you hotel. Good hotel, with television." The last thing I need is television, and I am wary of swindlers after all the horror stories I have heard. I push my cart through throngs of people—families sitting on the curbs, people with hands outstretched chanting "Madam, Madam," boys eager to push my cart—for a price, of course. I feel like a Martian—I cannot hide my ginger hair or my almost transparent white skin that hasn't seen the sun since Australia nearly a year ago.

One man steps forward to push my cart and grabs the bar before I can block him.

"Whered are you gowinck, Madam, whered are you gowinck?"

We have a struggle over who is in charge of the cart. He refuses to let go, even when I jam my elbow down on his wrist. Only when I jerk the cart to a halt and push my face a couple of inches from his and yell "Let go!" does he reluctantly release his hold on the bar.

When finally I reach the bus and gratefully leave my heavy pack for the driver to load, I realise moments later that I should have stood outside to make sure no one snatched it before we left. I sit on the bus agitated and unsure whether or not to get out and check.

When I arrive at the hotel, I carry my bags to the front desk and ask for a room. The clerk has to repeat everything at least twice because both my ears are blocked; the congestion from the cold has moved into them from the pressure of many take-offs and landings in the last 20 hours. "I want a room with toilet and shower," I explain, nodding my head up and down, "without air conditioning," shaking my head back and forth.

"Yes, Madam," says the clerk, swivelling his head. The movement fascinates me—the head seems to have little to do with the neck. It is like a bowl full of ball bearings balancing on a pin. He swivels and scowls at each of my responses. While I wait for him to fill out papers, a young Australian woman walks into the lobby wearing a cream-coloured silk blouse and billowing pyjama pants. "Ah," says the clerk, his face softening with approval. "Beautiful."

"I picked it up from the tailor today," says the woman, smiling as she twirls around to show the back. She looks radiant and relaxed, comfortable in herself and with her aloneness. Her ease contradicts so many stories of women travelling alone . . . . I am envious.

During the night I sleep badly, distracted by the mosquito net draped over me (no place to fix the ties, so it rests directly on my face), the sounds of traffic and the strong smell of mildew and old urine in the room. In the morning I repack my bags and venture into the street to hail a rickshaw. We bargain a price (he begins with double the figure that the desk clerk suggested) and then bump and weave among the potholes and the unlikely mix of traffic that jams the streets. Bicyclists bypass bullock carts, shiny chromed trucks roar by pedestrians balancing earthenware pots filled with grain on their heads. A taxi careens around a corner, spraying dust on a boy herding goats with a stick. Every sort of vehicle, from the most ancient (feet) to the most modern (cars patterned after European models, their bright colours conspicuous among the black 1950-ish design that has served as a standard for two generations), swerves among the others on the road. Although the signs are positioned for driving on the left-hand side of the road, a by-product of British rule, I quickly learn that this is only a general directive—drivers choose a side according to their fancy.

At the bus station, I press among the people and discover that a bus is leaving for Pondicherry in about ten minutes. Standing at the platform, I feel strangely calm, despite the stares of many passengers. Even a European man travelling with his son singles me out and touches my arm, looking at my pale skin. "You've just arrived, haven't you?" he asks. I look at his brown hair, bleached to blond at the temples, and his sun-faded pants and shirt. "Yes, just off the plane. How'd you guess?" I ask, already knowing the answer. "You're so white. I mean, even for a European."

On the bus I sit next to a Tamil woman. Through her few words of English (and my non-existent Tamil) I learn that she is going to visit her sister in the village where she is from. When we stop at a roadside stand for lunch, she insists that I eat something. Men and women with trays of greasy food pass along the outside of the

143

windows so that passengers need only extend a hand to make a purchase. By the third round of vendors I am hungry enough to buy a few of the balls of fried dough. They taste like stale flour soaked in rancid oil. I eat a few bites and offer the rest to my travelling partner. She refuses, insisting that I eat.

I get off the bus to buy a drink at one of the cold drink stands, rough but sturdy affairs made with dry, splintery wood. Every beggar within a quarter of a mile catches sight of me and begins to walk or hobble or drag him or herself towards me. The most insistent is an old woman without legs. She hauls herself onto the bottom step of the bus and rasps "Madam, Madam, Madam" until the bus driver shoos her away. I look at the woman next to me, perplexed, unsure what to do. "You could give her *something*," she explains, glancing at my clothes and backpack. Although by Western standards I live on modest means, here in India I am wealthy beyond most villagers' imagination.

Most of the passengers nap in the mid-day heat. The bus occasionally veers to avoid a bicyclist who wobbles into the loose sand at the last moment or skids to avoid a bullock cart coming from the opposite direction. Rice fields stretch for miles away from the road. Only tiny villages with thatched mud huts interrupt the flatness. Women pound saris against the rocks in the village ponds and then drape them over rocks or grass stubble to dry. Old men and women lie death-like outside their huts. Children squat on the edge of the road, streaming urine behind them. In the fields the men and women stop at mid-day, squatting beside stainless steel pots of white rice, dipping fingers into the bowl and then gracefully swirling their hand to their lips before a single grain drops. How could anyone sleep with so much life bursting all around them? And why is it that everything seems more vital here? As we pass from village to village, I realise that people here live without privacy; what Westerners pursue behind closed doors occurs here for all to see. They have no doors to close. Life is immediate, direct, without censure.

Arriving at the bus station in Pondicherry, I am unsure how to find Auroville, much less the settlement of Fertile where I will be staying with a couple named Jan and Johnny (where Alan stayed during his visit). I mutter some prayers as I wander around the bus station. "OK, Creator, please, please guide me in how to get to Auroville. I have no idea where to go."

I approach the cluster of auto-rickshaws at the end of the bus station and ask if anyone can take me to Auroville. "Fifty Rupees," explains a self-appointed spokesperson. "Fifty?" I ask, incredulous. The four-hour bus trip cost only Rs 15. I talk him down to forty and then pull out my map of Auroville, a line drawing that shows the various settlements within the community. "Fertile," I explain, pointing at the map. Coughs and scuffing and general looks of confusion. Finally another man looks up. "Fer-teel?" he asks. Thank Goddess, a translator. "Yes, yes," I nod. "OK, you go," says the spokesperson, pointing to a young driver. He wrestles the vehicle out of the jam of rickshaws and wheels it to the road.

We drive back along the same road that the bus followed, past the shops and buildings and shacks and villages that stand farther and farther apart until the rice fields once again dominate the landscape. We turn onto a dirt road that goes through a few more villages. We pass under bougainvillaea branches and shrubs and trees. I can tell that the driver is excited by the lush greenness and realise that, although he claimed to know his way, he has never been here before. He points excitedly at a round structure covered by a filigree of geometric concrete patterns, "Matrimandir, Matrimandir." I recognise the structure from slideshows about Auroville—it is the heart of the community, geographically as well as symbolically. The Mother, the woman whose vision began Auroville, wanted the Matrimandir to be a place of

'Concentration', for the development of the inner lives of the people here. And for a community of around forty settlements scattered over 25 square kilometres, the building of the Matrimandir over the last 18 years has been the only unifying project for the collective as a whole.

The driver manoeuvres through the maze of roads, finally homing in on the Matrimandir. When we reach a crossroads near the structure, he stops and turns around to look at me. I know no Tamil and he knows no English, and I know he's as lost as I am. I glance around at two Tamil men across the road; the driver jumps out to talk with them. I look over to the left and see a Tamil man speaking with a woman . . . brown haired . . . familiar. "Dee!" I call out. "Dee, is that you?"

I know only a handful of Aurovillians, people who have visited Findhorn over the last three years. I met Dee during her last trip to Findhorn, just this past autumn. "Thank you, Great Spirit," I say internally, "for looking after me."

Always Dee has a smile, and she wraps her arms around me when I step out of the rickshaw. "This is Rama Lingum," says Dee, introducing me to the man beside her. "He's one of the first Tamil members of the community. He's been with us since he was a young boy."

I shake hands with Rama Lingum and chat briefly with Dee, explaining that the driver has no idea where Fertile is. "Well, I think Johnny is teaching today," says Dee, "but he'll probably be back in the late afternoon." Rama Lingum offers to lead the rickshaw driver on his motorbike. Grateful for his help, I call back the driver. "Oh, Dee, I just remembered," I say as I climb back into the rickshaw. "I have a letter for you, from Eric (a member at Findhorn)—hand delivered." Dee smiles and promises to stop by to visit soon.

We bump along a network of sandy roads. Even Rama Lingum pauses to remember the way at certain points. Without his help I am sure we would never reach Fertile. After a precarious drop in a washed-out area followed by a particularly sandy bit (the driver looks greener and greener as the road deteriorates), Rama stops his motorbike at the mouth of a green, leafy forest.

Johnny walks down the path to greet us; I'm not sure what I expected, but his lanky, graceful strength is welcome. The first thing I notice after his sun-blonded mop-like beard and the cloth twisted around his head is his eyes staring into mine—more an open-eyed than a wide-eyed look which is so deeply evaluating that I involuntarily smile and look down to adjust a strap on my daypack before hoisting it onto my shoulder. While Johnny chats with Rama Lingum, I pay the driver who is nervously wiping the engine and innards of the auto-rickshaw. Feeling a bit guilty about the rough ride (Johnny mentions that most rickshaws refuse to go farther than the far end of this section of road) I give him an extra Rs 10.

Johnny gives me a quick hug, nods his head, and then deftly swings the heavy backpack onto his shoulder and turns to walk along the path into the forest. I follow his barefoot prints in the sand, breathing the scent of flowers warmed by late afternoon sun. Patches of sunlight, escaping the leafy canopy, dapple the path. Bird song, the 'Tswoooooweet' sonic boom sound characteristic of the tropics, filters through the trees. I pause to listen to a bird call, 'bong . . . . bong . . . bong . . bong bongbongbongbong', that quickens like a dropped ball.

After the desert-like sweep of rice fields and dusty villages, this forest is a bit of paradise. The path winds past an open-domed building with bits of machinery and dusty books—what was once a school, Johnny explains, and is now a workshop. To the right a horse stands tethered among the trees. A cow rests patiently in the shade of a lashed bamboo and timber shed, and her calf lies nearby.

Straight ahead is the buttressed trunk of a banyan tree, its base encased in red clay

145

built up to form a smooth raised seat. The branches twist from the trunk, reaching towards the main house—ferrous cement base with thatched roof rising two stories above—and spreading over the roof of the open kitchen and eating area. Chickens and pea hens scratch in the courtyard and the dusty area around the cow shed. While Johnny deposits my pack inside the house, one of the roosters, a young one with colourful tail feathers and a beautiful comb, scratches his feet like an impatient racehorse and then makes a dive at my legs. Stunned, I jump back and rub the long scratch on my thigh left by his spur. "That's a new cock," says Johnny, shooing the indignant bird away. "He's had a few fights with the old cock but hasn't won yet. He seems to have his own flock of hens that follow after him."

We sit in the shade of the banyan, among a semi-circle of assorted chairs. "Do you know the architect Christopher Alexander?" asks Johnny. When I shake my head, he explains that Christopher believed in having lots of different types of furniture instead of everything matching. He emphasises creating functional living spaces, inviting nooks and crannies, comfortable, useful spaces.

"Is Jan working at the school, too?" I ask as we settle into the chairs, drinking tea sweetened with palm syrup and laced with fresh milk. "No, she's in Australia right now. She inherited some property in Victoria, south of Sydney, and she keeps saying she'll be back on a certain date, but then something else comes up . . . like she was supposed to come back with our daughter Jina in late January, but then she got an order from the local zoning board that she has to clear a three-foot path all around the property line. And she likes it there. She's talked several times about moving back to Australia, but I know that I want to stay here."

"How do you feel about that, wanting to be in different places? That's been an issue for Alan and me."

"If she's happy there, it's fine with me. We're more partners than husband and wife—we work well together with the children, and I'm glad that she's happy where she is. I think she'll be back, though, but she'd better come back before the really hot season starts. You picked the coolest time of year—that's easier. Then when the heat comes you adjust to it gradually, but to come back in the middle of the hot season —wooouh. Forget it."

The conversation runs to news from the Findhorn Community and Alan and his work with the calendar, how he is producing a new 'Trees for Life' diary this year to reach more people with information about the world's forests and the vision to regenerate the Caledonian forest.

"But is he doing anything?" asks Johnny. "Like planting trees or putting up fences? I'm interested in what people are actually doing, not just talking about." I explain the focus is on raising funds right now and finding local groups to work with, but I take the point to heart. As I look around the settlement, knowing that twenty years before the earth grew only a sparse crop of grain, I know Johnny is a man of action, not idle talk.

We walk through the garden, planted during the monsoon season that usually runs from late August to early January. Most of the rain, though, falls in the last two months of the year. I have arrived just after the ending of the rains, but its effects still survive in the mould that invades stored clothes or paper and in the fresh bloom of flowers and plants.

"We plant the garden during the rainy season," explains Johnny, "and grow most of our vegetables during the winter and spring. After May it's really too hot to grow anything." I smile, commenting how Scotland has just the opposite problem—not enough warmth and light to grow a lot of vegetables.

At the back of the garden is a pump house made with limestone pillars that support a thatched ('keet') roof. Bundles of flowers and splashes of red paint still linger on the posts from the Tamil New Year celebration/harvest festival. Newly installed under the roof is a Sterling engine, fuelled by wood or grain. The engine generates energy to move the piston through the movement of air between a front fire-heated chamber and a water-cooled one behind it. The government sponsored the installation of the pump as an experiment to provide alternative energy sources in the villages. Since most villages have little or no firewood, the engine is designed to burn rice chaff which is in plentiful supply throughout most of India, particularly in the agriculturally based state of Tamil Nadu. Fertile, unlike most of India, is blessed with a source of firewood from the thinnings and dead trees in the forest. The trees here grow quickly, but by the same token they reach maturity and die back quickly as well, so although the forest is only about 18 years old (the planting took place over a period of years), already Johnny can harvest some wood from it.

Moving back towards the circle of chairs in the deepening dusk, Johnny points out a small house at the far side of a pond choked with waterlilies. "That's Jan's house," he explains, "where you'll be staying. You can move your things in tomorrow." Johnny moves around the kitchen, lighting lanterns and ladling bowls of soup from a stainless steel urn that sits on a two-burner gas stove. I hear a crunching in the sand on the path and then see a beam of light. "Ah," says Johnny looking up, "this is Claude. He's living with us while he builds a new house for himself. Claude, this is Judith."

"Bonjour, hello," says Claude. "Welcome. I do not speak English very well, but I try."

"Claude didn't know a word of English when he came to live at Fertile, but now he can speak pretty well," says Johnny.

"How could you live here in Auroville without learning English?" I ask, surprised.

"I lived in Aspiration, which is almost all French people. I could live just fine without English."

"Why are you moving?"

"Oh, I've had enough of that community. I was really a loner there; I did not fit in. But now I am moving into a place next to Aurolec, where I work."

"Is that the computer company that Auroville started?"

"Yes, yes, that is the one."

The three of us settle into chairs and talk as night falls. "The dark comes quickly here," explains Claude between spoonfuls of soup. "By 6:30, completely dark."

Through our conversation, the first of many in the dark evenings of the tropics, I come to know Claude and most deeply Johnny. Himal, a teenage boy originally from Hyderabad, also lives in Fertile. He is like an adopted son to Johnny and Jan. He wanders through the kitchen later in the evening and says hello. His greatest passion is horseracing, Johnny tells me, and he was in training as a jockey before coming to live in Auroville. Even in the dark Tanney, the horse tethered among the trees, nickers when Himal walks by—their deep connection grows more obvious to me as the weeks go by.

The story of Fertile gradually unfolds. The settlement developed from one banyan tree (the one with the clay seat around its base), surrounded by soil baked hard as brick in the hot south-Indian sun, into a lush forest filled with birds and animals that had not been seen in this area since the clearing of the forest many years before. Among the weeds that have returned with the trees I find the remains of buildings, their thatched roofs long since disintegrated, that were the homes or private hideouts of families and children who have now left Fertile, either to establish settlements elsewhere or to range beyond India. Originally three families pioneered the replanting of the Fertile forest. Wandering among the tall trees I find a foundation of red cement which Johnny later explains is the remains of their first house.

"Your house?" I ask, incredulous.

"Yeah, for the first few years, until we built this one."

The structure, about the same size as the round kitchen in their present house, was home to Jan and Johnny and three children.

"And you did all of the replanting work while you lived in that house?"

"Well, the other families helped, too. We shared the central kitchen area and the garden. We used to do a lot more with the garden, but I've been busy with the kids in the school. When Alan was here we had the school in the building over there," he says, motioning to the domed structure, "but now we have a central school at Aspiration where all the kids go."

"Do you still teach?"

"Well, I still teach maths and a woodworking class. The kids are into that—you know, they need to work up a sweat once in a while; they can't just sit in class all the time. They can get out some of their energy and put it into some kind of work. We have community work projects once a month. Rama Lingum always cooks something great for lunch; a lot of kids come just for that."

"So you work with other teachers in the school?"

"We-e-ell, sort of. They have meetings once a week, but I usually don't go. I just want to teach, not deal with a lot of extra meetings."

"Is that OK with the other teachers?" I ask, thinking of my experience in the Steiner School, knowing how important the meetings were for the school's running.

"Mmh, they usually make some comments about my being there, but I've got a lot to do around here. Himal does a lot of things—he's a really good mechanic and builder—but right now I'm doing most of the work here along with the workers. Mangini knows the place almost as well as I do; he's been working here for years. But there are some things I have to be around to do. Like the Sterling pump. We're still working out the bugs in it."

During the coming days I realise that Auroville as a whole is still 'working out the bugs'—it is very much a community in its youth, involved in building and establishing itself. The foundation work of reclaiming the land, though, is largely complete. The government of India annexed a patchwork of land spread over 25 square kilometres for the creation of Auroville with the idea that some day the stretch of land would be continuous. The 'promised land' was never deeded, however, and Auroville today is a checkerboard of local villages and community land.

Almost all of the land stewarded by the community has been 'bunded', surrounded by a low wall of mounded dirt shaped by hand tools in the wet season. This simple method conserves water and soil. In the village fields the water floods in the monsoon season and then races into gullies, sweeping away acres of topsoil with it. In one area the canyons carved by the runoff are over twenty feet deep. The bunded fields, however, hold the water in place until it gradually soaks into the soil. The combination of bunding and tree planting originally caused the local water table to rise. In the past few years, though, the monsoon rains have become less and less predictable, and the water table has stabilised or even dropped.

The Mother envisioned Auroville with a 'green belt' around it, a wide band of forest and agricultural land to support the community. Together with Roget, a French architect, she discussed at length plans for the community that was to be "a bridge between the past and the future. Taking advantage of all discoveries from without and from within, Auroville will boldy spring towards future realisations."

148

The Mother died in 1972, four years after Auroville's founding. She left behind copious writings including directives and inspiration for the budding community and sheafs of possible plans for the futuristic city. One person who was close to the Mother said she responded to almost all suggestions with childlike enthusiasm —"Oh, yes, put it in, put it in." The people remaining to carry out the vision are struggling to piece together her dream and enact it. For a community dedicated to making bold leaps, though, the land of India offers a hard landing.

Resources are almost non-existent in India, and funding even scarcer. Many of the buildings begun in the early days of the community when international expectations were high now languish half-complete after the funds ran dry. A friend once wrote that Auroville impressed him as a bunch of '. . . futuristic structures growing weeds'. As the days pass, my understanding increases—India moves at a much slower pace than the West, weighted by the demands of basic survival. People had tried to describe to me the slow pace of the country, the lack of material goods, the difficulty in communications, but the descriptions meant nothing until I arrived to live them.

The simple act of buying a flashlight, for example, means getting to Pondicherry, 13 miles away. For the majority in India, that means walking or riding a bicycle. I am among the privileged who can afford to rent a bike. The elite ride motorbikes. Only the unimaginably wealthy have cars. Once in the city, I weave through the traffic to the market at the centre of town. There, row upon row of stalls stretch through a warehouse-like building, each shop crammed to the brim with goods —stainless steelware or sugar, vegetables or cloth, grain or heaps of aromatic spices, all weighed, wrapped in paper and then tied with string; paper or plastic bags are an unknown luxury. With Johnny's directions I find the stall that sells soap and other medicinals, then move to the end of the first row where the glass lantern canes are sold.

The shopkeeper carefully wraps the thin glass canes and frowns when I put them in my backpack. "Car-r-reful," he warns. "Break easily." I nod and smile and walk to the third row to find batteries and a flashlight. Although India prides herself on having electrified 100% of her villages, the settlement of Fertile does not have electricity. Johnny has resisted it tooth and nail. The local electricity, or 'current' as it is called here, comes from a nuclear power plant, and Johnny refuses to support nuclear energy. In the evenings, we light kerosene lanterns and use flashlights to move around. Emboldened by my success in finding torch and batteries, I seek out a 'medicals' store—allopathic medicine is the rage now in India, a status symbol of modernisation—to ask for contact lens solution. The clerk stares at me. "Contact?" he asks, puzzled.

"For the eyes," I explain. He leads me to a shelf full of eyedrops for sore eyes. I smile and thank him and leave the shop. In India, it seems, contact lenses belong in the same realm as microwave ovens.

For over a week I make the trek into Pondicherry (or 'Pondi', as it is called locally) to visit the 'School for Perfect Eyesight'. Founded by a man living in the Sri Aurobindo Ashram in Pondi, an optometrist inspired by Dr Bates, the clinic is dedicated to improving eyesight for anyone who wishes to come. No fees are charged, but donations are welcome. Having worn glasses for nearly twenty years, I am eager to improve my sight, even if only partially.

Each morning I awake at sunrise, lying on the bed in the upper floor of Jan's house, watching the orange glow of the sun between the trees and listening to the first chorus of birds. I clamber across the floor made of lashed bamboo poles and climb down a ladder to the cool, red concrete floor below. Once dressed, I make a dash for the toilet, placed at the edge of the forest with its own keet roof, and then wash in the cistern at the back of the main house. Although we don't have running water per se, each day the Sterling engine pumps water up from the well bored nearly 100 feet into the ground and fills three different tanks in the house and kitchen through a system of pipes buried underground. Large plastic measuring cups sit along the lip of the cistern for dousing yourself with clean, cool water. The water runs across the floor of the open patio and into a drain.

The January mornings are cool, so I dress quickly and head for the kitchen where Johnny and Himal sit sipping tea and eating hot cereal, made from one of the grains grown in a field nearby. A couple of nights ago, in fact, Johnny slept on top of one of the piles of just-harvested grain stalks to guard them where they lay waiting to be threshed the following day. "Why do you have to guard it?" I asked as he slung a blanket over his shoulder and prepared to leave for the night.

"Because you can't just leave things in the fields."

"Someone would take it if it was sitting there?"

"Sure—the Tamils are known for being 'light fingered', but I figure it's my fault if something gets stolen. They're like children; if you tempt them, they can't help themselves, so I try not to leave anything valuable out in the open."

This morning I have a bowl of cereal, slip on my daypack, and push my bike along the sandy path to the road. The first and last part of the trip are the hardest, straining through the loose sand on this back road. Nearer the main bitumen road going into Pondi the track is a bit better maintained. At one time the road from the beach to the Matrimandir was hurriedly paved for the visit of Rajiv Gandhi, but now, a few monsoon seasons later, the tar is gone and the sharp-edged gravel eats tyres. I skirt the edge, veering to one side or the other depending on the number of bicyclists coming from the opposite direction or the size of a herd of goats prodded by village boys.

I finally reach the main road, but the luxury of a firm surface is offset by the challenge of avoiding trucks and buses that careen along at full speed, sometimes leaving downed bicyclists in their wake. Johnny told me about a young family from a nearby village who rode into Pondi to watch a movie one night. Indians have made an art of stacking people on bicycles. The women lean gracefully on the carrier rack, sari and sash unruffled; children sit one on the handlebars, one in the rider's lap, one or two in the rider's arms on the back. This particular family was about half-way into Pondi when a truck hit the cycle and killed the whole family. In a moment. Gone. As I ride, I know that life is abundant and cheap in India. The wall between life and death is thin and neither my skin nor my cultural background provides immunity. Life is more immediate in the villages, and so is death, and I have no more guarantee of finishing my journey than anyone else on the road.

The unlikely mix of traffic weaves along at a somnolent pace—a honk, a dodge, a glance, a weave, a weft, onwards. Slowly. "Make time your friend, not your foe," says the sign in the Bank of India in Auroville. "Even if haste is unavoidable, hasten slowly." Sri Aurobindo. Relax or go mad becomes my motto.

Dust. Everywhere dust. A boy smiles with joy as he crouches by the roadside, relieving his bowels for the day. A goat wanders by, chewing the tatters of a rag, stirring clouds of dust with its spindly legs. An old man sits corpse-like against a mud brick wall, limp, seeking shade from the morning sun. 9 a.m. Still cool.

10 a.m. Sweat beads break, the sun presses hot on my shoulders. Sewing machines clack in a rough wooden hut, tailors' feet marching on the treadles, feeding through cloth to make western-style shirts. Outside on a billboard is a chubby Indian man wearing sunglasses and a blue polyester leisure suit. Ultimate status

150

symbol is the camera slung around his neck. I feel sad looking at the bony, broad shoulders of Tamil men constrained in polyester button-down shirts. Johnny comments that polyester lasts longer, so the villagers prefer it—but in this climate it is mercilessly hot.

Weave, dodge, ring bell. I pass a group of schoolchildren walking along the road, waving for a ride to shorten their long walk. I slow for a young boy (he jumps on before I fully stop)—I barely feel his weight on the carrying rack. He waves to his friends and smiles at his good fortune—fewer miles on his bare-soled feet.

Close to Pondicherry. One village bleeds into another. Taxis vie with bullock carts and goat herds. Hundreds of bicyclists, bound for work in Pondi, jockey on the road. Never have I seen a collision—a sixth sense seems to magnetise vehicles out of the way at the last minute. Many people who have travelled in India have told me how supremely intuitive the Indians are. On the road I know where they honed their skills and how necessary intuition is to survival here. Inner listening is second nature, a given in the culture.

Dung and urine patchwork in the dusty roadside. Children playing, half-dressed, happy. Glimpses of women beating clothes in the courtyards that open into the main street. "Privacy is a Western luxury," says Johnny. And suddenly the little house where I am staying, surrounded by trees and the sounds of birds, seems opulent despite the lack of electricity or running water or fancy furniture. To a villager my backpack full of clothes and small things is more than they will ever see together at one time in their whole lives, and yet I pride myself on having discarded a lot of my possessions to travel 'lightly'. The scale between the haves and the have-nots is way out of balance. I knew it intellectually before, but now I am living the inequality, which is far more enlightening than any television image or university course or impassioned speech. Visiting a Third-world country should be part of every Westerner's education—it is humbling and stretching to know how three-quarters of the planet lives and to realise that my lifestyle in the West rests upon the backs of these people. And, believe me, those backs are bowed under the weight.

I ride past the brewery, which exudes a mellow smell of fermentation. The rest of Tamil Nadu has banned liquor sales, but Pondicherry is a state unto itself and allows drinking. A French colony until the 1950s, Pondi is much wealthier than the surrounding towns, partly because of its informal ties with France and the relatively large population of Europeans for its size, and partly because it receives government funding as a state and has an effective lobby in the National Congress.

On the left side of the road, the Indian Ocean rolls lazily, sky-blue water dancing with reflected sunlight. I turn to the right towards the School of Perfect Vision—the courtyard is a quiet oasis on a back street of Pondicherry. Walking up the wide concrete steps to the upper verandah, the airy cleanliness and order of the school centres me. The first sight on walking into the high-ceilinged, whitewashed rooms is a photograph of Sri Aurobindo and the Mother, his spiritual partner.

Aurobindo fled here for political asylum in the early part of the century to avoid British persecution for his revolutionary ideas. His crime? Speaking out for Indian independence from British rule. He did endure one trial, and during his year-long imprisonment for treason his inner skills blossomed. In Pondicherry he continued his copious writing and his inner explorations, perfecting them to a science.

Aurobindo was already into his later years when a Frenchwoman came to visit the ashram. From a wealthy middle-class family of artists and a strong background in intellectual thinking, she had an active inner life that defied her rational leanings. A few years later she returned to the ashram to work with Aurobindo as a partner in what they described as the 'great exploration', striving to perfect themselves in

151

order to make the leap to the next phase of human development. For Aurobindo and the Mother (as she came to be known) that evolution would be a leap in consciousness, not an immediate change in physical form. They approached this inner work with the exactness of scientific researchers, recording the results of their experiments and exploration. Their journals are fascinating and detailed accounts of this self-study in consciousness.

After Aurobindo's death, the Mother continued to run the ashram and pursue the inner exploration. *The Lives of the Cell*, written by Satprem, one of her closest disciples, is an account of her work with changing consciousness at the cellular level of the body. She also began work to realise a vision for a community that would be a collective rather than an individual effort to embody this human evolution that she glimpsed through her efforts with her own body and consciousness.

On February 28, 1968, with the blessings of the government of India and many other countries as well, the Mother read the Charter of Auroville on All India Radio as part of the community's inauguration ceremony:

Auroville belongs to nobody in particular. Auroville belongs to humanity as a whole. But to live in Auroville one must be a willing servitor of the Divine Consciousness.

Auroville will be the place of an unending education, of constant progress, of a youth that never ages.

Auroville wants to be a bridge between the past and the future. Taking advantage of all discoveries from without and from within, Auroville will boldly spring towards future realisations.

Auroville will be a site of material and spiritual researches for a living embodiment of an actual Human Unity.

To symbolise this Human Unity, children from many countries placed a handful of their native soil in a central, lotus-shaped urn. After the speeches and flourishes of international dignitaries, a handful of people, chosen by the Mother, remained to begin the building of this visionary community.

And what they faced was the bare, hard-baked soil of India, so solid that holes for trees could be dug only in the rainy season, and even then only with crowbars. They built simple bamboo shelters with keet roofs and subsisted on dahl and rice and suffered the range of tropical diseases like hepatitis (almost everyone has a weak liver) and malaria. The money for the building came from people's own pockets supplemented by money from the Mother. She kept a small purse in her room in the ashram earmarked 'For Auroville'. Anyone who needed financial assistance went to speak with her, to explain their project and the need.

The community struggled along, sustained by the Mother's vision and her words of guidance for the community. "Auroville is created," wrote the Mother, "to realise the ideal of Sri Aurobindo who taught us the Karma Yoga. Auroville is for those who want to do the yoga of work . . . . To live in Auroville means to do the yoga of work. So all Aurovillians must take up a work and do it as yoga."

Auroville has had a solid, articulated base for its collective purpose since the beginning. In contrast, the Findhorn Foundation developed organically, step-by-step, without a long-term vision fully revealed at the outset. After struggling for a whole summer with the members of Cluny Hill to articulate a vision for our part of the community, I envy the Mother's clarity. The Foundation has evolved a philosophy similar to that of Karma Yoga, to enact awareness in our daily work ('work is love in action'). But here in Auroville that 'work' is never delegated. No ready-

152

made work departments exist. Each individual must look around, see what needs to be done, and then fulfil that need. After chafing against the restrictions of work departments at Findhorn, I find Auroville completely the opposite—no one suggests anything about where to work or how. The choice is mine, and initially the freedom overwhelms me.

So the building of the city continued—slowly by Western standards, but remarkably quickly by Indian measure—under the protective wing of the Mother. Only four years after the inauguration of Auroville the Mother died, leaving the administrators of the ashram in Pondicherry in charge of the welfare of the community. Unlike Auroville, whose stated purpose was the practice of Karma Yoga, the ashram is devoted to Bhakti, the practice of devotion and worship of the Divine. "The ashram and Auroville are like a tree," an old man in the ashram once said to me. He was one of the few in the ashram whom I met who had actually spent time working in Auroville. "The ashram is like the roots of the tree, the foundation. And Auroville is the branches, the realisation of Aurobindo's vision."

Unfortunately, though, it was not this man and others like him who were designated to look after the ashram's affairs. The appointed caretakers had a large financial base to administer—many of the businesses in Pondi are run by the ashram —and a huge moral gap to fill, left by the departure of a great soul. Human-sized, they could not fill it. "We (Auroville) were like a young child," explained Dee one day. "At four years old, we were left in the care of a wicked step-uncle."

Over the coming years, the relationship between Auroville and the ashram deteriorated until finally the Indian government stepped in as an intermediary so that a final solution could be explored. The crux of the problem is that the Sri Aurobindo Society (the administrative body of the ashram, the infamous 'SAS' often referred to in Auroville community meetings) was given title to the land, yet they have little to do with the daily running of the community—although they would like to. In the early days after the Mother's death, they tried to impose their will by withholding funds directed to Auroville through the SAS. They also refused to recommend certain people for visa extensions. Aurovillians appealed to the Indian governmen, and after a long struggle finally found a sympathetic ally in Delhi.

The stop-gap measure of placing Auroville under the protection of the Indian government provided a respite for the community to establish some sort of internal organisation. It also forced Auroville to create a central body that the Indian government could recognise and communicate with. For a collective of individualistic anarchists, that task forced the community to look at how they wanted to work together. What kind of a structure could the collective create that fulfilled the government's needs and did not compromise their ideals?

When asked what kind of governing structure Auroville should have, Mother smiled mischievously and said, "I know this will probably be misinterpreted, but the closest I can come to describing it is 'Divine Anarchy'." She went on to explain that decisions should be made in the moment, according to one's understanding of Truth and the Divine, not according to a policy outline.

The way that those words are played out in Auroville, though, means that any form of organisation is suspect. Year after year Aurovillians suffered the same blight of meetings to try to come up with a central body that could make decisions within the community and interface with people outside. In the interim, self-appointed delegations would go off to Delhi to negotiate. Incensed that such delegations had not obtained the blessing of the community before going to speak for them, other Aurovillians would draft petitions to Delhi saying that these undersigned people in Auroville did not agree with this or that decision. No wonder

Delhi was confused, not knowing who to believe or who had the 'official version' of Auroville's position on various issues.

Sitting in some of these General Meetings, I observe the challenges that the community faces in realising its vision in day-to-day reality. The resistance to any form of organisation or authority is so great that even the idea of having someone chair a meeting is a relatively recent innovation. And that person has to be careful not to direct too much or someone else will stand up and shout and simply overrule them. The role of chair is appointed but not empowered.

The issue of men and women and their roles within the community surfaces from time to time. Someone points out that all of these delegations going to Delhi are men; how about including some women? In contrast, the internal governing body is composed mostly of women. Strong women. I am reminded of a cartoon with a series of pictures captioned 'The evolution of man', following the changes from Neanderthal times to the apearance of *Homo sapiens*. In the background of each picture a woman kneels, scrubbing the floor. Her status has not changed through the millennia.

One man raises his hand, hesitantly beginning, "I know this will probably be taken as a sexist comment, but here goes anyway. I think the women have more skill at dealing with our internal struggles. They're more tolerant, more cooperative. So I suggest, in all seriousness, that women form the Internal Council and men deal with the negotiations outside." I shake my head when I hear the discussion—here we are in the 'New Age', and women are still scrubbing the floors and taking care of business at home.

And then there is the complicated issue of different 'political factions'. Over the weeks of sitting in meetings I begin to differentiate the groups. The most obvious are the 'extremists', the small, tightly organised knot of people (all French) who believe that Auroville should never negotiate with the SAS or have anything to do with the ashram ever again. This places the negotiators in Delhi in a difficult situation—somehow the ashram has to be included in negotiations about land ownership and other financial questions. But for these people, the principle of not recognising the SAS is most important. Wicked Uncle has done me wrong and I will never speak with him again. Ever. Pout. Here enters the French temperament, alliance to an ideal carried to an extreme. To negotiate = compromise = weakness. They actually make such statements in the meetings. And they are expert at quoting bits of Mother's guidance to support their cause. Most of them work on translating and printing Mother's *Agenda*, a previously unpublished collection of writing from her later years. A lot of the *Agenda* is like the Bible—inspiring but contradictory. In the volumes of writing you can find some reference to support whatever position you want to champion. The 'extremists' spout about truth but slur a lot of facts. In a nutshell, their self-proclaimed mission is Truth.

For most of the rest of the community, the Mother's vision of Human Unity takes precedence, and humanity includes the SAS and each other, even the ideologues. The tolerance practised in the General Meetings is, for the most part, remarkable. Occasionally someone will get up and stalk out (usually, but not always, the Truth Seekers) but the majority stay to listen to all sorts of tirades.

This struggle to balance the ideal of Truth with the vision of Human Unity is perhaps the crux of what is going on within Auroville as a whole. How can I follow what I perceive to be the Truth and still recognise the sisterhood and brotherhood of the people around me, especially the ones who have wronged me somehow? How do I balance the gifts of the mind (the ability to discern, reason and penetrate) with the gifts of the heart (the place of synthesis, unity, oneness)? Although Aurovillians

154

probably would not use the terms 'mind' and 'heart', I perceive the inner battle raging within individuals, within the collective and on the planet as a whole. The collective is a microcosm of the whole planet. "The enemy is not outside," said someone in a General Meeting. "It is right here within the community, and we have to deal with it here and not blame something outside all the time."

The struggle can produce a gift, though. Every time that ancient dichotomy is unified, change takes place. According to the Mother ". . . it is impossible for any change to take place, even in a single element or in a single point of the earth consciousness, without involving the entire earth in this change; it's inevitable. Everything is tightly interwoven. And a vibration in one place necessarily has worldwide—I am not saying universal, I am saying worldwide—consequences."

One of the major areas where that kind of change is visible within Auroville, besides the return of the forest, is in the work with the local villagers. When I first arrived in Auroville I was surprised by the number of villagers who worked in the settlements. At first glance it looked like a re-enactment of British colonial days. Through talking with people, though, I find that for the most part the villagers are regarded as workers, not servants. Most Aurovillians consider it a service to hire as many people as possible from the local villages, to give them employment. The wages may seem ridiculously low by European standards, but it is the villagers themselves who set the fees and tell their employers how much to pay.

The Aurovillians also work alongside the villagers, something that shocked the local people at first. In fact, sometimes the workers *insist* on doing things. Mangini, the longest-term worker at Fertile, always runs over when I get out the bicycle pump and inflates the tyres for me. I guess I look pitiful to him, struggling over the pump. He deftly places it beside one leg and then leans toward it, straightens, leans. In a few pumps he is finished. He smiles, shakes his head at me and carries the pump back into the house.

The young girls who cook the lunch and generally look after the house and kitchen also take me under their wing. Each day when I return from Pondicherry, Samadhi and Shanti collect purple, sweetly scented blossoms from a shrub called 'December' to make a string of flowers for my hair. One day I ask Samadhi, through Mangini's translation, to show me how to make the garland of flowers. For about 15 minutes I struggle with the tiny blossoms; most of them wilt between my sweaty fingers. The row of flowers is loose and uneven. Samadhi gives me a 'have you had enough?' look and then takes hold of the string. Her fingers move effortlessly, flicking the string around the blossoms and pulling them into neat rows. In about three minutes she is finished and slips them through a strand of hair above the top of my braid. I nod and smile. No 'thank you' is necessary among the villagers; the words exist in Tamil but are reserved only for unusual situations, like the saving of one's life. Otherwise I assume that gifts are freely given, without obligation; hence, no need for thank yous.

After a bit of lunch—varagu, a local type of millet, and some soup (sambar)—I ride to Ivar School on the far western side of the community to teach songs and games to the Tamil children in Isai Ambalam ('Singing School' in Tamil). The school is one of several buildings used by the 'Village Action Group' which is dedicated to making links with and supporting the local villagers. The project is headed by Dee, who met me in front of the Matrimandir when I first arrived.

Isai Ambalam sits at the back of the property; in front are various worker collectives, started by Aurovillians and villagers together, now mostly run by the villagers themselves. Under the shade of the central building, village women knit sweaters and bead hanging lampshade covers that are sold to markets in Europe. Near the

155

front entrance is a simple building with awnings stretching from two sides—one shelters the leather-working collective, the other a kitchen that makes lunch for the schoolchildren and the people who live full time in this settlement.

I walk up the stairs of the central building to see if Dee is working at the typewriter I hear banging in the office. Dee looks up when I walk in, pausing to wrap a finger over her upper lip. "What's up, Dee?"

"Oh, I'm working on an 'Aurovillage Communicator'," she says, sighing, "trying to write about what's been happening here over the last couple of months. Sometimes it flows so easily, other times I have to really work at it."

"But you write well, Dee."

"No, I've always had trouble writing. But Mother says that if you can get the vital mind out of the way and let the super-conscious do the work, then all things are possible," she says, laughing. "And it's true," she continues earnestly, "if I can just write without thinking too much, it goes much better."

"Dee, that reminds me—today at the School of Perfect Eyesight, when they put the compresses over my eyes, I had this . . . well, I guess you could say vision, of the Mother, in beautiful pastel colours."

Dee laughs, her eyes alight. "So, you're like one of us now," she says, nodding her head.

"I know you're busy—I justed wanted to say hello. I'll leave you to it." I pull on my sandals and head down the stairway.

Ivar, a tall, bearded Dutchman, saunters from the central building and stoops under the awning to ladle a cup of tea, rich with milk and jaggery (crystallised palm syrup—an improvement over the heaps of white sugar used in the village). "Judith," he calls, "do you want some tea?"

We sit for a few minutes, talking about what is happening here among the people who form the staff of the Village Action Group and about his own challenges. Ivar's vision for Isai Ambalam was the beginning of what is now a busy settlement. He founded the school as a way of addressing the great need that he saw in the village. "At first I just lived in my hut over dere and planted trees," explains Ivar, pointing to the forest behind us, "but the villagers kept coming and wrecking what I was doing. I realised dat I had to look at what was happening in the village, why dey were so angry, before I could go on planting dose trees. So I started the school, for the kids who wanted to come. We didn't worry so much about reading and writing. The kids were learning songs—we did lots of performances. It was good for the kids, gave them self-confidence, which is really not dere in the villages."

"And what happened?"

"Well, the kids came, and they learned a lot, but people were upset when the kids couldn't write the words that they were singing. They knew songs in Hindi, Tamil, English, but because they couldn't write them, people didn't think dey were really learning. And I was getting into an ego trip. So now other people are working in the school; it's independent, I don't work with it any more."

"What do you mean, 'ego trip'?" I ask, puzzled. To me, anyone who has endured India and suffered through as much illness as Ivar has—at forty his face is deeply lined, his body gaunt—must have more than ego to keep him in this place.

"I can be King among the villagers, really King—I mean it. It's like that here. I can do almost anything I want. If I went back to Europe, I wouldn't have the freedom that I have here."

"Is that really what keeps you here?"

"I don't know. I came with the vision of planting trees, and I got sidetracked into this work with the villagers. I saw the need, so I wanted to do something. But now I think I want to go back to the tree-planting work."

Nearly every time I talk with Ivar, he has another plan for what he wants to do next, but each day he continues his work with the Village Action Group, keeping finances for the sweater-making collective and studying vernacular Tamil. Change in Auroville seems to be a long time coming, but once it starts, it is enacted quickly.

Although I come here in the afternoon to teach the children English songs, I learn a lot from them. Most of the children are 'harijans', 'untouchables', a designation supposedly outlawed when India gained independence, although in reality almost every village retains it. The children are very affectionate and loving; after a couple of days, they hang on my arms and the little ones wrap themselves around my legs, calling me 'Ama'—mother. Through their reactions to me (they know very little English, so most of our communication is non-verbal) I learn about village mores.

Dress, for example. When I wear a sarong wrapped around my waist over a pair of shorts, the children point and call 'Lungi! Lungi!' which is the men's style of dress. One day the young women who are teacher's assistants take the sarong and tie it over one shoulder and around the waist. "There," says Mangaleshmi. "Dthat ees better."

Three of the young girls, daughters of the village man who has kept watch over the Fertile forest for years—he makes sure that no one cuts the trees or herds goats in the forest to forage—live with their family in a small hut of their own near Fertile. When I cycle past them on the road, they sing choruses of 'Twinkle, twinkle little star', one of the first English songs I taught them. When I stop to join them, they hang on my arms. One day one of them reaches up to touch the eyelets in my jumpsuit, frowning and shaking her finger at me. A village woman would never wear anything that exposed the shoulders, much less tiny holes over the chest.

Some days after singing with the children and playing games outside, I meet with Karpagavelli who teaches music in the school. She has a violin that she bought to accompany the children's singing. After studying the basics for about a year, she wants to learn some tunes. Although she is eager, teaching her is like trying to shape set concrete. In return she teaches me some Tamil—how to count and conjugate a verb. And sometimes we ask each other questions about our lives.

"Are you free?" asks Karpagavelli one day.

"What do you mean by 'free'?" I ask.

"Can you live without a father or husband?"

I look at her for a moment—in my upbringing I never thought of living alone as a freedom; it was a choice, is a choice, that I can make at any time, and I cannot imagine living without it. "Yes," I reply quietly. "And what about you? You're 'free', aren't you? You don't live with a father or a husband."

"Yes, but you see, I went to school," she explains. "Most of the girls cannot go to school after they begin their menses. Or she can continue school, but she will have a hard time getting married—a man doesn't want a wife with more education than him. Unless the husband wants her for the extra money she can make."

"But it's her money, right?"

"No, no," says Karpagavelli, smiling. "He keeps it all for himself. And a woman addresses a man always in polite form, he addresses her in common form. The man eats first at the table, then the women and children."

"Why didn't you get married?"

"Oh, my family didn't have the money to pay for a dowry."

"Are you glad you didn't marry?"

Karpagavelli looks at her clapsed hands for a moment, and then looks up. "Now, yes," she says nodding. "But not twenty years ago."

The conversation stays with me a long time. I think about it during the ride to Aurogreen, a settlement near Fertile where Charlie and Suzie run a dairy and fruit orchard. Each evening I go over to milk one or two of the cows—the older mamas with mostly dry udders. Charlie milks the ones with bulging teats as quickly as I can empty one of the older cows. The same energy that speeds him through the milking fills the rest of his day, starting with milking at around 5 a.m., continuing through work in the orchards and fields, and ending a couple of hours after milking in the evening.

The frenetic pace has buoyed Charlie since he started this settlement over ten years ago. I am incredulous when they show me pictures of the area when Charlie moved in—only a few stunted palm trees stood stubbornly in the flat fields. He had a clear view to Fertile and the windmills of other settlements nearby. Today tall fruit trees—papayas, guavas, breadfruit, lemon, lime, star fruit, banana, and others —stand in the way. The settlement includes two barns, a guest house, a main house, Suzie's house, and one built by a couple at the far end of the property.

"See, I had a lot of money when I came," explains Charlie, "or at least a lot for India. So initially I could make some mistakes, like buying village cows that weren't very good, and still have some money left over. But now that's all gone, and the dairy really has to pay for itself." Nearly everyone I have talked to takes periodic trips back to their home country to earn money to support themselves, but Charlie is so involved in the day-to-day running of Aurogreen that he cannot easily pick up and leave.

While travelling in India, Suzie spent some time in the ashram in Pondi and eventually knew that she wanted to stay. For seven years she worked in the ashram's dairy before moving to Auroville. "What brought you to Auroville?" I ask, surprised that anyone from the ashram would leave to come to Auroville.

"I just knew it was time. I had some dreams about Auroville and sensed I needed to make a move, so I did."

Only reluctantly does either one of them answer questions about their life before coming to India. At odd times a reference might slip into a conversation, but in general the past is left in the past. Most people in Auroville are impatient and sometimes indignant when asked about their lives before moving here. The sense I have is that such questions are taken as an attempt to categorise. We have taken on a new life, so why talk about the old? We are on an equal footing here, not constrained by the past. "Each one must know if he wants to associate with an old world ready for death," writes the Mother, "or to work for a new and better world preparing to be born." From people's responses, I learn that part of that 'old world' includes life before moving to Auroville—BA instead of BC.

Among the people I have met in Auroville, only Johnny talks freely about his past, and even then perhaps only as a natural outgrowth of our long conversations that sometimes run until after midnight. He describes his early experiences in Auroville, living in one of the local villages (his respect for and understanding of the Tamil people is so deep that I come to regard him as half-villager himself), the politics in the community, and his thoughts about a range of topics from appropriate technology and sacred geometry to husbands who refuse to travel with their wives. "The way I look at it," declares Johnny when we talk about tired husbands who want to stay at home for vacation, "either all of life is a holiday, or none of it is."

But tonight Johnny is away at a meeting to organise a travelling exhibition about Auroville with Tamil kids from the school at Inspiration. "It's supposed to happen in late February," mutters Johnny, "but we haven't even got the registration for the vehicle yet. And I think they're going to try to get me to drive and bring along some tree seedlings. We'll see."

I decide to go to a concert tonight with Thomas, a German graduate student visiting Auroville who has just moved in at Fertile. He is researching the use of biogas in the local villages, spending his days interviewing the villagers who have the government-funded units and educating them in how better to use them. The concert, like most major evening events, is scheduled for full moon to make the ride through the network of sandy roads and paths easier as well as to celebrate the lunar cycle.

The sand glows silver in the moonlight. I follow the tracks of Thomas' cycle through the maze of hard patches in the sandy road—first one side and then the other. As we approach Bharat Nivas, the cluster of buildings dedicated for cultural events and site of the major administrative offices, we join a growing swell of silent cyclists, wheels whirring in the night. The bicycles and the occasional motor scooter converge outside the concert hall. We leave shoes outside the door and move into the simple round room, lined on one side with bookcases. The stage is a low platform decorated only with a bouquet of flowers and a banner that hangs behind. This room, the current gathering place for the General Meetings, is transformed tonight. Instead of sombre, slow-paced discussions, people talk quietly and wave to friends across the room. Only about 100 of the 500 Aurovillians regularly attend the General Meetings, so tonight I see many new faces among the audience.

The concert begins with a short speech about the musicians and the music that they will be playing—Pandit Shivkumar Sharma is a renowned player of the santoor, an instrument like a hammered dulcimer. Once relegated to folk music in Kashmir, it has been brought by Shivji into the tradition of classical music in India. In his hands the folk instrument has become a virtuoso's tool. A representative from Auroville presents both him and the tabla player with gifts as a way of welcoming them. In India such a moment of ritualised greeting is common, and I find it full of dignity and respect. In the West we give flowers after a performance. Here, the gifts are given before, like an offering. The action is appropriate to the way that the Indian people approach music. They have a fierce pride in their culture and ancient traditions that span thousands of years, a pride that contradicts their clamouring after Western goods and Western ways. In fact, the pride in culture, the different way of looking at the world, endures intact under the veneer of Western ways.

People listen to the music with concentration, sitting on the floor with eyes closed. The concert begins slowly with Shivji playing complex riffs, the hammers moving in a flurry over the strings of the santoor . He is definitely the 'mind' of the duo while the tabla player is the 'heart'. The tabla player drums on a round-bottomed clay pot. It looks like the kujar available in any village market, but the sounds he draws from it vary in pitch and timbre from staccato taps to deep bullfrog-like bellows.

The music plays me through the evening, touching memories and feelings inside. The magic of full moon and the sounds weave through the room full of people clustered on the floor, concentrating, listening, being transported. During a pause Thomas whispers, "Do you understand this? I can't hear any melody."

I smile quietly. "No, it doesn't have melodies. It's improvised, like jazz. The music is meant to create a mood, a meditation."

As the evening progresses, I sense that the musicians move more and more inside the sounds until they become the music. At the same time, the sounds move more deeply inside me. I can feel the taps on the tabla inside my heart, the riffs from the santoor passing through my spine. For a few minutes I have no thoughts, only the awareness of sound moving through my body.

The magic lingers when the concert finishes. The audience moves out of the hall, quietly sorting through the jumble of sandals by the door. Only a few snippets of conversation pass through the crowd streaming away from the pavilion, their cycle lamps fading into the distance like fireflies in the night. A few people exchange hugs or a brief touch on the arm. Physical affection here is rare and very sincere when given. At first I found the lack of hugging and touching very cold, a sort of stand-offish attitude. As time passes, though, I begin to see that people are very aware of giving each other space, to stand on their own, to strengthen as individuals. I support you by allowing you to stand on your own.

I find the same attitude permeates a group that meets weekly to learn facilitation skills, to try to introduce new methods into the General Meeting. Exasperated by the lack of skill in leading meetings in the community, and knowing that any innovation must be presented very professionally or it will be ridiculed and dismissed, the group formed to perfect their facilitation skills before venturing to offer them within the community at large. As the group worked together and matured as a unit, its members began to realise that their experience was affecting them personally as well. For a community built upon individual initiative, their work together in creating a supportive, growing group is pioneering, even revolutionary.

Dee invited me to come to the meetings, and the group asked me to share some of my skills. Through my participation, I begin to see more clearly the relative strengths of Auroville and the Findhorn Community. When we make 'group agreements', a new concept for most people is 'personal disturbances come first'. In most cases, unless the underlying personal distress is cleared, it will surface in the meeting in a covert (or sometimes blatant) form. "What do you mean by 'personal disturbance'?" asks someone.

"Well, like if I noticed someone looked really upset, I might ask them what's wrong and if they needed any support."

The group looks aghast. Forest, a soft-spoken English man with long, flowing dark hair, protests, "But most people would take that as an offence—that someone would ask them if they need support."

My turn to look aghast. "An offence? "

"Yes, like you thought they were weak."

"This is an interesting issue for me," adds another woman. "I've been looking at the Newcomers (first year residents) and how we generally don't give them support. It's as if we say, 'I had a hard time starting here, so they should too.' It's looked at almost like an initiation. Like someone came to the General Meeting every week for a month asking for people to help him with his new house. He got really upset when no one came. People just listened quietly and figured he would get it eventually that you just don't ask for help; you have to do it yourself. I kind of wondered whether or not to say something to him, but he understood eventually and quit asking. I wonder, though, if we need to make it so hard for the Newcomers."

"I'm worried, too," adds Anne-Marie, another visitor to Findhorn this past autumn, "that asking if someone is distressed will give them the opportunity to go on and on about their problems. I'm not so sure that would be good in a meeting."

"Probably not in a General Meeting," I offer, "but in a smaller meeting you can end up spending more time on reaching agreement than if you spent the time at the beginning clearing things. Then those issues don't block the rest of the discussion."

Over the weeks I begin to see that the Findhorn Foundation's strength is its ability to work in groups; it is a formidable guru of group process. On the other hand, though, it has little space for individuals who want to pursue their own creative ideas. Here in Auroville, the individual and his or her creativity flourishes while the ability to work as a group atrophies. They are sister communities with polar opposite strengths. My dream would be to wed the two, to have a community that supports individual initiative and has the ability to work effectively in groups.

I am tired when I return to Fertile after the meeting. I sit in the lantern light, sipping tea and swatting at mosquitoes. Each time I meditate and write down the guidance, I hear that I should take more quiet time for myself. The cold that came with me to India cleared but then was followed by another. Last week Ivar suggested that I try drinking my own urine. I giggled. He was serious. After years of illness, Ivar's bouts of boils and hepatitis and other diseases stopped when he began drinking his own urine. I thought about it for a few days and then decided to try drinking my urine to clear up the cold.

I peed in a cup and stood looking at it for a long time before I had the courage to hold it to my lips. Small sip. Actually not too bad—salty and slightly acidic, but tolerable. The next morning my cold was much better; by the third day completely gone. Yesterday, though, I awoke feeling slightly feverish, but went about my usual routine anyway. Tonight I feel wired after the meeting, but deep down is a tiredness that I can't seem to overcome no matter how much I sleep. And sleeping isn't always very restful, anyhow.

Last night I awoke to thumping downstairs in Jan's house and crawled to the edge of the ladder to beam my torch around the room. Two luminous green eyes gleamed in the corner—a civet cat, one of the species that has returned with the forests. Slow, almost slothlike and equally tatty in appearance, the cats spend most of their lives in the trees. This one ambled out the window and into the darkness of the surrounding forest.

Another night I awoke to banging in the small box-like set of drawers downstairs. Afraid that it might be a snake (a cobra had eaten some of the baby chickens a couple of weeks earlier), I waited until morning to open the lid. A shrew sat inside, licking her whiskers. A couple of weeks later the box was filled with shuffling and soft squeaking—I opened it to find a jumble of tiny pink, sightless babies, guarded by their sharp-nosed mother.

For years I have dreamt of living somewhere 'between outside and in', as I once wrote in a poem, and when Himal tells me that he found a civet cat sitting on my bed one day, I know I have arrived there. The termites, too, tell me that my dominion in this structure is short-lived—I find them eating away the books in Jan's glassed bookcase and building honey-combed homes in the corners of the house. Any human dwelling not continuously maintained quickly returns to rubble in the forest.

On Monday after the facilitation meeting I awake with a fever. My only appointment for the day is with Suzanne, who works with Merriam Hill, an organisation dedicated to researching and applying innovations in group work. A man called Peter Callaway began the work as a result of having a vision of a huge triangle connecting three points on the Earth; he was told that these three centres needed to be connected, that they had work to do together. After a bit of research, he discovered that three communities had been established on these points—Arcosanti in Arizona, the Findhorn Foundation in Scotland and Auroville in the south of India.

Callaway set about fulfilling the vision by establishing the Hexiad Foundation, which sponsored exchanges between the communities—that was how Dee first visited Findhorn along with a few other people from Auroville. A few years later he refocused the work to concentrate on improving group work in general. Suzanne and Vinnie, another woman from the States working with Merriam Hill, have come to Auroville to look at the development of group structure in the community. They have given a lot of helpful suggestions within the 'group on groups' and in the

General Meeting, too, after a couple of months of observation. This morning, though, in addition to talking about our work with groups and communities, Suzanne and I spend time connecting as sister-spirits as well. Through details of her life, I come to know her as a woman of heart and dedication, and I realise how much I miss the company of women and the open-hearted touch of a friend.

Vinnie, too, has stolen my heart. Another bright-hearted spirit, her short blond hair bristles with aliveness around her smooth tanned face, and her eyes are clear-blue electric. Her years of living on the land in Arkansas, single-handedly building and maintaining a farm, show in the strength of her body, in her graceful move-ments and calm speech. We make plans to meet at the beach later in the week but as the days progress so does my own fever, and I finally surrender to staying in bed until it passes.

While in bed, I alternate between relaxing and reading and feeling guilty. Johnny is trying to fix the pipes in the bore of the well for the second time in a week, and I wish I could be there to help. Three women from the village sit on the patio outside the kitchen, patiently winnowing and then grinding the grain harvested a couple of weeks before. They rhythmically toss the grain from the flat woven baskets into the air, swooooosh swish-swish, swoooosh swish-swish over and over again, allowing the wind to blow the chaff from the kernels. Another woman sits before the grind-ing stones, thin arms pulling the top stone round and round and round, her move-ments as precise and predictable as a machine. In fact, the monotony of the work seems to create a momentum that overtakes them so that the actions become auto-matic, and they are free to talk and sing and laugh as they work.

For days while I lie in bed they continue at the monotonous task, a constant reminder of my own lack of productivity. Wanting desperately to be well, I ask in meditation how I can speed the healing process. "The body is going through a mas-sive housecleaning," I hear. "Do not add to the burden of this endeavour by adding lots of movement or striving. Give the body a chance to rest. All appointments can wait—set the house in order, and then allow the cleaning to happen. Take this time to read, write, listen, lie on the Earth, just be. The fever will help take the doing edge off your plans. Relax, allow the body to move through this period. Eat lightly, drink lots of water, relax in sunshine, stretch gently, give thanks."

I feel utterly, presumptuously privileged to be able to lie in bed and recover . . . but what good am I otherwise? After a couple of days the fever continues, but I drag myself out of bed anyhow and make a trip to the clinic in Aspiration to see one of the homoeopathic doctors in the community. Along the way, among the outlying village fields, a Tamil man trots from the edge of a field, waving at me. Assuming that he wants a ride, I stop my bicycle and wait while he climbs on. With the added weight, I have to stand up on the pedals to get the wheels moving again. As soon as I settle on the seat, the man reaches under my arms and places his hands firmly over my breasts. Stunned, I pause for a moment and then jam on the brakes. "Illai, Illai!" I shout, No! in Tamil. Unruffled, the man jumps off the bike and continues walking.

I continue pedalling toward the clinic, amazed at how calm I am. As the initial shock disperses, though, I grow angrier and angrier at the gall of that man to grab my breasts. I could never even imagine grabbing a man's penis, much less carrying out the fantasy—why does a man think he can grab my body as he pleases?

I also chastise myself for wearing a sleeveless shirt—to a Tamil villager, bare shoulders are a come-on. But, damn it, I should be able to walk around naked and not be violated. As a woman, I cannot go anywhere on this planet and feel com-pletely safe to move and dress (or not dress) as I please. I struggle here in India between respecting their different view of the world, knowing that much of it contains great wisdom, and honouring my own cultural sense of rightness and fairness. How much to compromise as a sign of respect, how much to protest? And what is 'truth', anyhow, when stripped of cultural learning?

In India, for example, movies produced within the country may not include sexual scenes. They can, however, show rapes. So now films have an obligatory rape (instead of 'sex') scene. Despite the laws banning 'pornography' within India, videos—a current rage throughout the country—guarantee a steady stream of Western pornographic films. Everywhere in Pondicherry are posters of a black-stockinged, half-dressed white woman with the name of the film plastered over her bare backside—'Bedroom Eyes' or some such drivel.

Flooded with such images, no wonder Tamil men look at women, especially Western women, licentiously. The sexual excitement, though, directly contradicts a lot of the village mores, as I learned through teaching dancing to the teaching assistants at Isai Ambalam.

At Celestine's suggestion (a Sri Lankan woman who is the head of the school), I arrived on a Saturday morning to share some Sacred Dances with the teachers so that they in turn could teach the children. Isai Ambalam emphasises music and movement to develop the children's coordination and self-confidence. Although the teachers encourage the children, they rarely join in the movement themselves. I assumed this was because they did not know any folk dances to teach.

After demonstrating the first dance, I moved away from the circle to pick up my violin to play as they danced. Immediately one of the young women fled from the circle into another room and stood at the window crying. Despite pleas from Celestine and another assistant, she refused to join the circle. Puzzled, I continued to teach the dances to Celestine and the small cluster of men who remained. Only through speaking to Celestine after the session did I understand the girl's distress.

For many generations only courtesans danced. They bore illegitimate children to their keepers and then taught those daughters how to dance so that they in turn could make their way in the world, and so the cycle continued. Only in the early part of this century did a wealthy Brahman woman begin to break the stereotype by dancing publicly, legitimising women as dancers, not necessarily courtesans.

The villages are always the last to change, though, and such liberalism has not yet altered their mores. Even touching a man's hand, explains Celestine, is forbidden, unless he is part of one's immediate family. As long as Celestine and I stood on either side of the girls as buffers between the men, the young women felt safe to dance. But once Mangaleshmi was placed in a position where she had to hold a man's hand, she couldn't do it—the contradiciton with her upbringing was too great.

Innocently I had entered into teaching the dances, completely unaware of what a revolutionary act it was. My initial reaction was horror at what I considered prudish behaviour, the kind that third-graders indulge in when taught folk dancing in the school gymnasium. But as the larger picture of village life came into focus, I was no longer certain that overstepping this taboo would be beneficial to anyone.

Each 'innovation' has the potential to chip away at the solid village structure that has evolved over thousands of years, and the villages—not the national government —unite India. The concept of the country of India is a new one, just as the idea of 'Germany' only emerged at the beginning of the 20th century—previously the land consisted of small kingdoms that shared a common language. 'India', too, was a collection of separate kingdoms until British rule. One of the 'gifts' of the British reign was the introduction of a common language—English. Today the former countries of India, now states under the umbrella of a national government, retain their native languages and fiercely resist attempts to name any one of the local languages the official tongue of India.

The national government of India is still weak, effective only in so far as the local people are willing to support it. For the most part Indians are very emotional, and if convinced of a cause, they can riot for days before they expend their emotional charge. Only respect for a particular person and obedience to their requests seem capable of uniting the country. The laws passed centrally have little effect, largely because of the corruption that riddles the government from law makers at the top of the heap right down to police officers at the bottom who are expected to enforce those laws. Thefts or disturbances within the village are rarely reported to the police. The officers generally receive a cut for themselves and demand a bribe from the *victims* of the crime or threaten to throw them in jail. When an Aurovillian finally caught one of the local thiefs and reported him to the Pondi police, the Chief of Police slanted the report to say that a police officer had tracked him down.

Instead of the federal court system, the villagers rely upon their own village council. They deal with any misconduct internally, as they have done for generations. Stealing, for example, is a very serious crime. No one has locks on their doors —few have doors, for that matter. The strong moral code within the village is their only safeguard. When that code is broken, the worst possible punishment is banishment from the villages. Such exile means separation from one's family, and that is a terrible penalty. The law of the villages, though mostly unwritten, is really the glue that holds India together.

So as much as I may question some of the village mores, I see that they are the backbone of this country. If the village structure strains and finally breaks under the weight of Western 'innovations', I am not sure exactly what would hold India together. The place would be pure chaos, an endless, angry riot. I don't pursue the dancing—the revolution of thought and action will have to rumble slowly, gently, if it is to succeed without rupturing the spine of India.

On the reverse side, the Westerners who have come to live in Auroville often strain and sometimes collapse under the pressures of adapting to village life. About a week ago a Frenchman, married to a Tamil woman and living in one of the local villages, lost his temper and struck one of the villagers. The villager had trespassed into his carefully tended forest, replanted and nurtured with care for several years, and had started to cut some of the trees. Incensed, the Frenchman ran after him and started hitting him. The disturbance drew a crowd, and soon the Frenchman was surrounded by an angry mob of villagers ready to lynch him. At this point, someone ran to the Central Guest House in Auroville, the closest settlement, and pleaded with the only man there—a newly arrived guest named Brad who happened to be a friend of mine from the Findhorn Community—to come and help. Brad, although he is mostly blind, agreed to do what he could to calm the crowd.

He and Satya (yes, the same Satya with whom I struggled at Cluny Hill) hurried to the village. Someone placed Brad, arms crossed, between the villagers and the Frenchman. "I didn't say much—in fact I can't remember if I said anything," recalls Brad afterwards. "I was shit scared, but somehow the crowd started breaking up and left the man alone."

The Frenchman's actions did not escape the notice of the rest of Auroville, though. He had had a similar outburst a few years before. This time he was given a warning in the General Meeting to stop the violence or leave the community.

He is not alone in snapping under the pressures of living in India. I was told about one couple who arrived in Auroville, sure that they would be spending the rest of their lives here. They had sold their home and most of their possessions and had

164

come to India, prepared for the long haul. A couple of months later, while waiting in one of the endlessly long lines at the bank, the woman's accumulated frustrations reached breaking point, and she freaked out. After her breakdown, the couple left Auroville and returned to their lives in Europe.

Although when I arrived such stories sounded ludicrous—how could anyone accumulate that much frustration?—as the weeks progress I understand that one must truly relax and learn to tolerate vast discrepancies or go mad. Also, I notice that most people undergo some sort of illness when they arrive. I had watched the pattern of 'first year illness' at the Findhorn Foundation, seemingly a hazard for anyone entering a new community, but here in a tropical climate those illnesses can be more virulent. As my fever continues to rage, despite the homoeopathic remedies prescribed by the Aurovillian doctor, I realise that I had hoped to escape such entry pains here. Gunther, a German doctor and former Steiner teacher who was a guest at Findhorn, now spending a few weeks helping in the clinic here, comes to Fertile to check on me one day. He comments, "The anthroposophists would say you are incarnating here."

"Incarnating? I think I'm dying, Gunther."

He smiles. "Sometimes illness is a way of arriving in a place."

CHAPTER 9
Mother India

Over the coming week the fever increases and my head begins to throb, first only when I bend over and then continuously. Desperate for some kind of help, I go to Heidi, an acupuncturist who lives in a settlement nearby. Each day she comes to Fertile to give me a treatment. Satya also comes to visit, and I find that the old resentment that built during my stay at Cluny Hill eases and then disappears as we meet as friends, without the structure of the community to shape our relationship. Perhaps the months travelling with Brad have mellowed her; and I, too, have made room for her to be different, letting go of the authoritarian image of her that I created when she worked in Personnel. She tells me stories of her travels throughout India with her autistic son when he was a young boy. "The people all brought him food," says Satya, laughing, "but he would eat only peanuts and bananas."

"Why did they bring him food?" I ask.

"Because they could see that he was different, mentally handicapped, and to them that meant closer to God, so they brought the food as an offering, to honour him."

"Hmmm . . . we do just the opposite in the West, trying to hide people who are different, trying to ignore them."

She describes a retreat she did in the forests of the north, living alone in a simple wooden hut. "I didn't understand why the local people made such a noise walking through the forest—when I asked them they said it was to scare away the tigers."

"Tigers?" I repeat, incredulous.

"Yes. Then I was a bit nervous. I made sure that I kept the fire outside the hut burning all night after that."

As these and other stories unfold, I begin to see Satya's depth and strength. Her outward appearance is always elegant, and I find that her inner beauty matches the outer. Anyone who can meditate peacefully alone in a tiger-filled forest has my vote for bravery. I discover her compassion, too, when she shares her concern about Brad's daughter, recently diagnosed as a childhood diabetic.

That compassion flows to me as well when she comes to visit one day. The fever has continued for several days, and now pain rages in my head, inescapable in its intensity. A hurt knee or a sprained ankle can be almost overlooked, but when the pain settles in my head—a nexus of sensitive nerves—I feel caged, unable to escape it. Satya gently kneads my feet and holds polarity points until Heidi arrives with her needles. "You're hot," says Heidi, touching my face, "but only in the head," she notes, checking my arms and chest and legs. After inserting a series of needles, Heidi smoothes my hair and tells me to relax. Half an hour passes. Before the needles have brought some relief, but today nothing touches the sharp waves that rumble through my head. Gunther arrives, and later the young Indian doctor who works in the Auroville clinic. "Do you think she might have malaria?" asks Heidi.

The doctor checks me, asking about the fever, body aches, where the pain is in my head. "I can't tell where the pain is," I tell him. "It's in my whole head."

He decides it's not malaria, rather a case of acute sinusitis. He prescribes some sulfa drugs and Tylenol to deaden the pain. The clinic in Auroville is out of the drug, so he offers to ride into Pondi to buy it at a medicals store. For nearly ten years I have taken no allopathic medicine, but I hesitate only a moment before agreeing to take the drugs—I desperately want relief from the hammers pounding inside my head.

Within a couple of days the pain localises in my ears. At first I can control it if I swallow a couple of painkillers and lie a certain way in bed. I hold the position until my body cramps—I'm not sure what is worse, the cramping in the body or the pain in my ear. So I shift and the ears retaliate, the sharp pain cutting more deeply into the nerves. Ear pain is definitely worse, so I shift back, take more pills, wait an hour in agony until they take effect, and then doze for a few hours until they wear off.

Eventually even the pills don't touch the pain. By this time I have quit eating. Even getting up to go to the toilet is a struggle. Everyone else at Fertile is busy with their own work, so if I don't get up to fill a pot of water, no one will bring it. I am afraid that at some point I will be too weak to get up at all. Heidi offers to have me stay in her house for a couple of days, where she can more easily look after me. Deeply grateful, I accept the offer.

The nights are the worst. I live for the hour when I can take the pills again. During the days I chastise myself for being overwhelmed by the pain. Every time I open a book of the Mother's guidance, it falls on a page that describes how to leave the body and then press the 'Divine Force' down into it from above in order to strengthen it and overcome illness. No matter how hard I try, though, I cannot budge my awareness an inch above my body. I seem to be hopelessly mired in this physical form. The Mother writes about transforming her pain—in this case, a toothache—into bliss, allowing the focus of the pain to carry her into other realms. As the days pass, I realise that I have failed miserably in transforming anything into bliss; I am not even brave about the pain. I am just *in* pain. And slowly drowning.

In some ways reading Mother's guidance, along with *Autobiography of a Yogi*, only adds to my distress. The words are inspiring and I learn a great deal about the depth of India's spiritual devotion. During a time of stress, though, Mother's wisdom, expressed in different terms than I am used to, throws me into a lot of inner questioning and doubt.

"The ways to Spirit are many," I hear in meditation. "Can you honour them all? Your individual path is unique—can you stay true to your line? Honouring all ways does not mean *following* all ways, nor does 'unique path' mean staying clenched to a single tradition. Everything you read or encounter must be checked with the heart—that is your only barometer. The depth of change you are undergoing is not immediately obvious. Be patient and persevere."

I gradually lose track of days, but I know that the date to meet Alan in Africa is approaching quickly. I have been hoping to clear the illness in time to board the plane from Madras on March 2nd. I also want to take part in Auroville's 20th birthday celebration on February 28th, to experience the essence of Mother and her vision for Auroville.

The days pass mercilessly with no sign of improvement. Finally Heidi makes arrangements through Frederick, the unofficial ambassador of the community—he has a royal bearing and a knack for making connections in high places—to see the head of the Ear, Nose and Throat Division at Jipmer Hospital in Pondicherry. Heidi, bless her soul, makes arrangements for a community vehicle and a driver to deliver us via the bumpy tracks to the hospital. Fortunately one of the pain pills is working during the ride, but it soon wears off as we sit waiting for the doctor in a cold-tiled hallway, tinged with the bitter smell of antiseptic. Nurses swing in and out of the ward doors, faces knitted with frowns. Patients covered with stiff green sheets are wheeled back and forth in front of us, in and out of the operating theatre to our left—anxious going in and groggy coming out. Finally the doctor strides around the corner, plump and officious looking, and inserts an instrument in my ear. "How long have you had pain?" he asks.

"Ten days, maybe two weeks," I tell him.

"Ah, not long," he says crisply. Goddess, it's long enough for me.

"Admit her," he barks to the nurse recording his comments on a clipboard.

My mind blanks for a moment. The colour must have drained from my face, because the doctor swivels his head and smiles at me. "Do not wor-r-ry," he says, "we will cu-r-re you."

Heidi spends the next hour running back and forth between the front desk and the bench where I sit. I hum quietly, trying to ease the pain in my ears. "Thank you, Heidi," I tell her when she completes the last form. "I don't know how I would have made it without your help."

"Ah, don't worry. Just get better," she says smiling. "It is a good hospital, one of the best in India. I came here when I had typhoid fever—they're very good."

We deposit my bag in a metal cabinet next to one of the beds in a ward. A nurse stops by and looks at my sundress, barely covering the knees. "She will need other clothes," she comments, nodding to Heidi.

"OK, Judith, I will tell the people at Isai Ambalam that you are here," says Heidi. "Maybe they can bring some clothes."

"Thank you Heidi."

When she leaves, a small cluster of women and children gathers around my bed. I close my eyes and lean back against a pillow, praying that someone will come soon with more pain pills. When I open my eyes, the women are still there, staring, curious. I realise that I am the only white woman on the ward. One of them leans over the bed and touches the sheets near my arm.

"Where is your family?" she asks, perplexed.

"In the United States," I tell her.

"But why aren't they *here?*"

"Well, it is too far away, many, many miles from here," I try to explain.

"But they could fly," she insists. For a villager who has never been beyond the bounds of Tamil Nadu, distance is hard to describe.

As the day passes, I begin to understand her concern. In the bed across from me a

168

mother holds a young boy, about three years old, who has a piece of gauze stretched over an opening in his throat. She feeds and washes and cuddles him; the nurses only intervene occasionally to check his temperature or bring medicine. Everyone in the ward has someone who either lives with them in the hospital or comes to visit for long stretches each day. Family, not nurses, take care of a patient's basic needs.

Late in the afternoon no medicine has arrived, nor has any doctor come to check on me. The calmness that I have carefully maintained throughout the day begins to crumble. I find the doctor who is on duty in the ward and ask for Dr. Majunder. "He is probably gone for the day," she tells me.

"Gone?" I ask, panic rising in me. "But he hasn't prescribed any medicine for me or told me when I will have surgery."

"You will probably have oper-r-ration on Monday or Tuesday next week, and you may need exploratory surgery first."

"*Monday or Tuesday?!* But this is Friday. I'm supposed to lie here for three days without anyone seeing me or prescribing medicine?"

"You can go and talk to the doctor if he is still here."

"Where would he be?" My memory of the corridors and maze of swinging ward doors is hazy. Exasperated, the doctor leads me along the corridors to Dr. Majunder's office. He looks up, surprised, when we enter the room.

"Yes?" he asks. "How can I help you?"

After a few comments, he nods to the other doctor and dictates a prescription for medicine. When I ask when the operation will be, he shakes his head and replies, "Tomorrow."

"Will that be exploratory sugery?"

"Tomorrow," he repeats, swivelling his head more quickly.

"Thank you, Doctor." I have no idea *what* will happen tomorrow, but now at least I have a hope that *something* will.

Back in the ward, I close my eyes and try to meditate to calm myself. Internally, though, I am screaming at the Creator. "*Please* help me, Creator; I think I may really lose it this time. *Please* help me."

When I open my eyes, Dee and Ivar are standing at the bottom of the bed. From my perspective, they might as well have wings and be carrying harps—they are angelic presences come to save me from the horrors of this place. "Oh, Dee, Ivar, I am *so* glad to see you."

"Hi," says Dee, dropping a satchel of clothes on the bed. "I got these from Fertile. I hope it's what you need. I tried to pick up what I thought would be helpful."

"Oh, Dee, thank you. And thanks for coming, Ivar. How did you get here?"

"We rode in on the motorbike. But we can't stay very long. Dee needs to get back for a concert tonight."

"Oh, the flute player, the special concert for the birthday?" I ask, heart sinking as I realise that I will miss all of the events.

"Right. So do you need anything?"

I hand him the doctor's prescription. "She says that I can buy this at the medical store on the corner. And I'm supposed to buy 'grommets' for the operation."

While he goes to the store down the street, Dee smiles and chats with the women and children in the ward. Through her I learn that the mother and boy have been on this ward for three months. I look around, trying to imagine living in such a place for so long.

When Ivar returns, I begin to tell them about going to see the doctor, tears welling as I relive the distress. "Look," says Ivar, "if you want anything to happen, you're going to have to be patient. They're used to arrogant Westerners. The more you demand, the less they pay attention to you. If you want help, you're going to have to relax."

"And you're lucky," comments Dee. "In the hospital where I was with hepatitis the beds were right next to each other and people were sleeping on the floor in between. Here you have at least four feet between the beds. And you talk as if you were going to die. Come on," she says gently, "it's painful, but you know you're going to live through it. You won't die."

"When you start feeling sorry for yourself," continues Ivar, "go down to the emergency room. I can't tell you the number of times I've brought people from the village into that emergency room on the back of my bike. One woman had taken insecticide to kill herself—you know, the Tamils will commit suicide at the drop of a hat. She was already cold and mostly stiff, but they found the right remedy for her. If there is a remedy, they will know it. The only problem is whether the chemist has any. In the case of this woman there was one vial of the remedy left. One. And it saved her; she's still alive. And you should see the people who come in from motorbike accidents, parts of their bodies missing or wrapped in a bit of cloth. If you're really in pain during the night, you should go down and see what comes into that emergency room. Do that, just get up and go downstairs and look. Then you'll see how lucky you are. Come on, you can look at this as a challenge, an adventure."

My 'angels' take a pretty tough line. They refuse to support my self-pity. I choke back tears and decide I can endure. About an hour later I walk along the corridor with them towards the front entrance and reluctantly say goodbye. When I return to the ward, the lights are dimmed, and almost everyone, except the row of very elderly people, abandons their bed and stretches out on the bare tiled floor. At home the villagers generally sleep on the floor at night. Here in the hospital beds are for sitting on during the day, but not for sleeping at night.

I indulge in a few tears as I lie in the ward listening to the fan clacking overhead. My pillow is sodden by the time I fall asleep.

The nurse wakes me early to take my temperature—4 a.m. At 6:30 breakfast is served in a tiny room off to one side of the corridor. The women know the routine and jostle me through the line to the single tap in the room, meant for hand washing and drinking water. This morning's breakfast is iddlies, a special Tamil meal made with a fermented mixture of ground lentils and rice, steamed into muffin shapes. After days without much food, I can barely finish two of them. The women notice the iddlie sitting on my stainless steel plate. "Eat, eat," says one woman, pointing vigorously at the food. "Must have *strength*." I pat my stomach and puff out my cheeks. "Full. No more. You want?" The mother with the young boy is happy to have the extra food.

After breakfast one of the nurses comes by and tells me not to eat or drink any more. "Surgery this morning," she explains. My stomach clenches. This morning? So soon? Nobody even knows I'm supposed to have surgery today. "Nurse, about the grommets—will they be temporary or permanent in my ears?"

"Oh, permanent," she says, nodding her head with certainty.

Holy shit. I sit in bed, back against the wall, trying to relax and meditate. A stretcher wheels into the ward and stops at a bed across the way. Not my turn yet. "Creator, you've really got to help me this time," I scream internally. I feel more alone than I ever have in my life. Who would know or even notice if I died right now? Goddess, I wish Alan or someone from my family was here.

When I finally reach some semblance of quiet concentration, I offer a prayer once again. "It's just you and me, Creator, just you and me." And when the stretcher finally arrives and they swaddle me in a green hospital robe and ease me onto the

170

stretcher, the prayers continue as we wheel through the halls. "Please take care of me, Creator, please take care of me. If this whole illness is to teach me how to trust, to rely *just on you,* Creator, I've got the message, OK? So please, please take care of me. It's just you and me. That's it, Creator, just you and me."

And perhaps the whole terrifying event is to teach me how to pray. I recall the words of Wallace Black Elk who once approached a friend of mine and asked, "White lady, you know how to pray?"

"Well, sure, . . . I mean, I guess, . . . well, yes, I suppose I do," she stammered.

"That's the trouble with you white people," said Wallace. "That's just how you pray. Look, if you want something, you got to *ask* the Creator for it. You gotta ask *loud and clear.* You gotta pray so the Creator *knows* what you're asking for. You gotta ask *strong,* make strong prayers."

In that hallway I'm taking a crash course in making strong prayers. If I could attatch a speaker to my internal voice, the whole hospital would shake with the sound.

An intern explains the operation to me in the hallway. "It is simple," he explains. "We insert an instrument and make a small incision in the Eustachian tube. But it is very painful, so we will be giving you full anaesthesia."

"The doctor said I should buy grommets, but the medicals store didn't have any."

"Ahhh . . . well, it is all right. We will see what we can do."

"Will the grommets be permanent?"

"Oh, no, no, they stay only a short time and then we take them out."

Thank Goddess. When they wheel me into the operating theatre I'm almost relieved. Among the chrome-edged, round-cornered machines and instruments, I feel like I'm in a 1950s version of *Dr. Welby, MD.* The anaesthesia takes a couple of minutes to take effect. "I'm a bit nervous," I say to the nurse standing above me. She stops to touch my arm, her brown eyes full of compassion peering above the green gauze hospital mask. Those eyes are the last things I remember.

* * *

Whiteness. I am sitting with four presences, angel-like, far above the Earth. I sense my body far below me, but I'm reluctant to return to it. Here it is warm and serene. "It is time," says the one to the right. "It is time to return." Reluctantly my awareness shifts into my arm, pressed underneath my right side. I linger for a long time in a warm, whitish cocoon, drifting in and out of awareness. The sounds of the ward continue, faint outside this protective blanket. Eventually I enter fully enough to move my arm.

When I finally shift and open my eyes, Ivar and Celestine are standing at the end of my bed. "So, how are you doing?" asks Ivar.

I pause for a few moments, still groggy, and discover that something is missing —the pain in my ear is gone. I say this tentatively to myself, afraid it is a temporary phenomenon, lasting only as long as the anaesthetic. "Sleepy. And the pain seems to be gone."

"Good. We brought some things for you—some letters and more clothes."

"Thanks," I murmur. There is a telegram from Alan, asking whether I will meet him in Africa, or should he come to India now, or at the end of the trip? He hopes for a reply by three days ago. Shit. The telegram has been sitting at Fertile for several days. I am panicked, knowing that by tomorrow he will probably be in London, and I have no way of getting in touch with him. "Ivar, can I give you a telegram to send?" I have been composing one in my head for days, trying to second-guess

Alan's response to my first one, sent while I was staying with Heidi. "Yes," says Ivar, rummaging for pen and paper. Celestine reaches out to smooth my hair. I shift to lie on my back and look up at her.

A nurse whisks by. "You must lie on your side," she insists, rolling me back to the right. "The ear must dr-r-rain."

"How long do I have to lie like this?" I ask, already sore from the last however many hours.

"Oh, three or four days."

Oh, Goddess. I sink into the bed, defeated. Heaven looks better all the time.

"And someone will have to stay with her," she says, waving officiously at Celestine. "*He* cannot stay," she says, nodding to Ivar. "No men are supposed to be on the ward, but today I will allow it. So you must stay." She nods decisively at Celestine.

After a few moments of protest, Celestine agrees. For the next 18 hours, while I drift in and out of sleep, Celestine waits patiently by the bed, offering water and helping me struggle with a bed pan. "The nurse here," whispers Celestine in the dark ward, "wouldn't even help me find the bedpan. She just pointed at a closet over there and said it was in there, but they were all dirty. She was very upset that I was making her work, disturbing her sleep time."

I've never peed in a bedpan before, and I wet the sheets. In the morning Celestine helps me change them—the nurses certainly aren't interested. About noon the next day Celestine, my surrogate family, leaves, but almost immediately Brad and Satya arrive and stay for about an hour.

An intern walks by to check my ears. "When can I get up, doctor?" I ask. After a day and a half, my right side is definitely weary.

"If you like," he says, nodding to Satya and Brad, "I can give you pass and you can take her into Pondicherry for the afternoon."

I should have known better than to trust the nurse's prognosis. Gratefully I sit up in bed, but I have no desire to walk around Pondi in the afternoon heat.

After Satya and Brad leave, one of the women comes over and points at my bedside cabinet. Unsure of her intentions, I open the door—sitting inside is a watermelon that Celestine brought with her from the garden outside her 'capsule'—a simple bamboo hut on stilts with a keet roof. I had forgotten the gift, but the women haven't. At lunchtime I ask the cook to cut the watermelon and put it out on trays. The eating room is soon littered with spat-out seeds. When I move around the room with the tray, offering it to the women, one of the older ones grabs my arm and points at the sink, then nods at my hands. Of course, I must wash my hands before offering food. And never, *ever* offer it with my left hand, reserved only for toilet duties. That would be the greatest offence.

After lunch I walk around the ward, offering the remaining slices to the older people too weak to walk to the eating room. Soon the ward, too, is spattered with sticky seeds. The cleaning woman, though, seems unperturbed. She patiently moves through the room several times each day, daubing the floor with a wet mop.

The afternoon wears into the evening. I sleep fitfully through the night, chilly under a thin blanket with the fans whirring overhead. In the morning when I return from the toilet I find a pamphlet on my bed. I look around and realise that each bed has one of the colourful leaflets resting on the covers. Mine, though, is a special English translation—of how Jesus can save me from my sins, and a simplified version of the nativity story. An Indian nun, long blue robe sweeping the floor, walks by and nods as she leaves the ward. I understand suddenly why the nurses are called 'sisters'; I had not realised this was a Christian-run hospital. Through talks with

Johnny I have learned that the growing middle class view the Christian religion as 'more progressive' than Hinduism. Small surprise, then, that one of the most modern hospitals in India would have a Christian bent. New technology, new religion —they go hand in hand.

The doctor comes over to check my ears and make a few notes on her clipboard. "When will I be able to go?" I ask her.

"This afternoon, after Dr. Majunder sees you."

Halleluiah. After lunch he arrives with a crowd of doctors and interns trailing after him. "How ar-r-re your ear-rs?" he asks.

"The pain is gone."

"Good," he says, nodding approvingly. "See, you ar-r-re cured."

With a general scuffling and scribbling of notes the mob moves on to other patients. When they leave, I ask the doctor sitting at the ward desk if I can go. "Yes," she says, nodding without looking up, "you may go."

After the hassle of getting into the hospital, I am surprised at her casual dismissal. "Do I need to pay anything?"

She makes a few suggestions, and then I gather my bag from the bedside table and look around the ward. My legs are still unsteady, and I'm a bit nervous about the walk down the stairs and then along the street to find a taxi to take me back to Auroville. Again I wish for someone who could share the journey with me, but I know that I must make it alone.

After distributing the last of the lemons that Dee brought on one of her visits, I walk down the halls, feeling invisible walls crumbling around me. While moments before I felt almost trapped within the ward, now I feel strangely removed from the all-consuming routine. The young mother and her baby boy walk along with me to the stairway, standing at the top and waving until I pass from view.

The sun glares on the pavement. Everything looks bleached under the strong rays. People walk and hobble and hop along the street; some look like regular visitors coming for ongoing treatment, others like harried families struck by a recent crisis.

I'm not even sure which way to go to the main road; I wasn't really paying attention on the way in. A rickshaw driver notices me craning my neck around as I mill among the people. "Madam, Madam, where are you gowink?"

"Auroville."

"Come. I take you."

As we near Auroville, a wind blows sharply across the village fields, and I cover my ears with my hands—they are still sensitive. On the road to Fertile we pass Johnny, cycling along with a video camera in his canvas daypack. "Aha, you're back," he says simply. "I'm off to the school to do some video work."

"See you later," I call, waving.

Back at Fertile I walk slowly through the trees, knees watery after days in bed. I unpack my bag in Jan's house and sit for a while on the edge of the cot that Johnny set up so that I wouldn't have to climb the stairs into the loft. The two dogs who live at Fertile come to visit, tails pumping behind them. Himal calls from the house, "Are you OK now?"

"Mostly," I tell him. "The pain is gone, but I have to get my strength back."

Even the cat comes to visit, a sleek white creature whose immaculately groomed coat looks out of place amidst the loosely controlled chaos of Fertile. She is a princess among gypsies.

Dee comes by in the evening to visit. "I talked with Joan (one of the women in the facilitation group) and she said you are welcome to stay with her for a few days. Her house is very comfortable; you could really relax there. Do you want to go?"

"Thank you for checking it out, Dee, but I really don't want to move again right now. I feel fine at Fertile—I think I'll be able to relax here."

"OK," says Dee, shrugging her shoulders, "but she's willing to have you if you change your mind."

Later in the evening Johnny and Himal and I sit talking around the kitchen table, catching up on the news. At one point, when I ask about what kind of house Joan has, Johnny stops and passes his fingers through his hair. "Look," he says, raising his voice for emphasis, "you've got to be more adventurous. If someone offers to have you stay with them, do it. That's the only way you're going to see more of Auroville."

I'm a bit taken aback—Johnny rarely raises his voice, and I feel unjustly challenged. I'm still weak after the operation and all the pain, and now I'm supposed to go off and conquer Auroville? I sit quietly, not knowing what to say.

For the next couple of weeks I putter quietly—taking the dogs for walks, making rosella jam, spending a few days at Srima Beach, an Aurovillian settlement about five miles north on the main road. Celestine, from Isai Ambalam, is caretaking the property while Monika and Gionni are away, and invites me to stay with her.

During the days we spend most of the time on our own, reading, walking on the beach, writing. In the evenings, though, we linger over dinner under the electric lamps that hang from the latticework above. The house is open and airy, like something from a South Seas island, with three lofts built into the sloping latticework reached by a lashed bamboo ladder. When I climb the first ladder to the loft where Celestine is sleeping, my stomach lurches, and I have to stop to catch my breath. When I gingerly sit down on the floor next to Celestine, suspended over twenty feet above the floor below, she looks at me and shakes her head. "I thought European people weren't afraid of anything," she says, smiling.

"What do you mean? I have fears, too."

"Oh, most Europeans aren't afraid of the dark or sleeping alone or whatever. And Margo (an American woman working with the Village Action group), when she was grabbed by those men when she was riding her bicycle out here, she yelled and hit them with her bag until they left her alone. A Tamil woman would never do that."

When I return to Fertile, I mention to Johnny Celestine's comment about Westerners not being afraid of anything. Johnny draws his knees up to his chest and wraps his arms around them as he begins to describe the Tamil villagers' childlike fear of the dark, and some of their beliefs associated with night and the moon. "There's a superstition in the village," explains Johnny, "that you don't keep curd after an eclipse of the moon."

"Why not?"

"Well, I don't know where the saying came from, but one time someone here in Auroville did Kirlian photography of curd and some other food before, during and after an eclipse. Before the eclipse all the patterns of the food were clear, but during the eclipse they blurred. Afterwards all the patterns were clear again, except for the curd. So the villagers may not be able to explain exactly *why* they do something, but there's usually some truth behind a superstition."

Johnny also talks about other ways the villagers have helped Aurovillians. When he and Jan first lived in the village, Johnny would go out fishing with an African man who had a degree in oceanic fishing techniques. "He would experiment with nets and tides and hooks, but you know after months of fiddling with this and that we never caught as much as the villagers did. Eventually we learned to watch the villagers and go fishing when they did. You have to catch the tides just right in those boats. They're an ancient design, and you really have to know the tides to work with them. Anyhow, after we started following the villagers, we caught a lot more fish."

I ask about the villagers' approach to the fields, wondering if Johnny or anyone else has experimented with crop rotation or mulching or new varieties.

"In the beginning we tried a lot of things," explains Johnny, yawning and stretching his arms above him. "But after a while we found that the best time to plant was when the villagers planted; otherwise the crop was too late or too early. So when the villagers plant rice, we plant rice. The day they harvest varagu, we harvest varagu."

"So they really know the land," I comment.

"Yeah, and they can see us making mistakes, so when we come to talk to them about not using DDT on the cashew crops, they don't really have any reason to listen. They can see that they know a lot more about the crops and the planting times than we do, so why should they listen to us about insecticides?"

"But you have been doing educational things in the village, haven't you?"

"Well, we made some videos of the dead fish in the village pond after someone dumped DDT in it, but people were so excited about seeing themselves and their friends on the screen that they didn't really get the point about why the fish were dead, and that they were drinking the same water. I don't blame them, though. In the long run they do know a hell of a lot more about the land here than we do. And they have begun to notice that the insecticides are killing the insects that pollinate the cashews as well as the ones that damage them, so they are starting to cut back some."

"Are there still people who know the local herbs in the villages, for healing?"

"Yes . . . a few. There's still an old man who comes every year to take some berries off one of the trees back by the pump. Once I started a study, a collection of the local medicinal plants, trying to save the information before the old people died out. But I haven't done anything with it for a while."

"So there was a tradition of using local herbs here?"

"Sure. Some of them are still used. The villagers had to take care of themselves before Western medicine came. But then, too, a lot of the plants disappeared along with the forests. Now, even if there is a local remedy, the people want to go to the clinic and get a shot. If they don't get a shot, they don't think the doctor is doing anything, so that's what they go and ask for."

In Auroville the challenge of balancing Western innovation and village wisdom is ongoing. The incoming Aurovillians owe their knowledge of house construction with local materials, agricultural techniques and well digging to the local villagers. In a climate with little rainfall, water is precious and the digging of wells essential. One evening, sitting at the large, round cement table in the kitchen, I come across a 'Banyans and Palmyras' newsletter about Auroville's forest which Johnny edits. This particular issue is about well-digging in different greenbelt communities.

The two main reports mention windmills. If Auroville has contributed anything to village life, it is the development of windmills from local materials. Shortly after I arrived, I went to watch the installation of the one at Samriddhi. For months Alan had been pumping water by hand. Now with the windmill installed, life is relatively easy, with water always available in holding tanks. Auroville's windmills stand about 60 feet (20 metres) high, the head supported by a tower made of local wood. The arms that catch the wind are generally made of cloth so that they can be furled in heavy winds. Diego, Samriddhi's next door neighbour, a dedicated windmill fanatic, had just finished raising the head of his windmill another five metres—his replanted forest had grown tall enough to interfere with the wind currents.

Tinkering with the details, like type of sailcloth or adjustments in construction of the tower, continues, but the basic formula for the windmills is a success. In fact Auroville has more windmills in operation than anywhere else in India, and is now beginning to share its knowledge with villagers in other parts of the country.

Johnny and Diego spent a month in a village outside Bombay constructing a windmill out of scraps of this and that. For the most part, the people were apathetic about both the windmill and life in general. Before leaving them, Johnny made a simple speech: The windmill could become a symbol for the village. *They* would have to take responsibility for its maintenance or it would soon fall into disrepair. If they worked together, the windmill would continue to work for them; if not, it would soon fall apart. Johnny and Diego had succeeded in building the windmill out of almost nothing, but its continued success was up to the villagers.

So many projects in India reflect the same principle—fancy dams for irrigation and village water supply, funded by money from the World Bank and other sources, stand in various stages of decay. Often the knowledge for or interest in maintaining a high-tech dam simply does not exist in a village. The people may or may not be consulted about whether or not they want a particular project, and rarely—if ever —are they asked what *they* feel would improve their life. Ultimately it is they who have the greatest wisdom about what does and doesn't work in that particular area. The villagers have little input in the decision-making process and therefore no investment in maintaining the projects.

As I read these reports, I have a sense of the monumental effort that goes into establishing the settlements in Auroville. Everything starts from scratch, from the most primitive conditions. The Mother's vision was for Auroville to be a place where humanity could 'boldly spring towards future realisations', but I see that Auroville will have to live through all of the preceding ages first—just as a human baby repeats evolutionary development in its mother's womb. Here in Auroville the community began with Stone Age technology, working with simple tools and living in primitive shelters, and has rapidly moved to later eras. The foetus re-enacts millions of years of evolution in nine months; Auroville has re-lived most of the development of human civilisation in the last twenty years.

Now for the most part Auroville has completed the land reclamation, built houses and schools and meeting areas, and developed food supplies that are much more varied than the early days of rice and dahl subsistence. With the basic physical needs met, the community is beginning to focus more attention on its identity as a collective—the desire to learn group facilitation skills is one of the first steps. A catalyst for this process is the negotiations with the Indian government. Auroville is forced to explore its purpose and work as a collective, rather than continuing as a loosely knit, highly tolerant group of individuals. My sense is that the individual freedom and creative initiative which are Auroville's strengths will have to be blended with strong group skills before the community can become 'a living embodiment of an actual Human Unity'.

Sometimes when I sit in the cluster of mismatched chairs at Fertile late in the afternoon after walking the dogs, I try to imagine what this place was like when Jan and Johnny arrived. As I watch the lengthening shadows slanting through the trees, I think about the hours of labour needed to dig a hole with a crowbar for each tree and then to fill it with compost before planting. When the trees were in the ground, they spent hours during the hot, dry summers patiently watering the seedlings with water hauled on bullock carts from one of the local villages. And then the labour of digging a well and building houses and cooking rice and dahl over a fire and making a toilet and planting a garden and bringing groceries and kerosene on the back of a bicycle from Pondicherry . . . it's almost impossible to comprehend the amount of effort and commitment that was involved.

I sit listening to the birds rustling among the leaves as they prepare for the night. The sliver between afternoon and evening always brings on a contemplative mood, and tonight I ponder that I have never been involved in creating something from the very beginning, from scratch. Always I have joined in projects that were already in motion. Here, though, each settlement begins from absolute zero. I wonder if I would have the physical stamina to endure all the frustrations that India has to offer—scarce materials, the tropical climate, bugs, the deathly slow pace, the all-consuming work of meeting basic needs. I wonder if I could begin something even amidst the relative ease of a Western culture.

As the sun sets, colour bleeds from the forest. When the trees dim to grey outlines, I move into the kitchen shelter to light the kerosene lanterns. The late afternoon routine of milking at Aurogreen, walking the dogs, preparing their dinner and lighting the lanterns has become a daily ritual. Without electricity my life is shaped by the movements of the sun. With electric lights, the sunrise or sunset can go unnoticed, but here the passing of the sun must be respected and planned for.

In the evening a deep loneliness builds inside. I am still bitter that the trip with Alan did not come to fruition, and frustrated that I am not strong enough to leave India even if I wanted to. I take one of the lanterns and retreat to Jan's house for an hour's meditation. These quiet moments help to redress my inner balance, upset by my illness and emotional turmoil. Once I am still inside, I begin to hear the words of wisdom that both comfort and challenge me:

The disappointment is deep and bitter, but you were meant for other ways and paths. You cry because you thought you heard correctly the voice of Spirit and not your own desires—this is a bitter cup to drink, but one that eventually will sweeten. All the turns upon the path are not easy, but you have a choice to grieve over losses or to give thanks for new opportunities. No door closes without another opening. You can cry before the closed door of Africa, or rejoice in an opportunity to delve more deeply into India. The layers are peeling, the questions probing more deeply. Cry the tears if you must, but open your eyes to the gifts as well. Make good use of this opportunity; the choice is yours to make your own happiness.

For weeks I have been pondering why my *ears* were blocked—what wasn't I hearing? Perhaps the simple message was that I was to stay here, in India, not go to Africa with Alan. Was the emotional investment in meeting Alan in Africa so great that I needed illness to keep me away?

Shortly after climbing into bed a centipede stings me on the stomach. During the rest of the night I sleep fitfully, sure that bugs are crawling over me, but when I check with my flashlight I see nothing. In the morning I am still tired and doze a bit in the growing light. Slowly I move through my morning routine and into the kitchen. Sunday morning—special day. Today we have dosas, prepared like pancakes from the bubbling mixture of lentils and rice that Samadhi and Shakti spend most of Saturday afternoon grinding and preparing. Overnight the mixture ferments, doubling in size inside the large pot. The scent of dosas frying in a cast-iron skillet is reason enough to get out of bed.

Somewhere about the second dosa of the morning, a visitor walks into Fertile looking for Johnny who has already disappeared to film something. I invite Gus, a visitor staying with Heidi and Patrick, to stay for dosas. Himal, too, has gone for a horseback ride and swim at the beach, so Gus and I begin an uninterrupted conversation that lasts for hours.

Through the morning and into the afternoon we share our experience of travel and family and our inner lives. Gus has just arrived from Australia where he was helping to make a video about the Dreaming Camps that Guboo—an aboriginal elder whom I met at the Findhorn Foundation—holds each January in his homelands of Wallaga Lake, south of Sydney. I have been wanting to visit Guboo and take part in a Dreaming Camp, meant to be an experiential introduction to the aboriginal way of life. Here, in a tiny settlement in the south of India, Gus gives me the information. Chills of recognition run through my spine and my shoulders involuntarily shudder —Creator, you send information in the most unlikely ways.

In his gentle, almost self-conscious way, Gus tells stories about his experiences at Uluru (Ayer's Rock, as the European settlers call it) and the visions and inner experiences that came from his time in Australia. After weeks of solitary quiet, the sharing of lives and stories is both comforting and tiring—I have found a like-minded soul, but the talking exhausts me. After several dosas, the sun slants towards mid-afternoon before Gus leaves. I am reluctant to see him go, but have a sense that we will meet again.

Late in the afternoon I retreat to Jan's house for an hour of meditation. For a few minutes I lie on my back under the mosquito netting, watching wasps burrowing into the wooden poles of the roof above, sending piles of wood pulp that looks like incense ash cascading down on the bed. Breeze, sweet breeze, blows over my sweaty arms and legs. Only the chickens scratching among the dried leaves below interrupt the peace of this afternoon. Despite the calm around me, though, I am anxious inside, impatient to know in what direction I *am* supposed to be going, since I've had such clear feedback from the universe about where I *shouldn't* be.

When I relax inside, moving into a deep silence, I hear:

Be prepared to live empty-handed for a while, in a profound 'I don't know', before breezing ahead on some sightless path. Be still and empty, waiting, waiting, not content to be filled with any passing spiritual teaching, but rather waiting for a moment when the heart is naturally struck and the note reverberates, filling and 'wholing' the being. The way may seem jumbled and blocked, but delays may prove more profitable than any extravagant journey at this time . . . . You already see the folly of planning, or at least counting on, specific events. Plan and be prepared for change. The agenda may change in the twinkling of an eye. Poof—a new set of mysteries, joys, encounters. Questions tumble in your mind, polishing like stones, yet the mind is not the site of solution; check the heart. Look at life through the eyes of the heart and watch a miracle occur.

As the days pass and my strength begins to return, I take longer and longer walks in the morning and evening. During these walks I become more aware of the passing of winter and the beginning of spring. In the purity of first impressions, despite people's descriptions of the hot summers and continual wet of the monsoon season, somehow I never expected to be here long enough to notice the progression of the seasons. The rosellas that I picked in their first fullness are now drying, the stalks mostly bare and spindly, waiting to dry completely and release their seeds. Frangipanis, extraordinarily sweet-scented flowers with waxy petals of white or yellow or shades of red, bloom and drop their blossoms to the ground. Wild dates blaze red and then deepen to brown as they ripen in the common fields. Women and children spend their days moving slowly through the red-baked fields, harvesting the dates from among the spiny fronds. Sometimes a couple of the children run up to me with their hands full of the fruit, offering me some of their hard-earned harvest—their nature is to share whatever they have. I accept a few, and we smile at each other before they run off, splay-toed, through the hot red fields.

A couple of weeks after returning from the hospital I decide that I am well

178

enough to make the bicycle ride to Ivar School for the Village Action Meeting. Held every Thursday morning under the shady mango trees in the centre of the settlement, the meeting is an opportunity for all those who are working in various ways with the villages to come together.

Thursday morning I get up early, wash and have a quick bite of breakfast before swinging onto my cycle and pedalling through the Fertile Forest. About 100 yards from the end of the trees, where the path curves to the left, I am startled by the sound of hooves thundering along the path ahead. Before I can veer off the path, Tanny comes streaking around the corner with Himal riding on her bare back, his hands buried in her mane. Himal's leg smashes into the handlebar which bangs into my thigh and pushes the bicycle to the ground. We both sit in the grass, gasping and rubbing our legs. "Sorry about that," says Himal several times.

"It's OK," I say finally when the initial shock is passed. "I can still walk, but, shit, I can't ride. Do you always ride like that?"

"Yeah, well, usually nobody's in the forest . . . ."

I limp back to Fertile, barely containing my tears. When Johnny asks what happened, my composure snaps and the tears begin to flow. More than anything I am frustrated—I really wanted to start working again, and damn it, now something else has stopped me. If it's not one thing, it's another . . . why are things so damned difficult here?

When I take some time in meditation, finally quieting the tears of frustration, I hear: *Know that the path is worth treading and becomes more insistently 'hedged' as time goes on, more clearly delineated and protected. Thus, detours are less common and more difficult to accomplish.* All right, Creator, if work with Village Action is not for me, I won't try going again. But does the message have to come so graphically?

In the evening I help Himal apply some ointment to Tanny's leg. "I think she was hurt more than any of us," says Himal. "She stopped really quick, and that strained her leg."

After dinner Himal and I have a long talk about his life in Auroville and with his family both before and after they came here. After his parents left Auroville, Himal decided to return to the community alone. He tells me about living in Transformation, a settlement with a school, in a keet-roofed hut ('capsule'). "I was really scared sometimes at night by myself. And one night, God, I'll never forget it, these two thieves that live out in the cashew topes came and set my capsule on fire." He gives a blow by blow account of grabbing his most treasured things and jumping out of the burning hut.

"And I used to write some really good stories then," he continues. "Some of them got published in the kids' magazine that Johnny used to make. It was all writings and poems and stories and stuff by the kids. I still want to finish this one long one sometime." As we talk, I begin to see more of Himal's strength and depth than ever before. This evening something has opened between us; the collision seems to have made us more aware and more understanding of each other.

For the next couple of days I take short walks, working the stiffness out of my leg. Sometimes I stop to help the women who are hauling pots of water for families who have moved into the cashew topes, preparing to harvest this year's crop of nuts. Usually they are among the poorest of the village people, willing to work for very small wages. They build simple shelters among the cashew bushes so that they can guard the crop until it is ready for harvest.

One late afternoon while walking with the dogs through the Fertile forest, I come upon three women and a boy crouched around the base of one of the young saplings. As I approach, I see that one of the women is holding a machete and hacking at the base of the trunk. When I am about ten feet away, the tree groans and bends to the earth. The women look up, startled to see me. Two of them scramble towards the cashew tope behind me, dragging the boy with them, and the woman with the machete vanishes into the field in front of me. I run along the path after her, but can see no sign of her in the dusky light.

I run the last quarter mile into Fertile, calling for Johnny. When I explain what I've seen, he takes off down the path towards the cashew tope. We trot through the fields, dogs loping behind, until we see a campfire ahead. Around the fire sit a cluster of women and children, their saris drawn around their heads to ward off the evening chill. They look up as we approach, innocently nodding and murmuring, "Hello, Johnny." Obviously he is a well-known figure among the villagers.

Johnny begins a barrage in Tamil, striding around the fire, waving his arms and pointing at the ten freshly cut poles that lie in a pile behind them. They shake their heads and protest verbally when he begins to pick up the poles. We probably would make a clean get-away except that the women have tied a couple of goats to the poles, and Johnny has to stop to untie them. The brief interlude gives the women enough time to mobilise themselves. They gather around the poles and begin to yank them out of Johnny's hands. "*Judith,*" yells Johnny, "grab some poles and run!"

I pick up three or four poles and run about ten feet before the women catch up. We begin a tug of war, half of the women pulling on my poles, half on Johnny's, with children hanging wherever they can grab hold. Initially I can't keep from smiling—the whole episode is so ridiculous—but after a while I see that the village women are dead set on prising the wood away. Their 'ul-ul-ul-ull' screams are deafening, and their thin arms determined. For them, the wood is the basis for their shelter in the cashew tope, not just a supply of firewood. They are fighting for a home. *And* they thrive on drama.

When I can't budge the poles another foot, I resort to trying to trip the women with my foot. As I swing my foot underneath theirs, suddenly I realise that I have broken an unspoken rule—you don't touch me, I won't touch you. The invisible line overstepped, the children gather around me and begin to pound on my back.

By now we have struggled almost to the end of the field. Johnny, too, is making little headway. "Grab one pole," yells Johnny, "and run for your life. Go get Himal to help me."

I drop all but one pole, yanking it from the rest, and trot across the field and through the forest, yelling for Himal. Soon we are both running through the fields to the stack of poles that Johnny has gathered at the edge of the forest. We each grab a couple and retreat to Fertile.

That night I lie in bed for a long time before sleep comes. My wrists and arms are rubbed raw from the rough bark sliding back and forth across them, but most painful of all is the memory of my own violence. Just a month before I gave a presentation about conflict resolution in the facilitation group, and here I am, working with total confrontation. In my mind I try to recreate how I could have handled the situation. I wish now that I had just laughed and dropped the bundle of poles and joined hands with these women, but when I talked with Johnny about it afterwards, he commented that we handled it 'village'. "It's good to have some drama," he said. "It may keep them from doing it again. Just have to be sure not to hurt them. Generally they won't hit you if you don't hit them." If we had just reported it to the village and let the council handle it, the women probably would have been beaten and maybe fined (the money goes to the temple).

"Was it really such a terrible crime?" I ask, still feeling sick about it.

"Well, sure, cutting a tree is a very serious crime among the villagers."

"But where can they get wood for shelters if they don't have money to buy it?"

"Some years I loan them the wood at the beginning of the cashew season, and they bring it back when the harvest is through. But you have to let them know they can't cut the trees or the whole forest would be gone. They'll probably come tomorrow, acting really indignant and demanding the wood, maybe bringing some of their family from the village, making a big scene. Or, if it really wasn't theirs, they probably won't come at all. We'll see what happens."

During the night I keep an ear alert for anyone prowling near the stack of poles. Nothing. The next day no one appears from the village to protest about the confiscated wood. The immediacy of the event stays with me, though, and precipitates as a bout of raging diarrhoea and mild fever. This time I decide to relax immediately, before anything more serious can develop.

By the end of the week, I am recovered enough to make a planned trip to Tiruvannamalai, a temple town to the northwest. I spend three days in Sriraman Ashram, a small community focused on the teachings of Ramana Maharshi, a great teacher who lived during the first half of this century. This ashram is very quiet and well-ordered, making it a popular stop for Western spiritual seekers/travellers.

When I enter the hall for the afternoon *puja* before the tomb of Ramana Maharshi, I have the sense of a community focused on perpetuating the memory of a ghost. When the ceremony finishes, I walk across the courtyard and climb a short way up the mountain to watch the sunset. This mountain, Arunchela, is sacred to the Hindus, regarded as the navel of the universe.

When I return along the path, I'm hardly surprised to see a saffron-robed old man approaching. What is unusual, though, is his warm smile and peaceful nod of the head. "Good eveninck," he says. "I recognise you from the meditation hall. You sit for long time." He nods approvingly. "Ver-r-ry good."

We walk for a while together along the path. He points to himself and says, "Satyananda." I roll the name in my mouth and then clumsily spill it out. He smiles and points to me. "Judith," I tell him.

He begins to tell me stories about his life here at the base of Arunchela, of his time as Ramana Maharshi's personal attendant, the most joyful years in his life. After his beloved master's death, Satyananda took a vow of silence for nearly 20 years. Soon after his decision to speak again, though, he moved out of the ashram and into his own small hut.

"Why did you go?" I ask him.

"Too much fighting, too much politics. I was tired of it, so I came to live here," he says, pointing down the path. "Come, see where I live. I will show you. And I show you my photo album."

I am a bit unsure about following the old man—I've heard stories about licentious sadhus (renunciates) who were less than virtuous in their dealings with lone women—but he seems kind-hearted and gentle, so I decide to follow.

His tiny two-room mud brick house is mostly bare except for pictures of Ramana Maharshi. The altar, though, is crammed with cards and memorabilia from people who have visited him from all over the world. He pulls a well-worn photo album from beneath his simple cot and places it before me, nodding. Among the carefully pasted pages are many pictures of Ramana Maharshi, clothed only in a loincloth, his great height accentuated by the tiny attendant—Satyananda—who appears in each picture, as persistent as a shadow.

When I stand to leave, I feel my heart fly open, ignited by the simplicity of this man's devotion. He clasps my elbows and presses his cheek against mine and then leans back to hold my eyes for a few moments. Here, I decide, is the first Indian man whom I have met who really has a heart. Before I go he invites me to come for tea in the morning, and I promise to come at 10:30 (another legacy of British rule, the all important mid-morning tea break).

The next morning I stop to buy bananas at a local stand (higher price for Westerners, of course) to give to Satyananda and then walk along the dirt road that leads to his tiny house. Satyananda gratefully accepts the bananas and places them amidst the clutter on the altar. "Puja, puja," he says, smiling. While I sit quietly on the floor, he patiently opens selected containers from the pile of cookie tins that fill one corner of the room. He withdraws tea and powdered milk and then boils water on his single gas ring. While the water heats, he carefully arranges a handful of nuts and cookies on a small plate. My chest aches as my heart opens wide—for the first time, I realise, since arriving in India. We sit in silence, listening to the birds chirping in the trees outside until the water hisses in the pot. He carefully prepares the tea and sets the single cup before me. I look up, surprised—nothing for him? He swivels his head and motions for me to drink, so slowly I sip the sweet milky tea and eat the nuts and cookies on the plate. When I am finished we sit quietly for a few more minutes until I nod my head and tell him I must go. "Yes," he says, nodding, "lunchtime at the ashram. But I not eat today. Full moon. Special day."

"Yes," I say, remembering that many people will be joining in meditation today as an extension of the Harmonic Convergence. I plan to spend the hour of full moon in the ashram meditation room linking with friends and family around the planet.

"Today full moon, beginning Tamil month, and Friday," explains Satyananda, holding up three fingers. "Very important. Today I walk around Arunchela with visiting sadhu and man from France living here with us. You are welcome to come," he says simply. "Meet us here at 3:30. Long walk—13 miles. We maybe go to temple afterwards."

I thank him, moved by his invitation, and promise to come. I wouldn't miss for anything the chance to walk around the mountain under the full moon.

3:30 p.m. The sun is still hot when we turn off the dirt path and onto the bitumen road that runs in front of the ashram. We join a swell of villagers making their way from the centre of Tiruvannamalai back to their villages. They stop in ones and twos at the small Shiva temples that pepper the base of the mountain to 'make puja', a ritual of purification performed by the resident holy man. After about an hour we turn to the right along a dirt road that skirts the western side of the mountain, passing through villages and alongside well-kept gardens and fences signposted 'Swami So-and-So's Ashram'. This must be the Vatican Row of Tamil Nadu, I decide as we pass by the fourth or fifth one.

By the time we reach the town of Tiruvannamalai on the far side of Arunchela, the streets have darkened and the moon hangs just above the top of the mountain. After a simple dinner of dosas at a local restaurant and shopping for vegetables, we make our way to the temple. "Watch your things," warns Satyananda. "Many people in the temple tonight, lots of thieves."

The temple is thrumming with activity. Satyananda is in his element—the priests bow respectfully and smile when he passes. Obviously he is a well-known and well-loved figure. We sit for a while on some steps, eating milk candy and sharing it with the children and beggars thronging this area.

Eventually we move through the temple and into the dark streets, walking the last miles around the mountain and back to Sriraman Ashram. At the gate I wave goodbye to the others and return alone to my simple room.

"Thank you, Creator," I murmur as I undress and pull the single sheet over me, "for Satyananda and the mountain and the healing time in the temple." Before I turn off the light—a bare electric bulb that hangs from the ceiling—I open my journal, and it falls to the day before leaving for Sriraman Ashram: *The trip is a blessing, the crust will loosen on your fear of India, and know that inner work is vital during this time. The cause for movement is a great need to resolve a puzzle from long ago, one which you have not yet recognised. Some of the clues and pieces begin to come together.*

Tonight, lying in bed with moonlight slanting through the high window of the back wall, I sense the edges of that puzzle mentioned in the guidance. Until the last few days India has felt like an alien land, and I have moved through it like a space-suited Martian. The time here in the ashram, though, has awakened some sleepy, half-forgotten memory . . . if not of this specific place, then perhaps of this way of life, one of simple devotion and one-pointed focus upon inner development. Whatever the deeper learning is, I am aware in this moment that I have somehow landed in India; I have made peace with the spirit of the land and its spiritual tradition. I have found the loving heart in the stern disciplinarian of Mother India.

* * *

When I arrive back in Auroville, I spend an afternoon in Fertile before moving to Joan's house in Aspiration for a few days' visit. After only four days away, Fertile feels strange, foreign, perhaps in part because of the arrival of a new resident, a young German woman named Gudrun who has visited before with Diego. Then she was introduced as his new 'girlfriend', but from the way she and Johnny interact, I sense that now *they* are lovers. A lot seems to have happened during my brief absence, but I'm not eager to press for details. I repack my things and swing onto the bicycle, heading for the Saturday afternoon facilitation group meeting.

After the meeting Joan and I ride to her home in Aspiration. When we park our bikes in the immaculate tool shed, I know immediately that Joan's house will be as straightforwardly elegant and simple as she is—always her blond hair is neatly, but not studiously, arranged around her finely shaped, tan face. Her clothes, too, are simple cotton, but the colours and cuts always look distinctive on her.

She has carefully arranged my entry to her house to give the greatest impact. First she shows me the treehouse where she lived for two years before her present house was built. Compared to this, the new house is truly a mansion. Made of curving walls of mudbrick with beautiful patios sweeping out from the entranceways and surrounded by a narrow channel of water ("To keep the bugs from getting in," explains Joan), her home is stunning. On top of the house rise white stuccoed domes that give it the air of a temple. Later in the evening when the sun has set and the moon shines full in the sky, we climb through the upstairs bedroom window onto a terrace and then up a short ladder to sit on the lip of one of the domes.

The forests and cashew topes stand in relief under the icy light. We talk more about our lives, our dreams, the experiences that brought us to Auroville. Again I am struck by the dedication and persistence of the Aurovillians in bringing the Mother's dream into form. For two years Joan worked on the construction of the house, first shaping the mud bricks and then supervising the workers hired to complete the work. "How was that?" I ask, knowing that village men have little respect for women.

"Well," says Joan, smiling and leaning her head to the side, "sometimes it wasn't easy, but in the end they did listen, and we did finish the house."

Some of our talks touch our highest, deepest aspirations, our longing to find our true 'work', as people here in Auroville call it. We talk about what I have come to call 'tough love', the kind of love that refuses to support weakness.

"That's the love of Kali, the love of the Mother," comments Joan. "The other day I met a woman on the road who I knew was having a hard time—her boyfriend of about eight years had just left with another woman. When I saw her I said, 'Hey, lookin' good,' because she really *was* looking good. We stopped to talk, and I suggested that she might think about getting a massage to help her, but it's up to *her* to actually arrange the massage. I'm not going to do it *for* her; she needs to do it herself. I want to support her in being strong."

"Hmmmm . . . it makes sense. I never thought about it that way before."

She teaches me some of the nuts and bolts of living in India, too, simple things that I have overlooked without anyone to point them out. "I've been thinking about publishing a booklet for people when they first arrive in Auroville," says Joan. "You know, when I first came I had a sort of 'fuck you' attitude, I wasn't going to follow a lot of the village ways that I thought were sexist or whatever; but now I think a bit differently." Her voice rises in a sing-song cadence typical of an Indian's voice inflection. "We need to respect the culture that is here. We are coming into their country, we should learn to be aware of *their* ways."

During the days of my visit, I come to understand more fully the relationship of the Aurovillians with the surrounding villages as well as Auroville's internal structure. Joan works at the visitors' centre at Bharat Nivas, so she is much more in touch with the core of the community than Fertile is, which tends to be more focused on education and greenbelt issues. In fact it is Joan who first takes me inside the Matrimandir, the heart of the community.

Although I have visited the structure several times, never before have I climbed the ramp and entered the upper level of this massive round ball resting on its wing-like supports. After walking around another ramp that curves along the inner wall, we climb a scaffold and walk across the wooden planks that rest between supports. I have to pause to catch my breath and steady my watery knees—the ground is a ten-storey free-fall below me.

Once across the planks we enter the central chamber of the Matrimandir, a huge open room meant to be a place of concentration. Now the room is bare concrete, but Joan explains the Mother's vision for special colours and shapes on the walls and a single adornment for the centre of the hall, a crystal continuously illuminated by a single beam of light focused through an opening in the ceiling above. Earlier in the year the Ziess company, famous for its work with crystals and optics, announced that the specially commissioned crystal had finally cooled (a two-year process) and was ready for shipment.

Now the Matrimandir building crew is working on models for a tracking device that will follow the sun's movement and cast the single beam of light into the crystal. They also have been experimenting with the golden discs that Mother envisioned on the outside of the Matrimandir—one of the many designs that she and Roget, the French architect, collaborated on. The number of changes and additions to the plans in the years before Mother's death make the building crew's job more difficult. No one is clear about exactly which version to follow, and Roget's visits to consult with the community are brief and infrequent.

Sitting quietly inside the central chamber, the attention on details passes away. The vast open space inside the room lends itself to inner stillness; in fact, it demands quiet reverence. The wind moans among the pillars below and pigeons coo and chortle from their roosts among the scaffolding. Joan leaves me for a few minutes of silence, and I move inside, hoping to experience the essence of the Mother and her vision for Auroville. I have no earth-shaking revelations, though, only a quiet sense of inner peace and the vast well of inspiration from which the community draws.

When we walk down the ramp and back into the intense mid-day sunlight, I turn to Joan, curious about how the completion of the Matrimandir will affect Auroville. "The Matrimandir is like the soul of the community, right?" Joan nods her head in affirmation. "So completing the Matrimandir would be like incarnating the soul of the community."

"You could say that," says Joan.

"Do you think a lot of things will change when the Matrimandir is complete?"

"On an inner level, yes, I think we'll see lots of changes."

I wonder, too, what will take the place of the Matrimandir as the focal point for work together as a community. Even now, with most of the structure complete, the building crew makes periodic requests for people to join in a concrete pouring that might last from a few days to a few weeks. When the Matrimandir is complete, will people sink fully into their own settlements, or will some other community work take its place? Perhaps, too, by that time the group identity of Auroville will be solid enough that it doesn't require physical work to keep the community focused on its common purpose.

Once again my time in Auroville is nearing an end. I wonder if this time I really will leave or if . . . . No, I don't even want to entertain the possibility. I am grateful for the extra time I have had, to come to know Auroville more deeply and to make some sort of peace with India, but I have no desire to extend my trip any longer. After another flurry of telegrams, Alan wrote to say that he will join me in Auroville for the last ten days of his journey, and we plan to leave India together. A couple of days before his arrival, I make arrangements to take a taxi into Madras to meet his plane. The driver will take us to Mamallapuram, a shore temple town south of Madras, and wait for us overnight before driving us to Auroville. For weeks I have been looking forward to Alan's arrival, and that morning I am up early to pack and prepare last-minute details before the taxi's arrival at 9 a.m.

After dressing and packing a few clothes in my daypack, I move into the kitchen to rinse and fill my waterbottle. I set it on the table while I rummage in the cabinet for some bread and fruit to take on the trip.

"Get your bloody pisspot off the table!!!" screams Himal. The words land like a solid punch in my solar plexus. Shocked by the suddenness and the violence of his words, I stand for a few moments, adrenalin pumping through my body.

"It's not a 'pisspot'," I say finally, the words terse and even, "it's a waterbottle. And I just rinsed it and filled it with clean water."

"I don't care what it is. Keep it bloody well off the table."

"Right," I say simply, and storm over to Jan's house to finish packing. I realise that talking to him would be useless at this point, and I have little control over my body or emotions. My arms feel limp and watery, and I have to concentrate on what I am picking up so that I don't drop anything. Once the initial shock begins to wear off, I fantasise all kinds of clever responses. I wonder, too, what will happen when Alan and I return—Johnny and Gudrun plan to take a week-long backpacking trip in Mundalai, the rainforest on the western side of Tamil Nadu, and leave Himal in charge of Fertile. Obviously he has been nursing some grudges towards me for several weeks—his anger is far out of proportion to what actually happened.

I stand at the end of the path, waiting for the taxi with Celestine who will share the ride into Madras where she has some errands to do. I'm still a bit shaky when she arrives, and I explain briefly what happened. "I have heard a bit about that boy," comments Celestine. "Very spoiled, I think."

"I don't know, Celestine; I've had the feeling he was upset with me, but every time I asked him, he said nothing was wrong."

As the hours slide by, the immediacy of the encounter with Himal passes. We have lunch in Madras and then drive to the Air India office where I change my departure date to coincide with Alan's, and Celestine buys her ticket for Sri Lanka, to go home to visit her father. We part with a hug, and I ride alone with the taxi driver to the airport.

After about an hour the plane arrives. I stand for another hour waiting, growing more and more distressed as all of the passengers move through the baggage area and out the front door. No sign of Alan. Twice I ask the India Airlines clerks to check to see if Alan was on the plane from Kenya to Bombay. "Cannot do," says the clerk, shaking her head. "You must go to other airport, ask Air India."

I meet another family in the same predicament and go with them to the other airport a mile down the road. After a couple of initial rebuffs, we make our way to the woman in charge of something-or-other who tells us to wait for the next plane. "They probably missed a connection and will come on next plane."

So we wait for another four hours for the second plane. The taxi driver, aware of my distress, tells me in broken English that he has prayed to Ganesh, the Hindu Elephant God—Alan will certainly arrive on the next plane.

Again I stand near the front door, craning my neck to see the stream of people moving around the baggage pickup carousel. Well, Ganesh is a poor fortuneteller. When the hall clears and still there is no sign of Alan, I go to the desk again, tears welling over. "Please," I say, barely able to choke out the words, "can you check if he arrived in Bombay?"

Miraculously the clerk comprehends the request and calls up the information on the computer. "No flight from Nairobi today," she says looking up. "Not until day after tomorrow."

"Day after tomorrow?" I ask, dazed by the information. Have I misread the telegram? I pull the crumpled, sweaty paper from my bag and re-read it. No, he said today. I'm torn between being angry at him for mis-writing the date and rejoicing that he's still alive, not downed in a plane crash.

Still stunned and unsure of what to do, I go back to the taxi and sit for a few minutes, explaining to the driver that I need some time to think. Finally I decide to spend a couple of days at Mamallapuram and then return by bus to meet Alan at the airport. The driver tells me he knows the man who runs one of the guest houses in the town; he is sure that he can get me a room there.

We arrive after 11 p.m. The driver is as good as his word; although the manager is not in, the clerk opens one of the dormitory rooms and I gratefully slide between the thick cotton sheets.

Two days later I board the local bus and return to the airport. This time I weasel my way into the baggage hall to make sure I don't miss Alan. He escapes me anyhow, and I finally find him outside talking to one of the baggage clerks. Thank Goddess, he's finally arrived.

We hug each other for a long time—his arms are like rain in the desert, welcome nourishment after our months of separation. Through the hours of excited talk that follow, I learn that Air India changed the Nairobi-Bombay flight schedule after April 1st. Since Alan was far away from any form of communication in the mountains of Rwanda, he did not know about the change until he was ready to leave for the airport two days before. Incensed at their lack of communication—"I'm sure they already knew about the schedule change when they sold me the ticket a month before"—Alan had insisted they leave some kind of message for me at the airport in Madras. No such luck. And a telegram would have arrived five days after him. "It was incredibly frustrating. I knew I had no way of reaching you in time, so I was trying to send you inner messages . . . ." That's the reality of trying to send messages between two Third World countries. "But anyway, I'm here now," he says, squeezing my hand, "and I'm glad I made it."

We spend a couple of days in Mamallapuram, admiring the spectacular carvings chiselled into the cliffs, portrayals of stories and heroic figures from the *Mahabharata*, walking along the white sand beach and swimming in the sapphire blue sea. We take the local bus into Pondi, so crowded that we spend most of the ride upright, jammed between other passengers pressed into the central aisle. In Pondi we flag down a rickshaw driver who is willing to take us to Auroville. We arrive at Fertile just before dark—the place is deserted, the food cabinet empty. Even the gas stove is out of fuel, so we cook some grain over a fire and then crawl into bed.

At 1 a.m. we are woken by the whoops and hollers of boys stampeding around on horses and motorbikes, cracking whips and breaking lantern canes. We decide to ignore it, thinking that Himal and his friends have arrived for a late-night party.

The next morning we commiserate with Gudrun—she, too, was awakened by the kids' antics. I am surprised that she has returned before Johnny, but she explains that her cold got worse instead of better in the damp rainforest, and the bugs were more than she could bear, so she came back alone on the bus. Late in the afternoon I start to work on a bicycle that has been rusting at the edge of the forest—it needs some new parts and a paint job before it will be rideable again, and I want to renovate it as a parting gift to Fertile. I spend about an hour sandpapering the old paint and rust until Himal comes home. I want to ask him about the kids who came last night, and let him know that we didn't like the noise, but I'm also aware that anything I say might trigger a terrible response. I hang on the moment, and finally decide to say something.

"Hey, Himal, did you tell your friends they could come over last night? I thought you were with them, so we didn't say anything."

"Nope," he says curtly. "I was over at Auroson's house. Yeah, I said they could come over and have a party."

"Did you know there were people here? They woke up Alan and me, and Gudrun, too."

Gudrun and another woman sitting at the kitchen table look down at the seats, unwilling to take part in the discussion. I don't blame them—I'd rather go somewhere and talk in private, but Himal refuses. Something uncorks in me, a death wish perhaps, and I tell him how the kids were cracking whips and breaking glass and yelling—I demonstrate just how loud.

Himal looks down, takes a deep breath, and begins a carefully controlled, obviously long-rehearsed speech. "Judith, don't you think you've been around here a bit too long? I really think it's about time you leave. Look, I hate you, I think you're weird, and you hate me—don't deny it—so why don't you just go somewhere else for the last week you're here and enjoy yourself. Johnny said if it got to be too much with you around, I could *suggest,* I'm not *telling* you, just *suggesting*, that you go somewhere else."

Again the adrenalin starts pumping. We argue and yell for about 20 minutes, Himal accusing me of all sorts of things, from not being like Thomas, the graduate student, to shitting in one of the cooking pots, to never buying anything for Fertile.

He overrides any attempt to contradict him by yelling as loud as he can. Himal struggles as best he can to stay in his seat. "Look, Johnny taught me that I can't just run away when I'm talking with somebody, so I'm staying here as long as I can, but I have to tell you I've just about had enough. So look, make your choice. I'm *suggesting* that you go somewhere else."

"And if I don't are you going to send your friends over to harass us, like you did last night?" He had said before that that was part of why he invited his friends to party at Fertile, hoping it would disturb me.

"I didn't do that!" yells Himal.

"That's what you said a few minutes ago," I remind him.

He grins sheepishly and looks down, caught in the lie. "No, I won't send them over to bother you."

When the verbal brawl finishes—just as painful as any physical one—I debate for a while whether to move or stay. Since I returned it has been like living in a militarised zone, and I'm not particularly eager to remain, although I'm also reluctant to move all my things only a week before leaving Auroville. Most of all I hate looking like I've buckled in to Himal's request. Amidst the violent fantasies that begin to brew in my head about how to deal with Himal, I also feel betrayed by Johnny. I am shocked that he would have given Himal the go-ahead to throw me out of Fertile. Perhaps he, too, has been angry with me for weeks without saying anything. How can I expect to work out problems, though, if everyone refuses to talk about anything until it builds into a violent conflict?

I leave to milk the cows at Aurogreen, and while I'm there I ask Suzie if they have a space where we could stay if we need it. "Sure," she tells me, "our guest house is empty now. You can come by tonight and get the key if you need to."

When I tell her about the argument with Himal, she nods her head and comments, "You know, Auroville is a place to work out karma. It's not a place for a holiday."

Relieved, I return to Fertile to talk with Alan to see what he wants to do. Himal is still sitting at the table, ordering the workers around as if he were a sahib. Mangini looks up as he sifts the gravel around the kitchen, something that obviously hasn't been done, or needed to be done, for years. His eyes are filled with pained humour. Working for Himal has not been easy.

Himal calls Alan over and tells him he's welcome to stay. "Thanks, Himal, but you know we're together. I'm not going to stay here if Judith doesn't."

"Well, what do you have to say about all of this?" he asks Alan. "What do *you* think I should do?"

"Well," says Alan, pausing to weigh his words carefully, "one thing I've learned from living at the Findhorn Community is that I have to get along with people who are different from me. I may not like everyone who lives at Cluny Hill, but I recognise they have as much right to be there as I do. I trust that we have a common purpose, even though I may not like some people's personalities. And I also know that when I get angry or irritated with someone, they are mirroring something that's inside me, too. It's like I put an aspect of myself onto that person, or they trigger something that's already inside me. I have to look at myself and realise that it's something *inside* me, not the other person, that I'm angry or upset about."

Himal asks a question that tells me that he doesn't fully understand the idea of mirroring, but the tolerance of different personalities sinks in. Thank Goddess that Alan can speak calmly and lovingly right now; it's certainly beyond me.

That evening we decide to move to Aurogreen. I still have to go to Fertile occasionally to pick things up. When I return, Gudrun is moving into Jan's house —probably part of her eagerness to cooperate with Himal, so that she could have a

188

space to herself. Each time I walk down the path I feel my shoulders drawing inward, my stomach clenching. Sometimes I actually fear a physical attack. For the most part, though, my entries and exits go unnoticed—except by the workers who look confused about my absence. "You go somewhere else now?" asks Mangini.

"Yes," I tell him, "we're staying at Aurogreen."

"You and your man?"

I smile—the workers have been very concerned that I am without a husband. "Yes, Mangini, Alan and I."

He grins. "That is good."

Himal sits in one of the wicker chairs, legs splayed and arms crossed, ordering the workers around. He blusters like a little Raj. "Mangini," he yells, "there's more gravel here to sift." Mangini winces, almost imperceptibly, and looks up, shrugging his shoulders. I smile and wish him well.

Alan and I spend most of the week visiting people and attending meetings. We give a session on attunement with the facilitation group. After some explanation and a practice exercise, we attune with Mother, the essence of Auroville, to ask how this group can best serve the community at large. A lot of insight and inspiration comes from the meditation. Only Elaine, a French woman who has recently joined the group, is disappointed by the session. She reports that she got the 'feeling', but not the 'concept' of attunement. She had done the exercises in another context and so found the meditation confusing and disjointed.

In that moment I understand the French influence in Auroville more completely. Unless they can grasp something in an acceptable mental form, they cannot absorb it. Elaine doesn't seem to be able to see past the particular outer form, rather than focusing on the content or context. For her the exercises should always illustrate the same point rather than being the backdrop to many truths. This makes any new information difficult to digest. I also see in her the need to *resist*, to take a stand. Remember, flexibility = compromise = weakness. Such a culture. Imagine having nearly half a community bent on inflexibility (pardon the pun). No wonder the people at Auroville have so many problems getting along, making decisions, simply communicating.

Alan and I also visit the settlement of Verité for a short session on attunement. The group is one of the few in Auroville trying to work together as a cooperative team, and they are eager to learn more skills to keep themselves inspired and functioning well. Their enthusiasm has been flagging somewhat in the last few months, so we decide to attune to Mother and the essence of Auroville to look at Verité's purpose within the larger community, as well as anything that would ease their interaction as a group. During the meditation I have a strong sense of connection with Mother and Auroville, experiencing the greater energy of Auroville as very vital and clear. I also feel the vast potential waiting to be manifested through the community, and Verité seems to be a current 'hot spot' to actualise that energy. The group gains a lot of insight about how they can connect more deeply with one another and inspiration about their larger purpose within Auroville. Alan also suggests that in addition to their meetings revolving around work they consider having weekly sharings, to take time to connect on a personal level.

Later in the week, Johnny returns from his backpacking trip and comes over to Aurogreen to see how Alan and I are doing. At first I recognise the voice but not the face—I have never seen Johnny clean-shaven, and his face is completely transformed. "What's up, Johnny, how come you shaved your beard?" I ask quietly.

"Well, a lot's been happening with me while I was away. I've been looking at how I hide . . . and one way is behind my beard, so I decided to shave it off."

"What do you mean, 'hide'?"

"Well, how I don't work with people, how I usually have my own trip, working by myself. Like with the school. I want to look at teaching *with* someone else instead of doing it alone. I realised there aren't that many people I work with."

We talk about his experiences in the forest with the village of people who live mostly isolated among the trees, a very traditional group. After a while the conversation turns to my blow-out with Himal. "I want to suggest that in the future you talk more with visitors, maybe review their stay in Auroville every month. I can't clear a conflict with anyone if they refuse to tell me what's going on with them." For several days I've been trying to separate out my part in the conflict, and I apologise to Johnny for the illness and not being able to work. "I know it must have been hard," I tell him. "Sometimes I didn't even know myself, when the pain was really bad, so I know it must have been difficult for you."

"We-e-ell, it wasn't really a problem. I wish Jan had been here, she could have taken better care of you. You know I've got a stoic attitude about sickness . . . . And I knew things were getting tense between you and Himal, but I didn't know if I should say anything or not. And look, if you want to work with kids, you've got to let them know what you're doing. Like if you're going to do urine therapy, you ought to explain what you're doing and *why*. Then they'll respect what you're doing. But if you don't say anything, it's like you don't include them, and they rebel and don't respect you. The kids were really freaked out when I had hepatitis and was drinking my urine—the best way to deal with it was to tell them what was going on. And if you're going to be public about it, you've *got* to explain."

I didn't think I *was* being public about it, but I take Johnny's point to heart. I thought the best way to deal with the urine therapy was to be as quiet as possible about it, but I realise that my plan backfired. Better to be upfront at the beginning instead of trying to be inconspicuous. Why is it so hard for me just to be myself and take the consequences?

"Johnny, did you tell Himal it was OK to ask me to leave?"

"No," says Johnny surprised. "I never said anything like that. I've really got to talk to Himal. His father beat him a lot when he was growing up; I don't like hitting him, but sometimes it's the only way he'll listen. Fertile's . . . well, it's got out of hand. The place really needs Jan. She's the one who keeps it together. Not my sort of creative chaos . . . that's part of what I've been thinking about, too."

We stand under the trees, talking until the late afternoon shadows darken into night. I am grateful for the chance to clear my sense of betrayal with Johnny, and also glad for the insights about Himal. I no longer feel such a victim. I have more of a sense of my own part in creating the conflict, and more compassion for Himal and the background he has come from. When Alan arrives, back from a visit at another settlement, he and Johnny leave for Fertile for a long reunion conversation. I decide to stay at Aurogreen. Although my body is much stronger, I still have little stamina, and I am exhausted after a full day. Also, I have little desire to return to Fertile, so I climb up to the loft of the guest house and fall asleep.

A couple of days before our departure, I ride into Pondi to sort out a visa extension. The men behind the desks bluster, shuffle papers, smoke cigarettes; one man happily bounces his daughter on his knee. They are indignant when I insist that they do some work and complete my extension. Actually, I don't insist, I patiently persist. I refuse to leave the office, and I can see my passport sitting at the top of someone's pile of paper work. Hours pass. Finally the clerk sits with his hand poised over the passport and reluctantly lets it drop to pick up the papers. Tense silence for a few moments, then everyone in the office grins. "What is she?" asks one of the others. "American," he answers curtly.

"Ah, I should have known."

I look up innocently. "Haven't I been patient?"

"Ah, Madam, you kill us with your patience," says the clerk, shaking his head. The office erupts with laughter.

With papers in hand I go to Samadhi, the grave of Mother and Sri Aurobindo in the centre of the ashram. Whenever I am in Pondicherry I try to stop here. I find the shady courtyard peaceful, a good spot for quiet meditation. The flowers on the grave touch me, too, reminding me of the tobacco offerings made by Native American people. Some Westerners find devotion to a guru repulsive, but I interpret the flowers as offerings to the memory of a teacher's strength and wisdom, a way of giving thanks.

Relaxing against one of the courtyard walls, I meditate for a few minutes, knowing that this will probably be the last time that I visit Samadhi, at least for a while. My thoughts turn to Australia and memories of my trip with Alan over a year ago. I have the strange feeling that I might never escape from India, might never make the flight out of Bombay to Australia.

I have been pondering my illness, recalling that as a young child I had a lot of ear infections. I remember the doctor once threatening to put me in the hospital if I wasn't better in a couple of days' time. I got better quickly. Since childhood, though, I have had no trouble with my ears. Why would I finally end up in hospital, years later, in India? I ask internally about my purpose for being in India, the reason for the illness, what lesson it is that I need to learn at this time.

"Your spiritual childhood is ending," I hear. "You face the growing pains of adolescence, the fury and the anger, the raw hurt of your being. India comes to lay you bare, to expose those areas long hidden, long ago hurt and suppressed. You have a new opportunity to own your strength and find your place in the world. You *can* begin anew, patterns *can* change. Do not fear emerging into the world."

When I open my eyes a stream of bare-headed pilgrims is moving through the courtyard. Whole families make pilgrimages during their holidays (ah, holi-day, holy day—the word suddenly has new meaning). They shave their heads as a ritualised act of penance, cleansing the old, and then visit shrines, temples and holy masters as a way of giving thanks for the past year and preparing for the new. How different, I realise, from my childhood family holidays. We visited museums, battlefields, national parks and beaches. Sacred sites were not on the agenda.

The next day, our last in Auroville, Alan and I ride to Ivar School to return the bike that I have been renting and to say goodbye to the teachers and children who have been so much a part of my life here. At lunchtime we walk over to the bakery, about a quarter mile up the road, where Alan worked during his stay in Auroville. I want to buy some cookies to give the children as a farewell gift.

One of the men who runs the bakery is just pulling a tray of small round chocolate cookies from an oven; the other is moving loaves of sourdough bread from one rack to another to brown them evenly. Three workers from the village roll long sections of cookie dough and cut out the tiny rounds before placing them on huge baking sheets. All of Auroville's bread is produced in these wood-fired ovens. Bread is little known in Tamil Nadu, so the bakery was a contribution of European Aurovillians, in this case two Frenchmen. The local villagers, though, have developed a taste for the buns and bread baked here, and often a couple of barefoot village boys come to the door with a fistful of coins to buy something.

While Alan reminisces with the man who was working in the bakery when he was a visitor, I talk with the other baker. On one of my first days in Auroville I came here to ask if they needed help; the bakery, though, no longer uses visitors because the help was sporadic and they were always having to train new people, so they hired village workers instead. We sat and drank tea and talked for a long time. They were especially curious to hear about how the Findhorn Community was doing. Today it is my turn to ask him about Auroville and what drew him here.

"In this place," he explains, "I am really focused on enlightenment. I don't talk about it much, but that eez really what I am going for. To evolve. To become enlightened. Now in Paris, I could hide. You know, jump in zee car and go visit friends, listen to music, read a book. Here I have no distraction. I cannot avoid myself. Yes, we all come here to work. It eez not for holiday. Sometimes, yes, there are disagreements, difficult—how you say—interactions, but they are there because those things, that violence, needs to be cleared from humanity, from me. I cannot pretend to be 'spiritual' and ignore that violence. It comes up for me to *deal* with it, and it eez not always easy work. But that eez why I am here. To work, to evolve, to really become enlightened."

His words stay with me. Aurovillians rarely *talk* about their purpose for coming to Auroville; for the most part, they are too busy *fulfilling* it. Doing things. But through the conversation with the baker, I am once again in touch with the dedication of the people who come to live here.

If I could characterise communities according to the chakras (energy centres in the body), I would say that Auroville is focused in the sixth (third eye) and seventh (crown) chakras. Aurovillians are concerned with direct connection with Spirit through the higher mind and with the concept of Enlightenment. The Findhorn Foundation focuses on the fourth (heart) and second (emotions) chakras. Its members work with unconditional love, with the wisdom of the heart, with intuitive knowing and 'guidance'. Auroville supports by encouraging people to stand alone, in their own strength. The Findhorn Community supports by encouraging people to bond, to 'synthesise' into a group in which the whole is greater than the sum of the parts. Neither way is right or wrong; they are simply different approaches.

We spend our last evening with Joan, talking about Auroville, 'tough love' and our relationships. "It's so important what you two are doing," says Joan. "You know, the planet needs so much healing in relationships between men and women. Keep going, don't give up. You two really have something—your work together, the way you are together. Keep going, please."

I smile, a bit embarrassed. It's true that Alan and I have learned, finally, to work together, and during our time here we have felt a more solid love for each other than ever before. Part of the change is that after years of my reaching out towards Alan, following him on his journeys, for once he has come to *me,* changing his plans so that we could be together in India. But I'm still not sure that this is 'it'.

When we arrive at the airport, a lot of feelings for Alan surface. During our months apart, I had almost forgotten the joy of sharing my life with another. After weeks of stone-like closedness, my heart is literally pierced when we hug goodbye. As I watch him move through the passport check and into the terminal for his flight to London, I feel the empty, lonely ache return. I am on my own once again.

A day later, after spending a night in a hotel in Bombay, I return to the airport to board the plane to Sydney, Australia. I arrive a couple of hours early, only to find that the plane had been delayed nine hours. If India has one thing to teach, it is patience. I chuckle internally. Please, Creator, will I actually escape this time? And that is really how I look at leaving India—escape. Here my existence hangs much closer than in the West to the edge of life and death, fluttering like shirttails on a frayed, windblown clothesline. Disease and disaster lurk everywhere, but somehow *life* is more immediate, too. Kali, the Great Mother, gives and takes life in equal measure, humbling all beings as she turns the wheel of incarnation. For this round in India, though, I have escaped her final grip.

CHAPTER 10
Dreaming Camps

During the plane ride, little shocks of culture adjustment begin. Sitting on a toilet instead of squatting; trusting the water that is served; watching films with English subtitles, even American films. A lot of the journey, though, is spent with headphones on, listening to music, contemplating my time in India, and searching inside for my purpose in travelling to Australia. During my last weeks in Auroville I began to imagine and talk about Australia as another trial instead of an adventure. Sitting on the plane, I realise that I have had enough of trials.

When I ask deep inside what it is I *really* want from this journey, I know that my heart's desire is to connect deeply with the land and the aboriginal people. What I want, though, doesn't correspond to what I've already planned—to visit communities in the northeast of Australia and to spend a month with Mary Harris, a former Findhorn member, writing at her home to the north and west of Brisbane. I also want to visit the Rainforest Information Centre where Alan and I gave a workshop with John Seed last year—this is one of the groups that inspired me so much with their combination of inner work and activism.

But here, listening to Tchaikovsky and looking deep inside, I know that my primary interest is native people, not activist groups, although they are an important part of my life, too. The last trip to Australia was shaped largely by Alan's interests; this one will be *mine* to create, and I have a sense that it will be quite different from my first experience. At this moment I *choose* to connect deeply with the land and the aboriginal people, even though it contradicts all of my well-laid plans. I have no idea exactly how it will happen, but I know that is what I truly want.

In my head I go about planning the journey anyway, deciding to travel for the first month, visiting Uluru (Ayer's Rock), Monkey Mia—a beach on the west coast where wild dolphins come in to interact with humans—and Guboo's Dreaming

Camp that Gus told me will take place in Western Australia around the beginning of May. Perhaps the contact in the Dreaming Camp will be enough to fulfil my desire to connect with aboriginal people and the land . . . . In mid-May I plan to fly back to Brisbane on the east coast and spend the remaining two months visiting communities and friends before returning to the Findhorn Foundation.

In three months I have become so fully immersed in Eastern customs that entering Sydney airport is a shock—a pleasant one. Everything is sparkling clean. I look at people and they smile—amazing. Expecting the usual gruffness of the clerks in India, I am deeply shocked when the passport clerk looks up and asks, "How are you?" I stare for a few moments and then some deeply rooted, almost forgotten reflex brings the response, "Fine. And how are you?"

Within two hours of landing I arrive at Ken and Jan's house, friends with whom Alan and I stayed the year before. Ken is a photographer and forester who spent 13 years living and working in Malaysia, mostly in the rainforests. During our last visit, he had been back in Australia only one month. Now, just over a year later, he and Jan seem more at ease, much more settled. Their transition experience makes them acutely aware of mine, and they are very gracious about giving me space and time to adjust.

After depositing my heavy pack and showering (ah, bliss to have warm water cascading on my body instead of short dousings from a measuring cup!) I decide to go for a walk. Although Sydney is relatively warm, after the heat of South India I shiver inside my thin clothes. Never did I imagine when I handed Alan my grey wool sweater, with sweat trickling down my back, that I would crave the extra warmth in a couple of days' time.

Walking through the streets of Balmain, one of Sydney's suburbs, I am struck by the almost sterile cleanliness. No one squats by the side of the road. No cows or goats amble past me. Cars seem to have had their horns extracted, like errant wisdom teeth, and no air horns blast from passing buses. The quiet is almost eerie.

The greatest joy is being able to stand on the pavement, quietly looking in the windows of the shops. Here I am anonymous. No harried store clerk bellows "Madam, Madam, you buy, you buy?" No beggars come, their faces swollen and sallow, eyes distracted, with limpid hands stretched towards me, chanting *"Pice, pice, pice."*

And the variety of *things* in the stores. This truly is a 'thing' culture. No wonder Indian people return from the West with bulging suitcases. So many of these things just don't exist in India. Walking into a wholefood store I find rice cakes and tahini, beloved food that I have not seen for months. Or tofu. Or barley or tamari or whole wheat flour—so many things that I have taken for granted living in the West.

The sound of laughter surprises me. People walking down the street talk and gesture and *laugh*. Freely. Few have grim, contracted faces. Their bodies and expressions speak of a life of ease. Athletic, barrel-legged men look fearsome to me after months of malnourished, five-foot Tamils. An Australian man's neck is as large as most Tamil men's *thighs*. I'm not sure that I am comfortable with this overpadded, overmuscled race.

A few days later, the initial transition complete—though I still stop to gape at things from time to time—I buy a bus pass at the Greyhound station and begin my journey westward.

I board the bus bound for Adelaide, the major city in south-central Australia. From there I will change buses—or coaches, as the driver insists during his announcements. After the buses of Tamil Nadu, they are gloriously luxurious, complete with carpet under the seats, a toilet in the back, upholstered luggage bins, and even a VCR that works.

In Adelaide I change coaches and head north for Uluru, the great stone monolith that rises in the centre of the continent, and a sacred spot to the aboriginal people. Four years ago the Australian government handed Uluru back to the traditional stewards of the area, the Pitjanjitjarra, with the stipulation that they immediately lease it back to the government as a national park. Uluru National Park is the first park in the country jointly managed by aboriginal people and white European settlers and is, according to the guidebook, a great success. Besides, the government now has one of its greatest tourist attractions outfitted with native people—good for publicity and good for the purse.

During my time at Uluru, I make my first tentative contact with aboriginal people. Each day I go to the 'Muruku Centre', an area inside the visitors' centre of the national park that is a reconstruction of a traditional aboriginal camp. Mostly the older people among the Pitjanjitjarra look after the Muruku village and demonstrate the crafts. These few elders, explains the ranger, carry the role of teacher in their traditional society, so their interaction with the visitors to the park is a natural extension of their teaching duties.

When I'm not sitting around the open fire always burning in a corner of the village, I am out walking, absorbing the aliveness of the land, feeling the vastness of desert space and time stretch me. The silence eats into me, first slowing and then suspending the usual clatter of thoughts in my mind. After a week's stay, I leave Uluru knowing that my education in aboriginal culture has only begun—I have a long way to go before I can surrender completely to the desert's harsh wisdom or intimately know the people who have embodied it.

Five days later, after an overnight stop in Coober Peddy—the world's opal-mining capital—I arrive in Perth with hopes of finding Guboo and the Dreaming Camp. I try the phone number given to me by his contact in Sydney, but no one answers. After several attempts, I walk through the streets of downtown Perth to the Aberdeen Lodge, a grotty hostel that is fully booked. The only space is on the floor in a room with three men. I don't mind, though. I fall asleep early, exhausted after the long bus ride, and get up before anyone else. My plan is to take the bus to Monkey Mia, a day's journey to the north, spend a week with the dolphins, and then come back to Perth to catch the last week of the Dreaming Camp.

After walking a couple of miles to the bus station and checking my backpack in for the 9 a.m. bus, I try the phone number once more. This time someone answers —and that moment reshapes my whole journey.

Barry, Guboo's organiser for this Dreaming Camp, explains that the Camp began the weekend before and will continue only until next Sunday, not the four weeks that I had expected. When I ask for directions to get there, Barry offers me a ride. "I'm going back down today anyway, so take the train to Fremantle and I'll meet you there."

"Fremantle?"

"Yeah, that's the last stop on the local train going south out of Perth."

"Right. I'll see you around noon."

I hang up the phone, resting my hand on the receiver for a moment to reorient myself. "Now, if I'm down there this week, that means I can go to Monkey Mia the week after and still make my plane to Brisbane . . . if I change it to two days later."

I go back to the baggage counter to ask them to get my bag off the bus. The woman gives me a withering look. "Sorry, my plans just changed," I tell her. I hoist the heavy pack onto my knee and then slide my arm through before it can topple sideways. The airline has a reservation office next door, so I amble through the doorway to change my plane ticket.

Around 11 o'clock I walk into the local bus station, hoping to get some information about buses that run in the area south of Perth. The Greyhound bus pass doesn't cover this area, and I want to do some exploring after the Dreaming Camp.

I search the aisle of bus platforms and finally find the local bus company for the Southwest of Australia at the very end.

"Yes, can I help you?" asks an older woman, the only agent in the tiny office. I ask for a timetable and information about the Karri and Jarrah forests.

"You travelling alone?" she asks, wide-eyed. After years of solo travel I'm getting used to this question and patiently reply, "Yes, and I plan to do some backpacking in the Southwest." Somehow the conversation runs from murders of lone women in the forest to comments about people of colour, obviously a favourite topic.

"We don't like the Blacks, you know, and they don't like us, so it's no use wasting love on them because they just return it with spite."

I stare, dumbfounded. "But someone has to start loving, or nothing will ever change."

"Well, the Blacks, and I mean the Middle Eastern people, too, you know, if they want to come to this country, they ought to learn to be Australian. I mean, doing things their way in their own country is fine, but coming here they ought to learn how to do things like us. You know, when in Rome, do as the Romans do."

So much for the federal government policy supporting multi-culturalism. The inner attitude obviously has not been legislated into the total population. I murmur something about learning tolerance and weaving a strong fabric of diverse people, not a homogeneous mass of followers, and escape into the autumn sunshine, steps heavy with the weight of my pack. As usual, five minutes after the end of the conversation I think of the perfect response: "If you want to be Australian, why don't you learn from the aboriginal people?" She probably would have choked on her false teeth. I relish the thought.

About an hour later I meet Barry at the train station in Fremantle—he's wearing a T-shirt, sweat pants and flip flops. He looks like a sun-bleached surfer—laid back and muscled, driving an old Dodge station wagon painted with rainbows and the aboriginal land rights flag. "Benny painted it," explains Barry when I ask about the paintings. "Benny Zable. Or Benny Bubbles, as some people call him. You'll probably meet him at the Dreaming Camp. He's really into the Freeze campaign, doing street theatre and art work and stuff."

We find a parking place on the crowded streets, swollen with Saturday shoppers, and spend the next couple of hours buying supplies for the Dreaming Camp. Fremantle, I learn, is the 'alternative' suburb of Perth. Among other things it has the largest Rajneesh devotee population in Australia. Fremantle is also a fashionable shopping spot for those who live in Perth, especially since the town had a major facelift to prepare for the America's Cup sailing race held here in January of '87. The Market and International Foodhall are jammed with people. I like the community atmosphere; lots of people stand in small clusters, talking and laughing and hugging each other. The Market seems to be *the* place to be on a Saturday morning. We move slowly among the booths to buy bread and veggies and other supplies.

We drive back to the house where Barry is staying and pick up Colleen, an aboriginal woman who has also been travelling with Guboo and helping to run the Camps. When we pile into the fully loaded car, Colleen explains that she's feeling tired and is going to crash out during the trip. She pulls on a pair of Walkman headphones, closes her eyes, and tunes out for the remainder of the journey.

197

Barry and I have a long talk about aboriginal people, how we came to know Guboo, what we've been doing with our lives. Before working with Guboo, Barry was an executive in a corporation. And yes, in his early years he was a surfer, spending his days riding waves on the beaches of Bali and Oz (Australia).

We drive south through grassland country and then turn to the east, climbing a ridge and entering the forest. We pass through small towns, really just clusters of buildings with a grocery store and post office, until we enter the town of Dwellingup. Here, among the regrowth Karri and Jarrah outside the town, is the site of the Dreaming Camp.

The road winds through the trees along first bitumen and then dirt road. The old Dodge wagon rolls and pitches over the rutted track until we turn off on a side road signposted 'Nanga Mill'. Here the native Karri, Jarrah and Marri forest fades into a plantation of straight-backed pines—a bit of North America in the southern hemisphere. Forestry has become a multinational business, oblivious of the land or climate in its quest to grow popsicle-stick pines for paper pulp. And for heaven's sake, don't give them enough space to develop branches or any other identifying characteristics—it confuses the milling machines.

Among the tall trees smoke drifts in a purple-grey haze, filtering the mid-afternoon sunlight. About a dozen tents are scattered along the flat, pine-needle-covered clearing below. Two silk flags—the aboriginal land rights flag and a rainbow flag —hang from a line suspended between two trees. The lower half of the land rights flag is red (representing the land), and the top is black (symbolising the aboriginal people); in the centre is a yellow circle, which is the sun rising over the land and the aboriginal people. A picnic table stands under the flags, covered with a clutter of plastic containers and open packages of this and that. Cups, dishes and silverware are heaped next to a tub full of soapy water for washing at the far end of the table. Someone is stirring an iron pot that hangs from a hook built into the circle of stones around the fire pit. A short way down the corridor (an old logging road?) another fire burns, built on the smoothed, bare earth.

I wrestle my pack from the back of the car while Barry unloads the food. Colleen takes off her headphones and walks barefoot down the path to where Guboo is standing in a shaft of sunlight that cuts through the trees. His snowy white beard and shoulder-length hair are neatly smoothed around his broad, tan face. Half Chinese and half aboriginal, he could pass for either, but Guboo 'Good Friend' Thomas has chosen to pursue his aboriginal roots. Or, to be more accurate, he was *chosen* to serve as an elder of his people, the Yuin of southeastern Australia, a 'nation' of about 3500 individuals.

At eight years old his training began. Chosen or not, though, a man or woman does not become a full elder until they are at least 60 years old and have white hair—'wisdom hairs'. Wisdom, according to traditional lore, comes with age. If you've survived that long, you must know *something*. The training is long, too, because the Law—a simple name for the complex system of stories, teachings and unchanging rules that govern traditional aboriginal life—can take many decades to master fully.

I hoist my pack on my shoulders and begin to walk down the path towards Guboo. About half-way down a tall, bearded man grasps my shoulder and gives me a quick, awkward hug—not easy with a full pack on. "Welcome. So you made it from Findhorn. Welcome. My name is David."

"Hello . . . uh, thanks. My name is Judith."

We nod at each other and I continue down the path. Gus must have written from India that I was planning to come. Or maybe Barry called—no, there are no telephones out here. Must have been Gus.

While Colleen talks with Guboo, I wander over to the open fire where a young guy with dreadlocked hair, baggy white canvas pants and a tattered green sweater sits. "Hey, how's it goin'?" he asks when I approach. "My name's Leon." He reaches up a hand to clasp mine in greeting.

"Heya. I'm Judith . . . . Do you know a guy named Gus?" I remember him mentioning something about travelling with a friend named Leon.

"Gus? Wow, cosmic, do you know *Gus*?" Leon's eyes pop wide open, and his pleasant expression melts into open-mouthed wonder.

"Yeah, I met him in India. He told me about your trip to Uluru," I tell him, returning the grin.

We hold each other's eyes for a long while, smiling. "Wow," says Leon, shaking his head and laughing. "Wow. You look just like him. Yeah, I mean, you've got the same look about you. How's he doin'?"

We talk for a bit about Gus's travels, my own, and Leon's trip since Gus left him at Uluru. Talking with Leon, I feel like I've time-warped into the sixties, populated by Rastafarians rather than hippies, and it feels strangely home-like. I've always thought I was born about ten years too late.

Eventually I leave Leon and move across the camp to where Guboo still stands in the sunlight, arms crossed, quiet. "Hello, Guboo. I don't know if you remember me—my name is Judith. We visited Randolph's Leap together when you were at the Findhorn Foundation."

"Well hello, darlin', yes, I do think I remember you. Did you have a good trip?"

As I tell him a bit about my journey across Australia and the quick change of plans this morning, I feel my heart stretch wide open. Guboo listens quietly and then comments, "I was going to go to Uluru on the way across, but the time wasn't right. Had the tickets and everythin', but it just wasn't right. Have to be ready to go there. Can't just pick up and go when you want to. Has to be the right time." He looks over at me, grinning. "Where you goin' to set up, darlin'?"

"I don't know, Guboo. I haven't looked around yet."

"Well, there's plenty of room in my tent if you need a place to stay."

"Thanks, Guboo, but I brought my own tent."

"Well, you could set it up over that way," he says, pointing to the empty corridor behind us. "You know, everybody hangs around my tent at night. We should've set it up away from the centre of the camp. That way I could have some quiet at night."

"Guboo, you know wherever you set up your tent would become the centre of the camp."

"Yeah, those people are up most of the night—singin' and talkin' and playing the dig (digeridoo) around the fire. But now if you were set up out here, we could have some privacy."

I finally grock that he's looking for a bed partner, and I'm definitely not interested. My fully stretched heart retracts a bit. Why is it that all medicine *men* seem to have lower chakras that just don't quit?

"Well, come on," says Guboo, affectionately slipping his arm around my waist. "I'll show you around the camp, and you can find a spot." We walk along the corridor, stopping in front of a circle of clay shapes drying in the sunlight. "We did an exercise with these this afternoon," explains Guboo. "It's for opening the hahrt chakra. I have people focus on their hahrt," he says, emphasising the words by pressing his closed fist against his chest, "and then tell them to start shapin' the clay as their hahrt tells them. Beautiful. Really opens people up. Opens dere hahrts. That's what the Dreaming Camp is all about, darlin', openin' up the hahrt. So many people have lost touch," he continues, looking up at me. "That's what my work is about, why I have these camps. Renewal of the Dreamin'. That's why I'm travellin' around Australia this year, for the Australian Bicentennial. Bring the Dreamin' alive through the whole land. That's my vision. And seein' people open dere hahrts . . . that's what my work is about."

"I certainly could use it," I answer quietly. "My heart's been really closed since I left Scotland."

He looks over at me, laughs, and wraps his arm around my shoulder, drawing me towards him. I smile and stand up, offering my hand to pull him up. I'm not eager for kisses; I want to get my things set up—near the middle of the camp. "Well, come on then," he says, taking my arm. "I'll help you set up your tent. Where's a good spot?"

I wander around the camp, ambling toward the nucleus of tents—I'm not eager for unexpected nocturnal visits, and I assume that having other people close by will deter him.

"How about over here?" calls David, cutting a path between Guboo and me. "Here's a good flat spot. How about here. This good?"

His words are as frantic as his movements. He takes the tent from my hands and begins fumbling with the top loop of the tent bag. It knots hopelessly.

"Here," I say, reaching for the tent. "Let me undo it. And I'd like to look around a bit closer to the stream."

"OK, OK," stammers David. "You don't have to stay here. Just trying to help, that's all."

He follows me while I shuffle around the campsite, scuffing my boots over the ground to try to find a smooth spot. David talks incessantly. Goddess, now I have *two* men following me.

Finally I settle on a spot, and Guboo sits pouting nearby while David helps me put up the tent. "I was gonna do that," he says, pursing his lips and setting his chin, "but you just moved right in, David."

"Guboo, I'm just *helping*," says David, exasperated. "Is that OK?"

"Well, I said *I* was gonna do it."

He sits with his arms crossed, lips turned down in an indignant frown, until a small crowd gathers around him, sitting quietly in the warm sunlight.

"Almost time for the Humming Bee," he calls finally. He gets up and walks back towards the central fire, and the other people move to follow. "Time to get people together."

I look over at David and smile. "Did you know he was putting moves on me?"

"Yeah," he says, grinning. "He does it to every woman who comes into camp."

"Is that why you cut him off?"

"Yes. And I also wanted to talk with you."

"He's so much like Sun Bear," I comment, smiling as I push in a tent stake.

"How do you know him?" asks David.

"I lived at the Bear Tribe for about six months. They're still like family to me."

"Well, I would never sleep with a woman unless I knew that I wanted to be with her for at least twenty years. That's just the way I am." He tells me about a man who came to an earlier Dreaming Camp who had an incredible sex drive. He would invite someone into his tent and talk with them while he was in the middle of screwing some woman. "I find that really disgusting," says David. "I mean, sex is OK, but it's like prostitution to me unless it has emotion in it, too."

I listen to his unsolicited speech while I finish moving things into the tent, wondering why he is telling me all this. "I just want to let you know where I'm coming from," he says after a short pause.

"And what *are* you doing here?" I ask, curious about what brought him to the Dreaming Camp.

"I'm travelling with Guboo, doing a documentary on contemporary aboriginal people. I shoot and edit the film, he owns it and the distribution rights at the end. That's how I work. I always give the rights to the native people I'm working with."

"You've done this kind of thing before?"

"Oh, sure. I've lived with the Inuit off and on for the last twenty years."

"You mean the Eskimo?"

"Well, that's what white people call them, but that's really an insult to them. It means 'eaters of raw flesh', like 'barbarians'. Their name for themselves is 'Inuit'."

"What does that mean?"

"People. The people, that's all."

I admire the bracelet studded with turquoise on his wrist and ask him if it's from the Southwest in the States. "Yeah, Navaho," he says quickly. "That's where I live—northern New Mexico."

We continue the conversation at breakneck speed—within ten minutes he has promised to either loan or send me books and papers to read and addresses to contact. If any topic is mentioned, he knows about it. If I've done anything, he has, too—twenty years longer, of course.

When the tent is up and my pack moved inside, he leaves me to unroll my Ensolite pad and sleeping bag. I sit inside for a few minutes, breathing deeply and enjoying the changing mosaic of pine frond shadows moving on the walls. After a night on a sour, musty floor indoors, I am grateful to be in the tent again.

Shadows stretch long across the pine-needle carpet when I hear the sharp staccato crack of clapping sticks. "Dreeeeamtiiiime, Dreeeeamtiiiime," calls Guboo. Time for the Humming Bee, a ceremony to observe the passing of the day and night. "Now, when the sun starts to go down," Guboo explained while at the Findhorn Foundation, "the bees go home. If you want honey—very important bush tucker—you look up and see all these bees flyin', and you follow those bees home, and you find where they live. Sacred spot. Bees are very important. So we honour them with the Humming Bee."

People slowly gather in the clearing between the two fires until about twenty of us stand in a circle, from babes in arms to an 80-year-old white-haired elder. We hold hands quietly in the dusky glen.

"Now the Bible says, 'You shall have faith, hope and love—and the greatest of these is *love*.'" Guboo clears his throat and puts his arms around the people on either side of him. "So let's all come together in the spirit of love for the Humming Bee. Now, these circles can be a powerful healing time, so if you have anything that needs to be healed, you pray for that pain to be taken away. We've had some powerful healings during the Humming Bee. All right, we begin with 'AH' and then change to 'hmmmm'—you'll hear when. And then 'the best is yet to come'. So everybody begin—AAAAAAAAH."

The sound rises in the forest, harmonies blending and clashing among the chorus of voices. With my eyes closed, the sound begins to soothe me, shaking out the tension from days of travel. The 'hmmmm' fine tunes and smooths my frayed inner senses. When the hum dies away, I feel as calm and deeply relaxed as after a Toning session. Here, though, the effect is amplified by the group setting.

Guboo breaks the thick, satisfied silence, "And all the people said . . . ."

"THE BEST IS YET TO COME. WOOOOOOOW!" we reply in chorus.

Guboo begins to sing:

Love, love, love
Love on Earth
Love, love, love
Throughout the Universe.

Before each chorus someone calls out a new quality or being, from trees to dolphins to tranquillity, to include in the blessing. After about ten minutes, the singing
fades, and only the sound of the stream continues in the stillness of the forest.
Finally a toddler, clasped around someone's leg in the centre of the mob, lets out a
satisfied squeak. We laugh and pull away gently. Many people pause to curl their
arms around people nearby.

I pull back and quietly exit the circle. My time in India has made me aware of
how and why I give hugs. I realised that I usually give hugs because *I* want the
physical comfort and reassurance, not because I want to *give* a hug. Maybe I am
colder now, with a tightly closed heart, or perhaps I have learned that affection and
support come in many forms. Whatever the case, I rarely hug now unless I really
want to *give* a hug. And I am more truthful about asking for a hug when I need one
instead of covering the desire in a 'oh, *you* look like *you* need a hug' lie to myself.

I leave the forest and follow the gravel road down to a bridge where it crosses the
stream that runs along the edge of the campground. A trail stretches from the road
and wanders alongside the stream. About half a mile down the trail I find a wide,
slow section of the stream with a downed old tree half sunk into the water . The
green-blue leaves and the grey streaked bark of Karri and Jarrah trees lining the
banks reflect in the mirror-still water. The site draws me like a magnet, and I settle
onto the end of the old tree to absorb the stillness and watch the coming night.

A few minutes pass before I discern the outline of a shore bird—some sort of an
egret—standing on its long, reed-like leg, the other drawn high into its feathers. I
have to become as motionless as the bird before I can see it.

I breathe deeply and slowly open my arms to the side, not wanting any sudden
movement to ripple the silence. "Thank you, Creator," I murmur internally. "Thank
you for this place." Tonight I realise how much I have been longing for wilderness
to renew me again after months of desolate, hard-baked India. And silence. Even at
the top of a mountain in India, I could hear the roar of traffic in the streets far
below. Silence and privacy are rare luxuries on most of this planet now, and I intend
to enjoy them fully during the coming week.

The path is a thin sliver of grey among the trees when I finally swing off the log
and head towards the camp. I know where the camp is by the light of the campfires
spilling pools of orange light from the flames and sending sparks showering
upwards towards the stars. Everyone in the camp draws around the fire, like wan-
derers from the darkness seeking warmth and shelter in the night. Without the 'protection' of walls or electric lights to roll back the darkness, we are enveloped by it,
laid bare to its power. But staring at the fire, I can forget my vulnerability and the
vast sky above me; I can forget that this fire is a tiny mirror of the millions that
burn in the stars above. The fire mesmerises me, rooting me in this moment, this
place, this pool of light. Here. Now. Content to watch flames of blue and gold and
orange and green licking at the logs. Consuming them. And who feeds all of those
star fires, I wonder? Who tends the fires of the cosmos?

More logs are heaped on the fire—for warmth as well as light. Here in the
Southwest, the blaze of summer heat that burns the fields to brittle stalks has passed
into the first coolness of autumn nights. I pull on a sweater and down vest, drawing

close to the rim of the fire's heat. About twenty people sit around, strumming guitars and singing or talking quietly with friends. Another knot of people stands around the fire pit where I can smell a pot of curry boiling over the coals.

Lots of new faces circle the campfire, people who must have been out walking or swimming in the river when I arrived. Joining the fire tonight I feel self-conscious, aware of the friendships that have already evolved during the preceding week of the camp, and some that have formed before. I feel shy and reluctant to speak. I hate this initial period of moving into a group or a community—I know intellectually that the first moments of awkwardness will pass and soon be forgotten, but in the moment I am frustrated with the whole process. I am tired of beginning over and over and over again with new people. I wish that people could see immediately who I am without my having to explain; I remind myself that I need time to find out who *they* are, too. Slow down, relax, I tell myself. It takes time.

I join in the songs that I recognise, and offer some of the chants that I know. A lot of the songs, though, are new to me, and when I ask the couple sitting next to me if they know where they came from, they tell me they were composed during the 'Great Walk'.

"What kind of a walk?" I ask.

"The Great Walk. We walked for a month through the forest, from the south coast up to Perth. In fact, we walked through here. Remember that?" says the woman, smiling at the man next to her.

He nods. "I don't know if you can see it, but we all got really close during the Walk. Like family. People are so happy to see each other again," he says nodding at two women who are laughing and talking, hands clasped on each other's knees. "It only ended a month ago, and it's like it's still going on. The Walk was supposed to bring awareness about the trees here in the Southwest, but it ended up changing a lot of people's *lives*. I mean, I've completely changed direction since then."

"What's different?"

"Well . . . I feel connected with the Earth. *Really* connected. Just walking every day, feeling the trees and the path, the rain and sun . . . it does something to you."

"And the camps were powerful, too," adds the woman. "We'd sit around massaging each other's feet, singing, waiting for dinner, telling stories. People's hearts really opened to each other. It was like being in love with everybody and everything all at once."

As the days pass, I begin to get a clearer picture of the Walk—both its purpose and its effect on people. The original intention was to walk through the forests of the Southwest up to Perth in order to present a charter to the Western Australia government. The charter included positive suggestions about how humans could interact with the forest and land of the Southwest. The impetus for the Walk was people's great love for the forest and their desire to protect it from the woodchipping industry that is chewing up huge tracts of both regrowth and old growth forest.

That initial impetus of love spilled over into the bonds that formed during the Walk, both with the Earth and with fellow travellers. Now, a month after the end of the Walk, people gather together to sing, weaving their arms around one another and swaying from side-to-side. When someone from the Walk comes into camp for the first time, friends shout with joy and run to hug and greet them. Sometimes pairs simply sit together on the ground, crossed knees touching, foreheads pressed together, and fingers entwined on their laps. Their open love ripples through the rest of the camp as well—although a tight group, they are not exclusive.

Word has gone around already that I live at the Findhorn Foundation, and most of the questions are about the community, not me per se. Again I see the sense of hope in people's eyes. But some are sceptical, too, especially Guboo.

Although he likes to boast about his travels, and often makes a special mention that he was at the Foundation, he has little respect for the community.

"Darlin', what do you think of the community now?" he asks one evening.

I tell him about the Open Forum that has started, the beginnings of a structure for a loose-knit group of people who have come to live around, but not *within,* the Foundation. If the 'juice' of inspiration is flowing anywhere in the community, it is in the Open Forum. I also tell him about the renewed focus on inner work and the restructuring and streamlining of the Foundation's administration.

Guboo looks unimpressed. He purses his lips together, his brow creasing as he stares at the fire. "What did you think about the community when you were there, Guboo?"

"Everybody was just interested in sex, not spiritual things. Changin' partners all the time, runnin' around. The spirit has left the place—it's not there any more."

I sit back, silenced by the hypocrisy of his words. Linda, the woman in whose caravan he stayed during his visit, said she fought him off for a whole week. He pressured her to have sex with him, expecting that a bed partner came ready-made with the caravan. When he was unsuccessful, he became sullen and withdrawn.

His comments reinforce my view of the Findhorn Foundation—it is a highly polished mirror for myself. What I see in the community is a direct reflection of what is going on inside myself. If Guboo sees promiscuous behaviour, that tells me he's involved with his own sexual fantasies as well. Certainly many people who come to the community use their stay to work out issues of relationship—it is a natural side effect of opening the heart. And then, too, if someone looks closely enough, they are sure to find *every* type of behaviour represented in the collective. We are a microcosm of the world at large—we struggle with the same day-to-day and large-scale issues as the rest of the planet. So in the end, a person's description tells me more about *that person* than about the community itself. There is a grain of truth in all observations, but the angle of focus tells me about the observer.

Our conversation turns to Sun Bear and the Bear Tribe. "Well, we did a Dreaming Camp together a few years ago," says Guboo.

"How was that?" I ask. Having heard Sun Bear's impressions of their meeting, I'm curious about Guboo's reaction. When I last saw Sun Bear, after I had been in Australia, he commented that he hoped to return to Australia and meet with a few of the Elders some day. "Did you meet Guboo?" I asked.

"Yes, we spent some time together, but I'm looking for people who've got the Power. So maybe on my next visit I'll find them, but I'll have to wait until I'm invited down there again."

"Well," says Guboo, staring into the flames, "Sun Bear's more interested in women than in the Spirit. I don't trust him. Too much involved with women."

I grin at Guboo. "Really," he says, interpreting my smile as a contradiction. "He had a different woman every night of the camp. Made me look bad. Made the whole camp look bad. I don't trust him." He shakes his head, averting his eyes to the fire once again.

I smile quietly into the darkness. No wonder they didn't get along—they are too much alike. And I sense that Guboo has a well of power and knowledge that he would never reveal to Sun Bear as long as he didn't trust him.

Despite our differences of opinion, I have great respect for Guboo. In fact, for the most part I feel tongue-tied and reverent, not wanting to press too much or seem too greedy for information. There are plenty of other people in the camp who are expert at ploughing through the barrier of decency and asking lots of questions. I simply sit quietly around the fire, listening to Guboo's answers. Sometimes he ignores the questions and turns to the fire—either he has reached the limit of his desire to answer, or the question touched on some area of knowledge that he cannot reveal.

"You come into camp like a child," explains David one evening when I ask about Guboo's silences. "You come in knowing nothing about traditional Law. You have to learn to ask questions like a child. Otherwise he won't and can't answer."

"How come?"

"That's the way this culture is," says David. "Look, a lot of information can be given to someone only after they've been through a particular initiation. If you haven't been through it, you can't talk about it. You have to start at the very beginning. And a lot of information you have to learn by watching. Look at what Guboo *does*, not how he talks. Look at how he walks, how he picks up things, how he sits . . . just all of the things that he does. No one's going to come up and *tell* you how to do something. You have to watch."

The next afternoon David demonstrates his point. As we sit at the picnic table, sipping tea and talking, he stops to watch one of the young mothers with her son. "Look up there," says David, nodding at the path that runs along the upper slope. "Look how she walks with the baby."

Nothing seems unusual to me. The mother is holding the toddler's hand as he walks bowlegged and barefoot across the ground. When they get to the steps leading down to camp, she holds his hand while he half steps, half free-falls to the step below. Only her firm grip keeps the baby from tumbling head first down the stairs.

"See," says David. "She's trying to make the baby walk like *she* wants him to, not how he normally would."

"What would a traditional person do?"

"The Inuit would pick up the baby and carry him, or let him crawl the way he wants to. They would never drag a baby that way, trying to force him to walk like that when he's not ready."

I turn back to the mother, watching her movements with the child. I have never questioned how a culture teaches its children to walk—and I can see the wisdom in David's comments as I watch the boy tottering on unripened legs, struggling to keep up with his mother.

When I go back to the tent to reposition the solar panel (used to recharge flashlight batteries) towards the sun, Colleen follows to ask if I want to go for a walk. Surprised after her silence on the way here, I'm pleased by the offer. I've been hanging around the camp waiting for Guboo to appear to lead the heart chakra exercise with clay that he announced for late this morning, but any sort of schedule is really a vague outline. The days are free for each person to create according to his or her own inspiration. If you feel like doing something, you do it. If you want to invite other people to join you, you can. If you want to sit and wait for someone else to think of something, you can sit and wait. For a long time. Because the camp is a self-created experience.

For a lot of the 'workshop junkies' who have arrived at the camp, the lack of structure is maddening. They have come to learn about aboriginal ways, and they expect to be taught. Their way. With mimeographed handouts and chalkboards, lectures and question-and-answer sessions. Or 'sharings' and stories and songs for the more 'enlightened', weaned on 'alternative education'. But tell them that the day is theirs to create, and they dally for hours around the camp, eternally waiting for something to happen. One woman insists on knowing what's for dinner. "Well," says David, "there's a tent full of food over there. You can make anything you want with what's in there. We just ask that if you use the communal food, you add some from your supply."

"But don't you have menus planned for the week?"

David stares at her for a moment. "We brought enough food for the week. You can make whatever you want."

For the most part, the meals are wonderful. Whoever feels like cooking that day, and generally everyone voluntarily takes a shift every day or two, puts together a pot of vegetables and a pot of grain. Somehow it's always just enough to feed whomever is around.

After a quick bite of lunch, Colleen and I decide to follow one of the tracks up the mountain. As we walk along the track, I quietly admire the way that Colleen carries herself. Although we haven't spent much time together, I have been aware of her presence in camp over the last couple of days. She walks solidly, evenly, her broad hips and shoulders moving in a fluid motion, always in *relationship* with the Earth instead of bouncing on top of it. It's as if she is magnetised by the core of the land. Colleen is often silent in camp, but when she does say something, it's wise or soothing or sarcastic, and it's always appropriate and to the point. And she laughs often—a laugh that shakes her whole body and leaves her speechless.

Today as we walk our conversation ranges from growth workshops we have taken to struggles with family, from past lives to our ancestral background. Since leaving Scotland, I have found few people with whom I can speak so freely, and it's like a warm breeze in winter—I am grateful for the touch of another sister spirit.

"So where *is* your family from?" I ask Colleen as we pass through the Karri forest dotted with graceful, low-growing grass trees.

"We're aboriginal," explains Colleen. "And part of my family is from Scotland. That's why my skin is so light. But see, aboriginal people don't look at skin colour. You're either aboriginal or not. It doesn't have anything to do with your skin."

"I guess that's like black people in the States. Almost everyone has some white blood in them, from the slave-owners sleeping with the women. Yeah, and you're either Black or you're not . . . . Are you, like, half Scottish and half aboriginal?"

"We don't talk about half or quarter or sixteenth or whatever. You're aboriginal or you're not. It has to do with how you're brought up. Like I remember my father one day," she says laughing. "We had this fireplace in our house at the edge of town, and one day he got out the crowbar and ripped the walls out so that the fireplace was really big. Like a real fireplace. He couldn't stand it being all small and enclosed. And we'd cook damper in the ashes."

"What's damper?" I ask.

"Oh, it's like bread. Johnny cake we used to call it. My Mum made the best Johnny cake in the whole world. Some days that's all we had to eat, so I've had a lot of Johnny cake in my life. I'll show you how to make it when we get back to camp."

"Where are your people from?" I ask. Since arriving in Australia, I've learned that aboriginal people are not one homogeneous mass, just as Native American people are from many different 'nations' or 'tribes'. When Captain Arthur Phillip sailed into Botany Bay in 1788, there were over 500 different 'nations' on the continent of Australasia, each with a different language and cycle of stories and songs. Most people knew their own language plus several of the surrounding ones. The linguists still survey and record and transcribe as many of the languages as they can—frantically trying to capture them in written and audio form before they disappear completely. In some areas, especially in the desert, the traditional languages are still spoken on a day-to-day basis. And sometimes they still quietly persist where the linguists have judged them extinct.

"Well, most of them are from around Adelaide, where my family lives now. But I also spent some time in Tasmania, and I felt a real strong family connection with those people. There are some stories about the people from our area migrating to Tasmania, so maybe we are related."

"There are aboriginal people in Tasmania?" I ask, incredulous. When Alan and I spent time in Tasmania, we were told that the British had killed off all the aboriginal people on the island. They organised a hunting party with enough men to make a sweep, on foot, down the whole island. They shot and killed anyone they found along the way. At least that's the story I heard. It's one of the points of shame in the record of the British Empire. I tell Colleen the story, and she counters with her own.

"They took some of the people and put them on an island off the coast, thinking they would die if they were left there. A lot of the old ones did die—they couldn't stand being moved from their home grounds. But some people survived. There are stories of sailors coming and raping the women, so they called some of the children 'half-caste', but like I said, aboriginal people don't count half or quarter or whatever. And I think some people came from the mainland to live there, too. Anyway, there's a community of aboriginal people there. I don't know who told you they were all gone, but it's not true."

"Hmmm . . . I'm surprised. The people we were staying with were pretty aware —Greenies, working on campaigns to save the forests. I'm surprised they didn't know. You mentioned that the Tasmanian people might have migrated from the mainland—what do you think about the theories of aboriginal people migrating from Asia or Africa, like when the sea level was lower?"

"Yeah, I know that's what the anthropologists say. But one time I had this really strong sense of knowing that our people didn't come from anywhere. We've *always* been here. I think the other races probably left from *here,* not the other way around. Yeah, I've got this sense that if we came from anywhere, it was from the stars, not from some other place on Earth."

"You know the Cherokee in North America also say they came from the stars —from the Seven Sisters. That's part of their history."

"Well, it makes a lot of sense to me. That's how I feel deep in my gut—we didn't migrate from somewhere else; we've *always* been here."

Eventually the track we are following grows fainter and fainter until it disappears into a thicket of grass trees. We bushwhack our way along the slope and eventually meet the main road that leads to the bridge at camp. Our conversation turns to our own inner journeys, and our mutual desire to learn the wisdom of the medicine people, the healers in traditional society. "But, you know, Colleen, I don't know if I could ever really be accepted to learn. It's . . . it's so far away from the culture I grew up in. And I really want to learn from a woman. I think that's really important. So far it's mainly men I've come in contact with, and I really want to learn from a *woman* . . . but I don't know if it's possible."

"Yeah, I was hoping to learn a lot from Guboo, but I've realised he really can't teach me anything. He has the men's knowledge, and he can't teach me any of the women's ways 'cause he doesn't know them. Yeah, I'm lookin', too, wanting to learn some of the sacred stuff."

"But you have to go through initiation before you can learn, right?" I ask.

"Right, and that's not easy for someone who's not brought up in the traditional way . . . . We'll see, yeah, we'll see what happens. I've got a sense there are things coming for me."

The crowd at camp has thinned considerably since the weekend. Most people left on Sunday evening to go back to school or jobs. Late in the afternoon Colleen and I decide to start dinner, so we spend about an hour chopping vegetables and putting lentils on the fire to make dahl. Soon after dark (and the Humming Bee) we gather around the fire to eat.

This evening I spend some time under the awning of Guboo's tent—it has indeed become the hub of the camp. We sit in lawn chairs and gaze at the fire blazing in the fire pit where people are huddled for warmth. "Well, darlin'," says Guboo finally, "you enjoyin' the camp?"

"Yes, Guboo, it's a beautiful place here, especially the river. Very peaceful. I like the place where the log sticks out in the water—I go down there whenever I can."

"Good swimmin' hole," he says, nodding. We talk a bit about the camp, and Guboo asks whether I'm planning to go to the camp at Monkey Mia.

I look up surprised. "You're having a camp at Monkey Mia?"

"Yeah, the 10th to the 20th of June, I think it is. Barry knows. You should come with us, darlin'."

"I've been planning to go there . . . that would be a really powerful place to have a camp."

"That's right. I'm gonna call the dolphins in. Very sacred spot. Call in the dolphins like my daddy and grand-daddy did. You got to know how to talk to them —with the mind," he says, pointing to the middle of his forehead. "Got to talk with them here. And you approach them like elders. 'Cause that's what they are, like elders. It's gonna be a powerful camp. You think about comin', too."

We talk a bit more about the camps, and Guboo offers to have me come back to Wallaga Lake the following January for the month-long Dreaming Camp. "You could be in charge of one of the areas of the camp," he says nodding. "You know, make sure everybody's all right, all of that. And then, you know, I need a secretary, too. I'm plannin' to travel to the States next year, and I need somebody to carry my bags and drive for me, do those sorts of things, somebody to take care of me."

"Barry's not going with you, Guboo?"

"Naw, he's got his own work to do. You think about it, let me know."

"I will, Guboo, because I'll probably have more time next year. I'm planning on going back to the States, and I'd be happy to help you if I could. Let's keep in touch. There's still the chance that I might stay at the Findhorn Foundation when I go back this August. But if I'm in the States, I'd be glad to help."

Tonight Leon is playing the digeridoo around the fire. The 'dig' is a long, wooden tube, once a fallen branch in the rainforests of the north. Guboo calls them 'gifts from God, from the forest' because termites eat away the fallen branches creating a hollow channel inside. Someone finds the hollow log, cuts it to size, puts a bit of beeswax around the top edge to make it smooth on the lips and then the instrument is ready to play.

Leon has mastered the art of circular breathing, so he is able to keep a continuous drone going. He also adds howls and growls that resonate through the long chamber as he plays. The sound is grounding—I feel my body grow limp and heavy every time I listen. My mind quiets, as if the drone replaces the usual clatter of thoughts; I go into a light trance. When I sit near Leon, I can feel the vibrations running from the end of the digeridoo resting on the ground, through the soil and into my own body. The low, rhythmic roar is like a cross between waves breaking on the seashore and the twanging of a rubber band. It is very similar to the synthesised 'sound of the Earth' produced by a German physicist who figured out the vibratory frequency of the Earth and then speeded it up by octaves until it was an audible sound. When I heard the tape, I immediately experienced the same relaxed, concentrated peace that I feel when I listen to the digeridoo. The dig, too, is the sound of the Earth.

This evening, though, I do not listen very long. I've felt tired all day—I've had a lot of dreams lately, some of which leave me exhausted in the morning, so I have promised myself that I will go to bed early tonight. Not long after turning out the flashlight, I am sound asleep.

* * *

First light, pale purple in the early morning. I awake to flashes of lightning and sharp cracks of thunder that boom around the valley and shake the ground like an earthquake. My first reaction is delight. Thunderstorms are a rarity in Scotland —too far north for much electrical activity. I have missed the raw power of such storms and their energising effect upon the land. My second thought is of the large trees towering overhead which could act as conducting rods for the lightning. I remember well the warnings in childhood to stay flat on the ground and away from trees during a thunderstorm. Humans, too, can become lightning rods. There are enough trees here, I decide, that the lightning has many to choose from. I feel warm and secure in the sleeping bag, and I don't feel any leak in the tent despite the torrential rain. I decide to spend the day dozing and reading—at least until the storm passes.

10 a.m. The storm is still raging, and I hear digging sounds behind me. I unzip one of the tent flaps and watch Nat and Julie, whose camping site is above mine, cutting trenches in the soggy earth to drain the water from their half-submerged tent. Reluctantly I look closely at the ground around my own tent. A huge puddle is forming that has already seeped under the flap that protects the front vestibule. I sigh, close the flap and decide to get dressed. The storm feels like it's here to stay for a while, so I might as well make peace with it.

I pull on shorts, sweater and my long Goretex rainjacket. I leave my shoes inside the tent—no reason to get them wet now. They may take days to dry out. Once the rains start in the Southwest, and they've been unusually late this year, they can continue for the remainder of the winter. With some breaks, I hope.

Outside the tent I find the camp in full motion. The central area where the firepits are is completely covered by at least six inches of water. Colleen's tent is adrift, and she and her tentmate Jill are dragging out their sodden sleeping bags and clothes. Barry and Leon and Clay, another friend whom Gus had mentioned, are sweeping the pine needles into long corridors to re-route the flood down the steep slope towards the stream. Water is streaming from all sides to pool in that central area. The whole scene reminds me of Winnie the Pooh and the stick races they would have in the swollen stream after the spring rains. The rain has fallen long enough to become an adventure.

The quickest bonding for any community comes with storms or other shared hardships—it brings out the best and the worst in people, and enough understanding to tolerate both. After making narrow cuts around my own tent—just enough to reroute the developing rivulets—I join the excavation crew near Guboo's tent. Charlene is stirring the second pot of oatmeal that she has made today. Her shoulder-length brown hair is dripping at the ends, just like the water trickling from the ends of the pine branches. I walk over and wrap my arms around her waist from behind. She turns to give me a quick kiss. "How long have you been up?" I ask her.

"Since dawn," she says smiling. "I like this kind of weather. Everything's so green and alive. It's great!" She hops back and forth in an impromptu dance, splashing the puddles with her bare feet. She grabs my hand and twirls me around and gives me a hug. "You're amazing," I tell her, shaking my head. For me the rain is a trial to be endured, but Charlene seems to thrive on it.

"What?" she asks innocently. "I just like the rain."

Within an hour the pine-needle drainage channels are complete, and all of the drowned tents have been bailed and moved to higher locations. After a bowl of steamy oatmeal, I decide to spend the afternoon walking. At least I'll probably stay warm if I'm moving.

Reluctantly I decide that the rain looks serious, like it's planning to stay at least through the day, if not the night and beyond, so I pull on my shoes for the walk. Not far out of camp I find Charlene and Kree—a tall, willowy woman who is here at the camp with her seven-year-old son and her mother—collecting wood for the fire. Charlene stands chopping wood while Kree loads it into the car. Her feet seem to grow right out of the earth as her powerful arms swing the axe, without any wasted motion. She rarely needs more than two swings to split even the greenest logs. Charlene has a strong, solid grace about her that I have rarely seen in either a man or woman.

After helping load the wood into Kree's van, we notice what look like golf-ball-sized lemons hanging from one of the trees. We peel a couple and taste them and decide they *are* lemons. Someone must have planted them here; perhaps this was once a town. Just below us are what look like the remains of railroad ties and beyond is a bulletin board. I wander down and read the signs, which give the history of what was once Nanga Mill. A boom town during the logging days in this area, it was completely razed in the early sixties by a fire that destroyed the surrounding forest as well. After this, the Western Australia state government decided not to rebuild the town. Reluctantly the people left the charred buildings to be reclaimed by the forest and moved elsewhere. The forestry commission replanted what had been the town area with pines and created a picnic and camping site. They left the surrounding devastated forest to regenerate by itself.

The blazed trail that I follow climbs up through that regrowth forest, among banksia bushes and grass trees that shed plumes of spray when I walk past. Along the high ridge, Karri and Jarrah trees predominate. All of them look charred at the base. During my time at Uluru, I learned that the traditional stewards of the land used burning as an integral part of keeping the landscape healthy.

The desert people, and from what little I have read I gather the people here as well, have mastered the art of patch burning. Each season the aboriginal people living in the desert would burn small patches of land—to scare out small game when they were hunting, and to encourage the seeds that needed scorching before they would sprout. The patch burning also ensured that wildfires started by lightning or a careless campfire would burn only to the edge of another season's burn area. There the undergrowth would be sparse or green, free of dried debris.

When the Australian National Park Department took over Uluru (Ayer's Rock) about 25 years ago, the traditional people tried each year to convince the rangers to burn patches of land. "Don't worry," the rangers replied. "We know what's best for the land."

The aboriginal people, who had occupied that country for at least 40,000 years (a probably conservative estimate by anthropologists), persisted in trying to share their wisdom. Finally after a fierce brush fire that ran wild and destroyed a large section of the desert, the rangers began to listen. Now they, too, are learning about patch burning. But it is the traditional people who have mastered the art—how to read the wind, how to judge the angle of a ridge to stop the burn, what sorts of shrubs are burn-resistant. All of these factors allow them to control the size and intensity of

210

the fire. In this way the fires are kept small and relatively cool. Most of the animals can run to the edge of the burn without being killed. Heat-resistant trees are blackened at the base but not completely destroyed as they would be in a wildfire. Seeds that need fire to germinate sprout and cover the land with fresh green shoots that feed the animals. The cycle begins anew.

After about an hour of walking along the ridge I see smoke rising in the distance. Is it the campfire of a hardy group of walkers? As I approach, though, I realise that the smoke is pouring from the base of a fallen tree that is still blazing, the last remnant of a fire that has blackened a whole section of hillside.

Despite knowing that the forestry service practises patch burning, the smell of dampened hot charcoal and the hot black earth steaming in the rain frightens me. Maybe the fire was started by lightning last night; maybe it wasn't deliberate at all. And I'm about two hours' walk from the nearest human, much less the nearest phone.

I spend about half an hour around the base of the fallen Karri tree, heaping earth over the open flames. As soon as I smother one area of the fire and move to another, the first area begins to smoulder and then burn again. After a while I realise I cannot stop the fire alone, and I decide to return to camp and at least report it.

At first I half run, half jog through the rain-soaked trees, spurred on by the pervasive smell of woodsmoke behind me. After a few minutes, though, I realise that my panic is exaggerated. The burn went right up to the edge of an old logging road and then stopped—the open earth makes a natural firebreak. And if the rain continues—and there is certainly no hint of it stopping—the fire will eventually burn out. By the time I arrive back in camp, the first brittle edge of anxiety is gone. Barry assures me that the forestry commission probably set the fire, knowing that the rains were predicted. "But it's so easy to assume things," I tell him. "I'd rather say something just to be sure." He promises to report the fire the next time he is in town. If I go first, I'll call. Satisfied, I let go of the worry.

By the end of the day, most of the parents with small children have left. Julie and Nat pack their sodden tent and go. The only ones remaining are Kree and her son Jason and a father with his two children. For the rest of the week, the 15 or so people left in camp grow much closer. By necessity we spend a lot of time together under the only large shelters. We sit or stand under the verandah of Guboo's tent or under the plastic tarp that someone rigged over the picnic table where the food and dishes are stored. During the breaks in the rain, Guboo teaches us how to make clapping sticks from the scraps of wood that someone got at a local mill. The hard Jarrah wood makes a sharp, sweet sound when the sticks are finished. Guboo spends hours poking bent coathanger wires into the fire and burning designs into clapping sticks for people. Working with his hands, he is in his element.

As the days pass, I wrestle with the decision about whether or not to go to Monkey Mia. I could go up there on my own right after this camp and not have to change any of my plans. But to experience Monkey Mia as part of a Dreaming Camp would be extra special . . . and I still have a lot of places I want to visit and photograph in the Southwest . . . and a lot of people from this camp are planning to go . . . it would be like an extended family reunion. With dolphins thrown in for good measure. And I could stay there for at least ten days with the dolphins instead of the four or five I had originally planned. But what about all of the people I wrote to when I arrived in Australia? What about visiting the communities and writing the book? Am I allowing someone else's agenda to shape my own once again?

After a couple of days' deliberation, I finally decide to go with Guboo and crew to Margaret River, a town a bit farther south down the coast of Western Australia, right after this Dreaming Camp. Then at the beginning of June I will join them at Monkey Mia. If I listen deeply to my heart, I know that I have much more to learn about the aboriginal world, the Dreamtime, the ways of their traditional culture. And in the end I may learn even more about community, especially *traditional* communities, than if I went to visit the 'intentional' communities on the east coast.

In a sense, the Dreaming Camps *are* communities—communities of the moment, much like the camps of the traditional nomadic people would have been. A family group travelling together would stay for a while in one area and then move on. Their constant movement meant that no one area would be completely fished or camped or hunted out before it could regenerate. Their nomadic lifestyle distributed their impact on the sparse, worn land.

On Friday, the next to last day of the Camp, Colleen and Jill and I decide to make a *hungey,* an underground oven made by digging a three- or four-foot-deep hole in the earth, building a fire and tending it until it burns into a good bed of coals.

We try digging the hole along the corridor where the open fire was built, but about four inches down we hit bitumen—this must have been an old road. We move up to the next ridge and find softer ground. We use a tiny spade meant for digging latrines, but within an hour we have the pit dug. By the end of the afternoon the fire has burned into a thick bed of coals, and the food is wrapped in aluminium foil—small innovation on the traditional method. The vegetables—squash and potatoes and other hard vegetables—are lowered into the pit, covered with ashes and dirt and left to bake.

While we sit waiting for the food to cook, Leon begins one of his raps about Oneness, how all people are related, and if that is so, then he considers himself to be aboriginal. After all, Guboo 'initiated him into the Tribe', and he has a lot of reverence for the land and aboriginal teachings. So, in his mind, he's aboriginal.

I look over at Colleen; her face is red and hard. I can tell she's really pissed off. Although the Sunday hunting parties to 'shoot abos', a popular sport not so long ago in Queensland, have stopped, many old prejudices still linger. After years of persecution of aboriginals, suddenly the scales have tipped and it's *fashionable* to be aboriginal—at least among a certain population, mostly the growth-workshop-junkie sort. While ten or twenty years ago many aboriginal people were ashamed to admit their heritage, now the balance has shifted so that even Europeans want to call themselves 'aboriginal'. They're running after the identity that the traditional people are running *away* from. (See *My Place,* listed in the bibliography.)

"Leon," says Colleen, her voice carefully controlled, "you're not aboriginal. You might feel really connected with the land and do a lot of good things, but you are *not* aboriginal."

"And what about you, Colleen?" asks Barry, coming over to join the conversation. "You've got Scottish blood in your background. What about that part of your heritage? Isn't that part of you, too?"

"Barry, we've had this discussion before. Look, either you're aboriginal or you're not. It's the way you live, the way you're brought up. Yes, I have Scottish blood, but I'm aboriginal. We don't talk about half or quarter or whatever. That doesn't matter."

"If it doesn't matter, then what's the difference if I say I'm aboriginal?" asks Leon. "I'm part of the Oneness, so I can say I'm anything I . . . ."

David ploughs right through his words. "Leon, you're not aboriginal—no matter what you do. Look, I've thought about this very strongly, and . . . ."

"Piss off, David!" yells Leon. "Look, you stand around the fire every night raving about this and that, so why don't you let me talk now? Give some space for other people to talk, too."

"You're wrong, Leon. I refuse to listen to nonsense."

The two of them lock horns and have at it for a good five minutes. I finally move away to check the fire, and Colleen wanders off, too. Both Leon and David take their roles as self-appointed teachers quite seriously, and they hit each other's vulnerable points square on the mark.

When David and Leon finish, David comes over and sits on the ground next to me and starts explaining why he interrupted Leon. Finally I look over at him and break into his flow of words when he takes a breath. "Look, David, I agree with what you were saying about Leon not being aboriginal, but I don't think it's right to interrupt people when they have something to say. That's one thing I've learned at the Findhorn Community. People can share whatever they want to, and I don't have to react to it. It's *their* experience, not mine."

"Even when they're talking shit?"

I shrug my shoulders and go on with building the fire. I'm curious why David wants reassurance from me. I'm sure he can see I wasn't much impressed by their argument. I wonder, though, why he's worried about what I think of him. Through the week, we've spent time together off and on, talking and sharing our experiences. We've mentioned travelling a bit together after this Dreaming Camp and before the one scheduled at Monkey Mia; we both have places to visit in the Southwest. So maybe he's worried that I'll change my mind . . . . No, he's made it quite clear that he prefers to travel alone, so I'm sure he wouldn't care.

Shortly before sundown we check the vegetables in the fire. After a couple of hours in the *hungey,* they are baked. We all sit around the fire brushing grit off the sweet potatoes and squash and passing around lumps of butter. A new couple has arrived in camp—their entrance in a BMW couldn't be missed—and the woman is sceptical about the food. She looks up, smiling nervously. "What do you do with the dirt?" she asks.

Everyone else is munching happily. Colleen diplomatically suggests that she rinse it under the tap. "OK," says the woman brightly. She comes back in a couple of minutes, complaining that now the food is cold. Someone suggests that she find a pot and put it on the rack over the firepit. Ten minutes later she returns and finally settles onto her cushion (never mind just sitting on the ground), and opens a jar of mayonnaise. "Anyone want mayonnaise?" she asks, insistently passing it around the circle. No, no one wants mayonnaise. She tries a few times and then, satisfied with her philanthropy, settles back and eats her food. Or tries to. Her smile fades and she chews with half-covered disdain. She must think herself very brave to be eating with us commoners.

She spends most of the evening talking with Guboo. That's why she came, to pick his brain for sacred knowledge. Medicine men and women are 'in' among yuppies, and she's hot on the trail of a bona fide Elder. After a couple of hours, she emerges satisfied, having been blessed with his crystals and offered a job as his secretary.

When 'Mrs Mayonnaise', as we affectionately name her, proudly announces his job offer, I cringe with embarrassment. I took his request for a secretary seriously, and so has she. So have most of the dozen other women whom he has asked since I arrived in camp. In that moment I realise that Guboo's 'search for a secretary' is simply a way of drawing women in, to make them feel wanted and important. My ego fell for the ruse.

The last day of camp I go for a long walk to visit the 'King Jarrah' tree, the last forest giant left after decades of clear-cutting and wild bush fires. I almost pass by the tree—it has no marking—until I realise that I have seen no other as large as this.

In the misty rain, I lean my belly against the trunk, resting my cheek against the dappled bark. Five people could easily reach around the base of the tree. After resting for a few minutes, I look up the 200-foot trunk, and try to imagine a forest full of such giants. I have read that the early settlers took days to walk a couple of miles—the forest undergrowth was that dense. At a certain point, they turned back to the coast, defeated by the giants.

How could the loggers deny the magic of these trees? Who could resist their majesty? And how must this single tree, the lone sentinel among the regrowth forest, view the destruction of its kin? I sense that you are like an Elder, a repository for history and secrets and knowledge long forgotten, and now eagerly sought among the younger folk. Many come to the forest, like me, to view the wise old giant—to pay homage, to stand in awe, to imagine how things once were. Many come to visit Guboo, to pay homage, to sit in awe, to imagine how life once was in this land.

Three hours later, when I return to camp, only the nucleus of about ten people remain. Leon is standing near the fire, looking into the flames. He looks up when I walk into camp and nods. "Wow, I really felt the energy change in camp. Right at about 1:30. Everything changed. It's like the camp really ended right then."

It's true—the camp feels hollow now, as if the space has been stretched wide and then vacated, leaving a vacuum where hours before life was bursting. As if to signal the fading energy, after sunset everyone's electric torch dies. Only Colleen's has a dim beam, and we share it around to make our way back and forth between our tents and the fire. We gather around the fire for a final evening of songs and dances, hopping and clapping and singing longer than any other evening. I feel as if the walls between us have disintegrated over the past week, and I feel completely at home with all of these loving souls. We have talked and laughed and fought and sung and danced together, and now we are family.

The morning begins early, with Guboo walking around the camp banging the clapping sticks and calling "I LO-O-OVE YOU, I LO-O-O-OVE YOU." After the Humming Bee, we spend the next couple of hours dismantling the camp and loading everything into cars. Finally, we make a last sweep through the area to pick up bits of paper and trash left by us and other visitors. Looking at the plume of smoke rising from the dying embers of the fire, a newcomer would never guess that a day before the place was 'home' to a couple dozen people.

And somehow our departure without leaving a trace is very fitting. We have come to learn about the Dreamtime, the aboriginal way of living, and like the traditional people we leave as family bands, driving instead of walking, to meet again in a month's time at another large camp—Monkey Mia.

CHAPTER 11
Monkey Mia

Our travelling family band of Guboo, Colleen, Barry, David and I make our first stop in Margaret River, a town on the southwest coast famous for surfing and more recently for its alternative neighbourhood community. Guboo gives a talk and leads a Humming Bee at the local town hall. He also visits one of the local farms where the owner has had a very deep experience in the forest, and Guboo returns the following morning to bless the land. During this time, watching Guboo working hands-on with the land, I see him in his strength. I know him as the powerful spiritual elder that he is. Quietly he gives out his teaching—the wisdom could easily slip by unnoticed by those not paying close attention.

After a few days, Guboo and Barry and Colleen return to Fremantle for a couple of weeks' rest before the camp at Monkey Mia. David and I stay on in Margaret River for a Great Walk reunion planned to record all of the songs sung during the Walk. David has offered to video the recording session for them. The weekend is filled with laughter and singing and lots of hugs. The love generated during the Walk is still tangible and free-flowing.

David and I, though, have our challenges communicating. After the recording session we decide to hitch-hike down to Denmark, a town on the south coast, where several people who were at the Dreaming Camp live. Our main interest, though, is meeting Maxine, an aboriginal elder living there. We are given the address of two brothers with whom we can stay—both have visited the Findhorn Foundation and are the nucleus of the 'Cosmic Club', the tongue-in-cheek name for a local group that meets every full moon to meditate together.

A couple of times I sit down with David and plead to communicate more clearly. "Are you willing to let me into your world?" I ask him. He tends to organise things and then come back and report what he has arranged. I am furious, wanting to work

215

together. I'm not going to make the mistake of following a man around again. And his habit of ploughing into the middle of someone else's conversation continues. I remind myself that he is responsible for himself, that he is free to do as he pleases, but still some of his behaviour bothers the hell out of me.

The climax of our communication difficulties comes during our two-day stay in the Shannon Forest State Park, another regrowth Karri and Jarrah forest. Our last ride of the day brought us right to the doorstep of a wooden cabin complete with built-in bunks and chopped firewood outside the door. "Do you have food?" asked the man, a local farmer, when he stopped for us after dark. "Do you have a tent?" When we told him we did, he nodded and said, "If you didn't, I'd take you home for the night. You won't get a ride now until morning; I know, I sat out here all night long once." And after he drives out of his way to take us to the shelter, he gives us his address a couple of miles up the road and insists that we come to see him and his wife if we need anything. That's the sort of ride we've been getting all day—it renews my faith in the goodness of humankind.

After dinner the second night in the cabin, we start a discussion that turns into an analysis of all of my shortcomings, and I don't agree with some of the accusations. I crawl into bed, face the wall and resolve to leave on my own in the morning. I've had enough of trying to communicate with David.

I awake in the morning, still fuming. I walk down the hill to the outhouse without saying a word and then begin to pack my bags. I leave a crack open in the door between David and me—I will try talking with him one more time, and if we can clear our differences, I will continue to Denmark with him. Otherwise, I'm heading off on my own. David watches while I cram clothes into the pack and jerk at the zipper. I return all of the papers and things that he's loaned me. "Are you going?" he asks simply.

"I want to talk with you, and if we can't work things out, I'm going. On my own." He watches while I finish packing, and then we sit facing each other on the wooden benches. For over an hour we rage and talk and spar until finally I ask him, "Are you ready to *receive*? I see you giving out all the time, but are you willing to let in love? To receive?" My eyes pierce his. He squirms a bit but doesn't look away. We are silent for a long time before he answers. "Yes."

"And do you want to *know* me?" We've had long discussions before about how we interact with people, and I've learned that if David hasn't made the basic commitment to know someone—not as a superficial acquaintance but on a deep level —he has little patience or respect for him or her. The silence after this question is even longer and is followed by a long, ten-minute explanation that ends with "Yes, I want to know you."

"Do you *really* want to know me?" I ask again.

"Judith," he says, dropping his arms in exasperation, "didn't you hear what I just said? Yes. Yes, I do. Now I'll ask *you* the same question. Do you want to know *me*?"

I pause for a long time. Why do I seem to attract challenging, difficult people? Are they a mirror for me? I sit on the verge of some ancient pattern—I've never simply walked away from someone or something before, no matter how difficult or outrageous the situation. I refuse to give up on them or me, and the habit has cost me a lot of time and effort over the years. I am eternally patient with difficult people. Like working with frightened wild animals, I delight in winning their trust. Could I simply get up and walk out the door? For once, could I let go and simply leave? In my mind I make the movement, pulling on my pack, walking down the hill, standing by the road alone. Some unnamable force, though, draws me back. If I walked away, I would miss something. I don't know exactly what, but it's important. Agonising over the decision puzzles me, too. Never before have I struggled so much in a friendship. We don't even have the bond of a sexual relationship to hold us together, so why am I willing to endure it? But I still have the choice to walk away . . . .

I turn back to David and hold his eyes for a few moments, perched on a thin line between staying and going. Finally, the balance swings towards safety—maybe. "Yes, David, I want to know you, too. And I want to ask you something. How did you know who I was when I walked into camp?"

David pauses a long time, biting his lip. "I talked with Gus," he says finally.

"In India?" I ask. I can tell David is reluctant to reveal much of anything. I'll have to ask the right questions or he won't say a word.

"Yeah, the night after you met him."

"Did *he* know that you talked to him?"

"No."

"So you talked with his Higher Self, like when he was asleep?"

"Yeah, I guess you could say that."

After that morning, our relationship slowly deepens. The seed is planted, and during our time in Denmark it begins to grow into a firm friendship. Together we spend a few days visiting Maxine Fumagalli, the Elder of this area. It is Maxine who guides me in my first baby steps towards understanding the Dreamtime.

When I ask her a question about one of the local sites, an area along the coast once used as a campsite and fishing spot for the Nunga people (traditional people of this southwestern part of Australia), Maxine gives me one of her penetrating looks and asks, "What is Dreamtime?"

"Well, uh, I, uh . . . I'm not sure that I can put it into words," I stammer.

"Dreamtime is connected with a place," says Maxine slowly, holding my eyes. "Dreamtime stories are about particular places. It's the creation of that place and the teaching about it. And it's only about that place."

"So different songs and stories tell about different places?"

"That's right," she says, nodding.

"So that's why each area has it's own Dreamtime stories?"

"Yes."

David and Maxine have a long discussion about language when Maxine shows him some of the materials she put together to teach children Nunga in the local schools. "One time," she says, her deep-brown eyes sparkling with fun, "this white linguist man came to teach us some made-up language, since he had decided we didn't have one. He went on for a while about how Nunga was lost, and he would be glad to teach us Pigon."

"Was it anything like your language?" asks David.

"No, it wasn't even *close*. After a few minutes I got up and told him off in Nunga. 'This man is sick in the head,' I told everyone. I turned around and walked out, and so did all of the old people." She chuckles.

"Did the man know what you said?" I ask.

"Of course not," says Maxine. "He didn't know anything about Nunga; he didn't know people still speak it. They're just quiet about it, that's all."

The language myth is only one of many that are slow to die in the town of Denmark. When we arrived, our host told us with certainty that Maxine was the only aboriginal person in town. After a terrible massacre by the white settlers, he told us, the aboriginal people put a curse on the land, and none of them would return. Part of the beginning of the Great Walk, he says, included a dance organised

217

by Ken Colbung, one of the traditional 'stewards' of the area around Perth, and the lifting of the curse.

Walking around town, though, David spots half-a-dozen aboriginal people. "Look, Judith, look how they walk. Back on their heels. Look."

When I watch the couple walking down the street, I notice the same sort of rooted movement that I saw in Colleen. It's not so much the specific motion as the quality of their relationship with the ground. In comparison, the other people bounce stiffly on rigid legs. In the bakery, David asks another woman and her daughter if they know where Maxine lives. "Yes," they tell him quietly. "But I think she's out of town visiting her daughter."

Later, when we meet Maxine, we tell her about the comments we have heard, how no aboriginal people live in Denmark. "I don't understand," says David. "I saw at least six of them walking down the street yesterday."

"I know," says Maxine. "There are about thirty aboriginal people in town, but they don't want anyone to know they're black. They have light skin so they can get away with it. And one, she wears so much make-up . . . ."

"What about the curse that was supposed to be lifted at the beginning of the Great Walk? Do you think more people will come back now?"

Maxine looks down for a moment and narrows her eyes. "The Nunga people didn't put a curse on this land. The white people who lived on the edge of town said if any black people crossed over the stream on their property, they would shoot them. Word got around and enough aboriginal people were shot that they finally stayed away. That was the 'curse' they're talking about."

"A lot of people we met who'd been on the Great Walk said it was really important to them that you were there at the beginning. Some said they could feel your healing power, and a few people were physically healed just standing around you."

"Hmmmm . . . . ," says Maxine, smiling quietly. "You know, for years I've been calling my people to come back here, to come back to the land. It's not easy being alone, doing this. I've been working alone for twenty years, singing the land, calling for my people. And then these, well, I don't know what you call them . . . ."

"New Age people?" I ask.

"Yeah, I guess that's what you could call them. They've moved into Denmark and at first I was really bitter. I wanted my own people to come back. But over the years I've made peace with them inside myself—in their own way, they belong here too."

During this time, through our talks with Maxine and visits to various sites in the area, I come to see David in his strength. Gone are the communication problems and the diffuse focus that irritated me so much earlier in the trip. With Maxine, he moves peacefully and speaks with great wisdom. When we visit the sites, he sits calmly, using fine-tuned inner senses to access a lot of information about the land, the people and the history of the place. I realise that the fast-talking, dishevelled appearance that David presents at first is really a lot of static that covers a deep wisdom and caring. It is for these qualities that I have stayed.

We also visit a local architect who is a member of the 'Cosmic Club'. We've heard that his house is situated near a spot special to the aboriginal people. When we arrive, we discover that the house is right *on* the rock outcropping. In fact, he blasted part of it away to make room to build. I have a sick feeling most of the time we are inside. When he shows us the lower section of his home, we walk by part of the rock outcropping that he included in the construction of the house—it forms a wall along the far side of the living room. I put my hands out as we go past and feel a cool breeze moving rhythmically over them. "David," I whisper. "Feel this."

He stops for a moment, his hands trembling in front of the rock. "It's breathing," he says quietly. "The rock is breathing."

The woman living with the architect tells us about his sensitivity to the land. "He knew this was a special spot. That's why he built the house here."

"But why did he build it right *on top* of the site?" I ask.

She shrugs her shoulders. "I don't know. I teach yoga classes in the room over where he did some of the blasting. I hope that some of the healing from the classes helps to heal the place, too."

While we ride our bicycles back to our host's house, I ponder the white European way of looking at the land and 'sacredness'. Traditional people leave sites *alone* that they feel are powerful or special in some way. They visit such an area only for a special purpose, to show honour and respect for the power of that place. Europeans, though, don't have much concept of 'sacredness'. Perhaps our monuments and churches—human-constructed things—are as close as we can come to understanding what sacred is. Imagine blasting part of the Lincoln Monument or Chartres Cathedral to make room for a house. Such a spot feels special, so you want to live there. Why not? Because it is a place to be shared by all people, in which to remember greatness and reverence and a power beyond human manipulation. For traditional people, those sites are everywhere, written right into the fabric of the land, and they are places to be treated with great respect.

After nearly a week in Denmark, we visit Maxine one last time, on the night of the full moon. "No goodbyes" says David. "I'll be talking with you." Maxine nods and gives each of us a hug. We say very little as we climb into the car. Maxine stands silhouetted in the doorway until we round the bend and pass out of sight.

From this point on in our journey, it is as if we are passed from hand to hand. I'm sure that Maxine has helped to smooth our way. Even delays and detours turn out to be necessary manoeuvres to route us in the proper direction. When we arrive back in Fremantle, Nat and Julie, who invited us to stay in their house, appear to be out of town. For two days we telephone and stop by to ring their doorbell. Late in the afternoon we decide to try one last time.

Still no answer. As we turn away from the door, I have a funny sense that I can't name, as if the moments between each second are stretching. "Hold on for a minute, David. I think something's going to happen." I pause for a moment, and then shrug my shoulders. "I don't know what . . . ."

We walk out the gate and stop to pull a fig from the tree that grows in the front garden. I hear someone singing, and turn to see Tara, a young woman who was part of the recording session at Margaret River. "Tara," I call. "How are you doing?"

"Good. How about you?"

"Well, not so good right now. We were going to stay here with Nat and Julie, but they seem to be gone for the weekend."

"Well," says Tara, "good luck. Hope you find something. I'm going to meet a friend right now, so I have to go."

"Thanks. Take care, Tara."

We walk up towards the main street, silent, hoping for inspiration about a place to stay. "Let's check out Beth's house," suggests David. "Maybe Barry's there, and he might have some ideas."

About half a block down the main road we hear someone running behind us, and we turn to find Tara making a beeline for us. "You know," she says, panting, "I realised you could come and stay with me and my parents."

David and I look at each other, surprised. "Come on, I'll show you where it is. It's just up the road. You can see it and decide if you want to stay there. I have the room upstairs and a beautiful porch. Well, you'll see it."

Tara half walks, half skips up the road ahead of us—her bare feet seem to ride on unseen springs and her head tilts with the rhythm of her song.

She leads us through the house and shows us her room. "I'm staying with some friends tonight, so you're welcome to stay here. I've got to go and meet my friend now. Just bring your stuff over; the door will be open. You'll meet my mum and dad; they're staying downstairs. OK? See you later."

David and I stand on the upstairs porch, watching the sun sink into the Indian Ocean, arms wrapped around each other's waist. "Thank you, Creator," I murmur. "This is a wonderful place, at least for tonight. But we'll probably have to find somewhere else tomorrow."

David reaches over to lift my chin to his, and we pause for a long, gentle kiss. Over the weeks of travel since leaving the Shannon Forest, the boundaries between us have softened and been replaced with a deep respect and love. The 'snorting', as I call it, the arguments and difficulties in communication, still continues, but underneath there is an acknowledged solid base of love. And perhaps it is the strength of the love that allows us to rage without breaking apart.

We walk downstairs and head for the front door. Our plan is to repack our things at the house where we've been staying and hire a cab to bring everything back. In the front hallway ahead of us a door stands ajar, and light from a single lamp pours into the darkening passage. David stops, leaning his head in the door, and begins a conversation with the man sitting inside at a desk. I only catch glimpses of his reddish-brown hair and bushy beard—David is blocking most of the doorway. He begins a quick barrage of information about the Dreaming Camps and what he's doing with Guboo.

The man listens quietly, adding a 'um-hum' every once in a while. He really looks more interested in his book than in David, and I tug at the back of David's shirt to try to hurry him along. "Oh, sorry," he says apologetically, and makes room for me to lean against the far side of the door frame. He missed the hint, or chooses to ignore it, and continues on for a few more minutes. At a certain point, some indiscernible line is crossed, and Brad, as he introduces himself, invites us to sit down at the kitchen table.

We don't budge from the table for over four hours. Brad and Karen, his partner who appears after about an hour, have spent most of the past ten years living with traditional people in the desert. They are, I finally piece together, Tara's parents. During that evening and the rest of the days of our stay, they share some of their experiences in the desert. In a couple of days I learn more about the traditional aboriginal view of life than any book could ever teach me. And it's not only the words, it's also the way that Brad and Karen move, how they speak (or don't speak), how they look at the world. Most of all they teach me through their commitment.

For those ten years of work, Brad and Karen received no pay—except one year, when they were given two blankets. They simply went to live with the people, to help in any way that they could, with no preconceived ideas about what the people needed or wanted. Their approach reminds me of the advice Chief Billy Redwing Tyack once gave me after he spoke at Oberlin. Deeply moved by his talk and the struggles of his people, I asked if there was anything more than writing to my congressional representative that I could do. "Go and live there," he said sternly. "Just do whatever you can do, whatever you see needs to be done. But don't come and go. Some people come, work for six months or so, then leave. If you really want to help, you've got to live there, not come and go. That's how you can help."

That night after his talk I came as close to quitting school as I ever had. My heart was bursting with the desire to help, *really* help, in a way that would truly benefit native people. In the end I convinced myself that I would be of more use if I was trained as a doctor, and I decided to stay in school. I lacked the courage to follow my heart at that time. Now that desire is burning within me again, rekindled by my time in India and the Dreaming Camp, and by Karen and Brad's stories.

One sunny morning Brad and I simply sit on the porch. Karen joins us with her sketch pad—she's been studying at the local university for the past year to finish a Fine Arts degree. The silence is the soothing kind shared by people at peace with themselves. The vast silence of the desert seems to have eaten into them, especially Brad. Slowly he begins a story about something, and the conversation flows for a few hours. Every once in a while Brad reaches the edge of something and stops, shaking his head. "Damn, some day I'd like to have someone else I could talk to about these things . . . but, well, that's how it is . . . ." and then the story veers in another direction.

Through the days I gradually learn the importance of the Law. It is taught experientially, and once someone carries the knowledge of that aspect of the Law, they can discuss it only with others who have been through the same learning. The sacred teachings are written into the land that was shaped by the Dreamtime heroes and heroines and their activities as they moved across the land. If someone wants to teach a child a particular lesson, a particular story, they take him or her to the site, tell them the story that explains the creation of that area, and give the teaching that comes from the story. "They actually touch the Law; it's right there in the rock," explains Brad. "That's why it doesn't make sense to tell the stories in some living room in a city hundreds of miles away. It's so much better now that the people have returned to the desert. The kids are learning the stories where they should be taught, right there where it happened."

Knowing my desire to work with native people, after a few days Brad suggests that we *might* come out with him to the desert camp where he has been living to work a bit with a group of kids who are putting a band together. I've been agonising over not having anything to share with indigenous people. I can't think of any skills or knowledge that I have that would really be beneficial. David, as well as to some extent Brad, has been encouraging me to share music—violin, singing and my ingrown sense of sound and rhythm. Working with the band, I would have a chance to experience a traditional community first hand. "And who knows," adds Brad, "maybe you'll come out to work there some day. Anyhow, you'd have a chance to check it out." He needs to ask the aboriginal people, though—they make the final decisions about who does or doesn't come into camp.

We leave Fremantle a couple of days before the Dreaming Camp at Monkey Mia is scheduled to start, promising to stay in touch with Karen and Brad over the next few weeks. They are unsure of exactly when they will be going out to the desert camp; the timing depends on when the new four-wheel-drive vehicle that Brad has come down to Perth to pick up will be ready. The visit also hinges on the Martujarra people's decision about whether or not they want us in the camp.

Verna, Kree's mother, and a close friend from the last Dreaming Camp, drives us up the west coast in her combi-van. The trip takes longer than expected, in part because I have a raging bladder infection and have to stop every hour to pee. We sleep by the side of the road—Verna in the back of the van, David and I on the ground outside. As we travel north, the vegetation grows shorter and shorter, shrinking from the hot desert sun. This area receives much less rainfall than the Southwest. In this year of changing weather patterns, though, the west coast has had an unusual amount of rainfall. Just a month previously an unseasonal hurricane ripped across Monkey Mia and Shark's Bay, two tiny towns along the peninsula

221

that juts north and west into the ocean, before heading south to some of the major towns along the coast.

Tonight, too, the weather is unpredictable. At 9 p.m. we are nestled in our sleeping bags and the sky above is completely clear, the stars brilliant. At midnight a few drops of rain fall, and we quickly stuff our bags under the van until the shower passes. At 3 a.m. the rain begins in earnest, and we finally drag our wet bags into the front seat of the van and sleep sitting up.

In the morning the sun is bright in a sky fringed with high horsetail clouds; someone sleeping indoors would never know it had rained. By mid-morning we reach the turn-off to Shark's Bay. In another couple of hours we see the ocean, shimmering turquoise-blue, to the west. After a quick stop for groceries and mail (the post office is located in the back of the store), we turn onto the dirt track that bumps over 19 kilometres to the caravan park perched on the beach at Monkey Mia.

I smile as we approach the caravan park—such an unlikely spot for an incredible adventure in communication between dolphins and humans that has been going on for at least 25 years. Like the Findhorn Foundation, the phenomenon began quietly with a few people in the supremely ordinary environment of a caravan park. Until a couple of years ago, the entire road from the turn-off at the Overland Roadhouse was unpaved, and only the hardiest tourists made the trek. As the word got out about the wild dolphins who were coming in close to shore, the trickle of holiday caravans increased.

The caravan park owners began to worry about the dolphins' safety. The woman realised just how much she had come to love them when a ship went aground in the bay, and the coastguard declared that the only way to move it was to blast it out. "I knew that they couldn't keep the dolphins away from the boat—they would come in to see what was going on, they're so curious. I told them that if they wanted to use those explosives, it would be over my dead body. I really was willing to strap myself to the boat; I was hysterical about anything happening to the dolphins. And you know, suddenly I understood those people who are trying to save the forests. I'd always thought they were a bit crazy, but in that moment I knew why they did it. It was then I realised how much I had grown to love the dolphins."

About five years ago the caravan park owners collected enough money to set up a ranger station that would serve both as an educational centre to teach people about the dolphins and as a research station for the scientists who were coming to study the phenomenon. In addition, they have rangers on duty at all times, in the water, to talk with visitors about the dolphins and explain how to touch them without hurting or upsetting them. They are wild, free creatures, and need to be respected as such.

The park stretches about a quarter of a mile along the coast. Campers and caravans and a couple of more permanent bungalows are sandwiched side-by-side. The paths are covered with fragments of white shell to keep down the sand and dust. We drive through the herd of trailers to the far corner of the park reserved for tent campers. Already about half a dozen tents are up. Guboo and Barry are sitting in lawn chairs under the verandah of Guboo's tent, and Colleen is arranging the food and dishes in the back of the trailer—a new addition to the travelling caravan, the trailer has freed a lot of space inside the old Dodge station wagon.

Leon and Kree and her son Jason are sitting in the shade of Kree's combi-van. Nicki, also a veteran from the last camp, is radiant and tanned, her swollen belly protruding under her free-flowing caftan. At eight and a half months pregnant, she seems completely relaxed, unconcerned about being miles away from the nearest hospital, or even nurse, in case the baby comes early. Her matter-of-fact attitude about the pregnancy and her future as a single parent to a newborn baby, in addition to her seven-year-old son, amazes and inspires me.

Within a couple of hours David and I have our tents set up in the deep, soft sand among the low bushes that grow on the dunes. More people are arriving, searching out places to pitch their tents. Slowly, the camp is coming to life.

Late in the afternoon I walk down to the pier where the rangers have roped off an area where people can wade into the water to meet the dolphins. I stand for a few minutes, watching the pair of dolphins who are cruising back and forth in the smooth, shallow water. The bay is protected enough that waves rarely break on the shore—only at the turning of the tide is there much movement. I want to be sure that I am centred before I enter the water. Guboo's warning to approach the dolphins as elders runs through my mind; I don't want to barge into the water without preparing myself first.

Slowly I wade in, just up to my knees. Immediately one of the dolphins veers around and glides by, rolling onto her side so that she can look at me. I also hear the clicking noises that mean she is using her sonar-like hearing—she can 'see' my whole body, inside as well as outside, by making this kind of sound-scan. She—at least I assume it's a she—looks like 'Holey-fin', the mother, and now *grandmother,* of the dolphins who regularly come in to shore. The top of her dorsal fin has a small hole in it, and her face is mottled with white scars.

"Is this Holey-fin?" I ask the ranger, reaching out to stroke the dolphin's side as she passes by. Her body is warm and firm, like wet human skin, but even warmer.

"Yes, that's her," she says.

"How did she get those marks on her head?"

"Well, someone in a fishing boat found her beached on a sand bar at low tide. It was mating season, and sometimes they get so excited that they just forget about everything else. So she probably got stuck there at low tide, couldn't get back in the water. She got a bad sunburn from being out of the water so long, but actually a lot of the white patches have healed. She's looking pretty good now."

"Are you Sharon?" I ask. Already around camp I have heard about the aboriginal woman ranger who has a special way with the dolphins.

"Yes," she says, nodding.

"Ah—someone mentioned your name at the Dreaming Camp."

"Right. I've been down to talk with Guboo."

We stand quietly in the shallow water, watching the dolphins pass. "They don't seem very interested in playing," I comment.

"Usually by this time in the day they've had enough touching. Only two are in now—in the morning sometimes there are six or eight of them. But it's getting pretty late now. Sunset soon." She looks off towards the west. Holey-fin comes up just in front of Sharon, arching her back and opening her beak, shaking her head up and down and chattering. Sharon smiles and bends over, hands clasped behind her back, talking gently. Holey-fin moves in closer and rests her beak on Sharon's leg for a moment. With an almost imperceptible swish of her tail, Holey-fin glides backward and then disappears under the water. In a couple of seconds she surfaces again about a hundred feet away, with the other dolphin who has been cruising along the beach. Together they swim, almost like torpedoes, disappearing underwater and then skimming the surface for a moment before submerging again. "They swim so fast," I comment to Sharon.

She nods. "They can swim as fast as sixty or seventy miles an hour."

Reluctantly I wade out of the water—sunset is close and the dolphins have gone out to sea for the night. The sun hangs orange over the ocean, spreading a carpet of red-gold. The Humming Bee will start soon. Already I see a small crowd gathering

223

on the top of the steep hill that rises behind the tent camping area.

I stop by the tent for a sweater—the air is growing chilly already—and then climb up the sandy hill to where people are gathered watching the sun sink towards the sea. For this first night, we stand in a circle with hands clasped, giving our names and where we are from. A couple of people read poems and stories from mimeographed sheets that Guboo has handed out, including a Dreamtime story from the Yuin nation. After spending time with Maxine, the story has more meaning for me. I recognise it as an important creation story for the Wallaga Lake area.

Looking around the circle I realise that I have already formed opinions about several people. Again I sense the initial resistance to opening to a whole new group. I have been through it so many times at the Findhorn Community with the influx of new guests each week. Most of the members eventually close down and don't interact daily with the constantly changing stream of guests; they limit their attention to the guests who join them in the work department. To become emotionally involved with *everyone* who passes through the community would be too draining. I note my tendency to gravitate towards the people who were at the last camp, and consciously decide that I want to open to the new people who have arrived here, too. Otherwise, I will probably miss some gems along the path.

At the last camp, most people ate together, but here the cooking breaks into small groups of five or ten people. The caravan park owners don't usually allow open fires—wildfires are a danger in this desert country—but they make an exception for us. We drag an empty fifty-gallon oil drum to a sandy patch at the edge of the camp, and forage fuel from the woody shrubs round about. A couple of people come equipped with camping stoves, so the usual gathering point, the campfire, is dispersed among several fires.

As the evening progresses, though, the crowd around the oil drum grows. Guboo tells stories and leads songs. When Guboo tires, he motions to David to improvise for a while. David takes off on stories about the Inuit and Crow people, and when *he* tires, he motions to me to sing some chants. Woops, I wasn't expecting to be part of the sideshow. Leon plays the digeridoo, someone else plays the guitar, another man arrives with a violin.

I nearly pounce on him. David and I have been scouring Western Australia to find an inexpensive violin to buy to take into the desert with us. The dearth of instruments is astounding. Music stores selling *any* instruments are rare outside of Perth, the capital of Western Australia. Now that I am without a violin and have no way of getting hold of one, I appreciate music and long to play much more than when I have one close at hand. "Don't it always seem to go, that ya' don't know what you've got 'til it's gone," sings Joni Mitchell. Out in the desert, I know her truth.

In the mornings, after the Humming Bee, almost everyone spends time at the beach with the dolphins. Early mornings are best, before the real crush of people arrives. Around 11 a.m. each day a busload of day tourists from Shark Bay descends on the beach. They plough across the sand and into the water, entranced with the dolphins and the sea. "Once," says Debbie, a photographer and writer who has lived at Monkey Mia for nearly four years, "I watched this huge woman with one of those tent dresses walk right off the bus and into the water. She didn't even stop to take her shoes off. And her dress just ballooned around her in the water. She was such a sight."

The rangers sell fish only a couple of times a day—they don't want the dolphins to become dependent on it, and they move the time around each day to keep them guessing. But one sale is always timed to coincide with the bus tour. After a couple of days I learn to avoid the beach at this time.

"Here puppy, here puppy," calls one little girl holding out a fish. The dolphins seem to be especially excited when young children get in the water. I've seen Holey-fin nearly beach herself trying to get close to a toddler. But this little girl is determined to treat the dolphins like dogs. Despite warnings from the ranger, she pats them on the dorsal fin, a very sensitive spot, and splashes and shouts and lunges at them as they pass by. Usually the dolphins are infinitely patient with humans, especially children, but this little girl has exceeded their limits. As she chases after Sicklefin, one of the males who can be quite aggressive, he turns around, beak open, and chases *her* out of the water.

Sicklefin, who has been coming into the beach only in the last couple of years, has added a new element to the dolphin-human encounters. Before, when the crew was all female, such acts of aggression were rare. The males, though, bring a more boisterous, mischievous quality, and they remind the humans that these dolphins are *wild,* not trained circus animals, and they can be just as unpredictable as humans in their behaviour.

For the most part, though, the dolphins are extraordinarily gentle and loving. Besides allowing us to touch them, they are constantly radiating love. I can see the effects on the people who are in the water. Their faces glow. They smile and laugh delightedly when the dolphins pass by close enough for them to touch. Their eyes fill with wonder when a dolphin parks next to them and patiently waits while they stroke its sleek, warm side. The dolphins always seem to be on their best behaviour.

As I look down the line of people standing in the chilly ocean water, I realise that the humans, too, are on their best behaviour. People reach out ever so gently to touch the dolphins. The gracefulness that I see in the dolphins is most deeply imprinted on those humans who have spent a long time around them.

The ranger Sharon stands for hours in her rubber overalls and boots, watching over the dolphins. When they come near, she never moves towards them, hands greedily outstretched like many of the new people. In fact, she rarely touches them at all, but the dolphins gravitate to her, bringing bits of seaweed—small gifts and an invitation to play. She picks up the long strands that they leave floating next to her and stretches them between her hands. The dolphins gently clamp their beaks on the seaweed and sink back into the water. Sometimes they repeat the game over and over again, taking the seaweed and then dropping it to float next to Sharon. All of the movements are slow and graceful, like a T'ai Chi version of catch.

Debbie, too, has an ingrown gentleness around the dolphins. Her arms and hands move with the grace of a ballet dancer when she reaches down to stroke one as it glides past. The dolphins know her well and often one will 'park' next to her. Debbie slowly leans down and places her hands on its side, not stroking, just hold-ing quietly. It leans its back against her leg and rests peacefully for a minute or two before returning to its rounds, gliding back and forth in front of the knees of the other visitors. "It's like having 'safe spots'," says Debbie when our eyes meet. "They pick out people they know and stay beside them for a few minutes. They know they can rest without worrying about how that person is going to treat them. Then they go back out among the new people."

"How long does it take for them to get to know people?" I ask longingly. Each day I come down to the beach hoping that the dolphins will do something special just for me. I've been hearing stories about them healing people of different ail-ments (especially mental and emotional disorders), following people along the shore, swimming with them in the water. Even though I know it's ridiculous, I feel jealous when they pay special attention to other people.

"Usually about as long as it takes *you* to know *them.*"

"You can name all of the dolphins who come in?"

"Sure. After a while you can tell them by their markings. They have their own personalities, too."

"Why is it that they seem to love certain people and stay away from others?"

Debbie shakes her head. "It's hard to know. For the first couple of years I was here, I took it really personally if the dolphins didn't pay attention to me. I felt really rejected. But I began to realise that if I was upset or feeling down, they wouldn't come near me; they only came if I was feeling centred, aligned. Since I realised that, I always sit back there," she says, nodding at the sandy beach, "and centre myself before I get in the water. That's helped a lot. And now I don't take it so much to heart if they don't play with me."

"Hmmmm . . . that's just what Guboo says, to take time before going in the water. You know, I've noticed the dolphins just cruise by in the afternoon, they stay an arm's length away from everyone. Do you think they get tired of being touched?"

"Probably," says Debbie nodding her head. "I suppose it's like humans. You know how you feel when you've been touched too long and you want your own space? That's probably how they feel, too."

I stop to talk with some of the people from the Dreaming Camp, too. There *are* some gems among the crowd, a few whom I misjudged completely at the beginning. We walk back towards camp in the mid-day heat—my pale, freckled skin can only take so much sun.

We stand in the shady alley between two parked vans eating lunch, talking, relaxing. After a couple of days filled with visitors, Guboo has turned the flap of his verandah around to face the back, away from the parking area, so that he has a bit more privacy. Like the camp at Nanga Mill, the days are mostly ours to create. Today Guboo plans on leading a silent walk over the dunes to a hill that is supposed to be a powerful spot, the intersection of several leylines (energy meridians that usually run in straight lines over the land).

"Judith," says the woman next to me, pausing to clear her throat. "I want to ask you something, and I'm not sure exactly how to say it. It's about Guboo . . . ."

"Um-hum?"

"Well, this is hard to say, but I'm wondering, well, when he kissed me after the Humming Bee, we were just standing around talking, and he, uh . . . ."

"French-kissed you, right?" I finish for her.

"Well, uh, yes. Does he do that all the time?"

"Mostly with white women. I don't think he'd dare do it with an aboriginal woman."

Colleen rolls her eyes. "An aboriginal woman would just laugh at him and walk away."

"Oh," says the woman, relieved. "I thought, well, maybe I'd done something to suggest . . . ."

"You know, it's funny, isn't it, that as women we always take it on that *we've* done something wrong. When Guboo started coming on to me in the last camp, I kind of played along nicely until he got the idea that I wasn't interested. I wondered afterwards why I didn't just tell him to piss off and leave me alone."

"Yeah, I guess it's like we're trained to think we're guilty, that we did something wrong." She pauses for a moment, kneading her hands. "I guess it's kind of silly when I look at it that way."

"We've been thinking for a while about talking with Guboo, just the women. A couple of men have talked with him, but he mostly ignores them. 'Well, it takes two,' he says. But, you know, I think *we* need to talk to him, not wait for the men to do it for us. And maybe he'd listen more if it was in a group, instead of just one woman at a time. Do you want to be part of a group that talks with him?"

"No, I really don't think it would be appropriate for me; I'm writing an article about the Dreaming Camp and I'm afraid Guboo would think I was going to write something terrible. He might not talk as freely with me."

"How about you, Colleen?"

"Yeah, we've been talking and talking about doing it. I think it's about time we did."

"Well, let's pass the word around among the women and see who wants to join us. How about tomorrow morning?"

"Good. After the Humming Bee? We could meet together first, and then ask him to join us."

The word spreads among the women, and the next morning seven of us meet in the sand dunes just outside of camp. We attune together, quietly holding hands in a circle, and then Colleen leads us in a power exercise that involves movement and a deep sound from the belly. "I think it's real important that we're in our power for this meeting with Guboo. And this exercise is good to do every morning."

We're all a bit nervous. Guboo can be a formidable person when he's challenged. We discuss the best way to approach the meeting and finally decide to simply go around the circle and have each woman tell her story and express her concerns. Arguing or confronting probably won't get us very far, but telling our stories, from the heart, might.

Colleen leaves the circle to ask Guboo to join us. He follows slowly and crouches down in the circle, arms tightly crossed. His eyes are hidden behind reflector sunglasses.

Colleen explains the purpose of the meeting simply and respectfully, and then we begin around the circle, recounting our stories with Guboo. Initially he denies everything. "I didn't do *that*," he says, pouting and setting his jaw when I tell him how disappointed I was when he asked me to sleep with him within 15 minutes of arriving in camp. When I mention how he has asked so many women (and *only* women) to be his 'secretary', he protests, "But I have to have *somebody* go with me. And *you've* got a boyfriend." I want to say, "And *you* have a *wife*", but I restrain myself. "That's not the point, Guboo. I don't want to argue with you. I'm just wondering if you would act this way with aboriginal women."

Guboo doesn't answer. As we move around the circle, the stories become more poignant, the words softer. The women speak from a great caring for Guboo, not anger. It is this, not my righteous anger, that reaches Guboo. He sits silently, face stiff, listening to these women, but he doesn't argue.

"Is that all you have to say?" Guboo asks finally. We look around the circle and then nod at each other. "That's all," says Colleen. "Is there anything you want to say to us, Guboo?"

"What can I say?" he asks, digging his thumbs under his arms. "You all talk to me this way, what do you expect me to say?" He pushes back on his heels, stands up and stalks back to the camp.

We sit quietly, stirring designs into the sand with our fingers. "You know," says Mary Anne, "I couldn't repeat this in front of Guboo, but I want to share it with you." She stops to wipe tears from her cheeks. "When I was in Guboo's tent the other night—I'd brought him some dinner—he asked if I wanted to sleep with him, and I told him no. He kept asking, and finally I said, 'Guboo, if you have sex with me when I don't want to, that's rape.' He got this really sick look on his face, and he said . . . ." Mary Anne stops, her voice faltering as sobs push from her chest. "He

227

said," she gasps, "'Don't you *want* to be raped?'" Her face crumples, and her sobs come freely. The woman next to her wraps an arm around her shoulder and draws Mary Anne into her arms.

An ancient anger wells inside me. How long have women endured such repulsive requests? And how long have men been so cock-assed sure that they could pressure women to satisfy their over-sexed needs? I am repulsed by Guboo's comment —assuming that he did make it—and shocked that Mary Anne would quietly accept it. So much to heal, so many ancient wrongs to right, before men and women can ever even really see each other again. Both women and men have so many roles to unlearn before we can meet as equals, as brother and sister instead of as pimp and prostitute. And the 'spiritual' community certainly is not immune to the disease.

"Colleen," says Verna when the sobs have died away, "that was a really powerful exercise. You suggested it's good to do in the morning. How about if we meet every morning after the Humming Bee?"

"And maybe people have other things to offer," adds Nicki.

"I know some chants and different exercises," I say, "and I bet there are other women in camp who have things to share."

"We've been talking about having a women's circle in the camps," says Colleen, adding a swirl to the design she is shaping in the sand. She looks up at us. "Maybe it's time to start one. Guboo can't really teach us any of the women's knowledge, and we can't just wait for him or one of the men to organise it."

"Well, let's pass the word around camp," says Kree. "We start tomorrow morning, after the Humming Bee, right?"

The nervous agitation that filled the circle earlier in the morning is gone. Instead, I feel excitement and a defiant sense of empowerment flowing through us. "You know," I comment, "if talking with Guboo did nothing besides bring us together to start a women's circle, I think it's worth it."

For a few more minutes we linger in the sand, savouring our sense of kinship. Finally we hold hands once again for a few moments of silence to end the circle. Slowly we leave and scatter through the camp and onto the beach, passing the word among the women.

I leave for a walk along the beach, to be alone for a while. Confronting Guboo —and I have to admit to myself that it was a confrontation, even if we tried to do it with love—was not easy for me. In fact, my craving for harmony in my relationships with people is so great that I usually go out of my way to 'fix things up' after a disagreement. Isn't that woman's eternal role, the peacemaker? Internally I am torn between feeling I was right to own my truth and being angry with myself for speaking from anger. That's what hurts most, admitting that I wanted to speak from the heart, but instead covered my nervousness and fear with anger. How often I have seen myself and others do the same. But I should know better by now. And I ought to love myself enough to be able to forgive the mistake. On top of the anger, I batter myself for not loving myself enough. I stomp along the beach, repeating "I, Judith, love and approve of myself." But in the moment it's a lie, and the affirmation doesn't do a damn bit of good.

By the end of the afternoon I have worked myself into a state of deep depression. How can I ever offer myself to do *anything* if I am so imperfect? I talk myself into believing that I am a total fraud. I want to teach and work as a medicine person —who the hell am I kidding? My actions have missed my mark so badly that I cannot bear to evaluate them. I have become an outcast to myself, but no matter how small I crush myself, I cannot escape. Tears flow, but they don't flush away the bitterness. Pounding my fist into the sand dunes does nothing to expend the fury.

Finally, unable to escape the internal pain, I resolve to walk along the beach until the inner storm passes.

Less than a mile down the beach I see Colleen sitting above me in a valley between two sand dunes. "Colleen," I call, "can I talk with you for a bit?" I know I have reached a point inside myself where I have gone as far as I can go alone. I have descended into a chasm too deep to climb out of unaided. In this moment I side-step my usual pattern of 'I'm hurt, leave me alone, I'll fix it myself'. As much as I would like to hide my pain and anger, I know I cannot without destroying myself further.

"Sure. Come on up." Colleen moves over to the top of the dune and smoothes a patch for both of us to sit down. When I tell her what's been going on inside, she listens quietly and then turns away to look across the sea.

"Judith, I think we did the right thing. I'm not worried about what Guboo thinks."

"Hmmm . . . earlier this afternoon I went over to where he was talking to some people, and he wouldn't look at me. Even when I asked him how he was, he ignored me."

"Yeah," says Colleen, "he's not talking to any of us. I guess he's decided we're *bad women*." She laughs. "If he wants to pout, that's his problem. And, Judith, I think you've got a lot to offer the camp."

I look down, digging my toes in the sand, unconvinced. "Really. I wouldn't say that unless I meant it. I think we're too hard on ourselves sometimes. You've just got to get on with doing what you can do. And you've got a lot to offer."

I sniff and wipe my nose, maybe half convinced. But the turning point has come —from here I begin to climb. David's words come to mind, "When you *think* you're strong, you're really at your weakest. When you think you're weak, you're really at your strongest." Well, by that measurement, I must be reaching bionic standards.

When I walk back to camp, one of the women whom we met in Margaret River approaches me. "You said you know the Sacred Dances?" she asks.

"Well, I know the basic ones that we do at the Findhorn Foundation."

"Would you be able to teach them? I've got the tape with the music, but I can't remember the steps."

"Uh, well . . . ." I pause for a moment, fumbling for a foothold on my shattered self-esteem. "If people are interested, I would be happy to teach some dances."

"Great!" she says, smiling. "How about tomorrow morning?"

"OK . . . after the women's circle. How about 10:30?"

The next morning about twenty women and girls gather in the same sandy circle where we met the day before. This morning, and for the rest of the week, we sing, meditate and dance together, celebrating the power of woman. Colleen and I make a loose structure with plenty of free space for women to add their own gifts, and usually each day someone new jumps in with the perfect addition for that moment.

By the end of the week, almost every woman in camp comes to the circle, and some of the men try as well. Gently we turn the men away, explaining that the circle is a woman-only space. Reverse discrimination, perhaps, but how else can women maintain a space for themselves? Some of the men sit by the fire, as close as they can be to the circle without leaving camp, uneasy with our show of strength.

One morning someone suggests we organise a circle for the men. "I think they feel really left out," she explains.

"If they want to have a circle, let them organise it themselves," I say. "They don't need anyone's permission." Another ancient pattern—women taking care of the poor, inept males who can't take care of themselves. I'm not falling for it this time.

Later in the morning we gather again for Sacred Dance—this time along with the men. I have watched people teach the dances so many times that the demonstrations come effortlessly. I thrive on the dances—they uncork a well of joy in me that few other things touch. That joy must come through in the teaching, because people are eager for more. Sacred Dance becomes a daily part of the camp routine.

Through the week, the women's sessions lengthen and build in strength. Judith, a woman from Adelaide, leads a strong meditation one morning to connect with the power of the womb. Afterwards, Colleen shares a vision she had during the meditation of the Rainbow Serpent, ". . . which is female to me, and She was curled around our circle, surrounded by lots of babies. I got the sense that She was saying that each of us was like one of those baby snakes, and we should take the power of this women's circle with us and start new circles wherever we go, moving like the babies, planting seeds. It was a really powerful image." An involuntary shudder shakes her shoulders.

The last morning of the camp, the women's circle needs every gram of accumulated strength to contain the rage and pain that has surfaced in some of the women. The night before, despite a strict rule that no drinking or drugs are allowed in the Dreaming Camp, three drunken men staying in the caravan park joined the circle around the fire. Because they didn't have any open cans of beer with them, they argued that they *weren't* bringing booze into the camp, and parked themselves in front of the oil drum, refusing to budge. I left the campfire soon after, but for the women who stayed, their powerlessness to make the drunken, verbally abusive men move brought up a lot of past traumas.

Unaware of what had occurred after I left the campfire, the next morning I lead an exercise working with yin and yang power. My partner in the exercise can't bring herself to stand in the open, receptive yin position. Each time we repeat the movement, her arms swing inward instead of opening outward. When I reach out and gently guide her arms into the open position, she begins to sob. *"No, I can't,"* she gasps.

Colleen, too, has tears in her eyes. "OK," I say to the group, "it looks like we need to sit down and talk a bit. I think some women need our support." We sit down in the sand and place one woman in the centre. Her cries and sobs rip through the camp. "All right, Creator, you'll have to guide me on this one," I pray internally. I know that simply talking won't help—this woman has gone beyond the ability to verbalise anything. She lies curled in a foetal position on the ground, eyes closed, her hands clenched in fists under her chin.

On a strong intuitive flash, I ask the women to form a circle and place their hands around her, like a womb. When the sobs quiet, I ask if she is ready to be birthed. "Yes," she says shakily. Slowly and gently we unfold her limbs, singing a birthing chant as we move her from a tightly closed foetal position to a relaxed open one, lying stretched on her back. Her face and body are transformed, freed of the earlier pain.

When she finally opens her eyes, they are filled with wonder. She sits up slowly and rejoins the circle. I can tell that some of the women are uneasy about the strong emotions running through the group. A couple of them get up and leave the circle, obviously upset. I was aware that not everyone felt included in the impromptu healing session, but I couldn't split my attention between supporting the woman in the centre and holding the group together—and Colleen, my usual anchor in the group, is involved with her own distress.

"Does anyone want to share anything?" I ask. "I can tell there's a lot going on with people . . . ."

"I do," says Colleen, her voice shaky. I have never seen her cry before, so I know that something has disturbed her deeply. "It's about those men who were here last night. It brought up all kinds of things for me. I was really pissed off because it's like the same situation with all aboriginal people. When I was growing up, even though it was *our* house, white men thought they had the right to come whenever they wanted to. And here it's the same. We don't have any way of telling them to get out of the Dreaming Camp . . . ." The women in the circle nod, suddenly connecting with why she is so distressed. "It's not 'our property' here, so we don't have a right to tell them to move. And they say the same thing to aboriginal people all the time—'It's not your land, not your property.' And we're powerless to make them get out."

Verna raises her arm. "Look," she declares, "I'm sorry, but I've got to go. I can see colours swirling around the circle, and the energy's just getting to be too much for me. So don't take it personally, but I'm going."

The group is on the verge of disintegrating, and I suddenly realise that this morning, for the first time, we didn't do any kind of opening exercise—we never consciously grounded ourselves or created the boundaries of our circle. No wonder all kinds of energies and emotions are flying about.

We begin a Taoist breath exercise, breathing the power of the Earth up through our bodies, out to the world, opening our arms to receive, then grounding the energy once again. With our bodies energised and grounded this way, we sing a song of celebration for each woman in the circle, "Oh, Colleen (or another woman's name), Celebrate Colleen, Celebrate Colleen with an open heart . . . ."

To end the circle, we do a modified version of a Sufi dance, "May the blessings of Goddess (rather than God) rest upon you . . . ." We change partners until we have sung and danced and blessed each woman.

For the most part the storm has passed, and we sit contentedly together on the sand. "I want to acknowledge everyone for making it through this morning," I say. "It's easy to be part of a group or community when everything is happy and going smoothly. But to me it's a sign of a group's strength when it can support people through difficult times. That's when the real work in community happens. And we did it without running away."

One of the women looks up. "You know, I never thought about it that way. I was feeling like something really terrible happened this morning, but when you said that, I realised that this *is* a part of community. It's important to deal with people's distress, and I've always run away from it in the past. In fact, I almost left this morning, but now I'm glad I didn't."

Silent nods. "Thank you, Judith. And thank you Colleen, for organising the circles during the camp."

I look up, surprised. Without planning it, I realise we have been the major guides for the circles. Without saying much directly, we have been holding the energy of the circle between us. I get up to hug Colleen, and the women clasp their arms around us, forming a group hug to acknowledge our work. Tears well and overflow onto my cheeks—I am touched by people's genuine appreciation, even more so because it is so unexpected. Colleen's face, too, is streaked with tears when we slowly pull away.

As I step back, a sudden movement catches my eye—I look down in time to see a baby snake, about three inches long, burrowing into the soft sand. I stand for a moment staring, unable to speak. Immediately Colleen's vision comes to mind. "Colleen," I whisper, "did you see that?"

"What?" she asks.

"A . . . a baby snake. It just went into the ground, right at our feet."

Her eyes open wide. "Shit," she says, stuffing her hands in her pockets. "That's the kind of thing aboriginal people get scared about."

"What do you mean, 'scared'?"

"Well, maybe it's superstitious, but they don't like messing around with spirits. They *know* they're powerful."

For the next half hour we move among each other, hugging and saying goodbye, wishing each other well on our journeys away from Monkey Mia. Colleen is still talking with someone when I finish, so I go across the circle to where her clapping sticks are lying, wanting to take them to her so that she doesn't forget them. As I reach down to pick them up, a wisp of smoke rises from the sticks.

I pull my hand back, unsure whether I saw what I saw. Did I perhaps just disturb some sand with my feet? I push my foot to the side. Nothing happens. Uh-oh, I think the spirits are talking again. Quickly I pick up the sticks and place them at Colleen's feet while she continues to talk, and then I leave the circle.

Later in the afternoon, as I am gathering my things to go to the beach, Colleen makes her way across the sand to my tent, followed by Mary Anne and Kree and Verna and Nicki and Theresa—all of the women who were the nucleus for the women's circle. "Now, hold on a minute," says Colleen laughing. "We have something to give you." She holds out an envelope for me to open.

I'm completely void of words. I open the card, hand-decorated by Kree, and read the messages of thanks inside. Tears flow again—tears of gratitude for these women, for their strength, for their caring. How could they ever know, after all my self-doubts earlier in the week, how much this means to me? I reach out my arms to hug each one and find myself in the centre of a hug instead.

When I tuck the card inside the envelope and slip it inside my towel, ready to make a quick exit, Colleen puts her hand on my shoulder. "Oh, no you don't. You're not going to get away that easily."

"I don't know if I can take much more, Colleen. I'm not used to this."

"Well, you better get used to it," says Theresa. "I think it's going to be happening a lot more often."

"I still have something to give you, so just hold your horses," says Colleen, smiling. She reaches inside her deep pockets and pulls out her clapping sticks.

A chill runs up my spine and sends shivers through my shoulders. "Colleen, you've had those a long time . . . I know they're special to you. I can't take them."

"No, they're for you. I got a real strong hit earlier that I should give them to you."

I stare at her for a moment and then tell her what happened this morning when I bent down to pick them up. Again her eyes grow wide, and she draws in a sharp breath. "You take them. I'm sure they're for you," she says quickly.

I reach out to take the sticks, half expecting to see more smoke, but nothing happens. Gingerly, I take them in my hands and quickly deposit them in the tent.

We stand together for a group picture, all of us in a line. "Hey, there are *seven* of us," I comment, looking down the line.

"Seven," says Verna, "like the Seven Sisters." We look at each other and nod. "Seven Sisters . . . weren't they chased by some man across the desert until they ran into the sky?"

"I don't know, we'll have to look up the legend."

When the picture-taking is complete, I go down to the beach to spend some time with the dolphins. By now I know them all by name, and I am delighted at how many of them are in this afternoon. I feel full of love and gratitude, as if endless gifts are flowing in and through me. The dolphins must sense my joy—they play more than they ever have before. BB (Beautiful Baby) stays beside me for long periods of stroking. Snubnose parks next to me, belly pressed against my leg while I gently place my hands on his side. Even Sicklefin, the aggressive male, lets me touch him—long, gentle holds while he bobs in the water next to me. No stroking, though. I am wary of accidentally doing something that might upset him.

A few times he has come up behind me and hooked his tail around the back of my knee, mischievously pulling me off balance. Just that simple motion lets me know how much power the dolphins have in their tails. I've read that an angry dolphin can smack its tail against a shark hard enough to hit it out of the water. I've learned too, how strong and sharp their teeth are.

A couple of days ago, I played with Sicklefin, holding seaweed out for him to take. When the little girl beside me followed suit, her mother caught her arm. "Don't tease the dolphin that way," scolded the mother. "He'll think it's a fish."

I looked up for a moment and shook my head. I've come to the conclusion that the dolphins are fascinated by how much *humans* seem to love this game—they know perfectly well that the seaweed is not fish. It's a simple game they've developed that humans can play, too.

When Sicklefin dropped a piece of seaweed in the water, I assumed that he wanted me to pick it up. As I reached into the water, though, my hand moved into his blindspot. *Snap*, faster than I could follow the movement, he grabbed my hand in his beak, leaving a series of teeth marks ripped into my middle finger. I pulled my hand away quickly, shocked by the movement. The teeth were razor sharp, and I realised suddenly just how gentle these dolphins are *choosing* to be. Sicklefin stayed in front of me, awaiting my reaction. "That wasn't very nice," I said finally.

I didn't get out of the water, but the shock and the sting of the cuts in my hand left me feeling queasy. A couple of minutes later Sicklefin returned with another dolphin and rested his beak on my knee, looking up at me for a moment before swimming away. His movement seemed to be an apology, or at least a reassurance. I'm sure that he could sense my distress.

Today, though, Sicklefin is very loving. We play the seaweed game—carefully —and he even lets me place my hand on his side while he floats patiently next to me. I can feel the same grace flowing through my hands as I have seen in Sharon and Debbie, and I realise in that moment that the movements are graceful because they are inspired by *love*—my heart is bursting and the love overflows into my arms and hands, into the angle of my head and the bent of my legs. I am inspired to touch and hold and caress and play as I would a newfound lover or a newborn baby. It's like being in love, but not with anyone or anything in particular. It is love that loves through me, catalysed by the joyous, playful love that flows continuously through the dolphins.

The final gift comes a few minutes later when the new mother dolphin and her baby come streaking by. Usually the mother keeps the baby on her far side, away from the crowd of people, when she makes a pass along the beach. Like the mothers before her who have brought young ones into shore, she seems to be waiting until the dolphin is almost full grown before she allows people to stroke it. Babies acclimatised to humans too young have a tendency to be *over*-friendly and can become a nuisance.

Today the mother swims straight towards me, her baby gliding just behind her side fin, and only at the last moment do they part—just enough for the mother to press against the back of my legs and the baby to glide against the front as they pass. The simple movement fills me with wonder. I stand open-mouthed, like a child thrilled with the first discovery of a balloon or a flower or a butterfly. The world is almost intolerably beautiful.

The next morning the Dreaming Camp begins to disperse. Guboo had planned to stay an extra day to rest before moving on, but when other people decided to stay on, too, he changed his mind. The extra day would hardly be a day of rest if everyone stayed to be with him. Only David and one other person and I do not join the early morning packing. David and I plan to spend a few days here before heading north in hopes of joining Karen and Brad when they drive out to the desert.

The women gather for one final circle to enact our morning ritual—Colleen's power exercise. This time, though, we make our circle right in the middle of camp—very symbolic, we decide, for bringing our power out in the open. When we finish, there are tearful goodbyes as the women pile into cars and vans and trucks that roll across the shell-strewn driveway onto the dirt road.

Guboo has gone down to the beach for one last farewell to the dolphins. Despite all of the fanfare before the trip, Guboo has entered the water only once, and he never went through the ritual of calling in the dolphins that he talked about. The closest we came was a Humming Bee at dawn when about half the people from the Dreaming Camp went down to the beach, standing in a half circle that opened into the sea. In the middle of the humming, Snubnose swam unnoticed right to the mouth of the circle and quietly poked his head out. He stayed for a chorus of 'Love, love, love/ Love on Earth' before swimming away. Guboo wasn't there that morning, though—he was up on top of the hill, leading a Humming Bee there.

I follow Guboo down to the beach and sit next to him at one of the picnic tables. I've decided to try one last time to make peace with him before he leaves. At first he says little, obviously still bitter about our 'meeting' with him.

"Guboo, the reason I talked with you like that is because I care about you. You've talked about how Sun Bear is, and I don't want to see you doing the same thing."

After a couple of minutes his face softens into a smile. "I can't hold a grudge," he says finally. "I don't have it in me. Let's be friends." He offers me his hand to shake, gives me a quick hug and then sits back, his face suddenly drawn and tired. Usually his age never enters my mind, but in this moment I am fully aware of his eighty years.

Looking out at the sea, his forehead puckers and tears flow down his cheeks. "I love my people," he whispers. "I love my people. They mean so much to me. Some day I want to buy land, so my people have a place to go. That's important to me. That's important."

We sit for a few minutes, silent, looking at the sea. When I look over at his tear-streaked cheeks and touch his hand, I sense how lonely it must be for him to have such a love for the aboriginal people and to have a vision of being a bridge with the white European culture as well. In this moment I see him as a lonely old man with a huge dream to fulfil—the Awakening of the Dreamtime among all the people of Australia.

CHAPTER 12
Martu Dreaming

Although David and I thought we were coming into the desert to work with kids forming a band, just before leaving Port Hedland Brad mentions that he has talked with the Martujarra people about David making a video of the Rudall River National Park where they live and the Martu's reaction to the proposed uranium mine within the Park. "Might as well make use of your skills while you're out here," he says, nodding to David. "You'll have to present yourself to the people and explain what you can do, and they'll make the final decision. But I've been talking with them over the radio, and they're expecting you to come out. You brought your video gear, right?"

Back in Fremantle we had talked about how offensive cameras would be in a traditional camp, so the change in plan surprises me.

"Uh, well, yes I did," says David. "I almost sent it on with someone else. I didn't think it would be appropriate to show up with a camera, you know, like we talked about . . . ."

"Well, good thing you brought it," says Brad, slamming the car door. "You're probably gonna need it."

David and I sit in the back of the new four-wheel-drive Toyota that Brad picked up in Perth for the desert camp at Punmu, looking at each other with raised eyebrows. We expected a couple of quiet weeks, not a filming trip.

"OK," says David. "I do the video, you take the photographs, right?"

"Did he talk with you about this earlier?"

"Nope," says David, pressing his lower lip between his teeth and shaking his head. "This is the first I've heard about it."

A couple of hours later we stop at the last petrol station before the turn-off from the bitumen road. From here the Toyota and the fully loaded semi-truck, crammed

235

with groceries and petrol and windmill parts for the desert camp, will cover 850 kilometres on a pair of tyre tracks that run more or less east across the desert. Brad drives the semi-truck and Karen follows behind with the Toyota.

Three aboriginal men who live out in the desert camp—Razorblade, Desmond and another man—ride on top of the truck. Alcohol is strictly forbidden in the camps, a rule self-imposed by the Martu, so the men are getting their fill on the way back. They periodically toss drained beer cans along the side of the road. Karen cringes every time she sees a can arcing from the back of the truck.

"I hate that," says Karen, eyes focused on the road ahead. "You know, they're used to just dropping their garbage in the desert. In the old days, it didn't matter—everything decomposed. Now garbage doesn't disappear, but the habit is too engrained.

"Can you say anything?" I ask.

Karen shakes her head. "No, it's not my place," she says simply.

After dark we stop by the side of the track and gather fallen wood from the dry, spiny shrubs. Soon small fires flicker in the open desert, and shafts of light illuminate the surrounding trees. I sit wrapped in my sleeping bag, the winter night threatening frost by morning. I look up as Razorblade comes to join our campfire.

"White man don't care about me." Razorblade sits staring at the campfire, the orange light reflecting on his smooth, black forehead. David and I sit quietly listening to the story. He begins slowly, pauses to shake his head and then gathers momentum, the words cascading like sand from an outstretched hand. "He take this land, pollute the water with uranium and I die. I drink the water and I die. I eat the animals that drink that water and I die. This is my land. I belong to this land. If this land goes, I die. I got nowhere else to go, this my *home*. I die, and *he* don't care."

The old man before us speaks strongly, with a directness native to the desert people. Emboldened by beer, he tells the tale again.

Drinking uncorks the best and the worst in these people. Tonight it has opened the deep well of sadness about the destruction of their land.

"That's why we're here," says David quietly. "We're trying to do something so that white people *will* listen."

"Maybe you fellas trying to help," says Razorblade. "Yeah, you all right. But most white folks, they don't even know we alive. They don't care about us. Just want to kill our land, and us too."

The words hit me hard. I'm part of that white culture that has done so much damage to these people, and yet I have no desire to see the destruction continue, of either the land or the people who have learned to live in this hard desert climate. With all my heart I hope that we really can do something to help—and with David's skills in making videos, perhaps we can.

When Razorblade gets up to join the other sleeping men, we throw a log on the fire and slide into our sleeping bags under the wide open desert sky.

In the morning we pile into the vehicles and continue across the desert, pushing to reach the camp by sunset. The 'desert' is nothing like I expected. Tall eucalyptus trees, their white bark brilliant under the intense sun, grow throughout the area. Mulga bushes are in bloom, their yellow blossoms cascading in plumes from the branches. The winter rains have catalysed an explosion of wildflowers—in the distance we see patches of purple and yellow and blue. Camels lope along the road (they love to make dust wallows in the sandy patches of the road—great for them but treacherous for unsuspecting vehicles). Originally introduced by middle-eastern immigrants for transport and then left to go wild, the camels have adapted well to the Central Desert. In fact, Australia has the largest healthy herd of wild camels in the world.

Dingoes, also an exotic, though of a much earlier vintage, trot among the dunes. They were probably introduced to Australia by Asian visitors about 2,000 years ago. Kangaroos bounce among the mulga bushes. 'Bustards', bush turkeys, strut on the sandy red earth. The desert is bursting with life. And everywhere, eternally, are the flies—dive bombing eyes, ears, nose, open mouth, any available bodily orifice that they can manoeuvre themselves into. The only way to avoid them is to keep moving, squint the eyes and cover the ears. I know now why most desert aboriginal people wear hats, summer and winter.

This area is part of the land traditionally walked and hunted by the Martujarra. 'Martu' is their word for 'people'. Today the Martujarra and other people who 'belong' to the Central and Western Desert (they talk about belonging *to the desert* instead of the desert belonging to them) are moving away from the cities to re-establish 'camps' in their traditional lands.

About thirty years ago many aboriginal people left the desert to move to urban areas, often drawn by a longing to be with family who had moved there. Such bonds are powerful enough to draw an entire race of proud people into shanty towns on the edges of burgeoning cities. Family was not the only draw, though. Subsistence living in the desert is gruelling work, and the relative ease of a money-based economy fuelled by government hand-outs was appealing. The result, however, was appalling. Uprooted from a culture whose strength is a deep sense of place, whose essence is a bonding with the fabric of the land, the fragmented family groups sank into hopelessness and despair. Alcohol eased the immediate pain but atrophied any long-term solution to the dislocation.

Over the last twenty years the Martu have returned to their traditional lands to re-establish their culture on their own terms. In the Western Desert, much of the success of this movement is a direct result of the work of Don MacLeod. For the last fifty years MacLeod has been lobbying and, moreover, acting in behalf of the aboriginal people. His account of the treatment of aboriginal people by white European settlers in Western Australia, *How the West was Lost* (now a major film as well as a book), includes a history of the legislation passed—and then ignored—by the British and Australian authorities, as well as firsthand accounts of his work with the people of the Western Desert. The setting up of 'desert camps' was, in large part, his idea. It was MacLeod who originally inspired Karen and Brad to work in the desert.

The People return to the desert with new eyes. Far from a nostalgic re-enactment of their nomadic life, they bring elements of European culture that soften the hard edge of desert suvival, like four-wheel-drive trucks and solar panels to generate electricity for lights. Aboriginal people are pragmatic and not at all romantic about the challenges of surviving the harsh desert climate. If a certain technology makes life easier, they use it.

Moving into an aboriginal culture, I enter as a child. The community has so many unspoken agreements about behaviour and such a different way of perceiving the world. They look at a visitor like me as a well-meaning person 'who hasn't been grown up properly'. Adult-children are a bit more embarrassing than ordinary children because they usually take longer to learn and the weight of age makes toe-treading more conspicuous. Simple things, like waiting at the edge of camp and asking to use the watertap before walking through the camp or not joining an all-men's circle uninvited—all of these things so blatantly obvious to these people are new territory for me. I have to rely more on my intuition, trusting when I have a sense that something would be offensive.

'Please' and 'thank you' do not exist in this culture. Courtesy is expressed on an action level, not through words. If I want to welcome you into camp, I bring wood and build a fire. I do not spend energy on flowery 'Oh, how wonderful to see you's especially since 'hello' and 'goodbye' do not exist, either. The Dreamtime, the essence of aboriginal culture, is an endless weaving of past, present and future. "I came out of the Dreamtime, and I will return to the Dreamtime." I never really go away. So why should I bother with dates and linger over goodbyes? Once the Dreamtime has taken hold, I am drawn back endlessly in mind and body, pulled by an irresistible, timeless force. I am part of the desert, and the desert is part of me.

These people are deeply intuitive and have a whole-being sensing different from that of any European people I have experienced. As is true with most traditional cultures, learning stems from observation. I feel childlike in my ability to keep my mouth shut and learn to understand without directly being told how to do something. These people watch my actions and pay little attention to what I say, so different from the culture in which I have grown used to buffering situations with words. I realise how many Western people spend their lives 'intending' things and how rarely these intentions are actualised. The Martu are accustomed to few words and much action. They do not understand white people who come with 'good intentions' who never actually produce anything.

We arrive at Punmu just after dark. Our first stop is to see Ditch, who lives with his extended family next to the airstrip, about a mile from the rest of the camp. He is the 'boss man', the elder of the community, and any new visitor *must* stop to see him before entering the central area. He gives initial clearance; in the morning we will meet with the 'council' for final approval.

In the darkness I can make out only the outlines of people's homes in the camp, illuminated by the campfires burning at the mouth of the 'houses'. Actually, most of the homes are what the government calls 'transition housing', something in between a shelter and a hut intended to 'teach people how to live in a house'. I can't imagine what relationship they were imagining between the corrugated iron sheets bent into a tunnel-like shack and a house with four walls and a door and windows. And the metal must get intolerably hot in the summer when the temperatures rise to 50 or 60°C (over 150°F).

Children come running to the truck, and the old men and women make their way slowly across the camp, many of them carrying babies on their hips. "We been gettin' *hungry*," says one of the men who comes to talk with Brad. "Ran out of flour a couple of days ago."

"We-e-ell, you can have big mob feast tomorrow. Lots of tucker in the back," says Brad. David and I get out of the truck and stand quietly nearby. "Don't expect anyone to say much," warns Karen. "They've got no reason to. You don't have any role here . . . and you're not part of a family group, so they don't really know how to relate to you."

"Are they going to have a party to welcome you back to the community?" asks David. Although Karen has been studying in Fremantle for the last couple of years, she comes out during most holidays.

Karen shakes her head. "Blackfellas don't make much of it; they don't even really bother to say 'hello' or 'goodbye'. I like it; even when they see family they haven't met up with for a long time, they just walk up to each other and start where they left off. Saves a lot of energy."

Brad and Karen, David and I drive to a small building about a quarter of a mile from the centre of camp. This is where all of the 'support people', hired by a government organisation called the Western Desert Land Council, stay. In the last year they have hired Brad, so for the first time in ten years he is receiving some pay for his work. The building is placed a little distance away from the camp so that the Martu can go about their daily life undisturbed but close enough that they are free to walk over any time to visit. And they do, quite often.

Already when we arrive a group of men is sitting in the kitchen, talking with Brad's co-worker. Also in the kitchen are two women who are collecting stories from the Martu women about the Canning Stock Route as part of an Australian Bicentennial history grant. After a quick dinner, David and I move our bags into one of the bedrooms and unroll our sleeping bags. I am looking forward to a day of rest tomorrow after the long drive over sandy, bumpy tracks.

Next morning we get up soon after dawn, enjoying the small corridor of time before the flies get warm enough to begin their dive-bombing missions for the day. Around mid-morning, while we are sipping tea, Brad comes into the kitchen and tells us the people want to meet with us now. They are waiting up near the school-house.

In a few minutes we are sitting in a sandy hollow littered with cigarette butts. Flea-bitten camp dogs track around the circle, gently sniffing us before they settle into the sand. One stays next to me, belly up, eager to have her stomach scratched. We wait while the men assemble in a loose circle with the women scattered some distance back around the edges.

I glance quickly around the circle. Why are none of the women joining the inner circle? I know that within aboriginal culture men's and women's sacred 'business' is strictly divided. For thousands of years this division was honoured in a way that recognised the strength of each sex, a 'separate but equal' policy for the most part. Men of the highest initiatory status sometimes joined the women's circle, and similarly women of high degree occasionally joined the men's circles. I thought, though, that this meeting was 'community' business.

David and I describe the skills we have to offer in making a video, and David passes around some of the publications that he thinks might be helpful to 'get the word out' about what is happening here in Rudall River. Shortly after we finish, three men stalk into the circle, obviously in a hurry—a mining company representative and his hired help, an anthropologist and an archaeologist.

The 'Uranus' mining company rep unveils a series of photographs (complete with two token aboriginal workers prominent in the display) to explain how the company goes about testing to find deposits of '. . . gold, copper, silver, uranium, coal and diamonds'. Who is he kidding? With a name like 'Uranus', everyone knows they are testing for uranium. After a major uranium strike by CRA, a multinational mining company based in South Africa, others have secured exploration leases in and around the Rudall River National Park in hopes of finding more uranium. In fact, the company officials seem confident that the Western Australian government will gladly, even eagerly, approve full mining operations. Certainly the CRA 'exploration' camp has taken on an air of permanence, complete with two swimming pools and a staff of around 100.

This phenomenon of foreign multinationals finding a warm welcome in Australia strikes me as odd. Why is Australia so eager to have its natural resources exploited by outsiders? Even harder to understand is why the idea is even entertained in the Rudall River area which became a National Park in 1977. I begin to realise that in Australia the designation 'national park' guarantees nothing in terms of protection.

How can the Australian government argue that these developments support 'progress'? Whose progress? Certainly not that of Australians, white or aboriginal. South Africa, Germany and Japan, to name a few, will reap great benefits from the ravage of the land, but Australians will be left with a denuded, poisoned, irradiated landscape to call 'home'.

Uranus, an exploration company jointly owned by a Japanese and a German firm, is ready to explore a tract of land that overlaps the northwestern territory of the Rudall River National Park. To their credit this company is asking the aboriginal people to identify sacred sites to be avoided before they begin work. CRA never extended such a courtesy to the traditional inhabitants of the area.

During the presentation I turn to Karen and whisper, "Why can't these people just say '*No!*' to the mining company and ask them to get the hell out of here?"

"They don't have any land rights," says Karen, bristling with irritation, "no recognition by the government that this is their traditional land. They have no right to ask these people to leave." I swallow, my mouth dry with bitterness as I watch the exploration company enact this drama. This same company learned its lesson about including traditional people a couple of years ago when they started mining in the Northern Territory without consulting the local aboriginal population. The people organised a successful roadblock that stopped their operation. Presentations like these maintain a 'nice guy' profile that pays off for their own publicity and, to some extent, safeguards them from protests by the traditional people.

The company rep invites Ditch, the Elder of the community, to choose three men to bring with him in the company's six-seater plane. Ditch chooses his men and also insists that David and I come along to film the trip, an unexpected request that the company, in its attempts to be completely open and honest about its operations, cannot easily refuse. The rep, arms crossed and knees locked, considers for a moment and then curtly nods his head. "Yes, they can come."

Within an hour we are bumping along the rutted dirt road to the community's 'airstrip', a cleared, smoothed patch of sandy desert earth. So much for a day of rest. Up in the air I have an eagle's-eye view of the Martujarra homeland. The sand dunes undulate like shore-bound ocean waves across the desert, and the Rudall River snakes among them, usurping their regularity with its wandering, sinuous curves. Ditch points with pursed lips and then his finger. "There," he says, "that's what the white folks call the Rudall River." He tells me the Martujarra name for it, and I try to wrap my mouth around the unfamiliar sounds. Ditch smiles and nods.

I return my gaze to the desert below and detect a new pattern. Lines are cut into the land, some ploughing over a dune and ending without apparent destination. Later, driving over some of these tracks, I realise they were blazed by mining companies to test likely land formations for mineral deposits. They violate agreements the mining companies made to minimise the impact of road-building in the national park. The skin of the desert is fragile and slow to heal—such scars are deeply etched and long remembered on the face of the land.

After the plane lands I sit in the back of a pick-up truck in the withering mid-day sun awaiting the arrival of the plane's second shuttle. In the back of the truck is a cooler filled with drinks and food. These mining companies lack no comforts in the bush.

A helicopter and pilot wait nearby, hired for three days to facilitate aerial identification of sites, much faster than following the rocky, thinly etched tracks in four-wheel drives, though both methods are employed. During the three-day stint the chubby archaeologist engineers the seat allocations so there is never space for me in the helicopter. I soon discover that a woman is extra baggage in a mining camp.

Soon after David boards the helicopter to join Ditch and the archaeologist in some initial surveying, one of the company officials glances at me, scuffs his boot into the sand so that his hip juts at an officious angle and casually declares, "You can go back to camp now with Sam. He needs help cooking dinner."

I freeze in disbelief, suddenly acutely aware of my position as the only woman among 15 men. After a moment's pause I stare back. "It just so happens that I am a good cook, but I find that a very chauvinistic statement."

"Well, that's the way it is out here," replies the rep. I have been warned about sexist Australian men but, until now, have never met one. The only thing I ever cook while in camp is American-style biscuits on the open fire. Most of the men ignore the smoke-laced, greyish lumps. Serves them right for asking.

For their initial exploration camp the company has chosen a sacred site right next to a major waterhole filled with sweet water all year long. Ditch and the others quietly explain that traditionally this was an important meeting and camping site because of the abundance of water. The company has made a major transgression in choosing that site without asking permission of the traditional people.

"Oh, we'll just be here until Monday," says the rep innocently. Ditch nods. "That's all right, I guess." What else can he do?

After weeks of camping in the dirt and cooking mostly over open fires, I am awed by the comforts here. A diesel-driven motor produces electricity for lights and two refrigerators that house the masses of trucked-in food. A camper trailer contains stove, sink with running water, the second refrigerator and shelves filled with canned goods. Extending from the door of the trailer is a twenty-foot-long verandah with long tables and folding chairs. A campfire constructed with stones supports a grill used to cook huge steaks for dinner each evening. A shower replete with a two-sided canvas blind for modesty rounds out the camp. 'Roughing it' in style.

When David and the other men return, we put our 'swags'—blankets rolled inside a foam pad for sleeping—near the edge of the camp where Ditch and the other men are sitting. David tells me a bit about the helicopter ride, and how the pilot lost track of his position on the map.

"Mugi (one of the aboriginal men) told him exactly where he was and where to go. The pilot wouldn't believe him at first, because Mugi's never been up in a plane before. But Mugi knew exactly where he was."

"I thought the men said they hadn't been here since they were children; one of them said it's been almost forty years. How could they know where they were?"

David smiles and looks across the starlit dunes. "The stories; remember, they know the land from the stories."

During the next three days I spend most of my time in camp alone and/or waiting. The chubby archaeologist arranges the helicopter seats, Ditch directs me one way, someone else another. Soon all of the seats are filled, and I am drawn to the unavoidable conclusion that I am neither needed nor wanted. At first I take the exclusion very personally, feeling I have fallen into an ancient trap of being tolerated because I am attached to a man (following David, the video expert, as his assistant in charge of still photography), which I believe is partially true. I also realise, though, that the aboriginal *men* are taking the anthropologist and archaeologist to men's sacred sites where I, as a woman, am forbidden to go. With a strong background in women's issues, I am in a hard spot. How can I support these traditional people in the division of men's and women's 'business' and remain true to my own beliefs about women's worth? I ponder this and other issues as I wait in camp.

For one thing, I muse, the company hired only male archaeologists and anthropologists whose job, I learn, is to record and verify the sites identified by the aboriginal men. Reminds me of how a woman used to need a man's signature for financial transactions a few years ago—in the desert, you need a white man's signature to verify sacred sites. I begin to feel a certain kinship with these aboriginal men.

Traditional women will speak and work only with women, traditional men only with other men, so even if aboriginal women had come on this trip, they would have had no one with whom to share their knowledge. In some ways the lack of female anthropologists has protected much of the women's knowledge. For years male anthropologists flooding into the desert in search of PhDs assumed that only men had sacred knowledge because they were included only in the men's affairs, as is appropriate in a traditional aboriginal society.

This exposure had a two-pronged effect. First, despite their promises, the anthropologists made aspects of the secret sacred knowledge widely known. From the perspective of a traditional culture, this action weakened the knowledge. Women's 'business', however, was not exposed to the anthropologists and therefore retained its strength. Secondly, contact with European male anthropologists introduced concepts of Western patriarchal behaviour into the aboriginal men's attitudes, a stance that has strengthened through exposure to the Christian missionaries who have moved into the desert in search of 'heathen' souls to save. I recognise during my days of waiting at camp that this video, intended to represent the struggles of the Martujarra *people*, could easily become the story of the Martujarra *men* unless things start to change.

Back at the Martu camp Karen and I talk about how to include the women's voice in the video. Broaching a subject within the community requires sensitive diplomacy—it's important to begin with the right person in the correct manner. Eventually the word filters through, and the women quickly organise themselves to combine a planned trip to meet a woman ethnobotanist at another camp with a side trip to visit and video some of the women's sites.

During our two-day sojourn back at the central camp, David and I spend most of our time up at the school, a central hub for a lot of activity. Unlike most aboriginal reservations (very similar to American Indian reservations), the school is not controlled by a missionary or a white government official. Here someone from within the community serves as principal and head teacher. The community as a whole interviews and selects outside staff to work in the school. Right now two white women are teaching—and they candidly explain that they are learning far more than they could ever teach the children.

Their training emphasises teaching *children*—if you want to bring about change, begin with the young ones. In a traditional society, though, the *older* people are the teachers. If you want to teach new ways without damaging the traditional structure, you teach the elders and then they in turn teach the younger people. Now the old ways are thrown out of balance because the young children often know more about Western ways than their elders. If the Europeans had understood a bit more about the aboriginal culture, they could have introduced Western education much more easily by teaching the older people first.

At Punmu the school was designed to address the imbalance—*all* people, no matter what age, are welcome. Parents and grandparents crouch on the floor next to the children, colouring or copying new words that the teacher scrawls on the blackboard. Most of them already speak English, but writing is a new skill. The children learn both English and Martu for the first three years; after that time they learn a particular course in either English or Martu. Compared to the school I went to, the teachers are relaxed about time. They set general beginning and ending times for the lessons and the schedule is flexible to accommodate funerals or major gatherings with other communities.

In one of the offices outside the main classroom, David sits talking with some of the men. Among them is Yabaroo Gibbs, an aboriginal man who is often referred to by the white folks who know him as 'the philosopher of the Western Desert'. Yabaroo is not his usual name, though. When someone dies in the community, his or her name is never mentioned for a full year. All photographs or tape recordings of that person are destroyed. The silence eases the mourning for the community and also allows the person who is passing to move easily away from the tight family group. Anyone else with the same name becomes Yabaroo for the space of a year. Even words within the language that *sound* like the person's names are deleted or replaced during that time. These frequent changes are part of what makes Martujarra and other desert languages so difficult to master.

People's faces soften when they mention Yabaroo Gibbs's name. He has a gentle wisdom about him that is obvious even when he doesn't speak. Yabaroo spends a lot of time alone, thinking. A couple of times when David and I have been out walking, we have come across him sitting quietly on top of a dune, looking over the dry, red landscape. In a culture where people do *everything*—including walking to the toilet—together, his solitude is unusual. And so are some of the ideas that have come from his quiet contemplation.

Yabaroo talks of his vision to plant an orange grove in the desert. "We have enough water," he says, nodding his head slowly. "We got them wells. We just need people look after the trees. Need lots lookin' after, gotta keep 'em watered."

The trees would be a way of providing fresh fruit in the desert, making the people less dependent on the monthly food runs down to Perth. Although the Martu still have the knowledge of the 'bush tucker' that grows wild, the land immediately around their permanent settlement has long since been picked clean. They have to range farther and farther away from camp to gather food. Most of the bush tucker is extremely nutritious and very concentrated so that people don't have to gather huge quantities to sustain themselves. The supplies trucked in from outside, though, lack the nutritional quality of the local food. Now people subsist mainly on tinned corned beef and 'damper', a quick bread made with bleached white self-raising flour and baked in the ashes of the campfire.

Oranges would also supply vitamin C to help prevent the frequent colds and bouts of bronchitis that plague the Martu. "They can develop pneumonia at the drop of a hat," explains Karen. "And the kids always have running noses and stuffed up ears. Most of them have hearing loss from all of the infections."

Yabaroo knows that the trees would grow because Karen and Brad kept a garden near the shelter where they lived before Karen went back to school, under a shade woven out of spinifex grass. They grew beautiful vegetables. Children visiting from other camps that summer loved the fresh vegetables. Their parents commented on how healthy the kids were when they came home. If vegetables can grow, says Yabaroo, so can trees.

The next day about a dozen Martu women complete with swags, 50-pound canisters of self-raising flour for damper and a couple of children pile into the back of a Toyota for the day-long drive across the salt lakes and desert to Cotton Creek, another Martu camp. There they will meet the ethnobotanist and, we hope, make some side trips to film the women's sites. David and I perch on packs and blankets and cling to camera equipment as the Toyota lurches and bounces through the desert amidst the July eruption of colour and scent.

Four-wheel-drive Toyotas, *the* transportation in the desert, allow the Martujarra people to incorporate Western technology into their traditional lifestyle. Desert aboriginal people, with a culture distinct from that of the inhabitants of the rainforests in the North or the hardwood forests of the Southwest, had to maintain a nomadic lifestyle to disperse their impact over the fragile and inhospitable environment.

Movement ensured that no area would be overhunted or overcamped.

The vast storehouse of knowledge about how to travel in the desert, how to live together and where to find food and water is preserved in the people's cycle of songs and stories. These song cycles trace the people's journey through the desert, describing every rock, bush, waterhole and even specific areas to dig yams or other 'bush tucker'. The songs also depict the journey of Dreamtime ancestors, heroic beings who moved across the featureless desert and created land formations through their activities. For thousands of years the Martujarra literally have followed in the footsteps of their ancestors, claiming these sacred routes as their own and retaining the weave of the practical and the sacred through their journey.

Throughout the ride the women and children scan the landscape, pointing excitedly and laughing and talking. The conversation, though I cannot understand the Martu words, seems to focus on the land. Every once in a while Patricia, Ditch's sister and a strong force among the women, translates something for us. "Over there," she says, pointing to what looks to me like most of the other land we have crossed, "is wild onions. Bush tucker." She settles back against the pile of swags behind her. I realise suddenly that the track we are following must overlap parts of one of the Dreamtime paths across the desert.

The Dreamtime stories of ancestral heroes and heroines also teach sacred knowledge. A child begins to learn these stories simply. He or she visits a particular site, listens to the story and then touches the actual makings of that teaching. This rock, this stream, this cliff that I can touch and see and smell and taste is a repository for a vast, sacred knowledge. The stories of a people do not make sense away from their ancestral home. How can a child fully understand a creation story and its relevance hundreds of miles away from the outpouring of that creation? Sacredness is rooted in a place, in the here and now. The essence of sacredness is embodied in matter, the very stuff of creation. Spirit and matter are inseparable in an aboriginal understanding of the world.

The song cycle of the Dreamtime Ancestors also becomes a practical map for moving across the desert. After years of being away from their home country, a land perhaps known among the younger generation growing up in the cities only through the song cycles, the Martujarra people returning to the desert can walk with complete confidence to the site of a waterhole, the knowledge of its position retained in the song/story cycle, and uncover a layer of pavement to reveal the water beneath. Their knowledge is specific, site-specific, within inches. That is the power of their mental technology, preserved through oral tradition.

Trees and bushes grow thickly along the banks of the Rudall River. Despite first appearances, this land is rich with water—underground water, not far below the surface. The Martu depend upon this water, thanks to the digging of wells and the building of windmills to operate pumps. When they are travelling and hunting, they rely on the open water supply. They are acutely aware that waste from a uranium mine would contaminate these water sources, poisoning the Martu people both directly and indirectly through the animals that they hunt and the food that they gather. For the Martu, water *is* life.

And because the mining companies believe that the tailings from the uranium mines will cause only a small amount of local contamination, they have positioned the proposed dumping site right on top of a major underground river which flows south to Perth and other major cities in the Southwest. Australia is a relatively dry continent with only three major underground rivers. The radioactive tailings could contaminate one of those rivers and thus the entire watershed that it supplies.

A hush spreads among the women as an outstretched arm pinpoints the movement of some bustards (bush turkeys). One of the older women sitting in front, one foot bandaged and her teeth worn almost to the gums, smiles broadly, eyes twinkling as she raps her knuckles against the back of the driver's seat. The truck slows and veers off the track, edging toward the bustards who freeze, making no attempts to escape.

BANG! One shot crackles from the rifle resting on the half-opened door. The birds squawk and flap slowly away, just out of gunshot range. One simply squats down close to the ground, apparently content that it is hidden. The performance is repeated twice more that afternoon. Finally the bullet reaches its mark, and the old woman happily pats the wings of the limp bird slung into the back of the truck. "*Kookka* (meat) tonight. Goo-o-d tucker," she says with a deep-bellied laugh.

That evening as the sun is setting we stop to camp not far from the river. I love enacting this ancient ritual, smoothing a patch of earth, collecting wood for the fire that cooks the food and provides warmth in the chill of a winter night. Soon five or six small fires are popping, consuming the bone-dry dead wood of the desert. The night air is chill without the sun, and I am grateful for the warmth of my sleeping bag and the fire that casts shadows into the upstretched arms of the surrounding eucalyptus trees.

The camp begins to stir at first light. Days are measured by the rhythm of the sun. The Martu have names for all the subtle stages of the return of light, many more than just 'dawn' and 'sunrise', reflecting the importance of the sun and illustrating the Martu's supreme ability to observe the finest details in their environment.

About mid-day we reach Cotton Creek, another Martu camp where no 'whitefellas' live. "Stay in the vehicle," explains Brad. "We gotta introduce you to the people here before anything else happens."

The women jump off the truck, pulling their swags behind them. A huge crowd gathers around the Toyota to greet incoming family. One of the old men looks ancient—someone explains that he's come out to Cotton Creek so that he can die on the land, where he belongs, not in some mission. He can barely walk, but a cluster of children is always near at hand to help him.

Over the days in camp, I have come to understand that everyone is related to everyone else according to 'skin groups'. In the Martu culture, people belong to one of four different skin or family groups. These family groupings are the basis for the structure of the society as a whole. If I have a sister or brother in skin group A, for example, *all* people in that group are related to me as brother and sister. If I marry a man in skin group B, then *all* of the men within that group are related to me like husbands. That doesn't necessarily mean that I sleep with all of them. I could, but for the most part relationships are monogamous. The family grouping ensures that no matter where I travel in the desert—and this particular kinship system extends through most of the Western Desert—I would have someone related to me in each camp who would cook or hunt or share their shelter with me. Marriages are dictated by skin groups not only for convenience but also to keep the gene pool clean among a relatively small population.

One of the four groups would be my 'wrong side'. I could not marry anyone in that group. In fact, I could not acknowledge their presence in any way. Even eye contact is forbidden. During Brad and Karen's ten years in the desert, there are certain people who have never spoken with them.

"Never?" I ask Brad. I can hardly imagine living in a community of a hundred or less people and never making eye contact, much less speaking, with certain people.

"Well, once one of them stood nearby and kind of smiled at the ground—that was as close as they ever got to acknowledging me."

This system of skin groups is part of the Law, the unchanging guidelines that govern traditional aboriginal life. Adults brought up in this culture know the Law, and they understand the consequences of breaking it. Marrying a 'wrong side love', someone in a forbidden skin group, would be an example of breaking the Law. Minor transgressions are punished by beating or spearing—usually in the leg, although it could be anywhere in the body. Major transgressions of the Law are punished by death.

Aboriginal Law never changes; it stays the same. That is partly why aboriginal people have such a hard time understanding western European 'law'. What do you mean, yesterday I could park my car here and today I can't? What do you mean, 16 years ago I couldn't have a legal abortion and today I can? And why are you thinking about changing the Law *again*? These changes don't make sense to them. Law is Law; it has always been and always will be.

Within a half-hour of arriving David and I are asked to join the circle of men who form the council in this camp. Again we explain our skills and what we plan to do—to make a video that explains the Martu people's struggle with the mining companies. The men listen quietly while we speak. Sheba, a young camel hand-raised in the camp, circles around us and finally settles next to me. She snortles in my hair until one of the children growls at her and pushes her away from the circle.

"Lot of talk," says one of the men. "Always a lot of talk. We been talkin' with these mining camp people for *five years*. And talkin' with the government. Doesn't seem to do much good."

"Well," says Brad, "these fellas are gonna try to get the word out about what's going on here. Maybe they can understand it better when it's on TV."

They talk for a while and then finally nod in our direction. We are welcome to stay—on the edge of camp. After we have unrolled our swags, I head across the camp to the water tap that stands next to one of the houses. I'm careful about walking wide around the shelters—the boundaries between each shelter are not marked by fences, but rather by an agreed-upon, unnamed distance. As a newcomer I can only guess how far that is, and I'd rather walk a bit farther, zig-zagging among the shelters, than offend someone.

Despite my attention to the boundaries, though, I still feel uneasy walking through camp. Maybe I'm breaking yet another unspoken rule by entering the camp at all.

I ask Brad and Karen when I return if it was OK to walk through the camp. "Well," says Brad, "not really. But they'll tolerate it because you're a visitor. If you were coming to work here, they would *tell* you if you did something wrong, but since you're visiting, they won't say anything."

"Shit. Have we done anything else wrong?"

"Don't worry about it. You're gonna make mistakes"

"Listen to them laughing and singing," says Karen smiling, sitting in the shade of the truck. "They never sing like that in camps where there are whitefellas."

"Yeah, not many whitefellas come in here. They even made me wait a couple days on the edge of camp once."

"You had to wait outside?" I ask. Brad nods. "You couldn't even get water?"

"Nope," he says, shaking his head.

"But you could die out here without water."

"Yep. But that's your problem, not theirs. The proper way of coming into a camp is to stand on the edge until someone recognises you, acknowledges that it's OK to come in. You can wait as long as they bloody well want you to wait."

Later in the afternoon Fiona, the ethnobotanist who has been working with the women, comes over to talk with us. She and her working partner, a man who is also a botanist, are staying about a quarter of a mile down the road. A man and a woman working as a team move more easily in a traditional society than they would alone. For one thing, the woman can gather information only from the women, the man only from the men. Also, as a partnership they pose no threat to the carefully regulated family groupings.

Fiona talks a bit with Brad about some of the debates that have been going on about 'plant rights'. The ethnobotanists of the eighties are like the anthropologists of the forties—they are the newest wave of scientists to mine information from the aboriginal people. Instead of banking on the traditional people's store of knowledge in PhD theses (although they do some of that, too), they are involved in the lucrative business of seeking out new plants that might be adaptable for commercial growing. Already some companies applying for seed patents have come up against disputes about just exactly who 'owns' the rights to certain plant species. Certainly the traditional aboriginal people have never lived with a concept of 'owning' any of the species in the desert, and yet for thousands of years they have been the human stewards of this land.

To their credit, Fiona and her partner have been involved in projects to help the desert people preserve their knowledge in written form. Although most of the teaching is passed on through word of mouth, the traditional people now have some of their knowledge of medicinal plants and 'bush tucker' preserved in writing in case the oral tradition ever dies out. Judging from the way the old people work with the children, though, I doubt that this will be the case in the near future.

A couple of days later the women, several of the children and some of the men pile into the back of the truck for a few days' camping trip. By Martu standards the 'mob' (their word for 'group') of twenty people in the back of the Toyota is small —en route to large gatherings 35 or so people is the norm. The plan is for the men to visit the CRA mining camp for a close-up look at what is going on—with camera in tow, if possible. The women plan to visit a site nearby and have me video a discussion among them about what *they* think about the proposed uranium mine.

We stop along the way to video some of the spectacular rock formations and the wildflowers that sweep across the wide open landscape, blooming in swathes of purple. The grasses are reaching maturity. Their swollen seed heads hang golden, surging in wind-driven waves. The Martu women ooh and aah, pointing excitedly at the windswept grasses and the flowers, smiling and laughing and enjoying the abundance of the rain-greened land. Always they seem to be focused on the passing landscape, rooted fully in the moment.

David sits next to me, chattering about plans for his TV station, his children, writing for different magazines. Sometimes I nudge him gently and ask him to be quiet. Anything not related to the here and now, this moment, this place, is jarring. The open space, the endless sky, the vast sweep of colour and movement, and the silence . . . when we stop always there is the silence. Eating into me. Rooting me. Stretching me and contracting me into the moment all at once.

Even the older women don't seem to mind the rough ride as we lurch over the bumpy track. In fact, when we hit deep ruts that send us bouncing high enough to bang our heads on the top of the truck, the women laugh and rub their heads and bluster at Brad. "Jackamara (Brad's name in the camp)," yells one old lady, banging the side of the truck and shaking her head. More peals of laughter. They love every moment of the journey.

After a few hours' drive we stop to camp just beyond a river, still flowing weeks after the rain. A few bushes and clumps of spinifex and a sparse scattering of trees are the only vegetation on this sandy soil. Looking around camp, I notice bits of grass and other debris twisted in the base of the shrubs and realise that this must be the overspill area for the river during rainy times. After the recent rains, the sand is washed clean and flecks of clear quartz glimmer in it.

Red-orange light burnishes the ground. I realise that only about half an hour of daylight remains. Time to gather wood, roll out swags, mix flour with water for damper, put the billy can on the fire to boil water for tea. Time . . . sun time, star time, fire time . . . desert time. Past time, future time, now time, *all time, now time.*

For a moment I slip away to Monkey Mia, where David and I spent June 21st, the night of the winter solstice, in a cave about half a mile from the shore. Several people had had strong experiences in the cave during the Dreaming Camp, so we decided to observe the solstice in it, meditating and sleeping there—alone, since everyone from the Dreaming Camp had left the day before. That night I heard footsteps outside, but when I propped myself on my elbow to look out, nothing moved in the moonlight. Clapping sticks beat rhythmically; people shouted and babies cried. Nothing was *physically* present outside the cave. The movements and sounds were not frightening; the deep peace of the cave was too pervasive. They seemed to be a natural part of something that had happened, was happening, will be happening.

My Western mind could understand the event as a 'bleed-through' from another time into the present. But aboriginal people believe that all time is *now,* and for thousands of years they have moved and lived and thought about time that way. If form follows thought, an ancient esoteric principle, then this land of Australia is infused with a very different time sense than the linear pattern that operates in most Western societies. And that belief, that 'thoughtform', has literally taken shape in the land of Australia, obvious even to the far less sensitive incomers. If even I was aware of movements and sounds—and I consider myself to be hopelessly insensitive to 'otherworldly' happenings—the thoughtform must be very powerfully rooted in the land.

In the morning the men decide to take the truck to visit the CRA camp with video camera in tow. That means no filming with the women—we have only one camera. Initially I am disappointed, worried that the filming with the women might not be completed before we have to leave. In about a week's time—I can hardly believe it—I will be on the airplane heading back to Scotland to give a workshop at the Findhorn Community. Time . . . space . . . sitting here in the Western Desert I can barely imagine what the cool, wet summer breezes of Scotland must feel like now.

One of the young girls, Maureen, comes over to the edge of the circle where our sleeping bags lie. I nod at her and smile—yes, it's fine to come in. She sits down next to me, wriggling into a comfortable spot on the sand. "You want some damper?" I ask her. Her eyes glow. "With honey?" "Yooah—yes!" She looks a bit disappointed when I pull out the wholewheat damper—white flour is preferred —but the honey makes up for it. When she finishes with the sticky piece of bread, she starts to look through my backpack.

"Is all this stuff *yours*?" she asks, her eyes wide. I nod. "What do you do with *this*?" She pulls out a roll of dental floss. "For your teeth," I explain, rubbing the space between my teeth. She continues to rummage through the pack, holding up this and that and shaking her head. "All this is *yours* . . . ."

For the last six months I have prided myself on reducing my load of belongings to a large backpack and a day pack. As Maureen looks through my things, though, I realise that what to me is a small amount is much more than she would ever claim as her own. In a traditional camp, very little belongs to individual people. Everything is available for everyone else to use. If I put down a hammer when I'm finished with it, the next person assumes that I don't need it now, so they pick it up and use it. When they finish, they put it back in the same place or pass it on to someone else. If someone decides at the last minute to go along on a trip, and they jump in the truck without a swag, no one worries. There's always enough to share around. "I've gotta be careful now when I visit Europeans," said Brad once. "I'm so used to doing things that way—I figure if something is just sitting there, they don't need it. I forget that to them it's *stealing*."

Maureen takes out the hair brush and looks at my hair. "I'm gonna brush your hair," she announces. Ever since my arrival at Punmu, the children have been fascinated by my long, ginger-coloured hair. Whenever they see me, they jump up in my arms and then reach back to my hair tie and pull it out so that they can run their fingers through my hair. Maureen is bolder than most—she wants to brush it, too.

When she tires of brushing, Maureen looks over at a cluster of spinifex grass. She purses her lips in that direction. Desert people use their lips more often than their finger to point at something. "You seen the bird's nest over there?" she asks. I think of myself as a fairly aware observer of the Earth, but I have to admit the nest had escaped me. "Uh, no I haven't." She leads me to a tiny hole carefully woven into a bristly spinifex grass clump, home to one of the desert birds. "Want to see some more?" We walk along the track heading west out of the camp, and she points out half a dozen nests and other things that had been invisible to me.

On the way back through camp Carol, a young aboriginal woman, joins us. "This my sister," explains Maureen. "Blood sister?" I ask. Maureen looks up at me. "*Sister.* You know," she says frowning impatiently, "we all related, and Carol's my *sister.*"

A couple of other children join us as we walk in the other direction out of camp. I bring my camera to photograph some of the wildflowers, and the girls are eager to be included. They point out plants, explaining their uses, and animal homes that I would pass by, completely unaware.

Carol points to a jumble of rocks at the top of a rise nearby. "See? That's an iguana's home." She pulls back a stone. "See the print? Really clear, right there in front." I detect the faintest hint of a disturbance in the sand. I follow as the women and children move easily over the desert, reading the signs with a fluid grace and wisdom that show me how deeply their knowledge of this land runs.

I realise that the time away from 'school' is also a learning time, the natural setting for the women to pass on their knowledge. During these journeys they go for walks, gathering plants and seeds just as they have for thousands of years. The children follow along, absorbing the ancient lore as they watch the women's movements. The children really attend two schools—one within the walls of the classroom, and the other here in the open desert. They are learning both European and traditional aboriginal ways.

Although the Martu people mainly eat the food trucked in from the city, they could survive in the desert unaided if they had to. Their knowledge of Place has not atrophied, and these camping trips ensure that the children will have the traditional knowledge and skills to pass on to future generations.

When we return to camp, Maureen settles next to my pack to show Carol everything inside. While they do this, I take out a plastic bag filled with hair that I've been saving. Since arriving in Australia, I've been losing lots of hair every time I brush it. I'm not sure whether it's because of the dry desert air or if it is an aftereffect of my illness in India.

"You gonna make something out of that?" asks Carol.

"Yeah, I'm thinking about making a belt."

"You spinning the hair?"

"Trying to. I just rub it together on my leg, like this," I tell her, rolling the hair over my leg and then twirling it between my hands.

Carol watches for a while. "You want someone to show you how to spin it?" she asks finally.

"Sure," I tell her, eyes alight. Slowly some of the women come and settle around the fire. Patricia begins to prepare the hair, unknotting the twisted strands and pulling it into loose, fluffy clumps. "You have any oil or fat?" she asks. I pull some body lotion out of the pack. She nods and begins to work the lotion into the hair. "Now, go find some sticks," she tells me.

When the hair is ready, one of the old women comes and settles in the shade of a tree near the fire. Smiling and humming, she begins to spin, her movements sure and graceful as the hair twists from the end of the stick into a neat strand of yarn. She nods and hands the sticks to me. "You try," explains Patricia. I roll the stick along my knee, trying to imitate the old woman's fluid movement, but my hands fumble and the yarn twists too tight. The old woman laughs good-naturedly, her shoulders shaking. She takes back the stick and continues to spin the yarn. "What you gonna make with it?" asks Patricia.

"I'm not sure; I was thinking about a belt or something for around my head." She nods silently, her lips puckering thoughtfully.

Later in the evening, talking with Brad, I learn that hair belts are very sacred in this culture—they are made only at certain times, for special occasions. No wonder everyone falls silent when I mention making a belt. Although my actions violate one of their traditions, they are too polite to say anything. Their tolerance of my behaviour—although innocent—is remarkable.

Sitting around the campfire, David tells me stories about their trip to the mining camp. The men drove right into the CRA camp and then drove around for a few minutes before the miners caught wind of them and chased the Toyota with two cars and a bulldozer until cornering it.

"You know," says David, "Ditch is a really good person. You know what he did when the CRA guys stopped us?"

"What?" I ask, staring into the flames.

"The first thing he did when we got out was show them bush tobacco—what it looks like, how to dry it. Can you imagine that?"

I shake my head. I can visualise Ditch, the traditional steward of this land, quietly explaining to some strapping mining official—an intruder in this land who has never communicated with the Martu—how to pick the desert plants. Always his first instinct is to share, to be generous. Always the traditional people are generous. "So what happened when they stopped you?"

"We had a gun, and they had gun," says David. "We could see it in the bulldozer. It could have been a real confrontation; somebody could have been hurt. The men were *very* upset about us being there, especially with the camera. They only wanted us to take pictures in certain areas, 'show' places. They didn't want to take us inside buildings. When we asked them why, they said they weren't worth seeing. We *knew* they were because we'd already been inside."

"What was in there?" I ask.

"Tailings. They were storing tailings, and there was a sign that said 'Keep out. Contaminated area. This means YOU.' In one building they were doing their separation of the ore, and people were walking around with white clothes and masks on. And in the lunch room there was a sign about how many people had got sick from the uranium. When we asked them about it, they said, 'Very few people get sick, we

250

have them tested all the time so they won't get sick.' We questioned what they meant by 'few', and they didn't answer that. They also told us that they spend one *million* dollars every month to run the camp."

"So what did the sign say? The one in the lunch room?"

"The sign said what to do around the camp. You wash yourself before you eat, before you do this, before you do that; you do this, you do that. I'll have to show you on the tape. I stood there and filmed it." I can just see David nonchalantly filming with a hundred angry pairs of eyes boring into his back. "The sign is to tell people what to do so they stay healthy, so they don't get contaminated. It's also to show outsiders. And throughout the camp there were signs saying, 'Land Reclamation. No Trucks Across Here'. *Only* in the camp, not outside."

"So they were trying to make the camp look good?"

"Yeah . . . it was stupid. We went to one site about five miles away where the Western Australia government was testing the effects of dust contamination from the mine. The only trouble was that the mine *was on the opposite side of the mountain*," says David, laughing, "and the wind would have to blow *around* the mountain to get to this site. This was about five miles from the mining camp, so if the wind blew in the right direction, around the mountain, then it would show contamination. This was the *government* test So we walked up there and threw some dust up in the air to make sure there was some to measure. We laughed, we giggled. We couldn't believe the government's stupidity; it showed that they don't care and that everything that is done is a front."

"What else did you see at the CRA camp?"

"Well they didn't take us inside any buildings so we could see what was going on. They took us to where some of the ore was located—they picked it up from the ground to show us how strong the mine was. They also took us to the highest point overlooking the camp and pointed out what each building was for. As I say, they wouldn't take us in the buildings, even after we asked them again. We asked how many people were here working. Fifty men and fifty women, they said—they always try to make it equal. Apparently it's harder to get women. Then Brad asked them where the boundary of the national park was in relationship to their buildings, and they pointed to within 25 feet of the edge of the buildings."

"So were they inside or outside the park?"

"The buildings were just 25 feet outside of it. We asked where the dump site for the tailings was. They pointed in a direction away from the park and said it was about a mile in that direction. But we could see from where we were standing that the big bulldozers and trucks were running right through the park. The road ran *inside* the park. Their survey posts, marking where they were going to do exploration, were all in the park. They showed us on the map, which looked to Ditch and Brad and Mugi a larger area than that they had originally asked for.

"Didn't they get pissed off with all these questions?"

"Oh, sure, and they were really upset about the video camera. But they treated us to lunch in their commissary—they gave us all the big steaks we could eat, lots of food, just like the Uranus company. Afterwards we left the main camp and drove to two sites that were in development by CRA. *Both* were inside the park. This really upset Ditch, especially the new road development to one of the sites. It wasn't a plain old truck road, but a real, graded dirt road. It looked to Ditch and the rest of us like it was an auxiliary camp being built. On the way to this site, we saw three large road graders—they passed us on their way back to the main camp.

"How did the men feel about the visit?"

"Ditch and Brad felt they had accomplished something just by going there,

251

because they've been talking about visiting this camp and other mining camps for five years, and until then nothing had happened."

"But they were successful in getting the exploration miners out of Cotton Creek, right?"

"That's right. The people told CRA it was a sacred site, but they didn't pay attention. So finally the people moved in and set up camp . . . ."

"In the summer, right, when no one was expecting them to come?" No one moves *an inch* in the 150°+F heat if they can help it.

"Yeah, I think that's right. And then the miners finally left and never came back. Anyway, that's the only thing that's been done in the last five years to stop CRA."

"What about sacred sites?" After going with the Uranus company people to identify sacred sites, I wonder how careful CRA has been.

"They checked with the Strelly mob . . . ." (another community of desert people a bit farther to the north who work closely with Don MacLeod)

"But that's not the Strelly mob's traditional land, is it?"

"No, it's not, but a spokesman for the Strelly mob said they could go anywhere. When we asked about sacred sites, the CRA people said there were none because the man they spoke to said there weren't any. They only asked this one man. And they never checked with Ditch, whose country it was."

"Did they ever talk with the women?"

"Nope, and they were told not to talk with anyone at Punmu, either."

"Do they even know there's anyone living out here?"

"Well, I can only tell you what one of the geologists said. I asked what he thought about the nuclear waste that the government plans to dump in the Southwest—you know, the waste from France and other countries. He said he thought the Southwest was too populated, but dumping it in the Central Desert would be all right. When I asked him if he knew there were people out there, he said, 'What people?'"

"He really didn't know anyone lived out there?"

"Judith, these people don't even know that aboriginal people exist. That's what upsets Ditch and all of them so much. These people never consult aboriginal people about *anything*. You know, when we asked them about jobs, they weren't even interested in hiring aboriginal people for the simple jobs—even as janitors. That's what upsets them. That these mining people don't even recognise that they exist."

We sit quietly for a while and then crawl into our sleeping bags. The news from the camp is worse than I expected, and I don't have the heart to ask more questions right now. The story is so complex. Dealing with the mining company is difficult enough, but with the added complication of bickering aboriginal communities the potential to play people off against each other is so great . . . . I wonder what chance the Martu have of maintaining their land or themselves against a big company with a lot of money and a lot of silent, illicit backing.

The next morning we drive back across the desert, arriving in Cotton Creek just in time for a meeting with a woman representing a major international aid group. Almost everyone in Cotton Creek has left for a funeral in a nearby camp. The winter is called 'the dying times', and many older people 'cross over' during these months. A few community leaders, though, have remained behind to meet this representative, invited by the woman who has been collecting stories among the Martu women for the last few months. The Australian Bicentennial Commission sponsored her story-collecting project with a hefty grant that includes funds for a four-wheel-drive vehicle and a generous salary. Strange that a white woman receives thousands of dollars to collect Martu stories, but the people have to beg for money to buy their own vehicles.

The meeting begins as does any other Martu gathering—when the time is right. We sit under a corrugated iron shade, the women together on one side, a few men sitting in front. Ditch and Brad lean against a wall, and David stands poised behind the video camera in front of the half circle. The camel Sheba periodically ambles through the circle and snortles in someone's hair or inspects the video camera.

The woman talks about her group's work in South Africa and other places to help oppressed traditional people. She speaks of the injustice of the way the Martu are treated in their own country and how her group wants to help. She promises to send money if someone in their community wants to go directly to Canberra to talk to the national government, and she asks for suggestions about any other ways they can be of assistance.

The men squirm a bit. The talk continues. Finally someone speaks up.

"We've been talking for five years about CRA and the tourists in four-wheel drives that just drive right into camp without permission. Had one come by yesterday, just drove right in. Talking, talking, talking. These government people come, these white people, and they promise things, but it's all talking, talking. Nothing ever actually happens. We're coming to the point where we're tired of talking."

The story collector agrees. "The government should conduct an impact study on the uranium mines and the recreational vehicle traffic in the Rudall River area. They don't know what's happening out here." When in doubt, call for a study. That's how a bureaucrat defines action.

"That study's already been done," fumes Brad. "Studies don't do any good, they're just a waste of time and money, a way for the government to look like they're doing something. Let the Martu manage the incoming tourists, like guiding camel trains through the section of the Canning Stock Route* that comes through their territory. Then they could control people moving through their land and generate some income so they are not so dependent on government money. Enough talk, time to act."

Brad pauses, elbows propped on knees, calloused hands circling the brim of a worn leather hat. After ten years in the desert, he is tired of the fruitless attempts of people who come offering help. Martu hopes rise, expecting the promised help to arrive or the proposed legislation to be adopted. Sometimes the strain of disappointment is too great. People, especially the old ones, simply die.

"These people are tired of promises. We need people who are willing to act."

Slowly, quietly the international aid representative begins to change her approach. "We will do all that we can. We will try our best to help in whatever way is possible." 'Will do' changes to 'will try' changes to good intentions and more talk.

When the meeting finishes, the women gather around the truck. Patricia swings behind the wheel and the other women climb into the back. At last we are driving out to a women's site, to film the area and the women's view of the uranium mining. The women speak in Martu, explaining the importance of the sites. Although I cannot understand the words, I can see the land formations they are talking about—an unusual shape in the rock, a dramatic change in colour. "Now, over there," translates Patricia, pointing to a cliff, "you can see one side is dark and the other light? That's the story of the dark side and light side skin groups."

The four skin groups are divided into two subgroups—two 'dark' and two 'light'.

*A white settler named Canning blazed the track that later bore his name to provide a route for driving cattle to markets in the south of Australia. Completed around the turn of the century, the Stock Route was used for only a few years before it was abandoned. Today a new exotic species herds along the Canning Stock Route, the four-wheel drive enthusiasts out stalking adventure.

So the Law about skin groups is written here, right in the fabric of the land. On the way back to Cotton Creek, we stop at the base of another hill that rises from the smooth desert floor. "Take a picture of this," says Patricia. "It's a very important place, very important to us. See those marks, those lines that go across the side?"

Scanning the hill, I see what look like giant fingernail scratches etched into the rock, running horizontally across the entire southern face. "Are those supposed to be there?" I ask.

"*Weeah, no*," says Patricia. "That's where the miners did their exploration."

"But isn't that a sacred spot?" I ask. In every camp David and I are strictly told where we can and can't go. Here we have been told not to walk in this general direction, so I assume that it is a special area.

"*Yooah*. But we can't tell you about it; that's not our place—it's for the women who live here in Cotton Creek to tell. So you just take a picture, that's all."

In the morning Ditch and Brad spend a long time listening and talking on the short-wave radio. In the desert, the radio is the lifeline that ties all the widely dispersed communities together. Through it messages are passed between camps, telephone calls are made, and the all-important Flying Doctor service is contacted. In the desert communities, most of them at least a day's drive from any paved road, all medical emergencies are handled by the Flying Doctor service. Planes land on the community's dirt airstrip and pick up people within hours of a phonecall. Without this service, hundreds of people would die in the desert.

Today Ditch hears that his son was flown to Port Hedland with a case of pneumonia earlier in the week. He should be flying back to Punmu late this afternoon. Brad nods at me. "We might get you back to Punmu for that plane," he says. "Probably have to do a bit of talking, but usually they let people go out with them if they need to get out." I've been worried about making my plane from Port Hedland in two days' time. If anything delays us—a flat tyre, a broken axle, an overheated engine, all common occurrences in the desert—I will probably miss the flight. A ride with the Flying Doctor service would save a full day's drive across the desert from Punmu back to Port Hedland. But the possibility of leaving this afternoon jars me—I'm not ready yet to think about leaving the desert. Or David. Or Australia. My heart aches when I think about leaving any of the three.

Although the journey goes smoothly, we don't arrive at Punmu in time to meet the Flying Doctor plane, so Brad plans to drive to Port Hedland the next day to refill the community's petrol supply and drop me off at the airport.

We start late in the day and drive through the night. When we reach the bitumen road outside Port Hedland just after dawn, I'm not sure if I'm relieved or disappointed. The hours before the flight leaves in the late afternoon pass far too quickly. When I board the plane, I sit by the window and watch the desert hills rolling below me as we take off. My heart is ripping, pulled by the magnetism of that red earth glowing scarlet under the setting sun. Those hills have touched me, and now I am a part of them, or they are a part of me . . . I can't tell the difference any more.

During the drive last night Brad stopped a couple of times by the side of the track to make tea. While we sat watching the fire consume the splintery twigs, Brad asked how I felt about going. I hugged myself, and crouched closer to the flames —for comfort more than warmth. "I don't really want to go," I told him.

Brad nodded. "Yep, the desert gets into you. And once you've been out here, you never really go away. That's what they say, and I think it's true." He looked up, staring at me across the flames. "I bet you'll be back here. We'll see. Desert doesn't let 'em get away that easily. And that old lady has your hair . . . never know what she might do with that."

CHAPTER 13
The Here and Now

Now, after a long journey, I have finally caught up with myself, to the here and now of my life in western Massachusetts. From this perspective, looking back over my journey, I want to emphasise that my experiences in each community offer a *slice of life,* a picture frozen in time. I have attempted to capture the essence of each place, but be aware that the details have changed. At the Bear Tribe, for example, Ruth (Blue Camas) reports that most of the Tribe now have their own living space, either in different buildings on the farm or in houses in town. The Circle Center has been sold, so the publishing and catalogue businesses have been moved to the farm on Vision Mountain.

The Findhorn Foundation has adopted a new method of choosing the members who serve on Core Group, the central decision-making body. Each member attunes to the people they feel are most appropriate to serve on the group, and the names most frequently listed are selected. This modified sort of democracy is a leap from the time when Core Group itself attuned to new additions to the group. More participation and more trust seems to be blossoming in the community.

As I began work on the chapter about Auroville, I received a copy of 'Auroville Today', a newsletter sent by Alan and Anna-Marie, announcing the adoption of the 'Auroville Foundation Bill' by the Indian Parliament. The bill ". . . seeks to acquire all properties relatable to Auroville which are currently owned by several societies, trusts and other bodies (*chiefly the Sri Aurobindo Society—my note*) . . . . The Government . . . proposes to acquire these assets without payment of any compensation and vest them in the proposed Auroville Foundation whose primary objective shall be to encourage and promote ideals and programmes envisaged in the Charter of Auroville."

The legislation includes an International Advisory Council, already in existence, to continue its yearly review of the community and make recommendations. One of the issues most heatedly debated during my stay in Auroville was that of who would actually guide the day-to-day running of the community, and the Bill ensures that the residents of Auroville will govern themselves '. . . through appropriate autonomous arrangements, which will include Residents' Assembly and its Working Committee'. Finally, a Governing Body, chosen by the Government according to *individual application,* not through representation from specific societies or trusts (reference to the SAS again), will manage the Auroville Foundation.

The news excites me. Now, at twenty years of age, Auroville is granted her independence. I wonder how she will progress without the ongoing disagreements with the SAS over legal control, freed from focusing on the outside 'enemy'. Sri Shiv Shanker, the Minister for Human Resources who introduced the Foundation Bill, summarised Auroville's progress to date as ". . . a beginning and a good beginning. Educational research in Auroville has just started flourishing. Research in the Works of Sri Aurobindo and the Mother has also received a good deal of encouragement. Research in the field of alternative sources of energy has also made some headway. The experiment of establishing a new ecological balance has succeeded to a very high degree. Above all, the atmosphere of Auroville has begun to vibrate with activities of youth and the ideal of unending education is being promoted in every field of activity in Auroville."

The synchronicities continued. The day after I began writing about Australia, a letter arrived from Debbie at Monkey Mia. "Some sad news at Monkey Mia," she reports, "with three dolphin babies dying in two and a half weeks and now the three males—Sickle(fin), Snubnose and BB—are missing. Plus the Caravan Park is changing hands . . . . There's been a lot of changes since you were last here." The news jarred me. I have always assumed that the dolphin-human contacts would continue indefinitely, but the news of the deaths and disappearances shatters that assumption.

After an eight-month silence, just as I began to write about Karen and Brad, a letter from them arrived. Brad writes that Ditch and Patricia are planning to tour around Australia to speak about what is happening in the Rudall River area. He wonders if the video is ready—Ditch would like to have it to show the government people in Canberra. "Ditch's comment," writes Brad, "is 'They can't seem to *hear*, maybe they can *see*'."

During the writing of this book, I have relived the last six years of my life, and some of the writing has not been easy. While I was writing about my experiences at the Bear Tribe and the abortion, an extremely painful boil erupted over my left eye that grew and grew until both eyes were swollen shut. Obviously I was writing about something that I didn't like looking at. On Halloween the boil finally burst. My sister and brother-in-law, with whom I was living at the time, joked that they could put me on the porch to scare the kids away.

Other memories sparked sychronistic happenings. Satya called our answering service as I finished the section on the Findhorn Community. Dee wrote from Auroville while I was writing about India. Although I believe in synchronicities (especially when they happen to *other* people), their occurrence is always miraculous to me. All of these little happenings reinforce my knowing that thoughts are powerful; through our minds we touch each other as surely as if we stretched a physical hand across thousands of miles.

As I complete the story of my journey, many questions come to mind. For instance, what is the difference between an 'intentional' and a 'traditional' community? My first response is that intentional communities, those with a stated purpose like the Bear Tribe or Auroville, are *remedial* for a culture that has lost touch with how to live in a neighbourhood, how to support each other as extended family, and how to live with care and concern for the Earth. But are those intentional communities different in that they have a stated purpose for being together, one that has more far-reaching effects than satisfying the survival needs of the immediate group?

In most cases *yes*, but some traditional societies also had communities that were set apart for specific purposes. The Hopi village of Hotevilla is a notable example of a traditional community that has a stated aim. According to Dan Katchongva's telling of the Hopi story (or 'history' in the Western sense), the village of Oraibi in Hopiland originally ". . . was settled in accordance with the instructions of the Great Spirit . . . . The vow which we made with the Great Spirit obligated us to follow his way of life. He gave the land to us to use and care for *through our ceremonial duties* (italics mine). He instructed us and showed us the road plan by which we must govern ourselves. We wrote this pattern on a rock so that we would always be reminded to follow the straight road. The Hopi must not drift away from this road or he will take this land away from us . . . .

"Oraibi village was settled firmly. Migrating people were now gathering there and asking to be admitted into the village. The Kikmongwi and the high priests would always consider their request and base their judgement upon their character and wisdom. Those who showed signs of boastfulness were turned away and told to go to the south mesas where their kind of people lived. Only good people, humble and sincere in their prayers, were admitted . . . .

"Among the ceremonies of each group the prayer for rain was important in order for the crops to grow and produce an abundance of food. The people depended on this for their livelihood. Boastful people were not admitted so that the prayers would not be polluted.

"Oraibi was now firmly established. The pattern of the religious order was established. Cycle by cycle we paid respect to our Mother Earth, our Father Sun, the Great Spirit, and all things through our ceremonials. We were happy for we were united as one."

In 1906, as a result of internal struggles exacerbated by the presence of missionaries and government workers, the 'faithful' people—the ones who stood firmly by the prophecies and way of life dictated by the Great Spirit—were evicted from Oraibi. They re-established themselves in a village that they named 'Hotevilla', which ". . . was settled for one purpose, to stand firmly on the Great Spirit's instructions and fulfil the prophecies to the end. It was established by good people, one-hearted people who were actually living these instructions." This village keeps the traditional ceremonial cycles alive, ensuring the health of the land, the continuance of the seasonal cycles, and a proper relationship with the Creator. ". . . My law is only the Creator's, just one," explains Dan Katchongva. *"And no manmade* (sic) *law must I follow, because it is ever-changing, and will doom my people."*

According to Dhyani Ywahoo, a teacher of the Etowah Band of the Eastern Tsalagi (Cherokee) nation, her people maintained 'Peace Villages' throughout the southeastern part of what is now the United States up until the beginning of the nineteenth century.

"The Peace Village was one way the Tsalagi people saw to maintain peace and balance—to maintain villages *whose single purpose was to mediate the various aspects of mind, always aware of the whole* (italics mine). Through spiritual practice and diet the inhabitants of the Peace Villages radiated peace of mind, enabling *maintenance of harmony with the pulse of the Earth* (italics mine) Their voices were relied upon for mediation of what appeared to be conflict. Many were priests and healers, keepers of tradition for the entire nation. Most important, they maintained areas of sanctuary. The Peace Villages were places of sanctuary where no blood was shed, no harm was done. Any person, even a killer or thief, who made his or her way to the village and followed the cycle of purification within the sanctuary for one year could be forgiven all transgression. Each Peace Village was guided by the Peace Chief, one committed to preserving life and skilful in transforming consciousness. The principles of the Peace Village were such that even 'white criminals', non-Native criminals in flight from the laws of their own people, could find sanctuary there, and many did."

But perhaps the communities of today have a new vision, a new inspiration for that dream of peace. Isn't that what the 'New Age' is all about? Often, though, I am humbled by how *ancient* many 'new age' visions are. While at Auroville I spent some time in the visitors' centre looking at the special display that was created for the community's 20th birthday. Along with pictures of the inauguration ceremony and the Charter handwritten by the Mother was a poster with a small note from a book by André Chedid entitled *Nefertiti et le Rêve d'Akhnaton*. In 1369 BC Queen Nefertiti had a vision for what she called the city 'Horizon'. "Here is a place," she declared, "that does not belong to any prince, to any god. No one owns it. Here is the place for all of us . . . . The earth will find it, find its joy in it. In it the hearts will be happy." Foundation of the city of Horizon: 1369. Achievement of the city of

Horizon: 1366. Death of Akhnaton: 1354. Destruction of Horizon: 1347. Death of Nefertiti: 1344.

Nefertiti's vision is remarkably close to the Mother's: "Auroville belongs to no one in particular. Auroville belongs to humanity as a whole . . . . Auroville will be the place of an unending education, of constant progress, and a youth that never ages." In 1968 Auroville was inaugurated, 3,337 years after the founding of Horizon. Perhaps humanity is finally ready for the leap—Auroville has already surpassed Horizon's 22-year lifespan and shows no sign of fading.

Clearly this vision of humanity living harmoniously with each other and the Earth has been around for many, many generations. Numerous societies have expressed the vision in as many different ways. Now it vision is surfacing within the western European culture. Why here? Why now?

For thousands of years, our culture has been the champion of the individual. This individualistic focus has produced many heroes, many singular 'superstars' that have left equally spectacular 'things' as monuments to their effort. Buildings, paintings, books, poetry, political systems, instruments, inventions are their legacy. I view the movement towards community at this time not so much as a pendulum swing—a reaction against the cult of the individual— but rather as the snake curling around to bite its own tail, bringing the polar opposites together in a circle of wholeness. Now is a time for balancing, for synthesising ancient wisdom and current innovation, for marrying the individual with the collective.

With the Martu, a society dominated by a collective, cooperative view of life, I sensed a strength that I rarely have encountered among western European people. Despite the physical struggle to survive in the desert camps and the ongoing threat of destruction from uranium mines, these people approach life with joy, generosity, laughter and affection. The West now searches for ways to fill an aching inner void gnawed into existence by the demands of material development. The Martu, in contrast, approach the world with a rich inner awareness that is just beginning to come to terms with the shaping of the outer, material world mastered by the West. The Martu core is ancient and solid, but the challenges it faces threaten to crush the ways crystallised by tradition. The transition may be painful, but the people firmly hold faith in their ability to re-establish their culture in the desert camps. An increase in the number of babies born in the Martu camps reflects this faith in the future.

The Martu have returned Home, to their Place. That Home, however, is far from secure. Ironically a people seeking to re-establish their culture away from western European influence find that same way of life following them into the desert in the form of mining companies determined to make the 'wasteland' produce. The companies, though, may be surprised by the fruits of their efforts in the desert.

An aboriginal story tells of a nest of luminous, green eggs guarded by the Ant People. Any disturbance to this nest of eggs will anger the Ant People and cause great changes to the planet as a whole. The luminous eggs in this prophetic story represent uranium, a force that can unleash great destruction on this planet when uprooted from its place. I am reminded that prophecies come as warnings. A good prophet is one whose predictions of destruction do not come to fruition because the people heed the warning and follow a new course. Prophecies foretell events based on the assumption that we continue along our present path. We can change direction and alter the outcome if we choose.

If we choose. To me, that is the crux of the matter. What sort of a world do you, I, we *choose* to live in? One that supports the life, health and diversity of the Earth and all of its inhabitants? One that is bent on destruction, violence and oppression?

One with opportunities for people to express their love, joy and creativity? What kind of a world do you want to live in?

Our *vision* for the way we want to live is the catalyst for the form our life takes. The shaping of our own personal lives is the foundation for the shape of the world as a whole. For me, the excitement of living at this time on this planet is the awakening understanding that it is our own thoughts, the contents of our dreams and visions, which shape our world.

So I offer you the challenge: What are you willing to live for? Remember, you have to have a dream before you can have a dream come true. So dream big. Dream the most outrageously wonderful dream you can imagine. *Choose* to live in such a world. And then begin to build the foundation, step by step, with the daily actions of your life. If that vision includes living in a place that is healthy and fully alive, I invite you to live in a Gaian community.

Who lives in a Gaian comminity? *You do*, wherever you are on the planet. You can maintain an awareness of Place and Planet even in the midst of a concrete-covered city. One man writes about his transition from living in the country to living in the middle of London. For three months before the move he affirmed daily that no matter where he is ". . . the major portion of Earth's surface is covered with the wilderness of oceans, that the major part of Earth's land surface is still green, that soil and earth is always beneath him despite the intervening concrete and that the sky is always above him. Regardless of where he is, he is always a creature of the living Earth."

Whether or not you live in an 'intentional community', you are a resident of planet Earth undeniably linked with the other human, plant, animal and mineral beings around you. No matter where you live—in an apartment in Manhattan or in a mud-brick hut in the rainforest of Asia—you can apply the principles of Gaian living in your life.

Begin first by asking four simple questions:
1. Where am I?
2. What is going on around me?
3. Who is my neighbour?
4. What does a Gaian community *in this place* look like?

They undoubtedly will open up a host of other questions. The answers, I hope, will surprise you. I offer some of my own musings on the subject that may help spur you on your way.

1. Where am I? The crux of this question is knowing place. *Really* knowing it. From my street address to the last expected spring frost date, from the source of my drinking water to the yearly cycle of the owl that lives in the oak tree at the bottom of the field.

As a primer for evaluating how well you know your Place, see how many of the following questions you can answer:

* How many days until the next full moon?
* Where does my water supply come from?
* Where does my wastewater go, and (if applicable) how is it treated?
* Where is the source of electricity (if any) in my house? How is it generated?
* What is the geological history of the area?
* What is the history of the native people?
* What species are endemic to this area (ones that exist only locally)?
* What is the last expected frost date this year?

* What is the average annual rainfall?
* Name three indigenous mammals, birds and insects.

One time when I was driving home from Elgin, a town east of Findhorn, I picked up a hitch-hiker—a wiry Scot wearing a thin jacket on a cold, grey day. We didn't talk much, but towards the end of the ride I mentioned that I would be turning off the main road towards Kinloss and from there to the caravan park. "By Findhorn?" asked the man.

"Yes—I live at the Foundation."

"Aye, I belong to Findhorn," he said simply.

"Sorry?" I asked, not sure that I had heard properly.

"I *belong* to Findhorn," he repeated, "but I'm living in Forres now (a town about five miles down the road). If you leave me in Kinloss, it'll be easier to get a ride."

I dropped him at the corner and then turned down the road that skirts Findhorn Bay. Having just returned from Australia, I was struck by his words—they could have been uttered by a traditional person in the Western Desert. I have travelled around the world twice to find a people who really know their Place, who *belong to the land* instead of believing that it belongs to them. And here, right in my back-yard, is a man with the same understanding. He knows where he is. He knows where he belongs—he *belongs* to the place where he grew up, and even a town five miles down the road is no substitute for that spot.

I also began to look around me for the stories that are still an active part of the Scottish culture, especially among the island communities, but also among the people of the Highlands. Ask any Scottish youngster and he or she will undoubtedly know the tale of 'The Laird of Co' or 'The Seal Wife'. All mention *specific places*, towns that still exist. After my time in Australia with the aboriginal people, I began to see that some of the stories paralleled the Dreamtime stories—they told about the Creation of this land. "Long, long ago, and longer ago than that . . . . " begins the tale of 'Mester Stoorworm', which tells me that this story comes from the Creation time, the same era as that of the Dreamtime heroes and heroines.

'Mester Stoorworm', a sea serpent with a mouth '. . . a mile wide, and as to his scaly body it reached from horizon to horizon . . .' reminds me a lot of the Rainbow Serpent, Creator Spirit to the desert people, whose movement created the river beds, and thus the source of water and *life* in the desert. The story has all the ingredients of a best seller—greed, lust, bravery, the fool whose wisdom saves the day.

In the end, the wise young fool sails into the belly of the serpent (Sound familiar? 'Jonah and the Whale' is only one rendition of this ancient theme. I've found Native American cultures with a similar story as well) and sets its liver on fire. The result was ". . . terrible indeed, for the huge body of Mester Stoorworm was cracking and breaking into jagged lumps that were flung hither and thither along the surface of the water; until, when the turmoil at last died down, all that was left of Mester Stoorworm was a scatter of islands, which men *(sic)* now call the Orkneys and the Shetlands, and one larger island which is now called Iceland, and where the fire that Assipattle (the wise fool) kindled still burns under the mountains."

This is a wondrous Dreamtime/Creation story, from the land of *Scotland*. The tale also contains teachings—about the wisdom in the fool, the destructiveness of jealousy and the power of humility and sacrifice. I began to wonder what other 'Dreamtime' stories might be buried in the legends of Scotland.

Soon after this discovery, a woman from the States who had been studying with some of the Northwest Native American people came to visit the Findhorn Foundation. We had tea together one morning in the community centre at the Park.

"I've been learning their stories," she said. "I felt that was important, to know the native history of where I was living—and since I was coming to Scotland, and my biological roots are here, I thought I would look up the stories here, too." In the Northwest, she explained, the people would choose what *age* of song and story cycles they would use for a particular ceremony. "Their history goes back through four ages, and each one has its own story cycle."

"Hmmmm . . . that's like the Hopi," I commented. They, too, talk about the seven *worlds* of this Creation. According to Hopi prophecy, we are coming to the end of the Fourth and preparing for the Fifth. Their concept of time and the development of the world is much vaster than the history of 'Western civilisation' taught in most schools—our history barely scratches the surface of the 'time' accounted for in most traditional people's history.

"That's right," she said, excitement crackling in her voice. "And what I'm finding is that the Celtic stories are divided into four ages as well . . . ."

"Aha," I said, eyes alight. "Like beginning with a Creation era . . . ."

"Yes, and then the Dedannon folk—"

"The shadow people?" Some of the Celtic stories I read in preparation for the story-telling performance included tales of these people, who once lived above ground and then, rather than perish completely as a race, became shadows and moved underground to establish a kingdom there.

"That's right, and then the fairy folk, and finally the world we live in now."

The woman gave me another important insight about the native people of the Northwest—*power* within that society is measured by how much knowledge of the *history and traditions* a person has. "That's one thing that really impresses me about the Findhorn Community," she commented. "You all learn its history during the Orientation programme. I think that's so important."

"That's right; and most of it has never been written down, so I guess you could say we have an oral history tradition, too. Usually the people who have been here the longest and know the most about the community and its history are the ones who carry the most weight. The way I look at it, the more responsibility someone takes, the more power they have."

The woman nodded. "It's the same with the people I've been studying with. The ones who take responsibility—for teaching and for carrying the history—are the ones with the most power."

Our conversation reinforced my belief in the importance of a culture's stories. To know a place deeply, I need to know the nuts and bolts of the biological and geological history of the area, but to stop there would be to overlook a vast storehouse of wisdom that resides in the *human* population of that area.

The myths and legends of a people give many clues about the social structures active in a culture, the guidelines for interactions between humans as well as between humans and other species. A culture's concept of the Creator, for example, has wide-reaching effects on the society. A sociologist from the University of Pennsylvania, who studied egalitarian communities in the US in an attempt to discover what factors they had in common, found two similarities:

1. Shared child-raising (both male and female participation in parenting).
2. The presence of a female Creator in the mythology of the people (either both a female and a male figure *or* just a female Creator). None of the communities focusing solely upon a male Creator produced an egalitarian lifestyle.

Human relationship with the Creator is reflected within the culture—what He/She does becomes a blueprint for how I interact with other male/female beings within the human population. The stories and legends also provide clues as to how to relate with the plants, animals and minerals in my neighbourhood.

While in Scotland, I became acutely aware of the lack of predatory species. I wondered at first if this island country had evolved without them, but after some inquiries among the local environmentalists, I learned that Scotland did once have a healthy population of predators—bears, wolves and wildcats among them.

Their absence contributes to the over-large herds of deer wandering the Highlands. In addition there are thousands upon thousands of sheep. Introduced in the 18th and 19th centuries, the sheep replaced 'unproductive crofters', the local subsistence farmers who were forcibly removed by English landlords.

The remnants of the once vast forests of Caledonian pine trees in Scotland (cut to supply the factories of England, to build the ships that met the Spanish Armada, and to fuel Britain's many wars) could not withstand this invasion of grazing animals. Pine seedlings grow to an inch or two before being lopped off by hungry deer and sheep. Two-hundred-year-old pine giants stand in scattered clumps in the Highlands, but no young trees are growing to take their place.

What kind of history, I wondered, did the Scots have with the bear, the wildcat, the wolf? What kind of stories, what sorts of images did they feed to their children? What were the local legends about these animals?

I went to the library and returned with a stack of fairy tales. I rediscovered 'Little Red Ridinghood' and the wolf who 'cold-heartèdly' ate her grandmother and then devoured Red Ridinghood. Among the several versions popular in the nineteenth century, the Brothers Grimm avenge this cruel ending by introducing the hunter who kills the wolf by splitting its stomach. Out pops Red Ridinghood exclaiming, "It's so *dark* inside the wolf!"

In just this one story I found the projection of greed, violence and trickery onto the wolf. It was portrayed as a creature without morals, not only killing a 'helpless old woman' but eating the granddaughter as well, and as a malevolent trickster who fools the little girl into believing that he is actually her grandmother. Red Ridinghood sums up the cultural stereotype of the wolf when she describes the darkness inside the wolf, dark meaning evil and uncontrollable. The wolf became a repository for the human shadow, the collection of qualities that humans are loathe to face in ourselves.

Some might argue that these stories teach children morals and important social values. Steiner teachers contend that children must find *some* way of working through the fear and violence that exists in the world. Children who grow up without violent bedtime stories, who live in a world where the Three Little Pigs have a conflict-resolution session with the Wolf and return home as friends, act out their violence in other ways. Instead of working with destructive forces in the realm of fantasy, they must grapple with them in their day-to-day world.

My response, though, is that the images implanted in children become the fabric for their interaction with the world. The story of the 'big, bad Wolf' becomes an archetype that was applied to the flesh and blood wolf living in the forests of Scotland, Ireland, England, Germany and all the other countries where this creature was systematically wiped out. The legends still persist in Scandinavian countries, too, where one of the few remaining wolves, separated from its pack far to the north, was shot and dragged through the streets by triumphant hunters, despite an EEC law that protects the wolf as an endangered species.

In Britain the last wolf was shot in Scotland in the late 18th century. Two hundred years later I have a hard time even finding *stories* that mention wolves. Why the extermination?

When humans project undesirable, difficult-to-look-at qualities upon another being, the next 'logical' step in eliminating those qualities is to get rid of the being upon whom they are projected. The British people began a systematic removal of the wolf that lasted for centuries before they finally succeeded in stamping out the last of a beautiful, powerful species.

The Europeans who moved to the New World began the same systematic extermination. Their mission in the US is nearly complete. But humans lived on the North American continent before the invasion of European settlers. Why were there any wolves left to kill?

The answer can be gleaned once again from examining the stories and legends of the pre-European inhabitants, the Native Americans. The wolf is a respected teacher in the stories. Men and women go to the wolf to learn its song and over the years they learn a means of peaceful coexistence with it. 'Who Speaks for Wolf' is an ancient teaching story from the Oneida Nation. Part of the teaching addresses the human-wolf relationship:

THEY SAW that Wolf and the People could not live comfortably together in such a small place.
THEY SAW that it was possible to hunt down this Wolf People until they were no more.
BUT THEY ALSO SAW that this would require much energy over many years.
THEY SAW, TOO, that such a task would change the People: they would become Wolf Killers. A People who took life only to sustain their own would become a People who took life rather than move a little.
IT DID NOT SEEM TO THEM THAT THEY WANTED TO BECOME SUCH A PEOPLE.
(*Who Speaks for Wolf*, Paula Underwood Spencer)

And they did not become such a people. They chose instead to live with respect for the wolf. They moved to another location so as not to interfere with the already established wolf community. The story reflects and perpetuates a way of respect and wisdom, just as 'Little Red Ridinghood' reflects and perpetuates a way of fear and projection which led to the exterminaton of the wolf in European countries.

You can read fairy tales for yourself and find the image of the fox, bear, coyote, raven, lion, tiger, elephant and others exemplified within that particular culture. The myths and legends in essence give us a model for interacting with the world. We can examine our surroundings as a measure of the mythological background of the culture and then choose to continue, alter or replace this symbolic underpinning.

Important stories live among *all* of the people who have settled in an area —recent arrivals as well as native people. Which leads me into the second question:

2. What is going on here? The first clue I can offer is to look at the *resources* available in the community. Usually the phrase 'natural resources' brings to mind discussions of board feet, minerals to be mined and litres per minute flowing through a stream. By resources, though, I mean *re-sourcing,* all of the things that lead me back to the source, the *essence of place.*

As mentioned above, the traditional inhabitants, if you can still find them, are a rich storehouse of information about the area where you are living. And don't be too quick to assume that all of the native people in your area have died or been removed. The settlers of Tasmania have long lived with the myth that no aboriginal people exist on that island. I, too, was taught in school that the traditional people of southern Ohio—the Shawnee, Pawnee and other nations—had been killed or moved in the horrific marches to reservations in the west. "When did that end?" I asked my mother one day. "Oh, they were still being sent west on the trains in the twenties and thirties."

"*This* century?" I asked, incredulous.

"No," she said. "The 19th century. I can show you some of the records in the Courthouse downtown if you're interested."

A couple of years later, though, while living in Scotland, I received a newsletter from a group of native people in what is now northern Kentucky and southern Ohio. They are coming out in the open to teach their traditional language and craft skills to each other and any interested white settlers. Their people, they explain in the newsletter, never left their traditional lands. They made their way through Mammoth Cave, one of the longest continuous caves in the world, from western to eastern Kentucky. There the Amish people sheltered them and declared that they were 'white' so that they would not be included in the 'Great Removal' and taken from their traditional land.

Look carefully around you—search out wisdom among the *older people*, too. Once when I was visiting a friend in London, he mentioned a woman who had lived on his street for over fifty years. What a treasure that woman could be to the local residents—she must have a deep well of information and insight about the neighbourhood that comes only with time and patient observation.

In the town where I grew up, an older woman, still very active in her mid-seventies, spent a summer teaching me how to quilt. She knew my grandmother and great-aunt and the whole history of the family better than anyone among the younger generations.

The old people, especially in rural areas, have a knowledge of the land and the seasons that outstrips anything you could ever read in a book. Seek them out. Invite them over for tea. Make it a point to spend an afternoon weeding their garden or raking the leaves. The kindness usually uncorks a string of stories that repays the effort manyfold. They may tell you how the pond at the back of the wood got its name, how to dry sunflowers in the autumn, or where the watercress grows wild in an eddy of the creek. And if you linger even longer, they may tell you about the day they wrapped their arms around the old beech tree in the corner of the field and explained that it was time for it to be chopped down. Or the white ball of light that they've seen rushing through the stalks of corn on a hot summer's day. They might even tell you *their* grandmother's recipe for burdock root salve . . . if you linger long enough.

A lot can be learned on your own, too.

Here is a simple exercise:

Set aside an afternoon each week, or at least an hour, to explore an area where you live. You might begin by looking for a 'power spot', a place where you feel at peace, rooted, open and expectant. It might be a particular tree that grows in a park nearby or a boulder perfectly shaped to the angle of your back. Perhaps a lake or stream draws you, or a particular section of the beach. 'Look' with senses other than your eyes. Let your heart guide you—allow yourself to be drawn from the heart, as if by a magnet. Take off your shoes, close your eyes and let the intelligence of your feet in connection with the Earth guide you to a spot.

Once there, practise the art of sitting. Learn to observe, to the finest detail, the

life around you. Mark off a circle about a foot in diameter and observe it closely-
for an hour. Bury yourself in the earth or sand or leaf cover and experience life
from this perspective. Every once in a while—not too often, since most humans
seem to spend too much time verbalising—bring a notebook and write down all
of the words and feelings and impressions that come to you. Shape them into a
story or a poem. And most of all, give yourself time to be. Quietly. Thoughtlessly.
In these quiet, empty spaces the magic of the land can invade you unawares.

When you arrive back home, record your thoughts and observations. If you paint
or draw, you might want to keep a visual record of your special spot as well. Over
the days and weeks and years the record can become a source of vast knowledge
—reading back through it, you may surprise even yourself. "Ah, so the wildflowers
bloomed early after the flood . . . and that was the year the leeks did so well in the
garden . . . ." Eventually, like the older people rooted in your neighbourhood, you
will become an expert on Place.

Seek out the painters and poets, the visionaries and violinists, the crones and the
crooners. The Artists of a Place also reveal the character of the land and the concerns of the people. The land shapes a culture, and in turn the culture shapes the
land. Different native cultures, for example, used different colours to symbolise the
four directions. "It's no great secret why they chose certain colours," explained a
friend who has studied beading with a native teacher. "They used the dyes that were
available in that area."

Music and dance also are shaped according to people's relationship with the land.
Instruments evolved according to the materials available in that place—the digeridoo of the Northern Territory of Australia, for example, was unknown among the
people of the Southwest—the voracious termites of the northern rainforests that
hollow the fallen logs do not exist in the Karri and Jarrah forests of the south.

Alan Lomax, a folklorist, researched the difference between the dance style of
certain African and European communities. The African dances used shuffling
movements, an outgrowth of walking through relatively flat country, while the
European folk dances involved lifting the knees, a reflection of walking up and
down steep, mountainous slopes.

One time I flew from Denver, Colorado down to Phoenix, Arizona just as the sun
was sinking behind the curve of the western horizon. On this cold, clear late winter
afternoon the edge of the horizon split into bands of colour—crimson red bled into
orange and then yellow and green and pale clear blue before fading into the pur-
plish-blue of the darkening sky. For the entire journey I sat looking out the window,
entranced by the vibrant, translucent purity of the colours. As I watched them fade,
I realised that the sunset looked exactly like some of the Navaho weavings with
their bold stripes of warm red and orange and gold. I could imagine that the sunset
colours in the Southwest had inspired many weavers and painters among the native
people.

Poetry and prose also take on inspiration from a deeply rooted sense of place.
Gary Snyder is an advocate of poetry within a *bioregional* context. Bioregion, as
defined by The Bioregional Project of New Life farm, is ". . . a life region. A geographical area whose rough boundaries are set by nature (not humankind), distin-
guishable from other areas by characteristics of flora, fauna, water, climate, rocks,
soils, landforms, and the human settlements and cultures these characteristics have
given rise to."

Snyder describes a group of poets he calls 'home-growers', ". . . poets who live in a place with some intention of staying there—and begin to find their poetry playing a useful role in the daily life of the neighbourhood. Poetry as a tool, a net or trap to catch and present; a sharp edge; a medicine; or a little awl that unties knots . . . .

"Poetry is written and read for real people: it should be part of the gatherings where we make decisions about what to do about uncontrolled growth, or local power plants, and who's going to be observer at the next county supervisor's meeting. A little bit of music is played by the guitarists and five-string banjo players, and some poems come down from five or six people who are really good—speaking about what is happening *here*. They shine a little ray of myth on things; memory turning to legend . . . ." (From: Gary Snyder, *The Real Work*)

Gaian Communities have the potential to inspire what I call 'visionary artists'. Artists create for the sake of creating. Profound artists, the ones whose work shapes a culture, create for the sake of creating *because they have a vision*. Richard Bach, author of *Jonathan Livingston Seagull*, says he writes because he has to, not because he wants to. A book takes hold and won't let go until it is written. He is not particularly worried about how the book will be received or whether it will sell —he simply knows that he must write.

The yearning to create is a basic human condition, one that needs to be acknowledged and celebrated. Whether you knit or hammer nails into composting toilets or research biochemical reactions, if you approach your work with love and enthusiasm, you are creating something vital. And when that creative work is bonded with a vision for the Place in which you live, the potential to transform that Place, and therefore the Earth, is limitless. Change begins here. Change begins now. With you, with me, with the visions that we create and act upon. The future is now—it rests in our dreams, and needs only a nudge, a conscious act, to awaken it.

Brenda Uleland offers this inspiration for the creative genius lurking in all of us: "Why should we all use our creative power and write or paint or play music, or whatever it tells us to do? Because there is nothing that makes people so generous, joyful, lively, bold and compassionate, so indifferent to fighting and the accumulation of objects and money. Because the best way to know the Truth or Beauty is to try to express it. And what is the purpose of existence Here or Yonder but to discover truth and beauty and express it, i.e. share it with others?" (Brenda Uleland, *If You Want to Write*)

3. Who is my neighbour? This is one of the most important keys to unlocking the secret of a Gaian Community. When I look around and truly ask who my 'neighbours' are, I find the oak tree rising stark and gnarled beyond our screened-in porch, the grouse who forage among the fallen leaves, the woodpecker who drums on the old maple tree by the barn. The amethyst cluster sitting on the desk and the oil lamp and roll of stamps are neighbours. My computer is a trusted friend (without you, this writing would have stretched another three months, at least).

When I look at 'neighbours' and my closest of kin in this way, I find my sense of family extending far beyond my biological one, and then orbiting beyond the confines of a *human* family. It even grows to encompass those beings that most biologists would overlook in their definition of 'life'.

At the beginning of this year I chose an Ally, an essence of the Earth—the 'Deva' or perfect pattern of a particular species—to join me in my writing during the coming year. Although I use a deck of cards for the exercise, you can find Allies in your life by paying attention to the things that fascinate you. More about this in a minute. The Ally I chose to aid and teach me was *Tools*. When I first looked at the illustration of a gardening spade and rake, I smiled, remembering the first time that I had drawn this card.

Then I was disappointed—I wanted something that was *alive* to be my teacher, not a human-created object, a surrogate creation. Now, though, when I move inside the essence of Tools, I find them bursting with life. I sense that their life is enhanced with the application of human skill. Tools become avenues to extend my ability to create and express in the world—they are like extensions of my arms and mind and heart. The benefits are reciprocal: they enable me to accomplish work, and in turn I bring them more fully alive by channelling my love and creativity through them.

I know, for example, that my violin thrives on being played. As a violin ages, its tone sweetens and the sound moves from it with greater ease. It needs to be played, though. If a violin simply sits in a shop, the tone will never warm. It needs human contact, it needs to be *used*. After travelling for six months without my instrument, it sounded sluggish when I first took it from the case, and the strings were reluctant to stay in tune. I almost felt that it was pouting, jealous of being left behind. The more I played on the instrument, the more open and gracious the sound became. That violin, made by Luigi Fabris in his studio in Venice through the days of 1880, will outlive me. That tool for expressing sound and joy and rhythm will last perhaps another century beyond my own life—and I find that refreshingly humbling.

Soon after drawing the Ally of Tools, I was sorting through old magazines and came across a copy of an article called 'Honouring the Spirit of Tools' by Toshio Odate. The author described a workshop that he had taken with a Japanese carpenter. He began by showing the tools, and more importantly, the Japanese craftsperson's *attitude* toward tools.

When he began his apprenticeship, Odate explained, he did not touch any of the tools for a full year. His task was simply to watch—and to sweep the floor and ladle soup. Tools were not for playing with; they were for working, and the apprentices were required to understand the whole of the work before they ever picked up a single tool. Like the traditional people in the desert, his training came through *observation*. Once he had his own set of tools, he never let other people touch them—to him, that would be like touching his face unbidden. It would be an invasion of privacy. The tools had become a part of him, but only after they were 'tamed'. The master trains them, with discipline and tenderness, through his or her work.

Odate learned the skill that I have come to call 'deep listening', the ability to listen to beings who do not communicate verbally. Most Western humans, because of our conditioning to see ourselves as the only species capable of language (and thus, we have assumed, communication) have lost the ability to hear or sense *non-verbal* communication. Slowly, scientists have recognised communication systems in other beings that can mimic humans' present linear form of language communication, for example in chimpanzees, gorillas and dolphins. By releasing the limiting belief that *language* (spoken or signed) is the only possible communication form, a human becomes receptive to the state of deep listening. In this mode we can move beyond receiving linear, mental images to feeling or sensing impressions that can then be translated into thoughts.

Traditional Native American and Australian aboriginal cultures include this form of communication in their daily lives. In contemporary Western culture the work of Dorothy Maclean provides an inspiring example. Dorothy receives 'transmissions' from 'devas' (Sanskrit for 'shining ones'), the archetypal patterns of plants, animals, elements, etc. In essence, she has rediscovered the art of deep listening in sensing the wisdom of these beings and then translating the impressions into words.

All humans are capable of deep listening once we overstep the conceptual barrier of perceiving language as the only form of communication. Here is a simple exercise to open to this communication:

Find a plant, stone, shell or seed, anything that catches your interest (a fascination with something often signals your openness to learn from that being). Find a quiet place where you will be undisturbed for at least ten minutes. Place the object in the palm of your hand and sit quietly. Imagine that your body is made of butter and you are melting in the hot sun. Feel your breath moving into any tight spots in the body and releasing any tension. As the body relaxes, so will the mind. Gently focus your eyes and attention on the object in your hand. Be aware of any sensations in your body and any thoughts that pass through your mind. If you want to deepen the connection, visualise breathing the object/being in and out of the centre of the chest (the heart chakra). When you feel complete, breathe deeply and relax your attention.

When you first practise this exercise, five minutes may seem like a long time. Gradually lengthen your listening times as you feel ready.

The skill of deep listening can aid you in befriending the neighbours who live around you. Once you have mastered the skill of quietly focusing on an object, deepen your communication with the following exercise:

Find a comfortable position, preferably with spine straight. Breathe deeply and relax the body. Close your eyes and spend a few minutes exploring the shape and texture of the object. Rub it against your face, turn it over in your hand, smell it, taste it. Then open your eyes and focus on the object. Let your eyes go 'soft' —focus gently. Imagine breathing the essence of this being right into your centre. (Pause) Notice any thoughts or impressions that run through your mind, but allow them to pass, like clouds blown across the sky. (Long pause)

After a couple of minutes, close your eyes again. Now view this being in your mind's eye, with your inner vision. See it in detail. Notice the shape and colour and texture. Now move closer. With your inner senses, touch this being. (Pause) Explore the way it feels. (Pause) Now move even closer until you move right inside this being. Feel yourself merging, melting right into its centre. (Pause) Become one with this being, and begin to experience life as it experiences life. Look through its eyes, notice how you feel, how you move, how you interact. (Long pause) Now move through the cycle of a day, a season, or year—do it from within this being. (Long pause). When you are ready, feel yourself gently stepping back, moving away, moving slowly back into your Self. (Pause) Give thanks for this being and its work on the planet. (Pause) When you are ready, bring your awareness back to where you are sitting, into your body, and open your eyes.

You can practise this exercise with any being. Your power spot is a good place to do it, but after a while you can perform this exercise anywhere, with or without the physical object in your hand. The important part is the *merging*. To me, this is the supreme gift given to humanity—the ability to merge our consciousness with that of other beings. Over the years of guiding this meditation in workshops, I am continually awed by the power of this exercise. Often people begin their sharing afterwards by saying, "Well, I don't know if this is right or not—I don't really know anything about the dragonfly (or whatever it is), *but . . . .*" and they go on to describe perfectly the movements, habitat and life cycle of that creature. I have seen it happen so many times, that I *know* humans have the ability to resonate with other life forms. And that experience of connection can bring a lot of information, wisdom and healing.

You can use this exercise, for example, with a sick houseplant or tree in your yard. You may learn through the experience of merging with a fern that it needs a shadier spot and more water. You may find that a tree planted in a hollow doesn't like having wet feet. The experience of merging can also open your understanding of the *healing properties* of a being.

Once during a talk by Sun Bear, a woman asked him about the healing action of a certain plant. He stared at her for a few moments and then shook his head. "I don't understand," he told her. "You're a two-legged, just like me—why don't you go ask it?" We all have the ability to listen—we just need practice and *trust* in the things that we hear.

As an experiment, choose a herb whose medicinal properties you would like to learn about, preferably one that grows wild in your area or that you have in your garden. Use the merging exercise with the herb and write down your impressions. Afterwards look up the plant in a couple of herbal books. The information may surprise you. One friend commented, "Oh, this book only scratches the surface. It misses all of the deeper healing qualities completely." Most of those herbals, too, are simply recapitulations of earlier works dating back hundreds of years, not first-hand research, so take them as a guide and plumb the depths yourself.

Sometimes deep healing comes through the merging exercise itself. One time a woman in a workshop chose the Snake to tune in with. Because the group was large, not everyone shared their experience with their Ally. Afterwards the woman came to me, her face beaming. For twenty years she had been in psychotherapy because of her extreme fear of snakes. Although initially she had a very difficult time with the meditation, once inside she was able to move freely within the Snake and experience life as it does. "It was wonderful, being inside. I suddenly understood what it's like to be a Snake. And you know," she said, her eyes sparkling, "I'm not afraid of them any more."

Allies are teachers, helpers and supports. They are *never* destructive. There is no such thing as a 'bad' Ally. The Snake or the Wolf or the Spider or the Thunderstorm or any of the other beings of the Earth all have lessons to teach, wisdom to share. All of our neighbours on the planet are potential teachers and guides for our journey.

4. What does a Gaian community look like *in this place?* The essence of a Gaian Community is inextricably linked with Place. Within Auroville, for example, there are numerous examples of how its relationship with the land and the Indian culture shape that community. Houses take on a certain form and style according to the local building materials that are available. People plan meetings to avoid the middle of the day when the sun is at its strongest. Major evening events are scheduled around the time of the full moon to make riding along the dirt tracks easier. The community's attitude towards work is very similar to that inherent in the Indian culture at large—people create their own jobs. A woman and her daughter, for instance, look after the public toilet in Pondicherry. No one hired them for the job—they saw a need and they fulfilled it. Their pay is whatever tips the women who use the toilets give them—and usually people do slip a coin into their outstretched hands as they leave. In the community of Auroville, people are expected to create their own work. They must look around for themselves and see what needs to be done.

At the Findhorn Foundation the work hours are changed according to the seasons. In mid-summer, when the daylight hours stretch until after midnight and large numbers of guests flood in for the summer holiday season, work hours extend until 5 p.m. In mid-winter, though, when the sun sets around 3:30 p.m., work ends at 4 p.m. The extra time is a 'creative hour', to be used as people choose. For me most of those hours were spent quietly. The inward draw of the season was so strong that I needed quiet time to rest within myself. The change of light from season to season is dramatic in Scotland. I can understand why people were moved to build stone circles to measure the cycles of the sun and moon. Their passing is truly noteworthy, something to inspire wonder. Or, in the depths of a cold, dark winter, to inspire drink . . . .

My point with these examples is that a Gaian community is of necessity shaped by Place. A community that supports the life, health and diversity of the desert will be very different from a woodland one. The Inuit of the Arctic have developed a culture that is quite different from the rainforest dwellers of South America.

Gaian communities can flourish in the city as easily as in the countryside. During my travels I visited Imago, an urban neighbourhood community in Cincinnati, Ohio devoted to developing a 'humane/sustainable' culture where:

1. Human consciousness will deepen and become more perceptive, loving and wise.
2. People become more spiritually sensitive.
3. Humanity lives in ecological balance with the rest of nature.
4. Life will be sustainable, not dependent on non-renewable resources.
5. Humanity will become aware of its interdependency and will learn to cooperate globally.
6. The community will be an essential support system.

The neighbourhood community is slowly expanding as houses along the dead-end street go up for sale. About half-a-dozen families on the same street form the nucleus of Imago. Each night a different family takes a turn cooking for the other neighbours. They also meet the first Thursday of each month to celebrate the changing of the season or to participate in presentations that range from hypnosis to organic gardening methods. They share tools and surplus vegetables from their gardens and books and childcare and cups of flour. They are neighbours, an oasis in the desert of urban anonymity.

I've noticed, too, that wherever the land is regenerating, communities also are flourishing The town where I am living now, for example, is an area of regrowth forest in western Massachusetts. A hundred years ago farmers grazed cattle and sheep on these mountainous slopes—you can still see the remnants of the stone walls that lined the fields. Now the trees are coming back—graceful beech saplings and gnarly oaks, shiny-barked birches and sugar maples. And a different sort of people are moving into the area than the farmers of a century ago.

People wave from passing cars and stop to talk along the road. In the post office are notices about war tax resistance seminars and classes in building composting toilets. The 'Country General Store' has a billboard out front listing every sort of holistic therapy or workshop you could imagine. On the weekends people come to the store to swap new and used clothes at the 'Rags to Riches' shop. Two small neighbourhood food-buying co-ops meet each month.

Artists have invaded the area, too, as prolific as the spindly saplings in the regrowth forest. They come out in force for the Full Moon Coffeehouse each month. The local poet reads his work, the swing violinist who lives at the end of the road plays something from his latest album, and four high school girls sing 'Let peace begin with me'. Little children pad around in their footie pyjamas, visiting friends in the jam-packed town hall. Cakes and cookies and tea (including herbal, of course) are served at the back. The coffeehouse is an eagerly awaited event in the life of the community, especially during the winter months when cabin fever sweeps through the snowbound houses. The monthly meetings are a chance to see friends, catch up on the news and enjoy the creativity spawned in the local area. These gatherings have a larger purpose, too—each coffeehouse funds a different project, from landscaping the town commons to aiding hurricane-torn Nicaragua.

Wendell, the community where we are living, is one example of a Gaian community in the making. Take heart—the heresy can root anywhere, even in your own back yard. The seed for living a life in harmony with yourself, your neighbours and the Earth, lies within you. The vision, *your vision*, for the community and the world that you want to live in is yours to realise. Dream will become reality when we *embody* the life that we envision.

That, to me, is the essence of the journey—to embody those qualities that I want to see in the world, to become a resident of a Gaian Community right where I am. In this spot. At this time. The challenge is to become what I call a 'daily activist', someone who builds the kind of life she or he envisions through the *daily actions* of their lives. I'm not concerned with the protesters who spend their lives saying 'No' to the latest wrongs. They have their place and their work to do, but in the end their 'victories' only mean an *absence* of something. No nuclear power plant. No discrimination. No clear felling. The sad truth, though, is that these protests never *create* anything. At best, they leave a void.

The activists, in the true sense of the word, are the ones who are *enacting* a vision of a different kind of world. They have a vision firmly implanted in their hearts and minds that acts like a compass to keep them on course, to steer all of their actions towards the realisation of that carefully planted, well-tended dream. Never forget the power of the acorn, the elders remind us, when you view the oak tree. Plant the seed of vision within yourself, and tend it well. Dream and scheme and sing and dance and laugh into form that seed of living at one with all life. May that Dream blossom and bear fruit for the good of the whole of creation.

Information

Books and Publications

Berry, Wendell. *Recollected Essays: 1965-1980*. San Francisco: North Point Press, 1981.
Berry, Wendell. *The Unsettling of America*. New York: Avon, 1978.
Bloom, Michael and Pogacnik, M. *Leylines and Ecology: an Introduction*. Glastonbury: Gothic Image, 1985.
Caddy, Eileen with Liza Hollingshead. *Flight into Freedom*. Shaftesbury: Element Books, 1988.
Caddy, Eileen. *Footprints on the Path*. Findhorn: Findhorn Press, 1976.
Dadd, Debra Lynn. *Nontoxic and Natural*. Los Angeles: Tarcher, 1984.
Dadd, Debra Lynn. *The Nontoxic Home: Protecting Yourself and Your Family from Everyday Toxics and Health Hazards*. Los Angeles: Tarcher, 1986.
Findhorn Community. *The Findhorn Garden: Pioneering a New Vision of Humanity and Nature in Cooperation*. Findhorn: Findhorn Press, 1988 (first ed. 1975).
Friends of the Earth. *Seeds*. Pamphlet about the effect of seed patenting. Available from: Friends of the Earth, 26-28 Underwood St, London N1 7JQ, UK. Telephone: 071-490-1555.
Hanh, Thich Nhat. *Being Peace*. Berkeley: Parallax Press, 1987.
Katchongva, Dan. *From the Beginning of Life to the Day of Purification: The Hopi Story*. Taos: Hopi Land & Life, 1982. A free copy can be requested from: Hopi Land & Life, Route 9, Box 78, Santa Fe, NM 87501, USA. Paid for by voluntary contribution; this book is not sold.
Keyes, Laural E. *Toning: The Creative Power of the Voice*, rev. ed. Marina del Rey, CA: DeVorss, 1973.
Maclean, Dorothy. *To Hear the Angels Sing*. Issaquah: Morningtown Press, 1988.
Manning-Sanders, Ruth. *Scottish Folk Tales*. London: Methuen, 1976.
Margolin, Malcolm. *The Earth Manual: How to Work on Wild Land Without Taming It*. Berkeley: Heyday Books, 1975.
Morgan, Sally. *My Place*. Fremantle: Fremantle Arts Centre Press, 1987. Moving, humorous story of an aboriginal woman growing up in Perth, Western Australia, and her search to uncover her family's roots.
Mother and Satprem. *Mother's Agenda, Vols. 1-13*. New York: Institute for Evolutionary Research, 1981-88.
The Mother. *Living Within: The Yoga Approach to Psychological Health and Growth*.

Ed. A. S. Dalal. Pondicherry: Sri Aurobindo Ashram, 1987.
Odate, Toshio. *Japanese Woodworking Tools: Their Tradition, Spirit and Use.*
Newtown, CT: Taunton Press, 1984.
Satprem. *The Mind of the Cells.* New York: Institute for Evolutionary Research, 1982.
About Mother's work in her later years (translated from French).
Satprem. *Sri Aurobindo or the Adventure of Consciousness.* New York: Institute for
Evolutionary Research, 1984.
Savitri. *Sunward Rising.* Story of Auroville from a long-time member's perspective.
Snyder, Gary. *The Real Work: Interviews and Talks, 1964-1979,* ed. Scott McLean. In:
New Directions, May 1980.
Spencer, Paula Underwood. *Who Speaks for Wolf: A Native American Learning Story.*
Austin: Tribe of Two Press, 1983. Soon to be reissued as part of a trilogy of Learning
Stories by The Alexandria Library, PO Box 2021, Dallas, TX 75221, USA. *Wolf* and its
accompanying Teacher's Guide have been declared an exemplary educational program
by the US Dept. of Education.
Sun Bear (with Wabun and Barry Weinstock). *The Path of Power.* Spokane: Bear
Tribe Publishing, 1983.
Sun Bear and Wabun. *The Medicine Wheel: Earth Astrology.* Englewood Cliffs, NJ:
Prentice-Hall, 1980.
Ywahoo, Dhyani. *Voices of Our Ancestors: Cherokee Teachings from the Wisdom Fire.*
Boston: Shambhala, 1987.

Contacts

THE HENRY DOUBLEDAY RESEARCH ASSOCIATION
Convent Lane, Bocking, Braintree, Essex, UK.
Telephone: 0376 24083
Dedicated to furthering organic gardening practices and maintaining a 'seed library'.
Through the Association, you can become a seed guardian by growing and increasing
stocks of old varieties. Send them seeds over ten years old, from Britain or abroad.

SEED SAVERS EXCHANGE
Kent Whealy, Director, Rural Route 3, Box 239, Decorah, Iowa 52101, USA.
Major collector and distributor of 'heritage' seeds in the USA.

NATIVE SEEDS/SEARCH
3950 West New York Drive, Tucson, AZ 85745, USA.
Non-profit organisation devoted to conservation and promotion of native agricultural
crops of the southwest US and northwest Mexico. Listing of seeds for sale: $1.00.
Associate membership: $10.00.

BLUE RIDGE SEED SAVERS EXCHANGE
c/o Kim Domeratzky, Box 106, Batesville, VA 22924, USA.
Local seed exchange for the Blue Ridge area.

TALAVAYA SEEDS
PO Box 707, Santa Cruz Station, Santa Cruz, NM 87507, USA.
"Talavaya is a Hopi word for the time of day just before dawn, when the farmer goes to
his fields and the Great Spirit receives his prayers. Talavaya Center is a non-profit
research and educational facility that is working to save the pure strains of traditional
native seeds that can help feed the world."